M000296750

ADMIRAL
JOHN S. McCAIN
AND THE TRIUMPH OF
NAVAL AIR POWER

★ ★ ★ ★

Titles in the series:

Studies in Naval History and Sea Power
Christopher M. Bell and James C. Bradford, editors

Studies in Naval History and Sea Power advances our understanding of sea power and its role in global security by publishing significant new scholarship on navies and naval affairs. The series presents specialists in naval history, as well as students of sea power, with works that cover the role of the world's naval powers, from the ancient world to the navies and coast guards of today. The works in Studies in Naval History and Sea Power examine all aspects of navies and conflict at sea, including naval operations, strategy, and tactics, as well as the intersections of sea power and diplomacy, navies and technology, sea services and civilian societies, and the financing and administration of seagoing military forces.

ADMIRAL
JOHN S. McCAIN
AND THE TRIUMPH OF
NAVAL AIR POWER

★ ★ ★ ★

WILLIAM F. TRIMBLE

NAVAL INSTITUTE PRESS
ANNAPOLIS, MARYLAND

This book has been brought to publication with the generous assistance of Marguerite and Gerry Lenfest.

NAVAL INSTITUTE PRESS
291 Wood Road
Annapolis, MD 21402

Library of Congress Cataloging-in-Publication Data

Names: Trimble, William F., date, author.
Title: Admiral John S. McCain and the triumph of naval air power / William F. Trimble.
Description: Annapolis, MD : Naval Institute Press, [2019] | Series: Studies in naval history and sea power | Includes bibliographical references and index.
Identifiers: LCCN 2018042605 (print) | LCCN 2018043218 (ebook) | ISBN 9781682473719 (ePDF) | ISBN 9781682473719 (ePub) | ISBN 9781682473702 (hardcover) | ISBN 9781682473719 (ebook)
Subjects: LCSH: McCain, John Sidney, 1884–1945. | Admirals—United States—Biography. | United States. Navy—Officers—Biography. | United States. Navy—Aviation—History—20th century. | Aircraft carriers—United States—History—20th century. | World War, 1939–1945—Pacific Area. | World War, 1939–1945—Naval operations, American.
Classification: LCC E748.M1413 (ebook) | LCC E748.M1413 T75 2019 (print) | DDC 359.0092 [B] —dc23
LC record available at https://lccn.loc.gov/2018042605

All maps by Brad Sanders.

Book design and composition: Alcorn Publication Design

To Eleanor, Charlotte, and Clementine

CONTENTS

MAPS

ACKNOWLEDGMENTS

In the long process of researching and writing this book, I assumed more debts than I can ever repay. Jim Bradford at Texas A&M University first suggested that I do something on John McCain, persuading me that after I wrote about Glenn Curtiss and the early pioneers of naval aviation it was time to look at someone like McCain, who was derided by early aviators as one of the "Johnny-Come Latelys." With much trepidation I sent drafts of early chapters on McCain as commander, Aircraft South Pacific Force to John Lundstrom, the dean of naval air operations in the South Pacific in 1942. John, as well as James Sawruk, read the drafts and politely pointed out errors that—had I been more knowledgeable, experienced, and careful—I should have caught myself. Tom Wildenberg, my good friend and a superb naval historian, read most of the manuscript. His sharp editorial eye and admonitions to keep the focus on McCain vastly improved the finished product. At the Naval Academy, where I was the Class of 1957 Distinguished Chair of Naval Heritage for 2014–2015, my boss, Capt. C. C. Felker, helped me place McCain and the fast carrier task force in a wider strategic perspective, while colleagues Cdr. Davin O'Hora, Robert Love, and Jason Smith clarified my understanding of the Navy's command structure and World War II in the Pacific. I also owe much to the expertise of Barbara Manvel at the Academy's Nimitz Library, and Jennifer Bryan and David D'Onofrio in the library's Special Collections & Archives. Rick Russell, director of the Naval Institute Press, and Susan Todd Brook, senior acquisitions editor, offered encouragement and advice at times when I got distracted by other projects and responsibilities. The finished product owes much to the expert copy editing of Drew Bryan and the help of production editor Rachel Crawford.

I could not have written this and my other books without the services and holdings of the National Archives and Records Administration. At Archives II in College Park, Nathaniel Patch was unstinting in offering his time and expertise, which was essential for locating key Bureau of Aeronautics and Chief of Naval Operations files. He also made it possible for Auburn University to acquire Pacific Fleet message and dispatch files available only on microfilm. Eric Voelz at the National Personnel Records Center in

St. Louis cut through the red tape to make a copy of McCain's voluminous personnel file available to me. Over many years, no one has been more cordial and helpful than Jeff Flannery at the Manuscript Division of the Library of Congress. I am indebted to Dale Gordon, Tonya Simpson, and Curtis Utz at the Archives Branch of the Naval History and Heritage Command for making important collections available to me and other researchers after the NHHC came out of a prolonged period of reorganization. At the Naval War College, Douglas Smith and librarians Robin Lima, Dara Baker, and Dennis Zambrotta tracked down McCain materials that I otherwise might have overlooked. Hill Goodspeed and Marc Levitt at the National Naval Aviation Museum in Pensacola dug out the Thach Papers and other McCain-related materials for me. Carol Leadenham guided me to and through the McCain and other collections at the Hoover Institution Library and Archives at Stanford University. Brad Sanders somehow transformed my feeble penciled drafts into comprehensible maps and charts.

I cannot express enough praise for the encouragement and support from many colleagues and friends. In the History Department at Auburn University, former department chair Charles Israel carved out a semester's leave for me at a key point in the research and writing process. Morris Bian, Paul Casarona, Michael Kern, Angela Lakwete, and David Lucsko could not have been more helpful and supportive. Tim Dodge, Helen Goldman, and Dana Caudle in Auburn's Ralph Brown Draughon Library were instrumental in acquiring and copying materials from Archives II. Fellow historian David Burke expertly removed imperfections from many of the book's photos. Long-time friend and retired Air Force historian George Cully kept me on task by always asking me how much progress I had made on the McCain project. He also put me in touch with another retired Air Force historian, Daniel Harrington, whose work on Army Lt. Gen. Joseph T. McNarney led me to a crucial wartime agreement between the Army Air Forces and the Navy on the distribution of land-based strike aircraft. Tom Hughes at the School of Advanced Air and Space Studies at Maxwell Air Force Base and author of a superb biography of William Halsey allayed much of my anxiety about doing operational history. Over many years, my good friend Karen Babich opened her house on Chesapeake Bay to me on numerous trips to Washington.

My most sincere gratitude goes to the late Senator John S. McCain III for taking time to talk with me about his grandfather's life and accomplishments. My thanks go, also, to the senator's son, John S. ("Jack") McCain IV, himself a naval aviator, whom I met at the Naval Academy to discuss the book's focus and the significance of carrier task force operations in the Pacific.

Yet there is no one more deserving of my thanks and appreciation than my wife Sharon, who for more than forty years has been a cherished partner in my personal and professional life's journey. She uncomplainingly endured days and hours at archives around the country, copying uncounted files and photos. More than anything, this book is the result of her patience and loving commitment to our marriage and our family.

At places in the text, words in quotations that may be offensive to contemporary readers have been left unchanged for accuracy and historical context. All errors of commission and omission in this and my other works are, of course, entirely my own.

ADMIRAL
JOHN S. McCAIN
AND THE TRIUMPH OF
NAVAL AIR POWER

★ ★ ★ ★

The Airman's Admiral

On the morning of 19 November 1944, Vice Adm. John S. McCain, commander of Task Force 38, perched on the green leather transom off to one side of flag plot in the carrier USS *Hancock*'s island superstructure. Spare, almost gaunt, with blue eyes squinting from his weathered, ruddy face, McCain had been fidgeting in anxious suspense as he listened to radio chatter and scanned flash reports describing strikes against targets in the big Philippine island of Luzon while impatiently waiting for his boys to return safely. Lt. Cdr. Leonard J. Check, commander of the carrier's Fighting Squadron 7 (VF-7), along with Lt. Johnny Bridges, had just landed their Grumman F6F-5 Hellcats aboard the flattop and scrambled up to flag plot from the flight deck to see their boss. McCain had invited Check and Bridges to meet with him and describe their mission, a fighter sweep over Japanese-held Nichols and Nielson Fields south of Manila. In flag plot the pair found officers in khaki uniforms standing shoulder to shoulder around a large chart table scrutinizing the movements of the carrier task force and tracking enemy surface and air threats. Sharing the busy, crowded, and noisy space were chambray- and denim-clad enlisted men who monitored radios, manned radar repeater stations and communication desks, and transferred data onto plotting boards that provided officers with graphic combat information.[1]

McCain's Task Force 38 (TF-38) was the principal offensive component of Adm. William F. Halsey's mighty Third Fleet. At the time, TF-38 consisted of three task groups totaling twelve fast carriers and nearly six hundred aircraft, screened by four fast battleships and a host of cruisers and destroyers. McCain's force was responsible for providing support for troops under Army Gen. Douglas MacArthur as they fought through the central Philippines. Army Air Forces (AAF) fighters and bombers, plagued by downpours that transformed recently captured airfields into treacherous quagmires, were unable to assist their comrades on the ground. Much to his chagrin, Halsey realized that in this emergency TF-38 would have to make up for the Army's air power deficiencies, despite his units being worn down by months of virtually nonstop combat. McCain's aviators flew four strikes and 592 sorties on the 19th, claiming 16 enemy planes shot down and 110 destroyed on the ground. Actual Japanese aircraft losses were more modest: based on statistical analyses about 70 percent of the aircraft reported by the fliers were destroyed. In addition to damaging or destroying numerous small craft, the airmen sank an oiler in Manila Bay and two cargo ships near San Fernando north of Manila. TF-38 lost 19 aircraft and 12 pilots and aircrew killed or missing in action during the attacks.[2]

McCain wanted to hear more than statistics. "What did you see, and what did you do?" McCain asked Check as he downed a cup of coffee in flag plot. Check answered that he had come over the targets at 20,000 feet and, encountering no opposition in the air, dropped down to a thousand feet to bomb and strafe Japanese aircraft, many concealed in camouflaged revetments scattered around the airfields. When he and Bridges got word that Japanese planes were in the air north of Manila, they went on the hunt. They found their quarry lurking in the clouds, flushing them like ducks and quickly downing four before the others fled. McCain asked, "Did you bring all your lads back with you?" Check replied that two of his fliers had to ditch in the sea but had been rescued by destroyers. Bridges, who had been responsible for photographing the results of the strike, claimed that he and his flight division of Grummans had shot down two Nakajima Ki-43 Hayabusa ("Oscar") fighters. "How much damage did you do to Japanese shipping in Manila Bay?" McCain asked. Bridges replied that in his estimation the strikes had resulted in at least thirty-five large and small ships sunk or damaged. "You have performed one of the most dangerous as well as a necessary mission," McCain concluded. "Congratulations. Glad you are back." It was typical McCain. At every opportunity, he sought to meet and talk with those serving under him, not just because he learned more about operational successes and failures, but also because he truly cared about the young men he ordered into harm's way. They, in turn, appreciated his energy and enthusiasm and held him in high esteem as an "airman's admiral."[3]

Adm. John S. McCain was among the exclusive cadre of American naval officers who reached the pinnacle of carrier task force command during World War II in the Pacific, joining such luminaries as William F. Halsey, Raymond A. Spruance, Frank Jack Fletcher, Marc A. Mitscher, and Thomas C. Kinkaid. Much has been written about these figures, who along with officers in subordinate command posts have been assessed by numerous writers and scholars, the foremost being Clark G. Reynolds in his groundbreaking survey *The Fast Carriers*. McCain has not been ignored. Alton Keith Gilbert chronicled his personal life and professional career in *A Leader Born: The Life of Admiral John Sidney McCain, Pacific Carrier Commander*, and John McCain (the admiral's grandson), with Mark Salter, provided an intimate portrait from the perspective of a third-generation naval officer in *Faith of My Fathers: A Family Memoir*. Scholarly works by Clark Reynolds, John Lundstrom, and other historians have examined McCain's decisions and actions at critical junctures in the Pacific War. Nevertheless, McCain presents an opportunity for a deeper examination of organizational, administrative, operational, and technological change during a formative period in the Navy's history.[4]

Under McCain and other flag officers, naval air power, organized into multicarrier task forces, evolved from a tactical supplement to the battle fleet dedicated to sea control and protecting sea lines of communication into an independent strategic striking force. By the end of World War II, the aircraft carrier was capable of a sustained forward presence and could project power from the sea in ways no one could have imagined only a decade before.[5] McCain and others witnessed and took part in this transformation, which shaped and was shaped in the crucible of global war. From other historians we know the broad contours of this change in the strategic seascape, but only a few have filled in the particulars. The life and naval career of John McCain provides a lens to bring those details into sharper focus.

After graduation from the Naval Academy in 1906, McCain joined the Asiatic Fleet and saw duty in cruisers and battleships during and after World War I. His first command, the ammunition ship *Nitro* (AE 2), provided the opportunity to hone his leadership and ship-handling skills. Administrative and political experience came in multiple tours of duty in the powerful Bureau of Navigation (BuNav), where he became an expert in complex and controversial personnel and promotion policies. McCain went on to earn his wings at Pensacola in 1936. Then as now, to become a naval aviator was to join the ranks of the elite; that McCain did so at the age of fifty-two was a remarkable accomplishment that earned him the respect of many airmen who served with and under him. Yet to the service's zealous pioneers, McCain, Halsey, and other senior captains who became aviators were forever branded with the pejorative "Johnny-Come-Lately" or "JCL."[6]

That McCain came late to aviation was fortuitous. His seniority in the officer hierarchy and his experience ashore in Washington provided invaluable political connections at a moment when changes swept through naval aviation in the mid- and late 1930s. Treaty restrictions expired, crises overseas put nations on course to another world war, and money once more flowed into shipbuilding and aircraft production programs. Exercises, or fleet problems, in the late 1920s and early 1930s revealed much about both the strengths and weaknesses of the aircraft carrier. In 1937, as a senior captain with his prized wings of gold, McCain secured command of the *Ranger* (CV 4), the Navy's first carrier built as such from the keel up. With the *Ranger* he participated in fleet problems in the Pacific and the Caribbean in 1938 and 1939. In January 1941, McCain took over command of the Pacific scouting force, which was responsible for patrol aviation, centering on the long-range flying boats vital for strategic reconnaissance and scouting.[7] That experience, in turn, led to his command of all land- and tender-based naval aviation during the early phases of the Guadalcanal campaign in the summer and fall of 1942. McCain's wartime shore duty included tours as chief of the Bureau of Aeronautics (BuAer) and as the first Deputy Chief of Naval Operations (Air) (DCNO [Air]), before his return to the Pacific as a carrier task force commander in 1944.

Important combat and administrative responsibilities, which through seniority and experience came sooner to McCain than to the more junior air pioneers, earned him a reputation as an innovator and positioned him to make decisions about budgeting, planning, command, and operations at critical moments before and during World War II. That he made mistakes in combat and administrative commands cannot be dismissed, just as one cannot ignore his many accomplishments, both at sea and ashore. John McCain, as much as anyone in high command during the war, deserves recognition for bringing victory in the Pacific and securing aviation as the tactical and strategic heart of the new air Navy.

CHAPTER 1

From Mississippi to the Sea

John Sidney McCain was a child of time and place, of culture and community, of history and heritage. His life was rooted in rural Carroll County, Mississippi, on the fringes of the fertile alluvial Delta where in the last decades of the nineteenth century cotton ruled the economy and tradition counted more than wealth. In 1851, William Alexander McCain, John Sidney's great-great grandfather, bought rich farmland on the banks of Teoc Creek, eight miles northwest of the county seat of Carrollton. On the eve of the Civil War, William McCain was one of the wealthiest and most prosperous landowners in the county, his "Waverly" plantation worth at least $40,000, not including forty-three slaves valued at approximately $30,000.[1]

The details of the McCain lineage are hazy and wrapped in myth. A romantic tale, related by Elizabeth Spencer, John Sidney's niece, has the McCains fleeing Scotland in the early seventeenth century to escape retribution from Queen Elizabeth for their loyalty to Mary Queen of Scots. More accurately, we know that the McCain lineage goes back to the Ulster county of Antrim in the north of Ireland, where many Protestants from Scotland had settled in the early eighteenth century. From there the McCains, McKeans, and others of proud Scots-Irish heritage crossed the Atlantic to the colonies of Pennsylvania and Maryland by the 1720s. John Sidney's great-great-great-great grandfather Hugh McCain lived in Caswell County, North Carolina, during the 1770s. One of his sons, Joseph McCain, found a home in Rockingham County, North Carolina, where he lived until his death in 1840. Joseph's son, William Alexander, was born there in 1814. When the Confederacy went to war in the spring of 1861, William Alexander joined the 5th Mississippi Cavalry Regiment as a private. Some sources have his death in the service in 1863, although others claim he deserted and died in a Confederate prison in 1864. He was survived by his son, John Sidney, who had been born in Teoc in 1851 and was the eldest of William's and his wife Mary Louisa's four children.[2]

William Alexander's widow Mary Louisa and son John Sidney ran the Teoc plantation through the violent and economically trying years of Reconstruction and Redemption. John Sidney brought Elizabeth ("Lizzie") Young from the nearby town of Middleton into the McCain clan when they married in January 1877. John and Elizabeth's first child, William Alexander, was born in 1878, followed by Katherine in 1882, the year of grandmother Mary Louisa's death. John Sidney, their third born, arrived on 9 August 1884. Three other siblings, Mary, Harry, and Joseph, were born, respectively, in 1889, 1891, and 1894. William attended the U.S. Military Academy, from which he graduated in 1902, and went on to a distinguished career in two world wars before retiring as a brigadier general. Mary married Luther Spencer and had a daughter, Elizabeth, who became an award-winning novelist. In her memoir she portrayed a close and comfortable family life on the farm at Teoc and in the town of Carrollton, where her grandfather held various official county positions. She recalled that the McCains embodied strict Presbyterianism and enjoyed an elevated social position stemming more from pride and long residency than from wealth.[3]

There is nothing to indicate that young John Sidney experienced anything much different than did his niece Elizabeth as his childhood years passed in Teoc and Carrollton. He grew up in a house surrounded by books and a home generally free from the personal, emotional, and financial stresses that afflict many families, although his brother Joe suffered from bouts of depression and alcoholism later in life and died prematurely of an accidental gunshot wound. The McCains were familiar with firearms; family lore has it that one night young John Sidney heard a noise outside the house, woke up thinking he saw an intruder, and in his nocturnal confrontation blasted one of the trees in the yard. His early education was in the Carrollton schools, where he was regarded as a "star pupil" by the county superintendent of education. One of his jobs was telephone operator. He learned the importance of responsibility when in the midst of a severe thunderstorm he asked his father if he could shut the office and wait out the storm. His father's response: "Stick to your post, son."[4]

After graduating from high school in the spring of 1901, John Sidney matriculated that fall at the University of Mississippi in Oxford. His brother William had attended Ole Miss in 1895–96 before going to the Military Academy at West Point. John Sidney was at the university for only a year—1901–02—during which he took courses leading to a bachelor of science degree. Possibly because he wanted to follow in his older brother's footsteps, he decided to leave Oxford for West Point. To prepare for West Point's rigorous entrance exams, John Sidney took a test for prospective entrants to the Naval Academy, the results of which were good enough to convince him to choose Annapolis over West Point. With a letter of appointment from Senator Anselm J. McLauren of Mississippi, John Sidney passed a physical exam and was admitted to the Academy as a second-year midshipman on 25 September 1902.[5]

At Annapolis McCain discovered an institution undergoing a profound physical and academic transformation. Stately gray granite buildings were going up all over the "Yard," replacing dilapidated wood and brick structures on the banks of the Severn. Because Bancroft Hall, a dormitory massive enough to house the entire brigade of midshipmen, was still under construction and would not be ready for occupancy for another two years, McCain and others in the class of 1906 had to bunk in temporary wood frame annexes that were deficient in nearly all modern amenities. At the same time, the Academy had begun to implement a new and challenging curriculum that stressed science and engineering as the best preparation for officers in the new Navy of steel and steam. Yet the cloistered Annapolis culture—rooted in strict discipline, a hierarchical social structure, and an ethic that evoked medieval concepts of honor and privilege—had not changed. Nor had much of the academic tradition, which still emphasized rote learning over independent thought and informed reason. Nevertheless, the Academy engendered among the midshipmen a lifelong commitment and sense of selfless duty that carried through entire careers and lifetimes.[6]

Midshipmen paid a price in submission to a sometimes mindless conformity and traditions going back to the age of sail. Believed to "build character," hazing, or "running" as it was also known, was a form of institutionalized harassment officially banned but still common, with incoming "plebes" and other underclassmen the usual victims. Mids like McCain who shared rooms in the annexes were fond of rough-housing and pranks that could and did lead to disciplinary measures. In his first two years McCain earned demerits for such offenses as not placing his shoes neatly under his bunk, chewing tobacco, smoking, playing cards, and returning a library book late. A more serious offense occurred in December 1904 when he got fifteen days on the ancient frigate *Santee* for being "disrespectful to [a] superior officer." That year he earned 189 demerits. There were also health problems. Minor ailments landed him in sick bay in 1903 and 1904, but they did not threaten his naval career, as did an odd temporary hearing loss that caused the Academy to find him "disqualified for Naval Service" in March 1905. Fortunately, at the request of the Academy's superintendent, the Navy's surgeon general recommended and the Navy Department agreed that McCain's disability be waived and that he remain at the Academy through his first-class year.[7]

Each summer, midshipmen went on summer cruises, training exercises intended to familiarize them with the routines of shipboard life and inculcate them with the discipline and responsibilities associated with command at sea. Many of the mids regarded the excursions as rewards for the hardships imposed by academics and relief from the suffocating Annapolis culture. On 6 June, at the end of his first academic year, McCain joined the bark *Chesapeake* for the 1903 cruise. The ship's captain was Cdr. William Halsey, whose son Bill—two classes ahead of McCain at the Academy— was also on board, the first time in Academy history that father and son had served together on a practice cruise. The *Chesapeake* sailed from Annapolis to Gardiners Bay in eastern Long Island, then to New London, Connecticut, where McCain transferred to the *Indiana* (BB 1), a seagoing coastline battleship dating from before the Spanish-American War. The *Indiana* took the midshipmen to New York for Independence Day celebrations and on to the resort town of Bar Harbor, Maine. There McCain boarded the venerable steam sloop *Hartford*, famed as Adm. David Farragut's flagship at the 1864 Battle of Mobile, which carried him to Rockland, Maine, and back to Annapolis on 31 August. For the 1904 cruise McCain again embarked on the *Hartford*. From Annapolis on 6 June, the *Hartford* and other ships took the mids to Newport News, Virginia, then to New London, Provincetown, Massachusetts, and Boston before returning to Annapolis on the *Indiana's* sister *Massachusetts* (BB 2) at the end of August. The 1905 summer cruise was McCain's third and last. He sailed on the new monitor *Florida* (BM 9) from Annapolis on 5 June, steaming down the Chesapeake Bay to Newport News, where he and the other mids toured shipyards before continuing to Rockland, Maine, and Gardiners Bay. At Gardiners Bay, McCain transferred to the monitor *Terror* (BM 4), which exercised in Long Island Sound before joining the other training ships at Solomons Island, Maryland. All of the warships returned to Annapolis at the end of August.[8]

Along with his fellow midshipmen, McCain earned various nicknames, among them "Mac," "Lentz," and "Johnnie," but later the one that eventually stuck was "Slew." Where and how the name originated is lost. It may have derived from his peculiar "slew-footed" gait, or from his Mississippi background, where bayous were known as "sloughs" or "slews." Though popular and respected by his comrades, who chose him as petty officer in the Tenth Company, McCain did not distinguish himself as a scholar. In May 1903, at the end of the academic year, McCain stood 68th in a class of 160. His best work was in English, law, and modern languages; his worst in mechanical drawing and "efficiency." The following year he fell to 99th out of a class of 140, although he did relatively well in mathematics and physics courses. At the end of his third year he ranked 77th in a class that was down to 125, with good marks in mechanics and physics and poor grades in seamanship and conduct. His grades in naval construction and physics were about average for the class in the 1905–06 academic year, but his grades in navigation and modern languages were poor. On graduation he stood 80th in a class of 116. The 1906 yearbook *Lucky Bag* praised him for his humor and facetiously congratulated him as the "skeleton in the family closet" who gained "1 3/8" ounces during his time at the Academy. Indeed, at five feet seven inches and 134 pounds, McCain had put on nearly twenty pounds since 1902. Among his classmates who made flag rank were Robert L. Ghormley, Aubrey W. ("Jake") Fitch, John H. Towers, Leigh H. Noyes, Isaac C. Kidd, and Frank Jack Fletcher.[9]

McCain graduated with his class on 12 February 1906, at midyear due to the rapidly modernizing Navy's pressing requirement for junior officers. At the time, midshipmen did not immediately receive their commissions and routinely spent a year or two at sea as passed midshipmen—sort of apprentice ensigns—before being promoted. McCain's first posting in April was to the *Ohio* (BB 12), a 12,700-ton battleship mounting four 12-inch guns, which served as the flagship of the Asiatic Fleet in Manila. His first assignments were as boat officer and assistant to the ship's officer of the deck. Capt. Leavitt C. Logan, the *Ohio*'s skipper, rated McCain very good to excellent in his fitness reports and commended him as a "promising officer" deserving "favorable consideration" for promotion by the Academy's Academic Board. After five months in the *Ohio*, McCain transferred to the 4,400-ton protected cruiser *Baltimore* (C 3), where he was an assistant navigation officer standing day watches. He did well initially, only to run into trouble in November when the ship's commanding officer, Cdr. James M. Helm, suspended him from duty for allowing sailors to get drunk following a party at the Cavite Navy Yard. He further declared him "not up to the average standing of midshipmen" and that he "should not be ordered to any ship as a [regular] watch officer until qualified."[10]

The episode in Cavite and subsequent poor fitness report may have taken McCain out of consideration for a choice billet and relegated him to duty in the old gunboat *Panay*. Acquired from Spain by the Army and transferred to the Navy in 1899, the shallow-draft, lightly armed 160-ton vessel had performed blockade and patrol duty during the bloody and protracted Philippine-American War. Temporarily laid up in 1902, the *Panay* was recommissioned in January 1907 with Ens. Chester W. Nimitz as commanding officer. As the only two officers on the ship, McCain and Nimitz worked closely together and shared responsibilities. The *Panay* spent most of its time in and around the southern island of Mindanao patrolling against restive Moro natives and showing the flag. Nimitz recalled that Navy rations were short and that at times he had "difficulty feeding my crew." Generous Filipinos, however, helped with fresh food, supplemented by ducks shot by Nimitz and McCain. In the middle of a war scare with Japan, Nimitz and McCain avoided a protocol dilemma with their Army counterparts. "My second in command, J. S. McCain (06) and I had been well entertained by Army families in Zamboanga, and we planned a return party on 4 July 1907," Nimitz recalled. "When McCain and I compared our lists of guests (each of us had acted independently with invitations), we were shocked to see that we had invited people who hated each other & who would not mix. While pondering on how to resolve this problem, we received the urgent orders to depart at once for Cavite. This permitted us to cancel the 4th of July party—much to our relief." Years later, McCain recounted that the only excitement was when he "took part in one midnight raid on a Moro stronghold which was abortive, the Moros having received information through a supposed fifth columnist."[11]

In July, McCain left Nimitz and the *Panay* to assume duties as engineer officer on the *Chauncey* (DD 3), a 420-ton destroyer laid up in reserve at Cavite. Lt. Frank R. McCrary, the ship's commanding officer and later a naval aviator, liked McCain's "great interest and energy," despite his lack of experience and not having a full complement of personnel in the engineering department. He was particularly impressed with how well McCain and his men had replaced the destroyer's two propellers in twenty-four hours, a third of the time estimated for the job. McCain was promoted to ensign on 18 March 1908 while he was with the *Chauncey*. In his last fitness report, McCrary wrote that McCain had "shown the greatest interest in his work as chief engineer and has his department in better condition than it has been during my experience with the flotilla." Unlike many of his fellow officers and bluejackets, who contracted all manner of diseases while on duty in the Philippines, McCain escaped with nothing worse than a mild case of dengue fever, requiring only two days in the naval hospital in Cavite in September 1908.[12]

With orders assigning him to the Atlantic Fleet, Ensign McCain was detached from the *Chauncey* and reported to the 16,000-ton, 12-inch-gun battleship *Connecticut* (BB 18) in Manila on 27 November. The *Connecticut* was the flagship of what was known as the Great White Fleet, then roughly halfway through an epic fourteen-month circumnavigation. Originally intended as a means of demonstrating American naval power in the western Pacific, the world cruise appealed to President Theodore Roosevelt as a means of concentrating the new battleship Navy and flexing American naval muscles before a global audience. Roosevelt had personally seen the gleaming white battleships of the Atlantic Fleet sail from Hampton Roads in December 1907. They joined the Pacific Fleet in San Francisco in May and reached the Philippines on 7 November. The *Connecticut* departed from Manila in December and reached Suez in early January before being detached to Messina, Italy, to join the battleship *Illinois* (BB 7) in providing assistance to survivors of a devastating earthquake in Sicily. Naples and Gibraltar were ports of call before the fleet returned to a triumphal presidential review at Hampton Roads on 22 February.[13]

McCain spent a month at home in Teoc before reporting in May to the armored cruiser *Pennsylvania* (ACR 4) on the West Coast. That summer he took ten days' leave to marry Katherine Davey Vaulx in Colorado Springs, Colorado, on his twenty-fifth birthday, 9 August 1909. Thirty-one years old at the time, Katherine had been born in Fayetteville, Arkansas, on 8 January 1878, and was a graduate of the University of Arkansas. The marriage was evidently the culmination of an extended long-distance courtship; it is likely that she had met McCain when he was a freshman at the University of Mississippi where she was teaching courses in classical languages during the 1901–02 academic year.[14]

McCain left the *Pennsylvania* in December 1909 and reported to the armored cruiser *Washington* (ACR 11), where he served as an engineer officer for more than a year. In the fall of 1910, after spending most of its time on the West Coast, the cruiser steamed from California to Hampton Roads via the Strait of Magellan. During his tour in the *Washington*, McCain took and passed the examination for advancement to lieutenant junior grade, the promotion to date from 13 February 1911. That year Katherine gave birth to a son, John Sidney Jr. ("Jack"), on 17 January while she was visiting members of her family in Council Bluffs, Iowa, and McCain was at sea in the *Washington*.[15]

In keeping with the Navy's desire to have its officers broaden their experience by rotating in and out of sea and shore duty, McCain left the *Washington* in February 1912 for a posting at the Charleston Navy Yard. During a two-year tour, he was in charge of the Machinist Mates School, served on a board of survey, participated in various court martial proceedings, and earned promotion to lieutenant on 5 August 1912 (to date from 1 July). That September, while still assigned to the navy yard, he was detailed to temporary command of the 200-ton torpedo boat *Stockton* (TB 32) for a big naval review in New York on 13–15 October. McCain earned uniformly "excellent" fitness reports while he was assigned to the navy yard. In Charleston the McCains celebrated the arrival of a second son, James Gordon, on 17 February 1913. More shore duty followed on the West Coast before McCain received orders in April 1914 to report as executive officer of the *Colorado* (ACR 7), a 14,000-ton armored cruiser with the Pacific Reserve Fleet at the Puget Sound Navy Yard in Bremerton, Washington. There Kate gave birth to a daughter, Catherine Vaulx, on 13 January 1915, just before McCain went off to sea in the *Colorado* to patrol the west coast of Mexico during a period of revolutionary turmoil. While he was the *Colorado*'s exec, a board of inspection in 1915 attributed the "excellent" material condition of the ship to McCain's "thorough and efficient administration." He remained with the *Colorado* until he was detached on 11 September 1915 to assume duties as engineer officer on the armored cruiser *San Diego* (ACR 6), flagship of the Pacific Fleet.[16]

For the first year and a half McCain was in the eight-year-old, 14,000-ton *San Diego*, the cruiser steamed up and down the West Coast before being placed in reserve in February 1917. At the time, one of his superior officers commended McCain for the "splendid organization" of the ship's engineering department and remarked that he was "a most excellent officer." On the eve of the country's entry into World War I, the *San Diego* was restored to full commission and in July transferred to the Atlantic Fleet. At Hampton Roads in August, the ship joined Cruiser Division 2 and later served as flagship for the commander, Cruiser Force Atlantic. While with the *San Diego* McCain was temporarily elevated to lieutenant commander on 31 August. In late December, McCain took over as the cruiser's navigator, and on 16 January 1918 received permanent promotion to lieutenant commander (to date from 22 September 1917). Through the rest of the year and into the spring of 1918, the San Diego escorted transatlantic convoys from bases in Tompkinsville, on Staten Island, and Halifax, Nova Scotia. On 26 May, McCain was detached from the cruiser and assigned to duty with the Bureau of Navigation in Washington. A little more than six weeks later, on 19 July, the San Diego struck a mine laid by a German U-boat and sank off Fire Island, New York, one of the few American warships lost during the war.[17]

One of the most formidable organizations in the Navy's Washington bureaucracy, the Bureau of Navigation had, among other responsibilities, the assignment and advancement of personnel. As appointment officer with the temporary rank of commander, McCain's primary job was to keep officers' records and provide information to selection and promotion boards as well as to Congress. Early in his tour he had to deal with the complexities of demobilization as the Navy shrank from a wartime high of 31,194 officers and 495,662 men in 1918 to 10,109 officers and 108,950 enlisted personnel in 1920. A specific problem was the large reserve officer corps, in which there were many highly trained personnel with specialized experience whom the bureau wanted to retain by shifting them to the regular Navy. One of McCain's duties in the fall of 1920 was service on a special board to promulgate rules for such transfers and to draft congressional legislation to implement them fairly. Like many of his fellow officers, McCain disliked shore duty, but the assignment provided him with valuable administrative experience and a firsthand understanding of Washington politics. Equally important, the McCains, living together first in an attached three-story house on Newton Street and later in similar dwellings on Ontario Road and Twentieth Street in Northwest Washington, experienced years of stability that too often eluded Navy families.[18]

Based on his work at BuNav, McCain published a study of officer selection and promotion in "A Personnel Survey" in the U.S. Naval Institute Proceedings in January 1923. He used detailed statistical analysis to project that under the Personnel Act of 1916 there would be only 72 slots for 157 officers eligible for advancement to captain in 1927. Those coming up for elevation to commander and lieutenant commander were better off, with slightly more vacancies than officers available for advancement. But the situation was complicated by age requirements. As senior officers retired or left the service, officers in lower ranks took their places based on seniority, causing temporary age "humps" in the officer corps that would slow promotions through the early 1930s. There were also situations where age requirements and selection procedures held junior officers in their grades longer than necessary or desired. And it was not fair that a selection board might pass over a qualified senior officer who would have to retire in a few years for an equally qualified younger officer who would not age out as soon. McCain concluded that the Navy had earned the recognition and respect of the American public and Congress, who knew that "when ministers of state have anything to say they say it with battleships." It was essential for the Navy to have an equitable and "elastic" system that ensured a "reasonable flow of promotion at very small cost," acknowledging at the same time that no policy would make everyone happy and that there would always be "obstructionists" within and outside the service.[19]

In June 1921, McCain separated from the Bureau of Navigation and returned to the fleet, reporting to the battleship *Maryland* (BB 46), a 32,000-ton dreadnought boasting eight 16-inch guns then fitting out at the Newport News Shipbuilding and Dry Dock Company. When the ship was fully commissioned on 21 July, McCain took over as navigator. As sea duty went, it was thoroughly enjoyable. The *Maryland* was a "showboat," serving as flagship of the Atlantic Fleet, calling at Annapolis for the 1922 graduation ceremonies and at Boston for the anniversary of the Battle of Bunker Hill. In September 1922, the *Maryland* escorted the steamer carrying Secretary of State Charles Evans Hughes to Rio de Janeiro for the Brazilian independence centennial exposition, returning him to New York after a week of ceremonies. During his tour McCain earned promotion to commander on 31 December 1921. Only days later, he had to take leave to return to Carrollton, where his mother Elizabeth had suffered what he declared was a "general breakdown" and died on 17 January at the age of sixty-six. McCain left the *Maryland* in April 1923 and reported a month later to duty once again with the Bureau of Navigation.[20]

BuNav was McCain's professional home for the next three years. His assignment was to the bureau's office of officer personnel, whose director was Capt. William D. Leahy, later a fleet admiral and President Franklin D. Roosevelt's chief of staff during World War II. The immediate issue was the Equalization Bill before Congress in 1924. Drafted by a Navy board in June 1923 that included members from each of the staff corps (Engineer, Construction, Medical, Supply, and Chaplain), with McCain representing officers of the line, the bill linked staff officers to "running mates" in the line, thus providing them with opportunities for advancement equal to those enjoyed by line officers and ensuring they were promoted at the same time. McCain explained the situation in an article in the March 1924 *Proceedings*. Generally the proposed policy would give staff officers a better idea of their opportunities for promotion, which under present law was not easy to calculate due to the vagaries of the Navy's selection process. McCain explained that by averaging the chances of advancement line officers had over four successive years, staff officers might be better able to anticipate their futures in the service, and he provided data on how many medical officers would be qualified for elevation to captain by 1930. Some staff officers might have to mark time in their rank until their running mates caught up with them, but on the whole the measure "affords the same opportunity for promotion of staff officers whose promotion has lagged behind the promotion of their running mates in the line."[21]

As the Equalization Bill ground through the legislative mill, lawmakers called McCain to Capitol Hill in the spring of 1924 to explain details of the measure and why he believed it was important to revise the Navy's promotion policies. From 17 to 19 March he appeared before a subcommittee of the Senate Naval Affairs Committee chaired by George W. Pepper, a Republican from Pennsylvania. Nearly all the bureau chiefs who testified thought the bill would positively affect their uniformed personnel. The sole exception was Adm. John D. Beuret of the Bureau of Construction and Repair, who emphasized that Construction Corps officers opposed changing the policy because over the long run it would slow their promotions. Initially McCain was the subcommittee's de facto resource person, providing statistics, specific information, and correctives as needed as various senior officers came before the senators.[22]

When he was called to the witness table, McCain went through the bill line by line and explained how each of its provisions affected various officer grades and how the "running mate" system worked, illustrating specific contingencies when officers died or retired and assuring those present that nothing in the bill favored any officer or class of officers. He agreed to redraft the wording and organization of the bill that he and the senators believed would help clarify its major provisions when it came before the House. He stressed that the "secret of the whole thing" was that the bill provided long-term continuity that had been lacking in previous personnel legislation. The proposal also assured equality of opportunity for those officers as they advanced past the rank of lieutenant commander, where the selection process sometimes hampered the promotion of staff personnel. To those concerned about senior officers who might be forced into retirement at relatively young ages, McCain explained that his figures estimated that only 7 percent would have to leave the service before the age of fifty. And to Beuret's worries that the Construction Corps might lack a sufficient number of senior officers, he emphasized that "when this bill has become a law the Secretary of the Navy will be able to calmly and judicially consider the size of a corps as a balanced part of a military institution, and to so recommend to Congress, which will also be freed of the personal element in considering the question."[23]

A month later McCain spent three days before the House Committee on Naval Affairs, chaired by Pennsylvania Republican Thomas S. Butler. As he had in the Senate, McCain detailed the various provisions of the Equalization Bill, especially the "running mate" concept, which he saw as a "guiding principle" that underlay the promotion of all staff officers. Within two years of the passage of the 1916 Navy Personnel Act, he said, "discrepancies began to appear, and the line was moving ahead faster than some corps, and other corps were moving ahead faster than the line and other corps together." The present bill would solve those problems. Some on the committee fretted about the costs of the bill. McCain patiently explained that the measure would not result in a Navy top-heavy with expensive flag officers, nor would it result, as one congressman put it, in an "endowment insurance policy" for a plethora of retired admirals. McCain estimated that the total cost to the taxpayer would be on the order of $400,000 in retirement pay, not the $4 million that had been mistakenly presented by a Construction Corps officer. In the end, McCain believed "most emphatically" that the bill would eliminate friction between the staff corps and the line, and his appeals for efficiency, fairness, and homogeneity resonated with the congressmen, despite many of their reservations about costs and budgets.[24]

The General Board, as the Navy's principal planning body, was interested in elements of the Equalization Bill that specifically affected officer promotion and selection. McCain appeared before the board on 23 May 1924 to answer questions about BuNav's proposal to extend from thirty-four to thirty-five the years of service before mandating the retirement of captains. He explained that the intention was to allow captains who were high on the Navy List to stay in the service a year longer and thereby have an equal chance for promotion as some of their younger counterparts; when the regulation applied to everyone, he stated, "you have an absolutely equitable proposition." The fundamental issue was fairness, but there was also a political dimension. An officer further down the list who had been passed over knew that the reason was based on a selection board's assessment of merit and not his years in service. That officer was therefore not in a position to complain to members of Congress that the Navy had arbitrarily forced his retirement due to age in grade. McCain went on to urge the board to support the bill, which he optimistically expected had enough votes to move expeditiously through Congress.[25]

If McCain believed he had the General Board's support for the Equalization Bill, he still wanted to reassure a wider Navy audience of the potential benefits of the proposal. In an article in the May 1925 *Proceedings*, he used the Academy's class of 1907—big in comparison to the 1906 (McCain's) and 1908 classes, and one where because of its size some officers were not optimistic about their opportunities for advancement—as a case study of how the new policy of age-in-service might function. He assumed there would be no increase in the number of authorized line officers and that each year on average 9 percent of commanders would be passed over for captain in the present selection process. Presenting statistics, he traced how many commanders in the class of 1907 would be elevated under existing policies, which stressed seniority and accounted for vacancies that opened due to the retirement of officers in various age groups. A table included all 4,776 officers in the service from the most senior admiral to the lowest-ranking ensign, which allowed all commissioned personnel to estimate their chances for promotion under the present selection system and provided guidance for them once the new measure went into effect. The bottom line was that for most officers in the grade of commander and above, the revised policy would not affect their advancement to any major degree.[26]

Another opportunity for McCain to present his ideas about officer promotion came with the President's Aircraft Board in the fall of 1925. Appointed by President Calvin Coolidge in the wake of the fatal crash of the Navy airship *Shenandoah* (ZR 1) and the subsequent tirade by Army Brig. Gen. William ("Billy") Mitchell against both the Army's and the Navy's "criminal negligence" in handling aviation, the panel's chairman was Coolidge's old college chum and internationally respected businessman Dwight Morrow. Coolidge wanted the board to address the economic distress of the aircraft industry and to resolve once and for all the controversy between the Army and the Navy over the control of military aviation. He hoped as well to steal the march on Congress, which since March 1924 had its own select committee under Wisconsin Republican congressman Florian Lampert investigating a wide range of questions regarding the government's role in aviation. Among those serving on the Morrow Board was Georgia Democratic congressman Carl Vinson, who was also a key minority member of the House Naval Affairs Committee.[27]

Naval aviation was a specific consideration of the Morrow Board. Since the establishment of the Bureau of Aeronautics in 1921, its chief, Rear Adm. William A. Moffett, had sought to establish authority over aviation personnel. Moffett found himself in conflict with the Bureau of Navigation, which held an unyielding grip on the assignment of officers to sea duty and was reluctant to provide flight pay for what aviators regarded as hazardous duty. Moffett also fought a rear-guard action within the service with aviators who wanted to have a semiautonomous aviation corps, believing it would insulate them from what they saw as a hidebound and hostile "battleship Navy" dominated by the "Gun Club." To Moffett, who insisted that aviation was integral to the fleet, a separate corps was anathema, and he had to reassure aviators that he would protect their interests as line officers within the service.[28]

McCain appeared before the Morrow Board on 6 October. He acknowledged that senior aviators, "rightly or wrongly," felt they were being held back from important command positions and that young officers, forced to rotate between aviation duties and general line service, were unsure about pay and advancement. Moreover, he understood that a corps was a "protective promotion device" that assured advancement within their specializations. Yet he saw the possibility that line officers would tend to dismiss aviation as a combat arm if it were segregated into a separate corps, and airmen would find themselves removed from command authority. Aviation was, he insisted, an "integral and corporate part" of the Navy. In that respect, he agreed with Moffett. On the other hand, he adhered to the BuNav regulation that aviators periodically had to go to sea in line responsibilities if they were to advance into command positions. The chief stumbling block, as he viewed it, was flight pay, which aviators would have to forgo while they were at sea; a possible answer was to reimburse aviators with the equivalent of flight pay. He also suggested that the law could be amended so that selection boards based promotion recommendations on the fitness of more senior aviators within their specialization and not in relation to the performance of general line officers. These men would be held as extra numbers on the Navy List and be eligible to command ships.[29]

The Morrow Board exposed McCain to the challenges the Navy faced as it grappled with the implications of the new technology. The so-called

McCain Plan had merit as a partial solution to the dilemmas faced by the aviation community, yet such pioneer aviators as John Towers chafed at the prospect of being held as extra numbers in rank. Fully accepted by the president, the Morrow Board report virtually guaranteed that Moffett and the Navy won their battle with Mitchell to retain control of aviation, and its recommendations paved the way for aviators eventually to command aircraft carriers and other aviation-related ships and units. Nevertheless, it did not lead to an early compromise between BuAer and BuNav on a host of other differences, including flight pay, length of sea duty, and other personnel matters that were not fully solved until World War II.[30]

Finally passed by Congress and signed into law by the president on 10 June 1926, the Equalization Bill was in large degree a personal triumph for McCain. It rationalized and balanced the Navy's pay and promotion policies, which needed updating to reflect the increasing professionalization and specialization of the service. Not all officers were pleased, particularly those in the Construction Corps, who had to wait for many of their line counterparts to "catch up." Nor was Admiral Moffett. He worried that the law would siphon off to line duties specialist engineering officers in the Bureau of Aeronautics, and he intervened with the Secretary of the Navy to restrict a number of Construction Corps officers to engineering duty only. Even so, as late as 1939, constructors lobbied Chief of Naval Operations (CNO), Adm. Harold R. Stark, for changes in promotion policies. McCain wrote Stark that, contrary to some accounts, Construction Corps officers had not been discriminated against in the promotion process and that their continued agitation had been detrimental to the principles of equalization established by the 1926 legislation. Constructors, McCain asserted, "think that the poorest Constructor is better than the best Line officer" and that their elevation "remains under the dead hand of seniority." Not only should no Construction Corps officer be promoted ahead of his line officer "running mate," the number of captains in the Corps needed to be shaved back to 50 percent of the equivalent number of experienced line officers.[31]

In rationalizing the process, the law injected more rigidity into promotions than many were comfortable with, leading to revisions in the 1930s, but for the most part the policies remained in place throughout the remainder of the decade. Hardly exciting compared to other aspects of naval duty, personnel matters nevertheless lay at the heart of the profession. McCain's expertise earned him respect in the service and among key members of the House Naval Affairs Committee, including Carl Vinson, who later chaired the committee and became one of the Navy's chief advocates on Capitol Hill. Adm. Thomas Washington, McCain's first boss as BuNav chief, wrote that McCain's "knowledge of, and efficient handling of the whole subject won the confidence of the Senate and House Naval Committees, and thereby enabled the Navy to obtain much necessary and valuable naval personnel legislation, the credit for which . . . should be fully given to him."[32]

★ ★ ★ ★

Following his tour with BuNav, more sea duty came in April 1926 when McCain traveled across the country to Mare Island to take temporary command of the *Sirius* (AK 18), a relatively new 4,000-ton transport attached to the Naval Transportation Service. He commanded the ship for only four months before he took over in August as executive officer of the battleship *New Mexico* (BB 40) at Bremerton. The ship's skipper was Bill Leahy, with whom McCain had a fine working relationship from their years together at the Bureau of Navigation. An older dreadnought, commissioned in 1918, the *New Mexico* displaced 32,000 tons and mounted twelve 14-inch guns in its main battery. It was the first American battleship to employ turboelectric propulsion, whereby steam turbines drove generators that supplied electricity to powerful electric motors, thus saving space and eliminating the complex reduction gears used in more conventional systems. McCain was with the ship for more than a year and a half, a plum assignment that provided him with additional practical experience in the battleship Navy and earned him a reputation for efficiency. Under Leahy and McCain, the *New Mexico* was known as the "Wonder Ship" for its high standards of performance and many awards. One of McCain's fitness reports emphasized that "due largely to Commander McCain's efforts, the *New Mexico* has moved to first place in gunnery, engineering, and communications; and been complimented by the Commander-in-Chief for smartness, cleanliness, and material condition." In June 1927, while McCain was with the *New Mexico* homeported at San Pedro, Kate and the two youngest children—James and Catherine—joined him, taking up residence in nearby Long Beach. At the same time, much to his delight, he learned that his son Jack had received an appointment to the Naval Academy.[33]

William R. Smedberg, later a vice admiral, joined the *New Mexico* in San Diego. Shortly after coming aboard, McCain asked him, "Son, what would you like to do when you're on this ship?"

Smedberg replied, "Well . . . Sir, I don't know really. Anything that I'm told to do."

"What do you particularly like?" McCain continued. "Do you like navigation, do you like gunnery, do you like engineering?"

Smedberg said, "I'd like gunnery more than anything, Sir, and navigation, but I really dislike engineering."

"Fine," McCain said. "You'll be an assistant in the main engine room." For a year, Smedberg learned firsthand all there was to know about the ship's engineering department.

McCain also had heard that Smedberg had been a coxswain on a rowing crew at the Academy. Smedberg acknowledged, "Yes Sir."

"Well," McCain said, "starting tomorrow morning, and every morning when we are in port, at four or five o'clock you will take out the enlisted race boat crew, and then when you come back you take out the officer race boat crew, because we are going to win the races."

"So while my classmates were going up to LA and coming back at six o'clock in the morning," Smedberg recalled, "I was getting up every day at four and taking out the enlisted race boat crew and then the officer race boat crew, and we won both races that year."[34]

After leaving the *New Mexico* in February 1928, McCain went on to the Naval War College in Newport, Rhode Island, for postgraduate studies, a crucial though not necessary step for earning a captain's four stripes. Kate, James, and Catherine accompanied him to Newport for the academic year 1928–29. McCain joined forty-seven other Navy, Marine, and Army officers in the senior class, including three fellow commanders—H. Kent Hewitt, Alan G. Kirk, and Jesse B. Oldendorf—who went on to flag rank and important commands in World War II. The curriculum included intensive background reading in the classics of naval history and strategy by Alfred Thayer Mahan, Julian Corbett, and Herbert Richmond, with the focus on battles such as Trafalgar, Tsushima, and Jutland. Then, as now, the students employed the commander's "Estimate of the Situation" in the plans for and conduct of battles, played out in the college's war games.[35]

McCain's studies at Newport included two theses. His first was on a required topic that examined military strategy and foreign policy during a specific period in American history. McCain's topic was "The Causes of the Spanish American War, and the Naval and Combined Operations in the Atlantic, Including the Transfer of the Oregon." In a generally clear, chronological narrative, McCain traced the long-term causes of the war, foremost among them the decline of the "aged, decrepit, and decadent" Spanish empire in the New World, with the consequent power vacuums and uncertainty that led to tensions between the two countries and made conflict inevitable. The more immediate cause of the war was the revolution in Cuba, which Spain sought to suppress with "cruel and damnable stupidity" that aroused American public opinion, fanned by "yellow journalism," in favor of intervention. With the exception of Commo. Winfield Scott Schley's "Flying Squadron," the Navy adhered to the principles of war by imposing a blockade on Cuba and concentrating the battle fleet under Rear Adm. William T. Sampson to engage and defeat Admiral Pascual Cervera's cruisers at Santiago. McCain briefly discussed the importance of new technology in naval warfare. The threat of an attack by a Spanish torpedo boat momentarily disrupted the epic voyage of the battleship *Oregon* from San Francisco to join Sampson's force off Santiago. "The torpedo," McCain wrote, "was a relatively new weapon and had a young and enthusiastic following much like the air service now." Missing were the economic, social, and political dimensions of Manifest Destiny, Social Darwinism, and the New Imperialism, but on the whole the paper, which earned an "A," was a fair summary of American nineteenth-century foreign and naval policy.[36]

McCain's second thesis was on a topic he chose with the approval of the War College faculty: "The Foreign Policies of the United States." Better written and more carefully proofread than his previous work, the paper was a substantially finished product that combined solid narrative history with insightful analysis. McCain surveyed American diplomacy from the colonial era through World War I and the immediate postwar years. Consistent with Mahan, he stressed that the United States, especially after the completion of the Panama Canal, was an insular nation with global ties, and he emphasized the necessary connection between military and naval policies and strategies with national interests and diplomacy. He was especially critical of Woodrow Wilson, calling him a "visionary" who sacrificed national interests for the "noble dream" of the League of Nations. "Professors and schoolmarms read, but surely they never study history," he wrote. Wilson's political opponents were not much better. "The Republicans countered the idealistic appeal of the League by one equally appalling, namely Disarmament" in the 1920s. For the present and future, McCain believed that world peace was a chimera and that only a realistic foreign policy could ensure American security and prosperity. Closer ties with Britain were essential, although that country's imperial interests were not always consonant with

America's and the British would continue to be the nation's economic rival. Like many, McCain viewed China as a slumbering giant and an enormous potential market. Most critically, resource-poor and expansionist Japan had eyes on China and the Philippines and "must be regarded as a potential enemy who bides her time." McCain concluded that "in any subsequent embroilment we must keep one eye on Japan."[37]

After graduation from the War College, McCain returned to Washington in June 1929 with Kate, James, and Catherine to begin a two-year tour with the Bureau of Navigation. His principal responsibility was organizing and conducting the Navy's enlisted and officer recruiting programs, a priority as the new administration under Herbert Hoover committed to continuing Coolidge's policy of moderate naval expansion. Shortly after arriving at the bureau he was off on a trip to inspect recruiting stations in Pittsburgh, Cleveland, Chicago, St. Louis, and Cincinnati. Early the next year he journeyed to New York, New Orleans, and Memphis, followed in the late spring and summer by a tour of recruiting activities in San Francisco, San Diego, Hampton, Virginia, and Newport.

For the most part, McCain had never suffered from health problems, although he had been treated in 1920 for what doctors believed was a duodenal ulcer, seemingly cured after several months on a special diet. Then one evening in August 1930, he complained of severe abdominal pain, which doctors diagnosed as a perforated duodenal ulcer, necessitating surgery at the Washington Naval Hospital, a four-week convalescence, and one-month sick leave. Following medical exams he was determined fit to return to duty in November.[38]

Fully recovered from what might have been a career-ending illness, McCain received orders in February 1931 to go to sea in command of an ammunition ship appropriately named the *Nitro*. On the afternoon of 9 June, he hoisted his flag on the ship moored at Hingham Bay in Boston's Outer Harbor. Commissioned in 1921, the 10,600-ton vessel was outfitted to haul explosives for ships of the battle fleet. While McCain was in command, the *Nitro* performed unexciting but necessary duty, delivering cargo, passengers, and ammunition to navy yards and depots on the East and West Coasts and transiting the Panama Canal no fewer than nine times. On 25 September, while the *Nitro* was tied up in Norfolk, McCain was temporarily promoted to captain, followed in June 1932 by a regular commission to date from 30 June 1931. Other than a week refitting in dry dock at the Boston (Charlestown) Navy Yard in October 1932, the only letup in the ship's routine was a two-month transpacific voyage in 1933. The *Nitro* stood out from San Diego on 23 January to deliver explosives to ammunition depots at Pearl Harbor, Guam, and the Cavite Navy Yard in Manila before returning to Mare Island on 31 March via Pearl Harbor. McCain's service as captain of the *Nitro* was exemplary. A board of inspection that month reported that "the condition of the Nitro is such as to reflect credit on her Commanding Officer, Captain J. S. McCain, and upon the officers and men under his command."[39] Hardly a glamorous first command, the *Nitro* nevertheless provided McCain with invaluable experience in the realities of command at sea and firsthand knowledge of a wide variety of ports and naval facilities, while burnishing his reputation as a fair yet demanding skipper who was well-liked and respected by those serving with and under him.

McCain was detached from the *Nitro* at Mare Island on the morning of 1 April 1933 and returned to Washington for what was to be his last tour of duty with the Bureau of Navigation, whose chief was now Bill Leahy. McCain found in the capital a political atmosphere laden with uncertainty. In response to the unprecedented economic crisis of the Depression, the Hoover administration had stressed reductions in federal spending that stalled expansion of the Navy and led to a 15 percent reduction in pay, a promotion freeze, and cutbacks in recruiting. In a letter to Capt. Lewis B. Porterfield, commanding officer of the *Maryland*, McCain wrote that "I can not give you an indication of the trend of things. Comments are so confused, ideas so wild, and people's interests so engrossed in what may be called local affairs that I am darned if I know how the cat is going to jump." On the other hand, McCain had "high hopes" that the new Democratic administration of Franklin D. Roosevelt would rescind the pay cut but was less optimistic that Congress would do much to "thaw out" the promotion freeze.[40]

In early 1934, McCain wrote that he had to "pinch myself" in disbelief about what he perceived as a "complete flip-flop in Congressional sentiment" toward the Navy. Roosevelt had at first contemplated continuing Hoover's policies of austerity and fiscal restraint but soon recognized that federal spending was necessary to mitigate the economic crisis. An immediate response, endorsed by Carl Vinson as the new chairman of the House Naval Affairs Committee, was to build warships using emergency public works funds. Then in 1934 Vinson teamed with his Senate counterpart, Park Trammell of Florida, to pass a massive naval construction act that authorized expanding the Navy up to its treaty limits in numbers and tonnages of warships. Roosevelt enthusiastically signed the bill into law on 27 March. New ships needed more men. McCain's assignment to the bureau's Planning Division involved developing a long-range Force Operating Plan that addressed recruitment, training, budget allocations, and personnel assignments necessary to man the treaty Navy.[41]

McCain's responsibilities also included work on a new personnel bill that, among other things, extended the line officer selection process downward to include lieutenants and kept lieutenants who were not selected for advancement as extra numbers on the Navy List. He expected the proposal to open lieutenants' prospects for elevation and yield a significant reduction in the number of retirees, thus forestalling future congressional efforts to limit the number of retirees to save money. In an astute political move, McCain made sure that the bill allowed congressmen to recommend additional special admissions of midshipmen to the Naval Academy. The measure became law in late May 1934. Although it accomplished much in untangling the Gordian knot of officer promotion, some objected that the measure did little to help junior officers and nothing to weed out the "dead wood" in the Navy's more senior ranks. There also remained unsolved the need for aviators in all grades, and particularly those who lacked sufficient seniority to command major aviation vessels. Sadly, any satisfaction McCain enjoyed in seeing "his" personnel measure become law was tempered by the loss of his father, who had died of a heart attack in April.[42] McCain took a week's leave of absence to attend the funeral and burial next to his mother in North Carrollton's Evergreen Cemetery.

At some point while he was at BuNav, McCain took stock of his career. He had proved his qualifications at sea and ashore, been promoted on time, and had forged personal friendships and professional connections in Washington, where he had established a reputation as an expert on officer personnel policies and as a superlative political tactician. Yet as a fifty-year-old four-striper in 1935, he knew that continued shore duty might plunge him into a professional and reputational black hole and that he faced keen competition from his peers. From years in BuNav and his deep understanding of promotion regulations, he knew which captains were above him on the all-important Navy List and thus ahead of him in line for advancement. Flag rank was the top of the ladder, out of reach before mandatory retirement unless he could somehow gain command of one of the fleet's major warships, primarily a battleship and possibly an aircraft carrier. A flattop might allow him to jump over some of those ahead of him on the list, but regulations since 1930 mandated that before officers could command a carrier they had to undergo flight training and earn their wings as naval aviators or complete a less rigorous course to qualify as naval aviation observers. So, on 18 January 1935, after calculating the odds and deciding his future lay in aviation, McCain submitted a request to Leahy for orders assigning him to Pensacola for instruction as a naval aviator.[43]

CHAPTER 2

Naval Aviation

Aviation appealed to John McCain for reasons that transcended his ambitions for promotion. He had always been fascinated by things technical, and he recalled later in life that flight and the airplane had been one of his interests shortly after leaving the Academy. Moreover, his professional career had included practical engineering experience as well as an understanding of Navy personnel policies that directly affected aviation and aviators. In January 1928, while still exec on the *New Mexico*, McCain had submitted a request to BuNav asking to be detailed to Pensacola for flight training. He coasted through the required physical only to be rejected because he exceeded the bureau's then-current age restrictions for flying. Although his subsequent appointment to the Naval War College assuaged any disappointment he may have felt, he knew he was physically qualified to fly and that there likely would be future opportunities to put in for aviation.[1]

McCain's break came in early 1935. Expansion of the number of ships and aircraft under the Vinson-Trammell Act created a shortage of senior officers needed to command aviation ships, shore installations, and other air units. Ernest J. King, Charles A. Pownall, and Richmond Kelly Turner had earned their wings in 1927 and had gone into aviation commands, as had McCain's 1906 Academy classmate Aubrey Fitch, who joined the aviators' ranks in 1930. Most recently, in May 1935, Capt. William F. Halsey Jr. had graduated from Pensacola as a naval aviator at the age of fifty-two, adding another name to the growing company of "Johnny-Come-Latelys." As for McCain, Leahy waived the BuNav age requirement and quickly approved his request for aviation duty, which received the endorsement of King, now a rear admiral and chief of the Bureau of Aeronautics, on 22 January. Again he passed the medical exam. Other than the loss of teeth, which ultimately necessitated a full set of dentures, the medics found him to be "physically and temperamentally adapted for duty involving actual control of aircraft." His orders came through on 30 April, although Leahy allowed him to stay on temporary duty at BuNav for another six weeks. McCain admitted that

Kate did not "altogether approve" of his decision to go into aviation, but that "she is at any rate acquiescent." He reported to Pensacola on 20 June; Kate and twenty-year-old daughter Catherine joined him there in September.[2]

★ ★ ★ ★

Pensacola, situated on Pensacola Bay west of the small city of the same name in Florida's panhandle, had been established in early 1914 as an aeronautic station, where the Navy trained all of its aviators in the years before World War I. Naval Air Station (NAS) Pensacola expanded exponentially during the war. One hundred buildings were added to the facility, and thousands of officers and men underwent instruction, not only in flying but also in such associated specialties as radio and instruments. After the war the station contracted, yet still remained the Navy's principal aviation training facility through the 1930s. Changes in the flight training syllabus came in 1931. Officers were required to receive 282.75 hours of time in the air, some of which included night flying, aerial gunnery, bombing, and torpedo work, as they advanced through five instructional squadrons. Stearman NS-1 biplanes began replacing worn out and obsolescent Consolidated NY-1s and NY-2s in December 1934. Ground instruction featured 465 hours of classes in aerial navigation, aerodynamics, aerology, engines, gunnery, and communications. Amenities at Pensacola included a library, officers' club, various indoor and outdoor recreation facilities, and nightly movies.[3]

Six days after his arrival in Pensacola, McCain went up with Lt. (jg) John M. Duke on his indoctrination flight. According to McCain's grandson Joe, McCain insisted before the flight that Duke "treat [him] like any other student." Duke, coming to attention and saluting, replied "Aye, aye, sir." After an hour of aerial maneuvers, during which Duke was not sure whether his student remained conscious, they landed and McCain stumbled out of the cockpit. Duke again saluted and asked if he had done as McCain ordered and "not worry about you being a captain?" McCain returned the salute and replied, "You did just fine, Lieutenant." After excusing himself and retreating out of sight to vomit, McCain drolly commented to a fellow captain: "You know, you're never too damned old to get a lesson in leadership." Through the first month McCain showed himself to be an earnest if not outstanding student who progressed well, especially in landings; most important, Duke reported that he "realizes his mistakes and makes effort to correct them." McCain soloed on 26 July after an extra two hours of dual instruction.[4]

Over the next seven months McCain passed milestone after milestone in the flight-training syllabus. In September, Lt. Paul E. Roswall took over instruction from Duke, criticizing McCain's rudder control in turns and landing approaches and helping him through stalls and spins. His grades marginally improved into the high 2.0s and low 3.0s out of 4.0. McCain lost a week of instruction in September due to leg and neck injuries he suffered in an auto accident. Roswall reported after a flight in early November that McCain exhibited "considerable improvement in that all maneuvers were executed smoothly, [with] well coordinated use of controls." His formation flying was good, but he had trouble finding his destination on a preliminary cross-country flight. In January 1936 Duke took over again as McCain moved on to the float-equipped Vought O2U Corsair, in which he faced the challenges of takeoffs and landings in varying conditions of wind and water. Disaster struck on 20 February when he cracked up a Vought O3U-1 Corsair floatplane on landing after a solo flight, fortunately bruising nothing more than his ego. Not surprisingly, McCain was a "little nervous" on a subsequent check flight. Four hours of instrument flying began in early March, followed by five hours of instruction in torpedo aircraft later in the month and five hours of work in April with the two-engine Douglas PD-1 flying boat.[5]

In the middle of flight training McCain received orders detaching him from Pensacola to temporary duty with Vice Adm. Henry V. Butler Jr., commander, Aircraft Battle Force, to observe flight operations during Fleet Problem XVII, a fleet exercise in the vicinity of Panama. In general, officers at Pensacola did not like having their students' instruction interrupted, but in McCain's case, they agreed with the Bureau of Aeronautics that prospective senior aviation officers like McCain could benefit from experience with aircraft carrier operations. McCain left Pensacola on 18 April and reported to Butler on the carrier *Saratoga* (CV 3) moored at NAS North Island in San Diego on 24 April. Later that day Aubrey Fitch welcomed him aboard the *Sara*'s sister ship *Lexington* (CV 2), which together with the *Saratoga* and the recently commissioned carrier *Ranger* were to participate in the war games. During the next month McCain witnessed the carriers in flight and other tactical operations, with the highlight being a 21 May "attack" on Balboa and the Pacific side of the Panama Canal by Bill Halsey's *Saratoga* and a powerful surface force. The *Lexington* and *Ranger* supported battleships, cruisers, and destroyers in defending the canal. Halsey launched first, only to see his strike miss the opposing carriers due to bad weather; the

Ranger attacked in better conditions, badly damaging the *Saratoga*, before herself suffering hard hits by shore-based patrol planes and torpedo bombers. Following the exercises, McCain rode with the *Ranger* on the return voyage to San Diego, arriving there on 8 June.[6]

McCain returned to Pensacola on 11 June to resume instruction in bombing, navigation, and catapult launches, along with more instrument flying and cross-country flights. The time away from Pensacola did nothing to improve McCain's flying skills, which seemed to deteriorate, possibly because of his tendency to lose concentration. In the middle of July an instructor reported that he had a "generally unsatisfactory" flight with McCain; another instructor graded him low on precision landings and overall "aptitude." "The work of this student is not consistent," he concluded. "[A]t times work is fair but then seems to go into a slump." Roy Johnson, another instructor at Pensacola, recalled that McCain had problems landing within a two-hundred-foot-diameter circle. After a check flight, one of Johnson's fellow instructors commented, "Gee, he couldn't even land in the field, leave alone hit the circle." When Johnson asked McCain what had gone wrong, he replied, "The altimeter must have been out, Son." It turned out that the wind had shifted 180 degrees and McCain, descending from 1,500 feet, had lost all his reference points. The "bottom line," however, was that McCain did well enough as a student to be awarded designation as Naval Aviator No. 4,280 on 24 August 1936. Yet instruction continued until 10 September, when he completed two hours of night cross-country flying, which brought his total to 325 flights and nearly 289 hours in the air. He was then a little more than one month past his fifty-second birthday and fell just six months shy of Halsey as the Navy's oldest officer to earn his wings at Pensacola.[7]

★ ★ ★ ★

McCain had anticipated he might get command of the new *Yorktown* (CV 5), but his hopes for that ship—or any other carrier command straight out of Pensacola—went on hold until those ahead of him rotated out of carriers into other aviation billets. In the meantime, he learned that he would go to the Canal Zone as commander, Aircraft Squadrons and as commanding officer of Fleet Air Base Coco Solo. Two miles east of Colón on the Atlantic end of the canal, Coco Solo had been established as a naval air station in 1917, first as a submarine base and later as a naval air station accommodating flying boats assigned to wartime antisubmarine patrols. Due to the station's location at the canal, the Navy considered the facility second in strategic importance to Hawaii and after 1930 expanded the installation to include new hangars, a landing field, three seaplane ramps, barracks, and officers' quarters. In 1931, Coco Solo was redesignated as a fleet air base to reflect its shift from coastal defense to fleet operations. McCain took a couple of weeks leave before he and Kate sailed from New Orleans for Cristobal, Canal Zone, on the United Fruit Lines SS *Santa Marta* on 10 October. When McCain reported for duty nine days later, he found that the three squadrons permanently located at the base—VP-2F, VP-3F, and VP-5F— were transitioning from older twin-engine Consolidated N2Y flying boats to the new Consolidated PBY Catalina. Sadly, he also learned that on the thirteenth, during his passage to Panama, his younger brother Harry had suddenly died of an acute liver infection.[8]

In his new assignment McCain had responsibility for organizing a series of exercises in early 1937 that involved his three VP squadrons and the seaplane tender *Wright* (AV 1), which had come down from San Diego as Rear Adm. Ernest King's flagship. King, formerly BuAer chief and now commander, Aircraft Base Force, had responsibility for all sea- and shore-based patrol squadrons and was eager to see how they performed in both long-range scouting and attack missions. King congratulated McCain on earning his wings and welcomed him to his new command, confident that he would "gain first-hand knowledge of that important (and little-known) adjunct of the Fleet—the flying boats." For his part, McCain was certain that he had "a fine command, excellent in appearance and spirit," and that if he did a good job in Panama he would find in King a "powerful and enduring friend." At the end of February, in what the press claimed were the "most extensive air manoeuvers ever scheduled in this region," fifty aircraft from McCain's squadrons flew from Coco Solo to Guantánamo, Cuba, before splitting up to continue on to Puerto Rico and the Virgin Islands. McCain wrote to his brother Joe that the exercises, which did not end until the middle of March, involved more than nine thousand miles of flying. Communications and coordination with surface units were problems, but otherwise McCain reported to King that "all planes and personnel came out of the maneuvers in excellent shape." While McCain's son Jack, serving on submarines, and his wife Roberta were posted to Coco Solo, their son John S. McCain III was born on 29 August 1936. A photo taken shortly after John III's christening ceremonies shows grandfather McCain sitting next to son Jack and proudly cradling his youngest namesake.[9]

McCain had expected to succeed Aubrey Fitch in command of the *Lexington* after his tour at Coco Solo, but he saw the job go to another of his Academy classmates, Leigh Noyes. Instead, McCain received orders on 7 April 1937 to command the *Ranger*. In a sense, the *Ranger* was something of a consolation prize, although McCain told his son Jack that "I much prefer the *Ranger* to the *Lexington*." While the ship had neither the "sky line nor the prestige" of the *Lexington*, it was to McCain a "better boat for the purpose," meaning that it had been designed and built as a carrier, rather than converted, as were the *Lexington* and *Saratoga*. He and Kate sailed from Panama on the *Sixaola* for New Orleans on 8 May, stopped for a few days in Carrollton, and then drove the rest of the way to San Diego, where they arrived on the twenty-seventh. McCain reported to the *Ranger* in San Francisco on 1 June. The carrier had just taken part in week-long festivities marking the opening of the Golden Gate Bridge, after which the ship, with McCain still embarked, steamed with the *Lexington* and *Saratoga* to San Diego. There, at 1022 on 5 June, McCain hoisted his flag in the flattop, relieving veteran naval aviator Capt. Patrick N. L. Bellinger as commanding officer. Another aviator, Cdr. Alfred E. Montgomery, stayed on as executive officer, and Lt. Cdr. Matthias B. ("Matt") Gardner, a 1919 Annapolis graduate and a former member of the Navy's Three Seahawks flight demonstration team, came on board as the carrier's navigator.[10]

The *Ranger* was intended to fulfill Admiral Moffett's desire to pack the most offensive power into the smallest practical displacement, which at 13,800 tons allowed the Navy to build five carriers within the tonnage restrictions of the 1922 Washington treaty. The *Ranger* had been authorized by Congress in February 1929 as part of a naval expansion act that included fifteen cruisers, yet the ship was not laid down until September 1931 and not commissioned until June 1934. All ship designs are bundles of compromises. In part due to the insistence of aviators, the *Ranger* was initially to have a flush flight deck, clear of obstructions and featuring hinged stacks that carried boiler gases down and away from the ship. As completed, the *Ranger* displaced 14,500 tons, 700 more than originally planned, and had a small starboard-side island for ship and aircraft control. Eight 5-inch guns and forty .50-caliber machine guns provided antiaircraft (AA) protection. The carrier was 769 feet long overall, significantly shorter than the *Lexington* and *Saratoga*, but it had a larger open hangar deck and could accommodate up to seventy-two aircraft initially divided into two squadrons of fighters and two of scout/dive bombers, which recent exercises had shown could be effective ship killers. Yet the *Ranger* had its share of deficiencies, among them a top speed of less than thirty knots and relatively poor seakeeping characteristics, which sometimes limited its operations with the fleet.[11]

The *Ranger* stayed close to San Diego for several months, conducting routine flight operations off the southern California coast, during which time the fleet's air squadrons were redesignated to match the carriers to which they were assigned. For example, the *Ranger*'s units now included the number 4 as a suffix in their designations. In the reshuffling of aircraft among the carriers, the *Ranger* traded bomber units with the *Lexington*, and a scouting squadron came over to the *Ranger* from the *Saratoga*, now under the command of John Towers, mixing aviators from the carriers and temporarily disrupting unit cohesion. The carrier's four-squadron air group now consisted of VF-4 flying Grumman F3F-1s, VB-4 (commanded by Lt. Cdr. Paul Roswall, one of McCain's instructors at Pensacola) flying Great Lakes BG-1 dive bombers, and VS-41 and VS-42, equipped with Vought SBU-1 scout bombers. Another change came in July when three of the *Ranger*'s squadrons (VB-4, VS-41, and VS-42) went on board the *Lexington* to assist with the unsuccessful search for Amelia Earhart's airplane, which had gone missing on one of the Pacific legs of her round-the-world flight. Refresher training and carrier qualifications for Navy and Marine aviators continued through the end of August, resulting in mishaps, some serious injuries, but most important, no loss of life.[12]

Accompanied by the destroyers *Worden* (DD 352) and *Hull* (DD 350), the *Ranger* departed from San Diego on the morning of 4 September on a goodwill mission to Peru, where the United States was participating in the Inter-American Technical Aviation Conference in the capital city of Lima. The Peruvian government had asked to have American aircraft take part in celebrations dedicating a monument to the Peruvian air hero Jorge Chavez, who had died making the first flight across the Alps in 1910. The assignment was consistent with the Navy's traditional commitment to "showing the flag," which usually involved battleships or cruisers bristling with heavy ordnance. The *Ranger* itself did not exhibit such an imposing presence, but McCain was confident the performance of the carrier's air group would more than compensate for the lack of big guns. The passage south was routine, other than crossing the equator, occasioned on the morning of 13 September by the time-honored sailors' initiation of "pollywogs" into the domain of Neptunus Rex. McCain served as master of ceremonies, welcoming King Neptune and his court to the ship at 0845: "Your gracious majesty, the ship is yours," McCain proclaimed, issuing orders to the bridge to "break Neptune's flag" from the yardarm. McCain, himself a pollywog, endured the same occasionally painful and always humiliating ritual transformation to "shellback," as did the other neophytes on the ship.[13]

Early in the afternoon on the fifteenth, the *Ranger* anchored in the outer harbor of Callao, Lima's port city. Almost immediately, McCain and his fellow officers found themselves engaged in one reception, cocktail party, dinner, and ball after another. Laurence A. Steinhardt, the American ambassador and delegate to the aviation conference, visited the *Ranger* on the seventeenth before the ship got under way later in the morning for air operations. The next day, while steaming eight miles offshore, the carrier launched its air group, sixty-six planes in all, to overfly Lima and land at the city's Tamba airport. Observers were impressed that all the aircraft landed in twenty minutes and took off in seventeen; experienced naval aviators wondered "what these same observers might think could they see the normal operations as conducted at North Island." McCain welcomed Peru's president, General Oscar R. Benavides, to the *Ranger* on the twentieth, and on the twenty-third, delegates to the aviation conference toured the ship. Later that morning the *Ranger* put out to sea and launched its air group, which formed up with German and Italian aircraft to fly over the ceremonies unveiling the Jorge Chavez monument. Lt. (jg) Francis D. Foley, attached to VS-41, recalled that "we cruised serenely overhead at about 5,000 feet so they could see some decent mass formations. Then we went down to about 2,000 feet or 1,000 feet, then down to about 100 feet right over the ground, right down the field at full gun. It was quite a show." Following a reception for the *Ranger*'s officers hosted by Ambassador Steinhardt, the *Ranger* left on the morning of the twenty-fourth to return to San Diego, mooring at the naval air station dock on 5 October. President Benavides later awarded McCain a medal of the Order of the Sun–Knight Commander and the Peruvian Aviation Cross as tokens of his appreciation of the visit and of the *Ranger*'s performance.[14]

The *Ranger* spent the next three weeks in San Diego before leaving on 27 October for the Puget Sound Navy Yard. Flight deck repairs and maintenance in Bremerton lasted until 28 January, with the carrier returning to San Diego on 1 February. Six weeks later, on the evening of 15 March, the *Ranger* stood out from San Diego to take part in Fleet Problem XIX, a multistage war game involving attacks on and defense of the West Coast and Hawaii. The *Ranger* was a component of the White fleet, a task force under

Vice Adm. William T. Tarrant that included four battleships and shore-based VPs defending Southern California from Ernest King's Black fleet, which consisted of two task forces with three battleships each centering on the *Lexington* and *Saratoga*. Tarrant took the initiative at the start of the maneuvers on the sixteenth and dispatched the *Ranger* to scout to the north and northwest ahead of the battleships in the main body. McCain's aviators found the *Lexington* on the afternoon of the seventeenth and launched a strike, which, combined with an attack by San Diego–based PBYs, damaged the carrier so badly that it had to withdraw from the action. During flight operations on the nineteenth, the *Ranger* defeated an attack by Black destroyers and fought off Black carrier dive bombers. The initial phase of the exercise ended when White battleships caught up with and sank the *Saratoga*, which had been tardy in launching searches. For McCain and the *Ranger*, operations had generally gone well, although some of the carrier's aircraft were involved in landing and takeoff accidents caused in part by the carrier's poor seakeeping characteristics. Fortuitously, none of the mishaps resulted in injuries or loss of life.[15]

On 25 March, the *Ranger* accompanied other elements of the fleet from the West Coast to Hawaii for the next part of the exercise. This time the *Ranger*, *Lexington*, and *Saratoga*, plus nine battleships constituted the Blue fleet under Vice Adm. Edward C. Kalbfus, whose mission was to cover Marine landings on Maui and French Frigate Shoals, an anchorage about halfway between Hawaii and Midway atoll. King, as commander, Aircraft Battle Force, determined to make a surprise aerial assault on Pearl Harbor, defended by a Red fleet of cruisers, destroyers, submarines, and Navy and Army shore-based aircraft. On the morning of the twenty-eighth, the *Ranger* fired on and chased off snooping PBYs, which presumably reported the carriers' approach to Pearl Harbor. The next day, the *Saratoga* (minus the *Lexington*, whose crew had experienced an outbreak of tonsillitis) launched a successful predawn strike against Navy and Army facilities at Pearl Harbor. Meanwhile, McCain's aircraft supported the amphibious operation at French Frigate Shoals before meeting up with the *Saratoga* to cover the landings on Maui on the thirtieth, during which Red PBYs attacked and damaged the *Ranger* severely enough for the carrier to be declared out of action. Operations in bad weather led to the loss of several VPs and the deaths of eleven aviators.[16]

In early April, McCain's *Ranger*, anchored off Honolulu during a hiatus in the maneuvers, exchanged squadrons with Towers' *Saratoga*, as King brought the *Lexington* and *Saratoga* together into an autonomous striking force for the last stage of the exercise. King's Purple fleet was to assault the Green force, preparing in San Francisco for an offensive operation across the Pacific. The *Ranger* departed from Hawaii on the twenty-first, shaping a course for the West Coast with the mission to provide air cover for the Green battle fleet. On the evening of 25 April, the *Ranger* ran into an ambush by Purple destroyers. Left wounded and sinking by torpedoes, the flattop nevertheless managed to get off a retaliatory strike that sank all four of the attackers the next morning. Before the end of the exercise on 27 April, Purple carriers raided the Mare Island Navy Yard and damaged the seaplane tender *Wright* at Alameda as well as striking Green cruisers and other ships defending San Pedro.[17]

Back in San Diego, McCain and the *Ranger* conducted training and tactical exercises in California through the rest of the spring and into summer. Marine aviators completed carrier qualifications on the ship in May, followed by test landings and takeoffs by the new Brewster XSBA-1 monoplane scout bomber in July. In August, the *Ranger* began a series of antiaircraft drills involving a pilotless radio-controlled target drone. The radio-control program was the result of the Navy's interest in developing target aircraft for more realistic fleet gunnery training. Under Lt. Cdr. Delmar S. Fahrney, a Construction Corps officer and aviator, the program began as a high-priority program at the Naval Aircraft Factory (NAF) in Philadelphia in 1936. By the end of 1937, Fahrney's team had successfully flown a radio-controlled Curtiss trainer, and in the summer of 1938 the project moved from the East Coast to Otay Mesa, south of San Diego, for additional experiments. These tests included demonstrations involving McCain's *Ranger*, beginning with practice flights over the carrier by a remotely controlled Stearman-Hammond JH-1 on 15 and 16 August. On the twenty-second, the *Ranger*'s antiaircraft batteries practiced their skills on target sleeves towed by piloted aircraft before turning their attention to one of Fahrney's pilotless drones.[18]

The firing demonstration using the radio-controlled JH-1 drone began late on the morning of the twenty-fourth. After the JH-1 passed over the ship and was more than four thousand yards off to starboard, simulating a horizontal bombing attack, the *Ranger*'s antiaircraft guns opened fire. The plan was to maintain the drone on a steady course, with radio control from a Great Lakes TG-2 torpedo bomber, but problems with an automatic stabilizing mechanism caused the drone to maneuver rapidly in various directions.

Observers, of which there were a hundred on the carrier, including Ernest King, saw no AA shells from the carrier's starboard battery burst closer than a thousand yards from the target. On the next run, as the drone was about four thousand yards to port, the carrier's antiaircraft crews opened up, shells coming close but again scoring no hits before the airborne drone operator lost control of the aircraft and it crashed into the sea.[19]

McCain reported that the batteries had tracked the drone but "were never able to catch up" with it. The problem was that the centralized anti-aircraft fire control director had been programmed to track an aircraft in straight and level flight and not one rapidly changing headings. He stressed that "after the target reached a certain altitude on the approach it was necessary to train the director so rapidly that the [firing] solution obtained became virtually useless." The *Ranger*'s gun crews might have been able to hit the drone if it had not been changing direction and altitude, and McCain was confident that they would have succeeded in defeating a formation of aircraft making a straight and level bombing run. McCain concluded that the exercise, the Navy's first, was worthwhile, as "the anti-aircraft training received from firing on a target similar to a Drone is the most valuable and instructive firing that any ship equipped with an anti-aircraft battery can have." Moreover, he suggested that drones be employed in the future to simulate dive-bombing attacks. Rear Adm. Arthur B. Cook, BuAer chief, concluded that the tests verified the importance of the target drone program in ensuring "maximum war effectiveness" of shipboard AA "under *all* conditions."[20]

Routine training and gunnery and flight exercises occupied the *Ranger* through the end of the year, during which the *Saratoga*'s VB-3, equipped with Vought SB2U-1s, replaced the *Ranger*'s VB-4. McCain's carrier, accompanied by the *Lexington* and *Saratoga*, departed from San Diego on 4 January 1939 bound for Fleet Problem XX, a major fleet exercise in the Caribbean. The flattops passed through the Panama Canal and arrived in Colón on 13 January. Six days later, the *Ranger*, in company with the *Lexington* and the new fast carriers *Yorktown* and *Enterprise* (CV 6), sailed for Guantánamo and a series of bombing and other flight exercises between Haiti and Cuba. On 17 February, McCain's ship joined the Black (American) fleet at Culebra, Puerto Rico, for the start of the maneuvers three days later. Under the command of Vice Adm. Adolphus Andrews, and including five seaplane tenders, battleships, cruisers, destroyers, and a contingent of Marines, the Black fleet had orders to defeat the White force, representing a European fascist power that had gained lodgment in the Lesser Antilles and was supporting a revolution in a Latin American nation. The White fleet, commanded by Admiral Kalbfus, included the other three carriers, with battleships and other major warships, including the target ship *Utah*, which stood in for a convoy with reinforcements for the revolutionary forces. Kalbfus had 220 carrier aircraft, all under the command of Admiral King, along with 48 battleship and cruiser planes, and Andrews had the *Ranger*'s 72 planes, more than 160 seaplanes and PBY flying boats, and 62 shore-based Marine aircraft.[21]

Andrews, an aviator familiar with carrier warfare, determined to strike first, while Kalbfus, much to King's consternation, decided to hold his carriers close in support of his surface ships defending the *Utah* "convoy." The two sides' scouts found each other east of Trinidad and Tobago on the twenty-first. In the ensuing exchange, White aircraft sank four Black cruisers and damaged two others. McCain was now the "senior surviving officer" in charge of what remained of the Black force. On the twenty-third, Kalbfus unleashed King and the *Lexington* and *Enterprise* to search for and attack what was left of Andrews' fleet, now northeast of Puerto Rico, while McCain's aircraft spent the day in fruitless searches and an attack on two White destroyers that was aborted when Andrews found the ships had already been declared out of action. But Black VPs out of Culebra, San Juan, and Samaná Bay in the Dominican Republic subjected King's carriers to nearly a full day of attacks, while themselves suffering heavy losses. On the twenty-fifth, the *Ranger*, employing a new high-frequency radio direction-finding apparatus, located a carrier north of San Juan, which scouts subsequently verified to be the *Enterprise*. McCain launched a strike at 0645 that mauled and sank the carrier, although at the cost of fifteen airplanes from the *Ranger*'s air group. Later in the day, the *Ranger*'s SBUs put a White destroyer out of action, but eight of McCain's attackers were damaged by AA fire.[22]

On the twenty-sixth, the *Ranger*'s aircraft attacked marauding White submarines, one of which sneaked past the defending screen to score a torpedo hit on the zigzagging carrier. Although the ship was damaged, it was able to continue flight operations. *Yorktown* aircraft found and attacked the *Ranger* at 0730 the next morning as the carrier was steaming away from the main body of the Black fleet. The strike failed due to accurate AA fire, and two hours later the *Ranger* launched fifty-two dive-bombers to attack battleships in the White fleet just when the exercise ended shortly after noon on the twenty-seventh. Andrews' Black force had exacted a price, but it was unable to bring the White fleet to a decisive battle, with the consequence that the convoy got through as Kalbfus had planned. In his summary report, McCain concluded that carriers "remaining with or in the close vicinity" to the fleet were vulnerable to daylight attacks, implying that they could better defend themselves if they maneuvered independently. McCain added that carrier commanders needed to consider launching attacks early rather than waiting to coordinate actions with the main body; a carrier commander had to weigh the possibility "of losing our aircraft either on their carriers or in the air by delaying their attacks."[23]

Much still remained to be learned, yet Fleet Problems XIX and XX demonstrated that control of the air was vital and that fast carriers operating independently of the main body of battleships and cruisers could attack opposing ships and defend themselves against air attacks as well as inflict damage on shore targets, even if the latter were heavily defended. More specifically, the *Lexington*'s and *Saratoga*'s strike on Pearl Harbor in the 1932 exercise showed how vulnerable that fleet base was to surprise air attack. Nevertheless, the attackers were likely to pay a price when they faced land-based air. Both exercises revealed that long-range, heavily armed shore- and tender-based PBYs could find and damage an enemy fleet covering amphibious operations, although prolonged search and strike missions took a toll on aircraft and airmen. At the same time, carriers were shown to be vulnerable to gunfire and torpedo attacks from surface ships, especially at night, when they were unable to launch defending aircraft. The 1939 maneuvers in the Caribbean underscored the importance of concentrating air power in early strikes on the enemy's carriers and the effectiveness of dive-bombers and torpedo bombers, provided they had sufficient fighter escort. Otherwise they were likely to suffer heavy losses.[24] These lessons were not lost on McCain, who would face them when he and the air Navy confronted the reality of war less than four years later.

McCain's *Ranger* lay at anchor in Guantánamo Bay on 4 April when Admiral King transferred his flag from the *Lexington* to the *Ranger* to observe flight operations and tactical exercises over the next couple of days. The *Ranger* and *Lexington* left Guantánamo on the eighth, joined later by the *Yorktown* and *Enterprise* for tactical maneuvers en route to Norfolk. The carriers arrived there on the twelfth. McCain took three days' leave before the carrier shifted to the Naval Operating Base at Hampton Roads on the twentieth. A week later, on 27 April, the *Ranger* got under way for New York City, where the carrier and other ships from the Atlantic Squadron were to take part in the opening ceremonies of the World's Fair. After anchoring overnight on the twenty-eighth off Long Branch, New Jersey, the carrier steamed up the Hudson and moored at Pier 32 on the afternoon of the twenty-ninth. Among the twenty-eight warships present were the Navy's first carrier *Langley* (CV 1), which two years before had been converted to a seaplane carrier (AV 3), the battleships *Tennessee* (BB 43), *New York* (BB 34), and *Texas* (BB 35), along with elements of Cruiser Division 8. McCain and other officers were nearly exhausted making courtesy calls on civic leaders and taking in the sights and sounds of the fair and the big city. He wrote to King: "We are having a hot time in New York. Everybody is nearly dead all ready [*sic*]. I fell off the water-wagon, bounced a couple of times, and I am now back for good. . . . We average over 100 officers, day and night, for some entertainment or another." The *Ranger* hosted close to 60,000 visitors over two weeks; no fewer than 14,344 boarded the carrier on 13 May. On the morning of 17 May, the *Ranger* left New York and its air group flew off to NAS Norfolk. The flattop moored at Pier 7 at the Norfolk Naval Operating Base at 0801 on 18 May and remained there until the end of the month, when it transferred to the Norfolk Navy Yard at nearby Portsmouth to begin a much-needed overhaul.[25]

With the *Ranger*'s crew mustered on the flight deck at 0930 on 3 June, McCain read his orders to report to San Diego as commanding officer of NAS North Island and relinquished command of the carrier to Cdr. Ralph F. Wood. McCain's two years with the *Ranger* proved invaluable. He gained intimate knowledge of carrier tactics, especially understanding how fast carriers could function defensively with the fleet and independently in offensive strikes against enemy ships and shore installations. Despite its limited size and speed and seakeeping deficiencies, the *Ranger* demonstrated that small carriers with full air groups could still be useful provided they enjoyed sufficient protection from the battle line and cruiser and destroyer screens. The reputation McCain earned from the aviators serving under him was just as important as his inauguration to carrier doctrine and operations. Lt. James S. Russell, one of the flying officers on the *Ranger*, recalled that McCain invited aviators to the bridge to stand watch and later allowed them to step in as officers of the deck. The routine cemented McCain's personal connections with airmen and helped integrate them into shipboard procedures and operations; he was "all for passing the knowledge down to the younger generation, which we greatly appreciated," Russell remembered.[26]

McCain did not report to San Diego until 1 July. His command at North Island had seen the pioneering developments in naval aviation by Glenn Curtiss and Lt. Theodore G. Ellyson in early 1911. During World War I, the station had been a center for flight training before shifting to fleet support and aircraft and engine repairs and overhauls during the 1920s and 1930s. Under McCain's command, North Island was a large and diverse organization. In addition to airfields, airplanes, and aircraft maintenance and overhauls, the station was responsible for supporting the carriers attached to the Battle Force, Pacific Fleet. Training of all kinds was also important. When BuNav questioned procedures for recruiting enlisted men for technical education at the North Island Naval Training Station, McCain responded that they had been carefully selected and would quickly assume badly needed ratings in aviation. Inspection of the Fleet Training Base on San Clemente Island took him away from his desk in February 1940.[27]

In 1940, McCain helped oversee the expansion of NAS Alameda to perform extensive aircraft maintenance, repairs, and operations with assistance from North Island. Frank McCrary, McCain's former commanding officer in the *Chauncey* and now a captain and commander at Alameda, wanted to make sure that BuAer recognized the service McCain and his people provided in identifying and requisitioning shop equipment, laying out tools and machinery, and recruiting the personnel needed for the new shops and offices. BuAer chief John Towers responded that he was pleased "that the personnel of the Naval Air Station, San Diego so wholeheartedly contributed extensive time and labor in assisting in the establishment of the Naval Air Station, Alameda."[28]

Aircraft and aviation materials passed through North Island to operational commands, including Patrol Wing 2, in Hawaii, commanded by Pat Bellinger since November 1940. Bellinger did not have sufficient material either for training or to support the long-range flying boats needed to cover the search areas for which he was responsible, and he pleaded with McCain to send more equipment and aircraft. Shortly after the New Year, 1941, McCain wrote to Bellinger to tell him that "we are raising heaven and earth not to say hell, to get the stuff you need." He reminded Bellinger that he, too, lacked aircraft and personnel: "Just to let you know that other people have troubles, our planes are flying from 12 to 14 hours a day, and this week I have got to let up because of impending exhaustion of machines and pilots." On the other hand, he was optimistic that the training programs at North Island for pilots and radiomen were showing positive results.[29]

While McCain was dealing with diverse administrative responsibilities at North Island, the General Board in Washington was determining the characteristics of the next class of fast carriers. Although there was still some sentiment for a small carrier similar to the *Ranger*, the emerging consensus was for a ship displacing at least 20,000 tons, with a speed in excess of thirty-two knots and capable of operating a seventy-two-plane air group divided into four eighteen-aircraft squadrons. A fifth, or "spare," fighter squadron could also be accommodated. At first leaning toward the smaller carrier, McCain had second thoughts and came around to supporting a bigger design. Based in part on his experience with the *Ranger*, he had become an advocate of armoring carrier flight decks, reasoning that a ship, especially a small one jammed with armed and fueled aircraft on its flight and hangar decks, was a conflagration waiting to happen. In a memo to the Secretary of the Navy on 1 March 1939, he recommended that future carriers maintain their entire air group in the hangar deck, protected by flight deck armor sufficient to resist a 500-pound bomb. At that time, he was thinking about a *Ranger*-size carrier operating close to the battle fleet. Later, pointing to contemporary British designs that incorporated armored flight decks, he believed more protection was needed as carriers "took the fight to the enemy" in the Pacific and encountered fierce opposition from land-based air. Among the tradeoffs, which he fully acknowledged, was that the carrier would have to be significantly larger and heavier due to the additional hull and superstructure required. Jack Towers, in contrast, argued that the carrier's aircraft were its best defense and that any bomb exploding on the flight deck would destroy all of the aircraft spotted there. Towers won. The design of the new 27,100-ton *Essex* (CV 9), approved by the Secretary of the Navy in February 1940, lacked flight deck protection, but it did feature a hangar deck incorporating one and a half inches of armor.[30]

McCain became eligible for promotion to rear admiral in the fall of 1939, only to learn that the flag selection board had passed him over. It was a big disappointment, but it was not unusual for senior captains slated for flag rank to be passed over the first time around; John Towers suffered the same fate in December 1938 before Roosevelt pushed him through as BuAer chief in 1939, a job that automatically came with flag rank. McCain surmised that the board had not been fully aware of his administrative accomplishments, some of which he admitted had involved controversial decisions regarding personnel. As for his ship commands, he wrote to a friend that his "record at sea is second to none whatever." When McCain came up before the board again in the fall of 1940, he decided to be pro-active and seek the support of officers he had worked for and with. Ernest King, then serving on the General Board, believed his fitness reports for McCain spoke for themselves, but he added that McCain's administration of Coco Solo had "been a brilliant success" and that during the recent fleet exercises he had "handled his forces with skill, decision, and good fortune." Adm. Thomas Washington, former BuNav chief, applauded McCain for his "ability to meet and overcome the difficulties" associated with demobiliza-tion following World War I and for working with Congress on naval person-nel reform. Under McCain the *Ranger* and its crew "were well organized and worked efficiently, smoothly and quietly as clockwork." "I consider him a very efficient and able all round Naval Officer," Washington concluded, "of fine judgment, and an officer who loves his profession [and] who carries out any duty assigned to him fully and well." McCain also had Leahy's endorse-ment: "The performance of duty of Captain McCain, during all the time that he was under my command at sea and on shore, was of a high order of excellence. His duty in connection with personnel and with legislation affecting Navy personnel . . . when I was Chief of the Bureau of Navigation was of definite value to the Navy."[31]

Support from King, Washington, and Leahy carried weight with the selection board when it voted in December to elevate McCain to rear admiral. Following procedure, the Secretary of the Navy recommended McCain's promotion to President Roosevelt, who approved it on 23 Janu-ary 1941. Events moved swiftly. On the twenty-first, McCain had received orders detaching him from command of North Island and assigning him as commander, Aircraft, Scouting Force (Comairscofor), effective on the day of his promotion. The new posting was consistent with the decision to create what were known as type commands: that is, forces headed by flag-rank officers linked to types of ships and aircraft rather than to functions in association with fleet operations. Accordingly, McCain pinned on his stars and hoisted his flag as Comairscofor on the twenty-third, relieving Rear Adm. Arthur L. Bristol; simultaneously he assumed additional duty as com-mander, Patrol Wings (Compatwings), U.S. Fleet. McCain was quick to thank King. "Suddenly and unexpectedly," he wrote on the twenty-third, "I find myself trying to fill shoes which are much too large for me, even though they are four years old. I hope I assimilated enough under you to make a suc-cess of this job." Four days later, he was off in a PBY to NAS Seattle with two members of his staff to inspect Patrol Wing (PatWing) 4, the first of many trips he undertook during his tour as Comairscofor.[32]

McCain's new command was far-reaching and included responsibility for all Navy patrol aircraft operating on the West Coast, Alaska, and Hawaii. For his chief of staff, McCain turned to Matt Gardner, whom he respected and knew well from their time together in the *Ranger* and who was currently exec in the *Wright*, then being fitted out as a flagship. Other aviators joined McCain in San Diego. Lt. Herbert D. Riley, who had served with McCain in the *New Mexico*, came on board as McCain's aide and flag secretary, while Lt. Cdr. Joseph F. Bolger reported for duty in February as McCain's operations officer.[33]

One of McCain's first priorities was to familiarize himself with and determine the requirements of the various units under his command. One of the most important was Bellinger's Patrol Wing 2 in Hawaii, which counted six VP squadrons with about sixty PBYs based in Pearl Harbor and Kaneohe, a new facility on the northeast coast of Oahu. Tender-supported flying boats also operated on a temporary basis from Johnston, Palmyra, Wake, and Midway Islands, but Bellinger still lacked men and material and was unhappy that his command was not getting them as quickly as necessary. McCain commiserated with him that the "picture you paint is not a happy one" and that "you can count on every bit of assistance that I can give so don't hesitate to call on me for what you think I may be able to do." Bellinger and Pacific Fleet Scouting Force commander Vice Adm. Wilson Brown were anxious to know about facilities, personnel, and aircraft in Alaska and on the West Coast that could support their operations in Hawaii and the Central Pacific. The base at Sitka, Alaska, McCain reported, was in good shape, scheduled to go into full operation by 1 April, with hangars, seaplane ramp, office, maintenance, and other facilities needed to support a six-plane squadron, which McCain believed should arrive on or about the first. Another base, at Kodiak, Alaska, was still under construction, with a hangar and two seaplane ramps expected to be finished by June, but it would not be ready for full squadron operations until the summer of 1942. McCain estimated that the base at Tongue Point, Oregon, at the mouth of the Columbia River, with a ramp, apron, hangar, and maintenance and repair shops, could receive a six-plane squadron in June. Seattle, headquarters for PatWing 4, was "practically complete" and capable of supporting four twelve-aircraft squadrons with all necessary support facilities; by 1 April it would be ready for a squadron with six PBYs. The station at Alameda was partially completed and could be equipped for a nine-plane squadron by 1 April, assuming North Island provided interim repair and maintenance support. North Island itself had three VP squadrons with twenty-four flying boats making up PatWing 1 and was in McCain's estimation big enough to handle sixty aircraft if necessary.[34]

Long-range scouting and reconnaissance were the principal missions of the VPs under McCain's command. In an article in *Flying and Popular Aviation*, he wrote that patrol flying boats were largely self-sufficient and could operate from both established naval air stations or from more primitive advance bases, "sustained by mobile tenders which have been designed and provide for this particular purpose." "These aircraft," he added, "advance the visible horizon for the Fleet commander by hundreds of miles—distances equivalent to several days steaming by high-speed surface craft. In this service of information for the Fleet, patrol planes are the long range 'seeing eyes' of the Navy." Yet this "was by no means their only function." McCain recognized that the long-range patrol plane was also "equipped to carry heavy loads of bombs, torpedoes and mines," making it "the dreadnaught of the Navy's air arm" and providing the Navy with augmented "strategic offensive utility."[35]

McCain's public enthusiasm for the offensive capabilities of the long-range flying boat contrasted with his understanding of the VPs' operational limitations and technical and supply problems with torpedoes. When Adm. Husband E. Kimmel, commander in chief of the U.S. Fleet, suggested that flying boats might be equipped with torpedoes for attacks on enemy shipping, McCain looked into the matter. He concluded after corresponding with Adm. William H. P. Blandy, chief of the Bureau of Ordnance, that "many factors, most of them material, stand in the way of achieving a workable set-up for the service use of torpedoes by patrol planes." Only 116 of the 2,000-pound Mark 13 aerial torpedoes were available, "hardly enough even to afford adequate training," let alone for distribution to the fleet, nor were there adequate facilities for storing and maintaining the weapons. Moreover, American torpedoes had to be dropped from altitudes of ninety feet or less. McCain wrote that "it is my personal conviction that patrol planes are of the greatest value in long range scouting operations. Their procurement is slow and costly and as they would be extremely vulnerable while delivering a torpedo attack in clear daylight I would be most reluctant to see them sacrificed unless the sacrifice were justified by the urgent importance of the immediate objective of the attack." Torpedo attacks at night and in low visibility brought the advantage of concealment and surprise, provided the torpedo could be released at an altitude of 200 to 300 feet, which reduced the risk of flying the airplane into the sea.[36]

Blandy responded that McCain was mistaken that only 116 torpedoes had been assigned to patrol aircraft; instead there had been 316, with nearly 400 more to come in fiscal year 1942, not including those to be sent to new aircraft carriers. He did concede that more needed to be done about augmenting torpedo-servicing facilities ashore and on seaplane tenders. He also admitted that torpedo development had been slow, not for any technical reasons, but because "there were few U.S. naval aviators who were really interested in torpedoes." The European war and British experience had shown that the "torpedo is the most deadly weapon which aircraft can use against well protected heavy ships." Blandy cautioned that the claims by foreign navies about torpedo performance tended to be exaggerated. Recent intelligence indicated that the British estimated only 50 percent effectiveness from torpedoes launched from 140 feet, compared to 80 percent from the Mark 13 released from that altitude. To a degree, Blandy was disingenuous about the effectiveness of the Mark 13. Even with the addition of breakaway wood stabilizers that allowed the weapon to be dropped from higher altitudes and speeds, the Mark 13 suffered from serious control and reliability problems that persisted until 1944.[37] McCain, while seeking to enhance the offensive potential of VPs, would have to take their technical and operational shortcomings into account when he was thrust into a combat command in the early phases of the Pacific War.

Much of what was feasible in the spring of 1941 to enhance the capability of the aircraft, bases, and personnel in McCain's command rested on decisions at BuAer in Washington, where Towers as bureau chief faced conflicting priorities. Not only did he have to meet the Navy's requirements for more aircraft and trained airmen, but also the demands of Britain, which needed patrol aircraft to fight German U-boats in the desperate Battle of the Atlantic. In April, Towers won approval for more airplanes, including 50 Martin PBM Mariners, 150 PBYs, and 50 big four-engine Consolidated PB2Y Coronado flying boats. Herbert Riley returned in late June from meetings in Washington with good news about additional aircraft for McCain's command. He was pleased to hear that there had been recent increases in aircraft orders and that new factories were being built for big flying boats. For example, Boeing was manufacturing 90 twin-engine PBB Sea Rangers, which he judged was a "tremendous craft," Consolidated had begun work on the PBY-6, and Martin had

an order for 180 new PBM-4s. McCain estimated that the additional production would eventually give him 200 aircraft, allowing him to maintain an acceptable level of training, and that he would gain an additional
training squadron.[38]

McCain was away from San Diego on temporary duty much of the time.
In April, he flew to Hawaii to inspect PatWing 2, followed by a trip to Washington in May to meet with officers in BuAer and BuNav about aircraft procurement and aviation personnel requirements. On 15 July, McCain and
four of his staff were off in a PB2Y from San Diego for an eight-day tour
of PatWing 4 bases in Seattle, Sitka, Kodiak, Dutch Harbor, and Tongue
Point. In his follow-up report to Kimmel, he emphasized that other than
Dutch Harbor in the Aleutians, where construction had just begun, the
Alaska bases were ready for the limited operation of patrol aircraft, although
much depended on weather conditions that affected both visual and instrument landings. A weather radio station had just been set up at Kodiak, and
McCain highly recommended establishing a similar station at Dutch Harbor. It was also possible, he suggested, to use Russian weather reports, either
through a cooperative exchange or by eavesdropping and deciphering their
codes. He flew again to Pearl Harbor on 6 August to meet with Kimmel and
Bellinger before returning to San Diego on the morning of the tenth.[39]

McCain and his staff worked closely with the Army Air Forces (AAF)
in getting urgently needed aircraft and personnel from the West Coast to
Hawaii. Secretary of War Henry L. Stimson praised McCain for his command's assistance with the flight of twenty-one B-17s from San Francisco
to Hawaii on 13 May 1941. The commanding general of the Fourth Air
Force commended McCain and his people for their contributions to flight
and communication plans and stationing guard ships on the route from San
Francisco to Hawaii. McCain replied that "we were very glad to be of service," adding that naval aviators under his command were impressed with
"the performance of the Army personnel responsible for [the] planning and
execution" of the mission.[40]

Because of the strategic importance of Hawaii, Bellinger's PatWing 2
remained uppermost in McCain's priorities. He undertook another long
inspection tour of the Pacific in October, leaving San Diego early on the
fourteenth and arriving at Pearl Harbor that evening. From the fifteenth to
the twenty-second he was with Bellinger and PatWing 2, and he then visited
NAS Kaneohe and other bases before returning to San Diego on the morning of 24 October. McCain and Bellinger collaborated on the movement

of twelve VP-22 PBYs to Midway and shuffled other aircraft, squadrons, and supporting ships to and from Palmyra and Johnston Islands. They also worked out a schedule to ferry PBYs from Hawaii to Alameda for overhauls that could not be accommodated at Pearl Harbor. Their work paid off. Eighteen patrol planes arrived in Hawaii on 28 October, followed by twelve on 8 November, and twenty-four more on 23 November, bringing Bellinger's total inventory up to eighty-one by early December. McCain thanked Bellinger for his reports, which gave him a "much better understanding now of your difficulties" than he had previously. He assured Bellinger that it was his "intention to build up spares for your planes to the extent which will permit a distribution in your outlying bases so that plane movement may take place without the immediate support of a tender." Seaplane tender construction and conversion were not proceeding as well as McCain liked, although the 8,600-ton *Curtiss* (AV 4), built from the keel up as a seaplane tender and commissioned in November 1940, had come out to Pearl Harbor in May, and the *Tangier* (AV 8), a relatively new Maritime Commission cargo ship recently converted to an 11,760-ton tender, arrived in November.[41]

On 5 December 1941, just two days before the Japanese attack on Pearl Harbor, McCain wrote to Admiral Brown in Hawaii about his plans to assist the Army in air maneuvers scheduled for 11 to 16 December. Due to the lack of aircraft and personnel and the "pressure of time and circumstance," he could not spare more than three patrol planes from Alameda, which were to provide warning of approaching "enemy" forces, and perform search-and-rescue duties as needed. Communication facilities in McCain's command were also to cooperate with the Army. To McCain it was important for the Navy to be "included in an operation of such consequence," even if it meant pulling airplanes and personnel away from training for a week.[42]

Like many on the West Coast, McCain learned of the Japanese attack on Pearl Harbor late in the morning on Sunday, 7 December. He knew that "immediate and effective measures must be taken to organize and employ available forces at San Diego," and he called his staff and officers of the Eleventh Naval District to a conference shortly after noon to discuss plans and how they would be put into effect as soon as possible. On the thirteenth, he reported to Rear Adm. John W. Greenslade, Twelfth Naval District commandant, that he had at San Diego two patrol plane squadrons (VP-43 and VP-13) with fourteen aircraft, and one training unit with seventeen dive-bombers and fighters. Four submarines and nine destroyers were also available, although they were not in his command. McCain's VPs and

AAF long-range bombers under his command scouted the area southwest of San Diego out to 550 miles, leaving after dawn and returning after sunset. The intensity of operations had worn down his aircraft and aircrews to the extent that he warned it might be necessary to limit flying in the near future unless he was able to train Army fliers to take over much of his command's long-range patrol mission.[43]

In Hawaii, Bellinger's PatWing 2 had lost forty-six patrol planes, more than half his serviceable force, in the Japanese assault. Units at Kaneohe alone suffered twenty-seven PBYs destroyed and six damaged, leaving Bell-inger with only two patrol planes at that base. Only two patrol planes were left undamaged at Ford Island, where hangars and other ground facilities had also been grievously damaged. In the aftermath of the catastrophe, and in response to Bellinger's critical shortage of patrol aircraft, McCain proffered an objective assessment of the material and strategic situation in the Pacific. He agreed with Bellinger that "our lack of the sinews of war is deplorable, particularly in view of our long anticipation of such event." It made no sense, though, to complain about circumstances that were beyond his or Bellinger's control. It would be better "if we forewent vain regrets and based our actions on the ultimate which we can wring from the equipment avail-able to us with due consideration to provisions for the increases to come." That the "major naval air effort" appeared to center on the approaches to Hawaii bothered him, in part because he believed the available resources would be better used if they operated from advance bases. Given the present circumstances, Bellinger's limited number of search aircraft could be used more effectively if they flew from bases in Hilo, Maui, and Molokai and if they were deployed into coordinated outer and inner search patterns, pro-viding 360-degree coverage out to 550 miles. He suggested that Bellinger take a close look at the search plans he used in San Diego, with overlapping sectors that allowed coverage through 160 degrees with a maximum of ten aircraft. Bellinger might be able to accomplish something better using no more than twenty-seven aircraft per day.[44]

McCain also conveyed some of his ideas and concerns to Towers in the aftermath of Pearl Harbor. He valued Army shore-based bombers for their long range, endurance, and potential offensive power and suggested to Towers that the Navy acquire such aircraft rather than rely on the Army as operations moved out into the Pacific. Army fliers lacked the discipline and training of their Navy and Marine counterparts, and Army ground troops were on edge: "you take the air here at the risk of your life now, the Army being quick on the trigger," he warned Towers. Above all, McCain itched to get into the action as soon as possible. He had reminded Greenslade that his command was "seagoing at present" and that he did not want to be "tied to shore." Further, he had recommended to Kimmel that war plans called for Bellinger to go out to Midway and for him to replace Bellinger at Pearl Harbor, only to have Kimmel refuse his request. He told Towers that "myself and Staff want to go west." Towers replied that "I consider it more important for you to stay on the job at San Diego to take care of Aircraft Scouting Force's many important problems at that end, leaving Bellinger to run the job in the Islands." McCain would remain ashore for the time being.[45]

McCain faced a myriad of problems amid the confusion that ensued on the West Coast following the Pearl Harbor catastrophe. He worried, unnecessarily, about a Japanese carrier attack on the West Coast, which Towers rightly dismissed as improbable, although he conceded that a "submarine might pop up some dark night either in Coronado Roads or Santa Monica Bay or both, and lob a few shells into a well chosen objective." McCain replied, "I think you are wrong about air attacks." He agreed that the Japanese could not be everywhere, but they "still seem to be fairly ubiquitous" and were "certain to stage an attack on this coast if for no other reason than foofaraw." He also denied that there was any "hysteria" on the West Coast and that the civilian population had "absolute confidence in the Navy." He went on to stress that the number of aircraft available to him for "either inshore patrol or offshore search" was insufficient and that more airplanes were critical to fulfilling his requirements. The arrival of another patrol plane squadron, VP-44, at Alameda helped, but McCain also needed the Army to commit more of its heavy and medium aircraft to long-range searches or allow Navy personnel to take over AAF aircraft for such missions. In March, he wrote to his friend Capt. Francis S. ("Frog") Low, operations officer for King, who had succeeded Kimmel as commander in chief, U.S. Fleet (Cominch), that "it is criminal waste and stupid folly not to use our magnificent trained and skilled crews and pilots in B-17s and 24s." The Navy had to make it clear that he had "complete control of all aviation" in his command, "without qualification." By April 1942, McCain was delighted to report to Towers that a squadron of Army Lockheed A-28 Hudson twin-engine medium bombers at Alameda and another squadron of Consolidated B-24 Liberator four-engine heavy bombers at North Island "belong to us, lock, stock and barrel."[46]

West Coast operations and activities within McCain's command consisted of routine long-range searches and convoy protection missions by

Scouting Force VPs and shorter-range antisubmarine patrols by First Marine Air Wing scout bombers. In February, VP-13 augmented VP-43 in San Diego. There had been excitement in late December when two of McCain's patrol planes investigated a suspicious vessel trailing a Navy oiler about five hundred miles offshore from San Diego, only to have darkness fall before they could identify and attack the ship, which was believed to be supporting Japanese submarines. Most searchers returned to base after spotting more whales than enemy submarines. Even routine operations came at a price. On 13–14 February, three Navy Grumman F4F Wildcat fighters on a ferry flight from Tucson to North Island flew off course and went down in the mountains east of San Diego. Ensuing search missions resulted in the loss of one of McCain's aircraft. On the evening of 20 March, McCain left in a PBY on an inspection trip to Pearl Harbor, arriving there after an overnight flight from San Diego. Three days later, McCain boarded one of the Coronados for the return flight, but the flying boat had to turn around and return to Pearl due to engine problems, and he did not get back to San Diego until the morning of the twenty-sixth.[47]

Sitting in his office at North Island in the early spring of 1942, John McCain could reflect on where he and aviation stood as the Navy began to implement its strategy and plans to fight a two-ocean war. Since earning his wings at Pensacola, he had mastered the many complexities of naval aviation, whether shore-based, tender-based, or carrier-based. He had been in command at Coco Solo in the Caribbean and San Diego in the Pacific and, most important, expertly took the *Ranger* through extensive fleet exercises in 1938 and 1939, some of which involved multicarrier formations. He had made friends in the upper echelons of the Navy's administration, foremost among them Ernest King and William Leahy, and he had, perhaps grudgingly, earned the respect of Pat Bellinger, if not that of Jack Towers. To a degree, he had overcome the prejudice "brown shoe" naval aviators had for "black shoe" officers who had entered their exclusive club late in their careers. Yet he knew that no matter how crucial and valued his job might be ashore in San Diego, he was isolated far from the action as it began to unfold in the Central and South Pacific. He did not know, nor could he anticipate, that a rapid series of events and decisions would soon overtake him, ultimately bringing a combat aviation command at a critical time as the tides of war shifted on the other side of the Pacific.

CHAPTER 3

South Pacific Command

President Franklin D. Roosevelt was exasperated. Nearly three months had passed since the disaster at Pearl Harbor, and American military and naval forces had seemingly done nothing to counter the unbroken run of Japanese victories in the Pacific. At the end of February, in an effort to shake things up in the Navy—the service he had long considered his own—Roosevelt called on Secretary of the Navy Frank Knox to identify the forty admirals he considered "most competent" to prosecute the naval war. Knox assembled a committee of nine high-ranking and experienced flag officers. Among the members of this "unofficial selection board" were Ernest King, recently elevated to commander in chief, U.S. Fleet, Chief of Naval Operations Adm. Harold R. Stark, Vice Adm. Randall Jacobs, chief of the Bureau of Navigation, and Rear Adm. Harry E. Yarnell, a retired carrier commander working as a special adviser to the Secretary of the Navy. King and Stark were the board's automatic choices. Other members of the panel were eligible as well. To be included in the remaining thirty-eight an officer had to receive at least five votes.

Knox summarized the results of the committee's survey in a memo to the president on 9 March. Five officers received nine votes (some of whom were virtually unknown to the public or who had mostly held staff positions); six gained eight votes (notably Vice Adms. William F. Halsey Jr. and Robert L. Ghormley); seven had seven votes (including Rear Adms. Frank Jack Fletcher and Jake Fitch, both members of McCain's 1906 Academy class), Capt. (in the promotion list for rear admiral) Marc A. ("Pete") Mitscher, and Rear Adm. Richmond Kelly Turner; nine had six votes; and eleven earned five. McCain was one of those receiving six votes. Two officers who went on to outstanding careers, Chester W. Nimitz, former chief of the Bureau of Navigation who in late December with the rank of admiral had taken over as commander in chief, Pacific Fleet (Cincpac), and Rear Adm. Raymond A. Spruance, an experienced cruiser division commander and expert naval strategist, did not make the cut.[1]

Meanwhile, King, who wanted to know which officers should receive senior aviation commands, had called on BuAer Chief John Towers for his recommendations. On 2 March, Towers presented King with a list. To be selected the men had to demonstrate experience, professionalism, aggressiveness, toughness, and "modernized conceptions" of aviation. They did not have to be aviators. McCain was among the flag-rank officers or those in line for promotion on the list, which included Towers himself and five other early aviators, as well as seven latecomers. Towers also named Fletcher, even though he was a "black shoe" and not an aviator.[2] King's and Towers' recommendations improved the likelihood but did not guarantee that McCain would be among those flag officers chosen for major wartime operational assignments.

★ ★ ★ ★

As decisions about Navy combat leadership evolved in the late winter and early spring of 1942, the United States and its Allies considered the optimum course of action in Europe and the Pacific. Anglo-American strategists had agreed on a Germany-first grand strategy and concurred about the importance of maintaining the lines of communication through the South Pacific to Australia and New Zealand. But there the consensus evaporated. While Army chief of staff Gen. George C. Marshall and the British called for no more than a holding action in the Pacific, Gen. Douglas MacArthur, commanding Army forces in the theater, wanted a vigorous offensive, as did King and others in the Navy leadership.[3]

King had his eyes on the South Pacific. There, strategically located on New Britain in the Bismarcks, lay Rabaul, which the Japanese had occupied and begun developing as an impregnable fortress that could act as a fulcrum for further southern advances. In particular, King recognized the strategic importance of the island of New Caledonia, an outpost of the French empire mostly known for its plentiful nickel deposits, coffee plantations, and cattle and sheep ranches. King knew that a Japanese foothold there might place the empire's long-range bombers within reach of Sydney and Brisbane, Australia. He also knew that New Caledonia and the port facilities in the capital of Nouméa were valuable as a potential staging point for establishing forward bases closer to the British Solomon Islands, Rabaul, and other areas held or menaced by the Japanese. To secure New Caledonia meant garrisoning Canton Island south of Hawaii, Bora Bora in the French Society archipelago, and the Samoan Islands with Army troops and Marines. In the interim, after

a pause in their onslaught in the Far East, the Japanese had begun planning to widen their defensive perimeter beyond Rabaul to Port Moresby in
Australian-held Papua New Guinea and Tulagi in the Solomons.[4]

In February, King went even further in his commitment to the South
Pacific. He proposed extending the American presence to Tongatabu in the
British Tonga Islands and to the British-French island of Efate in the New
Hebrides, more exotic names and places likely to be sucked into the vor-
tex of global conflict. Because King's objectives obligated an even greater
deployment of military and naval forces that threatened to delay the offensive in Europe in 1942, the Joint Chiefs of Staff (JCS) met with Roosevelt
in March to consider the matter. King interpreted the results of the meeting
to be an endorsement of his plans for the South Pacific. Later in the month,
the Joint Chiefs approved a compromise between Marshall and King that
placed MacArthur in command of the new South West Pacific Area (Sowespac), leaving Nimitz in charge of the remainder of the vast theater.[5]

Not only did King's decisions highlight a strategic debate between the
Army and the Navy, but they also accentuated differences between him
and Nimitz. Basically, the two disagreed about where the Navy should concentrate its strength during the initial phases of the Pacific War. In what
the historian John Lundstrom called a "defensive-offensive" strategy, King
argued that once the Japanese offensive had been thwarted in the South
Pacific, the island chains west of Samoa could be used as advance naval
and air bases to support an American counteroffensive. Nimitz, in contrast,
believed that priority should be given to the Central Pacific. Steeped in
decades of thought about a naval conflict with Japan articulated in War
Plan Orange, he concentrated on defending Hawaii, Midway, and Johnston
Island, followed by an offensive through the mid-Pacific culminating in a
decisive fleet action somewhere near the Philippines. Nimitz worried that
any operations in the South Pacific would divert scarce assets, especially
carriers, which he needed to protect Hawaii and hold the line against any
Japanese offensive in the Central Pacific.[6]

By March, there were only three flattops in the Pacific—the *Lexington*,
Enterprise, and *Yorktown*—each the center of a numbered task force consisting of the carrier and its defensive screen of cruisers and destroyers. The *Lexington's* sister ship, *Saratoga*, had been torpedoed in January and was under
repair on the West Coast. Fortunately, the new *Hornet* (CV 8) was in San
Diego with Mitscher's Task Force 18 and would soon be available to bolster Nimitz's carrier forces. Also in San Diego was McCain as commander,

Aircraft, Scouting Force. On 12 March, Nimitz informed King that after a discussion with McCain he planned to "order McCain to command Task Group formed on Hornet," presumably to operate in the South Pacific. Yet just a day later King told Nimitz that the *Hornet* and Mitscher were to join Halsey and the *Enterprise* in a combined TF-16. Puzzled, Nimitz learned to his dismay on the nineteenth that the *Hornet* and the *Enterprise* were integral to a risky and highly secret plan to strike Tokyo and other Japanese cities with Army B-25 bombers commanded by Lt. Col. James H. Doolittle.[7]

McCain probably never knew that due to the unusual circumstances of the Doolittle Tokyo raid he had just missed getting a carrier task force command. Instead, he became part of a reorganization that redefined his command on the West Coast. In the shakeup, which occurred in March, McCain was removed as a subordinate officer under the Scouting Force at Pearl Harbor and instated as commander, Aircraft Southern Sector, Western Sea Frontier, a unified command with responsibility for all air components—both Navy and Army—operating from north of Los Angeles to Ensenada in Mexico's Baja California. This arrangement lasted barely a month until King determined that he wanted a single air command for the entire West Coast. Accordingly, King, now Chief of Naval Operations as well as Cominch, agreed to McCain's proposal that he (McCain) become commander, Aircraft, Western Sea Frontier, under which there would be separate Northern and Southern Sector patrol wings, while at the same time wearing the hat of commander, Aircraft, Southern Sector and keeping his headquarters in San Diego.[8]

Not long after McCain received his new orders on 3 April, King once more stepped in with further changes to the West Coast air commands. After warming his chair at North Island for only a week as Western Sea Frontier aircraft commander, McCain was designated commander, Patrol Wings, Pacific Fleet. Effective on 10 April, the new job took him out from under the Western Sea Frontier and placed him in the Pacific Fleet, where his boss was now Nimitz. Soon thereafter, on 27 April, McCain was detached from his Patwings command and ordered on 1 May to report to Nimitz in Pearl Harbor for assignment as commander, Aircraft South Pacific Force (Comairsopac). In this regard McCain was part of a major Pacific command reorganization that had been brewing for well over a month. At the end of March, Roosevelt had approved the Joint Chiefs' proposal to divide the Pacific into two separate commands, with the South West Pacific under MacArthur as commander, South West Pacific Area (Comsowespac). Nimitz, in addition to his job as Cincpac at Pearl Harbor, became commander in chief, Pacific Ocean Areas (Cincpoa), divided into the North, Central, and South Pacific. The nominal line of demarcation between MacArthur's and Nimitz's commands ran between the Solomons and New Caledonia.[9]

With Nimitz's concurrence, King picked Ghormley to be commander, South Pacific Area (Comsopac), with responsibility for all naval and military resources in the area. One of McCain's superiors and a former classmate at the Academy, Ghormley was intelligent, thoughtful, and diplomatic; he had previously been posted to London, where he deftly handled secret Anglo-American naval collaboration before the United States entered the war and was in line to take command of American naval forces in Europe. Instead, Stark took that post after turning over the CNO position to King, which left Ghormley free to assume an operational command.[10]

It did not take Nimitz long after becoming Cincpoa to realize that King had been right that the next Japanese moves would indeed be in the South Pacific. Nimitz relied on Ultra intelligence, derived from a synthesis of observations from decrypted Japanese coded messages, radio-equipped local Australian "coast watchers," radio traffic, and enemy ship movements. By May, Nimitz had sufficient information to know that the enemy was readying an offensive aimed at Port Moresby and the Solomons. Close to all-important New Caledonia, the Solomons beckoned like sirens to Japanese and American strategists and naval planners. Sprawling over 675 miles southeast from the Bismarcks, the chain included the big island of Bougainville to the northwest, with Guadalcanal and San Cristóbal the major islands anchoring the southeast extremity. Nimitz now agreed with King that if the Allies thwarted a Japanese offensive in the islands, they not only secured their lines of communication through the South Pacific but also acquired steppingstones to claw their way through the archipelago to Rabaul.[11]

Nearly three years in San Diego with multiple command and administrative responsibilities gave McCain an understanding of the complexity of shore- and tender-based patrol plane operations. He had also acquired a staff he knew he could rely on as he looked forward to his new and challenging tasks in the South Pacific. It was no secret that McCain chafed in his desk job and relished the opportunity to get out to the theater and into action. King wanted McCain in the new job knowing that he had a reputation for aggressiveness and that he had the know-how and experience to consolidate the disparate ships, aircraft, and base facilities needed to stabilize the region's defenses.

McCain soon learned that he was not going to get everything he wanted or needed in his new command. On 29 April, he wrote to Capt. Donald B. ("Wu") Duncan, King's air operations officer, to ask him what personnel, ships, and aircraft would be available to him in the South Pacific. McCain also suggested to Towers that the *Curtiss* be dispatched to San Diego to pick up him and his staff, as well as a number of airplanes for transfer to Pearl Harbor. The *Curtiss* would then continue on to the South Pacific, where it would serve as his command ship afloat. For mobility in such a widespread theater he wanted a twin-engine North American B-25 Mitchell medium bomber or a twin-engine Lockheed Hudson as his flag plane. It was soon apparent that he would not get the *Curtiss*, nor were many of his staff going to accompany him, despite their preference for following him out to the South Pacific. And Towers was in no position to assign an airplane to him. The reality sank in that he would have to make do with what he had when he got to the front line. He admitted to Duncan that if necessary he could operate on a shoestring and that he believed King's motto to "*Do better than I think I can with what I got*" applied to his situation.[12]

McCain turned over his Patwings command to Bellinger and flew out from San Diego in a PB2Y on the evening of 1 May for Pearl Harbor, arriving there early the next morning. In ten days of meetings at Cincpac headquarters with Nimitz and his staff, he was brought up to date on plans and operations to thwart Japanese offensive efforts in the South Pacific and learned that for the time being he would report directly to Nimitz while Ghormley established his new command in Auckland, New Zealand. On the morning of 13 May, McCain and members of his staff boarded one of Nimitz's Pacific Fleet Coronados for the flight out of Pearl. Ghormley and his staff accompanied them as they island-hopped to Nouméa, where they landed on the morning of 18 May. Two days later, at 1800 local time on 20 May, McCain hoisted his flag as Comairsopac aboard the seaplane tender *Tangier* anchored in the Great Road, Nouméa.[13]

To carry out his mission, McCain had only the *Tangier*, which had been at Nouméa since 3 March, and the 1,600-ton destroyer *Meredith* (DD 434). Skippered by Cdr. Wendell G. Switzer, the *Tangier* and its PBY-5 flying boats had carried out vital search-and-rescue missions during the Battle of the Coral Sea, 7–8 May. In that engagement, the first between two carrier forces, TF-11 and TF-17, both under Fletcher's tactical command, had fought the Japanese to a draw and ended the threat to Port Moresby. Nevertheless, the Japanese remained determined to maintain and expand their presence in the southern Solomons, where they had taken Tulagi and smaller islands nearby. When McCain and his staff arrived, the flying boats had returned to routine daily surveillance and antisubmarine patrols north and west of Nouméa, reaching as far as the Santa Cruz Islands, but short of the Solomons. McCain's capable chief of staff, Matt Gardner, now a commander, handled much of the administrative details. On McCain's staff was another aviator, Lt. Cdr. Frederick Funke, a 1927 Academy graduate who also carried over from San Diego. Weeks went by before yeomen, a quartermaster, mess stewards, and all-important radiomen and other communication personnel arrived at Nouméa.[14]

It did not take long for McCain to discover that radio communications were one of his most pressing problems. Not only was there a dearth of trained personnel, but the radio circuits were easily overwhelmed by the volume of traffic, while the heat and humidity wrought havoc on delicate electronics, and frequent tropical storms caused static and restricted the range of transmission and reception of the underpowered units. One patrol plane officer recalled that "the radio down there was very, very peculiar" and that "you could hear all kinds of things going on back in the States, but you couldn't hear the planes that you wanted" without considerable frequency shifts. In a handwritten note on 1 June, McCain explained to Ghormley that "communications here are a complete mess" and that he "badly needed" more and better radio equipment. Knowing that Ghormley had much to think about in his new job, he ended his message: "Damn it [I] don't see why I should worry you with my troubles as you must have plenty of your own." From his headquarters in Auckland Ghormley replied that he was "going full speed down here under very limited facilities" and that he was "doing his very best to get communications straightened out."[15]

The *Tangier*, lacking space, air conditioning, and communication gear, was not well suited as a command vessel, but McCain was under orders to remain afloat rather than secure accommodations ashore. Regardless, adequate facilities in Nouméa, with a population of only ten thousand, were few and far between, and McCain and his staff had neither the time nor the inclination to become embroiled in potentially contentious negotiations with local authorities. After the fall of France in 1940, the collaborationist Vichy government attempted to establish its jurisdiction in Nouméa, meeting resistance from a local populace sympathetic to exiled General Charles de Gaulle and the Free French. The New Caledonians ultimately rallied to the Free French cause in the fall of 1940, but the political climate remained unsettled when the first American troops arrived in Nouméa in March 1942. Tensions between the governor and a de Gaulle–appointed colonial commissioner wary of American and Allied infringements on French sovereignty boiled over into civil disturbances at the moment McCain assumed command. A combination of prudence and delicate political circumstances, therefore, dictated that McCain and his headquarters stayed onboard ship.[16]

In addition to aircraft, bases, and personnel in Nouméa, Comairsopac's sphere encompassed Bora Bora, American Samoa, Fiji, Tongatabu, and Efate. McCain understood the urgency of getting his command in shape and realized that he did not have much to work with. Immediately available at Nouméa were the 12 PBY-5s of Patrol Squadrons VP-71 and VP-72, attached to the *Tangier*, and 20 Grumman F4F-3A Wildcat fighters from Maj. Harold W. Bauer's Marine Fighting Squadron VMF-212. Altogether McCain scraped up a miscellany of 157 aircraft, including 116 fighters, 12 Marine dive-bombers in Samoa, and 12 Royal New Zealand Air Force Hudson bombers based in Fiji. The Army's 67th Fighter Squadron, with Bell P-39s and P-400s (the export model of the P-39), was also part of McCain's command.[17]

Within this embryonic joint force McCain counted five Army Boeing B-17 Flying Fortress four-engine heavy bombers, operating from an unimproved airfield at Tontouta not far from Nouméa. Army airmen worried that subordination of their bombers to the Navy "would establish a poor precedent" and undermine the principle of unity of command. In a compromise of sorts, the AAF agreed to the integrated command structure, provided their air units were directly under McCain and not under a more junior Navy officer. Thus the AAF retained unit integrity and control over training, indoctrination, and operations, all of which fell under the command of Maj. Gen. Millard F. Harmon as commanding general, U.S. Army Forces, South Pacific. McCain understood that this arrangement maximized the flexibility of the diverse and scattered forces under his command while still allowing him discretionary control over local units under specific tactical and operational circumstances.[18]

By the third week of July, additional Army aircraft had arrived from Hawaii, flying out of Tontouta and another relatively undeveloped air base at Plaine des Gaiacs on New Caledonia's west coast. AAF bombers were subsequently organized into the 11th Bombardment Group under the command of Col. LaVerne ("Blondy") Saunders. Despite the efforts of the AAF's publicity machine to demonstrate otherwise, high-level bombing had been singularly ineffective at the Battle of Midway. B-17s based on the atoll flew 205 sorties during the battle without securing a single hit, while carrier dive-bombers sank all four of the Japanese flattops. Belatedly recognizing the problems of bombing maneuvering warships, Army fliers shifted to attacking ships at low and medium altitudes—usually no higher than 10,000 feet—and if possible doing so with six to nine airplanes in formation. McCain found the big bombers especially useful, with the range and payload capacity to reach the southern Solomons from New Caledonia and having the defensive firepower to hold their own against Japanese fighters.[19]

Although residual Navy resentment from the AAF's Midway grandstanding threatened to poison interservice cooperation, and McCain doubted the Army was fully committed to the theater, the two rivals generally complemented one another under McCain's leadership. In one of his first recommendations as Comairsopac, McCain urged that to ensure "effective early readiness" of Army bombers, pilots from the Lexington be assigned to New Caledonia to help with training for attacks on warships at sea. McCain considered Saunders "a natural leader and by instinct a first class fighting man. I know of no one better in the air or on the ground." Saunders was grateful that McCain gave him "unlimited command," which he considered "a very pleasant surprise." The only major complaint from Army aviators appeared to be that their Navy counterparts did not provide adequate indoctrination on how best to conduct long-range maritime searches.[20]

McCain's schemes to use his aviation units, especially Navy and Marine aircraft and crews, generally adhered to concepts and doctrine developed in the 1930s. American planners understood that due to treaty limitations they had only a relatively small number of aircraft carriers to provide the fleet with air power as it advanced across the Pacific. VPs were therefore essential. Operating from advance bases, the flying boats provided long-range reconnaissance and scouting as well as a modest strike capability. Marine fighters took care of base defense against long-range bombers and carrier aircraft.[21]

Yet there were never enough resources. On 21 May, after an on-site survey of the command and his own assessment of the situation, McCain reported to Nimitz that for the "adequate defense of bases in South Pacific area" he needed six fighter squadrons and four dive-bomber squadrons (each with twenty-five airplanes), plus eleven medium and heavy bomber squadrons (each with a dozen aircraft). "As soon as personnel and planes are available," he wanted another fighter squadron, one more dive-bomber unit, two more medium and heavy bomber squadrons in Nouméa, and a fighter squadron at Efate, 715 miles from the Solomons. Altogether, he sought more than 390 additional aircraft. And that was not all. Long a believer in the ship-killing capability of aerial torpedoes, McCain asked Nimitz to dispatch a sufficient number of the weapons to arm his PBYs, as well as the attendant maintenance equipment and personnel. He also informed Nimitz that his exhausted patrol plane crews were "currently operating on practically [a] day on and day off basis which cannot be continued much longer" and pleaded with Nimitz for three more complete VP flight crews and additional pilots to reinforce his existing complements.[22]

In subsequent correspondence to Nimitz, McCain further elaborated on his estimate of the situation in the South Pacific. He was pleased to serve under Nimitz and applauded him for the victory at Midway: "Congratulations and three rousing cheers!!!" But he was less thrilled with matters in Fiji, where the senior New Zealand aviator, while "an excellent subordinate," was not cut out to take over a major command. In his estimation an Army Air Forces officer would be better suited to the job. Efate, where the airstrip appeared to be in "hopeless" shape only a few weeks before, was nearly ready for limited use due to the heavy expenditure of both "brain" and "brawn." He anticipated that Bauer's VMF-212 squadron would soon be based on the island. That said, though, getting more warplanes into Efate and other islands depended on the availability of pierced-steel planking (known as Marston mat) for temporary surfacing of new airfields. Given sufficient men and material to establish them as air bases, McCain believed that the Pacific islands under his command could be a "great boulevard for planes" and crucial for supporting an offensive in the theater.[23]

Because McCain's letters arrived "in the middle of the Midway job," Nimitz took nearly a month to respond. He agreed that more aircraft and men were needed in the South Pacific and was willing to do what he could to funnel them to McCain. "I am doing all I can to support aircraft increases throughout your area," he wrote, adding that "the going is still very slow, but we shall continue our efforts." He planned to have replacement carrier air units sent to McCain as soon as shore facilities and personnel were available, but it would take time. "The aircraft torpedo situation is bad," Nimitz admitted. Due to production shortcomings and the heavy expenditures of torpedoes in the Midway operation, "we have had no choice other than to hold back on torpedoes for your area." Yet personnel and equipment were on the way, "so I think you will be all set by the time we are able to give you the necessary torpedoes." On another optimistic note, Nimitz hoped to allay McCain's concerns about the problems in Fiji. He assured him that the Army was sending a major general to command all forces in the area and that Ghormley would detail an American air officer to the island to provide liaison with the New Zealanders. McCain thanked Nimitz for his "word of encouragement in the action being taken to fulfill our crying needs—particularly in the matter of an appreciable, permanent air unit at each of the major South Pacific bases."[24]

In a letter to Frog Low and Wu Duncan, McCain was forthright about the problems he faced and the opportunities he saw in the South Pacific. "The job as a whole in these parts," he stressed, "is a pioneer's job in a very crude sense, but I will disturb neither one of you distinguished gentlemen with the troubles inherent in the situation." He regarded island bases as mutually supporting "anchored carriers" that could be easily defended using air power, which he saw "in large measure" as a "substitute for ships, guns and infantry." But aircraft and aircrews had to be "drilled, exercised and ready" or those bases were vulnerable to enemy attack, and "the greater the diversity of planes and pilots the greater the difficulty" in ensuring their readiness. Army aviators were eager and enthusiastic, but they had a lot to learn about naval warfare, and "transient" AAF squadrons were of limited value in meeting immediate needs. AAF long-range aircraft were "magnificent weapons manned by green crews" that could do enormous damage to Japanese shipping and bases, whereas "the PBYs are poor ships manned by skillful crews." In the wake of the Battles of the Coral Sea and Midway, the Japanese were "staggering." Advancing bases as far and as expeditiously as possible was essential, especially in planning to move into the southern Solomons, where McCain believed the Japanese had yet to consolidate their gains.[25]

McCain understood the importance of scouting, searches, and tactical intelligence to fleet operations. He had specific ideas about how the limited assets under his command could be used to best effect, especially for early warning of a Japanese move "supported and implemented by carrier borne aircraft" from their major base at Truk in the Carolines or from the Marshall Islands. In a 19 June message to the commanding officers at Samoa, Bora Bora, Fiji, Tongatabu, and Efate, he outlined how they should organize and carry out searches. Ideally scouting should be extended to at least 650 miles, while keeping in mind that "the performance of the available planes," weather conditions, and crew fatigue had to be considered in planning coverage and frequency. Here McCain faced the realities that doubling search range meant quadrupling the area to be covered and that it was not possible for searches to be continuous. Unless flight crews rotated every other day, he warned, "the emergency, when it occurs, will find an exhausted outfit." He recommended that all VPs moored at their buoys had to be ready to take off with fifteen minutes notice day or night. Once contact was made with the enemy, it was the *"essential task"* of the search plane "to maintain that contact," for "once it is lost for a considerable length of time, the show is off until [contact] can be regained." Consistent with his philosophy of command, McCain stressed that his recommendations were a "guide," not a "directive," and that "full initiative in meeting situations is hereby accorded and expected of responsible commanders concerned and their lower echelons."[26]

To "avoid a set pattern" of searches and to provide more coverage, McCain recommended that some sorties could be sent out late in the day and return at night, using radar to penetrate the veil of darkness. To McCain radar was a "heaven-sent opportunity" that augmented visual surveillance and afforded his aircraft the opportunity to locate, identify, and attack enemy carriers at night well before they were in position to fly off dawn strikes. Like many of his contemporaries, McCain was overly sanguine about the technology and did not fully understand the state of the art in radar at the time or comprehend its manifold limitations. Catalinas fitted with ASV (air to surface vessel) radar, for example, had to fly at altitudes between 1,500 and 2,000 feet to maximize the sets' performance. Airborne radar at the time demanded intensive regular maintenance, had trouble identifying small craft, and under the conditions in the Solomons could not always pick out ships against the background of islands and land masses. Most important, the technology demanded trained operators, which in 1942 were in short supply. Nevertheless, while not a panacea, airborne radar was a critical technological advantage McCain's aviators had over their Japanese foes.[27]

Information from Pearl Harbor, much of it derived from Ultra, was useful in illuminating the strategic picture, yet McCain found immediate operational intelligence harder to come by in the late spring and summer of 1942. McCain expressed his frustration: "In the late spring of 1942, there was, literally, no intelligence worthy of the name. Pilots were briefed in several instances from National Geographic Society maps. There were no publications or recognition manuals on the Japanese Air Force, and the best information on the Japanese Navy was contained in sadly out-of-date and incomplete editions of Jane's Fighting Ships." His long-range landplanes and flying boats did what they could to report on enemy ship and aircraft movements and supply aerial photographs, all the while hindered by contrary weather conditions, a lack of experienced aerologists, and abysmal radio communications. McCain believed that F4F-7 fighters fitted with cameras "could be employed to great advantage" and on 22 August asked Nimitz to provide them. Nimitz ordered photo planes sent from the West Coast as soon as possible after 1 September, and a few came to McCain from carriers.[28]

In an effort to close some of the gaps in operational intelligence, McCain sent out two PBYs from VP-71 to Indispensable Reef on 9 June to investigate a pair of Japanese Nakajima Type 97 ("Kate") torpedo bombers from the carrier Shōkaku that had gone down in the Battle of the Coral Sea. They were disappointed to find that the Japanese aircrews had done a thorough job destroying code books and cockpit instruments, but they did recover radio equipment and provided detailed descriptions of the design and construction of the aircraft.[29]

Another imperative, as McCain had emphasized in his letter to Low and Duncan, was to push aircraft operations as far forward as possible. A step in that direction took place on 25 May when, as McCain had planned, three F4Fs from Bauer's VMF-212 began flying from the airfield at Efate, followed by thirteen more Wildcats four days later. Advance bases, however, were not easy to build in the constrained circumstances of the South Pacific, where construction personnel and equipment were in short supply. Fighters, for example, could operate from the six-thousand-foot rolled and packed-coral strip at Efate, but bombers could not move in until Marston mat and asphalt hard-surfacing were laid down. Not until 9 July was the field at Efate ready for use by B-17s. Construction of a seaplane ramp, apron, and attendant base facilities were well under way at Havannah Harbor in Efate by late May and were ready for "limited operations" by the middle of June.[30]

Matt Gardner, after he had returned to the States from the Solomons, summed up the difficulties of constructing bases. "Here in the midst of civilization," he explained in a January 1943 interview, "it's difficult to conceive of any place where there is absolutely nothing. Robinson Crusoe should be required reading for anyone who is setting up an advanced base in the South Pacific Islands." "There is nothing there—everything they eat, everything they wear, every place that they live has to be brought in from the United States," he emphasized. "There is no such thing as living off the country in the South Pacific, unless you live on cocoanuts alone." Simply offloading supplies in the absence of piers, docks, and cranes was challenging, and materials could not be hauled inland without roads, which themselves had to be hacked out by bulldozers and other heavy equipment brought in over "very poor landing beaches." No storage tanks, pipelines, fuel trucks, or trailers were available; gas had to be manhandled to the field in fifty-five-gallon drums. Persistent downpours turned the black soil into sticky muck. Nor was there ever enough time. Usually deadlines were set at "the eleventh hour, and *then everything must be done yesterday.*" Gardner credited McCain for his improvisational accomplishments: "When there isn't anything to be done, he's the kind of fellow who does something."[31]

Espíritu Santo, north of Efate in the New Hebrides and 135 miles closer to the Solomons, became one of McCain's most important advance bases. The tropical island—and McCain—entered the realm of popular literature with the publication of James A. Michener's semiautobiographical Pulitzer-Prize-winning novel, *Tales of the South Pacific*, in 1946. The "Commander" (Michener) observed that he "knew Admiral McCain in a very minor way. He was an ugly old aviator. One day he flew over Santo and pointed down at that island wilderness and said, 'That's where we'll build our base.'" The "Commander" concluded that "everyone agrees that Santo was the best base the Navy ever built in the region."[32]

Michener took some literary license, especially in according McCain with unique insight in identifying Espíritu Santo's advantages. A day before McCain took over as Comairsopac, the commander on Efate had informed Nimitz that Espíritu had a superb harbor and was ideal for the development of a seaplane base and airfields. Ghormley added that the "importance of ESPIRITU SANTO to US cannot be over accentuated." McCain quickly followed up with plans to use the Segond Channel on the south side of the island for VP operations. On 28 May, the New Zealand light cruiser *Leander* covered the landing of five hundred Army troops under the command of Brig. Gen. Harry D. Chamberlin, who occupied the area adjacent to the channel in what Gardner described as "a deterrent to the Japs taking it." McCain emphasized the urgency for getting the fighters farther north in a letter to Ghormley on 4 June. "In regard to construction of air field on Espíritu Santo," he wrote, "there is one weighty point: i.e. the Marine VF at Effate [sic] can reach and can fight for about one-half hour before it is necessary to return for fuel." A day later, he and members of his staff visited the island to inspect sites for the construction of airfields.[33]

In a letter to Vice Adm. Herbert F. Leary, who commanded naval forces under MacArthur's South West Pacific command, McCain wrote that it is "my opinion that we have not pushed northward far enough. I think we could, and should, occupy Santa Cruz and Vanikoro, as well as begin construction of air fields on Espíritu Santo." Ghormley, though, worried that moving too quickly to establish an airfield on Espíritu might consume scarce resources and divert Marines to defensive rather than offensive functions. He cautioned that "I am hesitant to over extend ourselves. . . . We must be careful in regard to dispersal of our forces." He did not want McCain to think he was "trying to throw a wet blanket on initiative," but he wanted to ensure that McCain "stop, look, and listen" before taking further steps. Capt. Daniel J. Callaghan, Ghormley's chief of staff, thought a move into Espíritu Santo might make it a target for Japanese attack and possibly occupation. He commented on 10 June that "personally I think an airfield would be most helpful on E. Santo, but none should be built until sufficient AA personnel and equipment are there to protect it. Otherwise it's just an invitation to our yellow enemies to 'Come and use it.'" McCain countered that in his estimation the move to Espíritu was "safe" and a "fair gamble." He believed that special construction units accompanied by experienced engineers could have the field available for Army bombers relatively quickly. Not until 19 June did Ghormley finally take over as Comsopac with headquarters in Auckland. It had not been easy setting up the command so far from home; at one point he echoed McCain's earlier comment that everything had to be done on a "shoe-string," a term that later came to apply to the entire Solomons campaign.[34]

Finally, on 5 July, Cincpac agreed with McCain and assigned "highest priority" to completing construction of the airfield at Espíritu Santo. With help from Army personnel, the site had already been laid out in the coconut groves and jungle, roads bulldozed and graded, and construction equipment, fuel, and ammunition brought in, yet incomplete taxiways and other deficiencies limited the field to no more than eight heavy aircraft. The first B-17 from Colonel Saunders' 11th Bombardment Group landed on the five-thousand-foot airstrip on the twenty-ninth. McCain reported to Ghormley that "construction [of] this field in such limited time with meagre equipment and facilities [was a] truly remarkable achievement exemplifying the can do spirit of personnel concerned."[35]

With characteristic enthusiasm and resolve, McCain wanted his forces to engage the Japanese whenever possible without jeopardizing his units' primary search mission. He realized that although the attacks were not likely to cause much damage, there was also not much risk of Japanese opposition. Most significant, it was, as he said, a "matter of morale—the boys are getting pretty tired of slogging along on daily patrols." On the night of 28–29 May, three PBYs from VP-71, in coordination with four PBYs from MacArthur's South West Pacific command, worked over Gavutu, a small island just south of Florida Island, north across Sealark Channel from Guadalcanal. Radio signals from the *Tangier* simulating those emanating from a carrier task force deceived the Japanese into thinking that carrier planes were responsible for the attack. The Catalinas bombed and set fire to oil storage tanks and dock facilities, but on the return flight they ran into nasty weather and in part due to poor radio reception wandered off course and ran out of fuel about 120 miles east of Nouméa. One was badly damaged in a forced landing in heavy seas and sank. Another PBY drifted ashore on a nearby island and was destroyed; the third made it safely back to Nouméa after being refueled. Fortunately, no flight crew were killed or injured.[36]

The Gavutu raid included a flight over Guadalcanal, where intelligence indicated that the Japanese might be planning to construct an airfield. McCain reported to Ghormley on 2 June that "a careful reconnaissance" of the location had been made "in full moonlight and at leisure, and the pilot stated emphatically that had there been so much as one truck in the area he must have seen it. There was no indication of any construction having started there as yet." McCain added that even though nothing had been found on the island, "we *are* concerned definitely with the proposed air field installations on Guadalcanal, which might and probably would be the source of extreme discomfort to us. When and as such a field is in the process of construction, a commando raid on Guadalcanal would seem very much indicated." Even better would be to use B-17s or B-24s in long-range day and night interdiction raids on Japanese shipping. As McCain guessed, less than a week later the Japanese began preliminary construction on an airstrip at Lunga Point on Guadalcanal's narrow northern coastal plain.[37]

McCain's forces continued offensive operations against Japanese positions in the Solomons for the next month. Without the Army's heavy bombers, McCain had to rely on his PBYs, which could not be used in daylight missions where they might encounter Japanese fighters. On 31 May, seven PBYs carried out a raid that targeted Tulagi, where they bombed fuel dumps, destroyed a seaplane, and "silenced" antiaircraft artillery. PBYs hit Tulagi again on 29 June and 6 July. Four Catalinas went after shipping off Tulagi on the night of 10–11 July, only to be thwarted by bad weather. McCain was always eager for action and abhorred flying a desk in Nouméa. He personally got a taste of offensive operations when he hitched a ride on one of three PBYs from VP-71 flying a night high-altitude bombing mission against Tulagi on 25 June. Although rain and clouds rendered the targets "impossible to see," the flying boats dropped eight 500-pound high-explosive bombs on a village with "results unknown." One Catalina officer recalled that McCain "never allowed any publicity. He would just show up before launch time and quietly climb aboard the aircraft."[38] That McCain flew on this and possibly other combat missions exemplified his natural inclination to lead from the front and his strong ties to the officers and men serving under him. They reciprocated with mutual admiration for his loyalty and courage. McCain's superiors liked having a fighting admiral on the scene too. Yet they might not have been pleased that he had flown on combat missions, for had he been captured or killed the Japanese would have enjoyed a substantial intelligence and propaganda coup.

Twice in June, McCain and Gardner flew to Comsopac headquarters in Auckland to confer with Ghormley about expanding the base at Espíritu Santo and other matters. There were also inspection trips to Fiji in late May and to Efate in early July. A big change took place on the afternoon of 20 June when McCain transferred his flag from the *Tangier* to the *Curtiss*, commanded by Capt. Maurice E. Browder. The *Curtiss* had arrived at Nouméa four days previously in company with the *McFarland* (AVD 14), an old 1,200-ton four-stack destroyer converted in 1940 to a fast seaplane tender. A day later, on the seventeenth, Cdr. Norman R. Hitchcock's *Mackinac* (AVP 13), a purpose-built 2,600-ton tender, joined the flotilla at Nouméa. McCain was pleased. The *Curtiss* was much better suited to accommodate him and his staff, the ship's flag country including space for separate radar, radio, and chart rooms. Furthermore, even though the *Tangier* rotated back to the West Coast, McCain had realized a net gain of two ships; three tenders could service more aircraft than could two. On the other hand, he was not so happy that the *Curtiss* did not deliver the torpedoes he had requested nor any of the personnel he urgently needed to service and arm them.[39]

McCain appreciated the additional ships, but he also needed more patrol planes. On 29 June, Nimitz ordered Bellinger to ensure that McCain's command got a total of thirty PBYs. Bellinger protested that dispatching the aircraft to the South Pacific would leave fewer than sixty PBYs in Hawaii, many of which were nearing the end of their service lives. Unless extra PBYs previously earmarked for the British were forthcoming from Consolidated, it was in effect a zero-sum game. Nevertheless, Bellinger soon complied, informing McCain on the thirtieth that the first of eighteen flying boats would go to Nouméa no later than 2 July, with the others to follow in flights of three per day through the rest of that week. A portion of the new aircraft allocated to the South Pacific were twelve PBYs of Patrol Squadron 23, sent out to relieve VP-71 and its personnel to return to Hawaii.[40]

Nimitz also wanted to know if airfields on New Caledonia were sufficient to handle a minimum of two carrier air groups while the ships lay over in Nouméa. In response to Nimitz's orders, McCain conducted a survey in late June to determine Nouméa's overall suitability as an advance base for flattops and their aircraft. McCain determined that two carriers could be moored in the harbor and that the field at Plaine des Gaiacs and another at Koumac northwest of Nouméa were "serviceable" for the carriers' aircraft, even though communications were poor, there were no antiaircraft guns for protection, and there was no housing for flight crews. The field at Tontouta had to be expanded and could not be made ready for large numbers of Navy aircraft before 1 September.[41] Although it would take time and effort, Nouméa subsequently proved its worth as a supply and repair base for the American carrier forces operating in the South Pacific.

The buildup of McCain's forces came about mostly as a consequence of the spectacular and in some ways unexpected American victory at the Battle of Midway on 4–6 June, which relieved the immediate threat in the Central Pacific and allowed American planners to recalibrate their South Pacific strategy from the defensive to the offensive. The immediate stimulus came from MacArthur, who on 8 June proposed a swift assault on Rabaul. The idea, if not the timetable or the prospect of Army leadership, resonated with the fiery King, long the champion of an offensive in the theater. Following more wrangling at the top levels of the American command structure, General Marshall engineered a compromise whereby the JCS agreed to a three-phase campaign. In the first stage, under Nimitz, Navy and Marine forces would take Tulagi in the Solomons and Ndeni in the Santa Cruz group; the next two stages, led by MacArthur with Navy support, included an offensive on the north coast of New Guinea and a thrust toward Rabaul. A necessary accommodation in the first phase was the decision to nudge the Sopac area west one degree to longitude 159 degrees east, thus including the southern Solomons within Nimitz's Cincpoa jurisdiction. Only later, in the first week of July, as it became apparent that the Japanese had indeed begun building an airfield at Lunga Point, did the planning specifically include an amphibious landing by Marines to secure the island and employ it for further offensive moves in the Solomons.[42]

With the expansion of Cincpoa's area of responsibility, Ghormley and his staff now had to plan for the Tulagi-Guadalcanal operation. Yet Ghormley, with no operational experience and cautious to a fault, was not well-suited to take charge of the audacious South Pacific offensive. The historian John Lundstrom concluded, simply, that he "was in over his head." McCain, on the other hand, was optimistic and committed to moving forward. He wrote to Harry Chamberlin at Efate that he was "1000 percent for the Guadalcanal operation," while recognizing that "I fear it will meet with the disfavor of our superiors, not in principle but at the present time in particular." Fletcher, due to his tactical experience and leadership of carrier task forces at the Coral Sea and Midway, was a natural to head the carrier and surface naval forces now under Ghormley's command. Rear Adm. Richmond Kelly Turner, King's assistant chief of staff for plans, was the amphibious force commander. Just as smart as Ghormley but without his superior's tact, Turner had the skill, experience, and confidence needed to accomplish what promised to be a complex and risky venture.[43]

The landings were tentatively scheduled for 1 August, allowing less than a month for the detailed plans to be finalized. At Cincpac headquarters in Pearl Harbor, Turner, Fletcher, and Spruance, a "black shoe" who had commanded a carrier task force at Midway and was now Nimitz's chief of staff, joined Rear Adms. Aubrey Fitch and Thomas Kinkaid in the planning process. By 5 July, they had completed a framework for the operation, which Nimitz forwarded to Ghormley on the sixth. Code-named "Watchtower," the Solomons operation included seizing Tulagi ("Ringbolt"), adjacent Florida Island, and Guadalcanal (the famous "Cactus"). McCain's VPs had one principal mission, succinctly stated: "prevent our striking forces from being surprised by an enemy carrier group." For this purpose, McCain knew it was essential to forward-base his tenders at Ndeni, 365 miles from the Solomons, and Malaita, only 80 miles on the other side of Indispensable Strait from Guadalcanal.[44]

Building on Nimitz's outline, Ghormley and his staff in Auckland completed their operational plan (Op Plan 1-42) on 15 July. Ghormley's recommendation to put off the operation from 1 August to 7 August (D-day), allowed more time for a rehearsal to take place in the Fijis on 27 July, for Turner's transports to arrive in New Zealand with the necessary men and equipment, and for more land-based air power to be brought in. Fletcher's Expeditionary Force was made up of TF-61, with three carriers (the *Saratoga*, *Enterprise*, and *Wasp* [CV 7]) and their escorts, and TF-62, Turner's command, which included the reinforced First Marine Division under Maj. Gen. Alexander A. ("Archie") Vandegrift. McCain became commander of Task Force 63 (CTF-63), with responsibility for all land- and tender-based aircraft deployed for reconnaissance, scouting, and attack operations in support of the Expeditionary Force. These activities would be coordinated with scouting and bombing aircraft from MacArthur's South West Pacific command operating in the area west of the Solomons. More specifically, in order to "render aircraft support on call" during the landings on Tulagi and Guadalcanal, Ghormley's plan called for TF-63 aircraft to be at Ndeni by 5 August and at the Maramasike Estuary on the east shore of Malaita on D-day. Ghormley counted on McCain to provide three VP squadrons, Saunders' 11th Bombardment Group, the 67th Fighter Squadron, the New Zealand Hudson unit, a Navy scouting squadron, and Marine fighter and observation squadrons.[45]

After studying Ghormley's operational plan, McCain recommended changes, foremost among them a delay in the timing. He argued that he could not bring his overworked VPs up as quickly as Ghormley had proposed and requested that the plan be modified to give him an extra day to do so. Ghormley agreed. On 20 July he circulated a dispatch in which he indicated that the plan had been revised to allow McCain's tenders to begin flying from Ndeni on 6 August and from Malaita on D-plus one.[46]

On 25 July, McCain and his staff put the finishing touches on the operational plan (Op Plan 1-42) for TF-63. The plan underscored Cincpac intelligence that the Japanese had intended to reinforce, consolidate, and build installations in the Solomons, including Tulagi and Lunga Point on Guadalcanal. TF-63 was divided into seven separate task groups (TG): TG-63.1 consisted of AAF Martin B-26 Marauder twin-engine medium bombers and a squadron of P-39 fighters; TG-63.2 was made up of the 11th Bombardment Group and its B-17s. Both AAF task groups flew out of Plaine des Gaiacs, but the B-17s were to move up to Espíritu Santo as soon as the airfield was ready. The *Curtiss* (TG-63.3) was to proceed to Espíritu Santo with ten VP-23 PBYs, arriving there early on 4 August and beginning reconnaissance operations the next day. The *McFarland* (TG-63.4) would be at Ndeni with seven VP-11 and VP-14 PBYs by 5 August (D-minus two). On 8 August (D-plus one) ten VP-23 aircraft would come up from Espíritu Santo to join the *Mackinac* (TG-63.5) at Malaita.[47]

McCain's surveillance plan included details on the search patterns to be flown by his aircraft in the days before, during, and after the landings. On D-minus two, PBYs from New Caledonia were responsible for sector 5, flying 700 miles to the north as far as Ndeni, while the VPs from Espíritu Santo covered a wide swath of ocean (sector 3) east of the Solomons. B-17s from Espíritu handled sector 2, which took in the Solomons as far up as Santa Isabel and New Georgia. A day before the landings and on D-day itself the *McFarland*'s aircraft from Ndeni would search sector 5, shifted from Espíritu and now ranging 650 miles northeast of the Solomons toward Truk and the Marshalls. On D-plus one, the *Mackinac*'s VPs from Malaita were to extend sector 4 another 350 miles north and northwest to 318 degrees. Basically, McCain's plan envisaged B-17s operating in sectors where there might be enemy fighter opposition, while the long-legged but more vulnerable PBYs covered open ocean areas. None of McCain's searches arced far enough west and north to take in the northern Solomons, which were to be covered by South West Pacific aircraft. Adhering to well-established scouting doctrine and practice, the airplanes would leave at first light, reach the extreme limits of their searches before dusk, and return at night using radar to sweep for any lurking enemy ships. Presumably they would detect and possibly strike a Japanese carrier force slipping through the cordon after sunset on the sixth, well before it could attack the invasion force at dawn the next day.[48]

Comairsopac's communication plan demanded initiative, imagination, and coordination to be fully effective in a rapidly changing and complex operational environment. The system comprised five radio circuits or "nets." Net "E" linked Nouméa, Espíritu Santo, and Efate, the principal bases supporting long-range reconnaissance and bombing missions. Net "A" connected all the TF-63 commanders, while Net "B" tied in the commanders of Task Groups 63.3, 63.4, and 63.5 (the *Curtiss*, *McFarland*, and *Mackinac*) but excluded their attached VPs. Net "C" was the most comprehensive, including all shore facilities, ships, TF-63 task group commanders, and search and strike aircraft. In contrast, Net "D" connected only Airsopac bases with New Zealand aircraft.[49] Reflecting the efforts of McCain, his staff, and above all the bluejackets manning radio shacks ashore and afloat, the electronic communication system was much improved over what they had inherited two months before, and it had the potential for swiftly disseminating contact reports from reconnaissance aircraft. On the other hand, the network was complex, the overlapping circuits were not fully integrated with one another, and the system remained subject to the limitations of the technology and vagaries of the tropical doldrums.

As McCain and the other subordinate commanders completed their plans for Watchtower and began assembling their forces, Ghormley called a meeting of the high-level officers involved in the operation. The conference took place at Tongatabu on 27 July, the day after Fletcher's TF-61 and Turner's TF-62 had come together off the island in preparation for the landing exercises at Koro in the Fijis. The assembly was not to be confused with a gathering of Nelson's "band of brothers," subordinates who knew instinctively what the hero of Trafalgar demanded of them. For reasons still hard to explain, Ghormley declined to attend. Substituting for him was his chief of staff, Daniel Callaghan, who flew from Auckland to Suva in the Fijis. McCain and three members of his staff came in to Suva on a PBY from Nouméa on the twenty-sixth, joining Callaghan, Turner, and Vandegrift on the destroyer *Hull* for the passage to Tongatabu. Climbing the accommodation ladder on Fletcher's flagship *Saratoga*, McCain suffered the indignity of being plunged "waist deep in the ocean" as the big carrier wallowed in the Pacific swells.[50]

★ ★ ★ ★

The *Saratoga* meeting, punctuated by a series of testy exchanges between Fletcher and Turner, revealed more division than consensus as the Navy approached the first South Pacific offensive. Of most concern was the air coverage, both from Fletcher's carriers and from McCain's shore-based and tender-based aircraft. Naturally, Turner and Vandegrift wanted to have air superiority over the objective and to have as much air support as possible for as long as necessary. Fletcher and McCain understood this, but because they were also aware that a surprise strike by Japanese carrier and land-planes was a distinct possibility, they had to commit a percentage of their aircraft to searches and defense of their ships and bases. Turner comprehended from the meeting that if for some reason McCain's aircraft could not carry out their searches, Fletcher would assign some of his carrier planes to "short-range scouting" missions. Fletcher's carriers and their air complements were therefore indispensable for the operation, but they could not be tied to the beaches for an indefinite period. So the most contentious issue to the planners then—as well as to historians today—was the length of time the carriers remained in the vicinity of Guadalcanal. Based on his tactical experience, Fletcher, more than anyone else, knew the inherent danger of keeping his carriers in place too long and determined to withdraw them no later than three days after the landings (D-plus two). No one considered this to be a problem at the time, since Turner and others believed the Marines' transports could be offloaded within forty-eight hours of the initial assault, leaving the cargo ships to be discharged at a more leisurely pace.[51]

Regardless of how long the flattops loitered after the landings, much of the weight of air support for Watchtower rested on McCain's shoulders. His immediate priority when he returned to Nouméa on the twenty-eighth was mustering his limited offensive air power to fulfill an ambitious commitment he had made at the *Saratoga* conference to accelerate strikes against the Japanese. The following night, 29 July, three PBYs from VP-23 carried out a raid on Gavutu, hitting aircraft on the water and damaging shore installations. On the thirtieth, nine B-17s struck the still unfinished Japanese airfield at Lunga Point. Three Catalinas hit Tulagi on the thirty-first, and the next day, 1 August, ten B-17s blasted Tulagi and Lunga, destroying a Japanese flying boat and shooting down two Mitsubishi ("Zero"-type) floatplane fighters. The heavies returned to soften up Lunga on the second and fourth and assaulted Tulagi on the third and fifth. One B-17 went down after being struck by a Zero-type floatplane over Lunga on 4 August and another was reported missing following an attack on Guadalcanal on the sixth. Meanwhile, the *Curtiss* anchored in the Segond Channel at Espíritu Santo on time on 4 August, and the next day the *McFarland* launched search operations with five PBYs from Graciosa Bay at Ndeni.[52]

McCain also faced the dilemma of providing continuing fighter protection for the Marines on Guadalcanal after the carriers left. The escort carrier *Long Island* (ACV 1) was to bring in a Marine air group consisting of a squadron of F4Fs and a squadron of Douglas SBD Dauntless dive-bombers from Pearl Harbor, but not before D-plus four at the earliest, and more likely D-plus six. Turner wanted F4Fs at Lunga as soon as possible, but McCain knew his Wildcats did not have the "legs" to reach Guadalcanal from Espíritu Santo and that Fletcher could not deliver them to Guadalcanal because the Marine aviators were not sufficiently trained to fly from carriers. Therefore, on 27 July he proposed that Fletcher fit the Marine fighters with auxiliary fuel tanks. If that were not possible, McCain had a backup plan. When Fletcher's carriers departed from Guadalcanal, two of their fighter squadrons could stay behind to operate temporarily from Lunga, while Fletcher

supplied fuel tanks to VMF-212, the Marine outfit that was staged forward
on Efate. That squadron could then fly to Guadalcanal at about the same
time the *Long Island* arrived with its fighters. Fletcher's fighters could fly out
to the *Long Island*, which would return them to their carriers sometime after
D-plus six. It was at best an awkward scheme rooted in the supposition that
the airfield on Guadalcanal would be ready within a few days of the landings. Of obvious concern to Fletcher was that McCain's proposal critically
depleted his carriers' fighter complements.[53]

Another problem was that the Marines discovered that even under
optimum circumstances they could not fit the tanks to their old F4F-3As in
less than ten days. McCain came up with still another alternative: borrow
fourteen F4Fs with auxiliary tanks from Fletcher, which would be flown by
the Marines from Efate to Guadalcanal to augment the two Navy squadrons
Fletcher had already donated to the cause. After the *Long Island* delivered
its Marine fighters, the ship could take all the Navy aircraft back to the
carriers. Now headquartered with his staff on the 8,400-ton auxiliary transport *Argonne* (AG 31) at Nouméa, Ghormley forwarded McCain's plans
to Fletcher and Turner on 2 August, reassuring Fletcher that the presence
of any Japanese carrier forces meant the fighters would be "immediately
released" to him. Lundstrom called McCain's proposals "harebrained."[54] On
the other hand, one might view them as imaginative solutions to complex,
nearly impossible tactical and logistical problems and a lapse in preparations
for the quick insertion of land-based fighters. No one dismissed his ideas out
of hand, and in any case no one at the time seemed to have any other ideas
about how best to ensure adequate fighter cover for the operation after the
flattops pulled out.

According to Ghormley's chief of staff Dan Callaghan, the consensus
from the *Saratoga* conference was that many details remained to be worked
out, that there was insufficient time for adequate planning, and that there
was no alternative other than "to whip plans into shape as rapidly as possible." Further evidence of the inadequacy of the preparations and the
hurry-up, ad hoc nature of the whole enterprise was the rehearsal at Koro,
postponed a day to the twenty-eighth. With no firsthand intelligence of
the island or its surroundings, Nimitz and his staff chose the site more out
of concerns about secrecy than anything else. Despite reservations that the
nearly impassable reefs surrounding the island would cause difficulties for
the landing craft, the exercise began as scheduled, only to have Turner ter-
minate his part of the operation prematurely because he could not afford

to lose valuable men and equipment. Fletcher's aviators went ahead with practice observation, bombing, strafing, and other support flights on the thirtieth. Unsatisfactory as it was, the exercise did provide badly needed experience for the amphibious force and gave the carriers an opportunity to test their support procedures in preparation for the real thing a week later.[55]

Fletcher's sharp eyes caught what John Lundstrom has referred to as a "hole" in McCain's D-minus one plans for searches in two sectors to the northeast of Guadalcanal: 3 (Espíritu Santo) and 5 (Ndeni). Because the flying boats would return well after dark and rely on radar—which was far from perfect—Fletcher thought it entirely possible that a Japanese carrier task force could remain to the northwest outside the previously searched sectors and make a night approach to Guadalcanal undetected. He informed McCain about the problem on 29 July. McCain notified Fletcher the next day that he understood the potential problem and would "comply" by changing the timing of his searches, but only if the "weather forecast indicates favorable navigational conditions." He also promised an update of his search plan to include prompt reports about areas of sectors that were not covered by his VPs, thus allowing Fletcher's carrier aircraft to provide additional searches as needed.[56]

By the eve of Watchtower, McCain had built up a force of 277 aircraft, impressive but shy of what he wanted and deficient in some of the most capable and modern types, not to mention being distributed over hundreds of thousands of square miles. Among the forces available to him were 26 PBY-5s from VP-11, VP-14, and VP-23, 49 Marine F4F Wildcat fighters from VMF-212, VMF-111, and VMO-251, and 25 Vought OS2U floatplanes (10 of which were in Samoa). McCain also had at his disposal 29 B-17s, 22 B-26s, and 79 F4F, P-39 and P-400 fighters. Eighteen Hudsons from the Royal New Zealand Air Force were also available.[57] McCain's resources were both varied and thin, presenting the worst of all worlds in terms of capabilities and coordination while he and his men anxiously awaited orders to begin the operation the next day. Guadalcanal was the first offensive operation of the Pacific War and the largest amphibious operation undertaken by American forces since 1898. While there was ample confidence among the naval leadership, there was no assurance that this or any other similarly ambitious and risky operation so far from friendly shores would yield a successful outcome.

CHAPTER 4

Guadalcanal

M cCain's Task Force 63 Catalinas and Fortresses had primary responsibility for long-range reconnaissance in the days and hours immediately preceding the 7 August landings on Guadalcanal. By the end
of the day on the sixth (D-minus 1), PBYs from the *Curtiss* at Espíritu Santo
and the *McFarland* at Ndeni had completed their patrols, as did the B-17s
from the AAF's 11th Bombardment Group, all responsible for covering the
southern Solomons and the vast ocean areas to the north and east of the
archipelago. McCain reported that there were no sightings of Japanese ships
or aircraft in any of the sectors they probed, although AAF Fortresses flying
from New Caledonia were unable to search sector 1 because of the weather.
The searches came at a cost. One of VP-23's Catalinas, piloted by Lt. Maurice S. Smith, slammed into a ridge on Espíritu Santo, killing all eight of its
flight crew; a VP-11 PBY flying out of Ndeni went down at sea while searching sector 5; and a B-17 was lost "due to navigation error," although its crew
was recovered the next day off the east coast of Espíritu Santo.[1]

Overnight, Fletcher's TF-61 and Turner's TF-62, aggregating seventy-
nine ships of all types (including three Australian cruisers), 234 aircraft on
three carriers, and a Marine invasion force of 19,000 men, closed on Guadalcanal from the south, undetected. Col. LaVerne Saunders of the 11th
Bombardment Group, who had attended the 27 July *Saratoga* conference
and observed the assembled forces at Tongatabu, was astonished: "It covered
the whole South Pacific and I do not know yet why it was [not] discovered
before D-day." The answer, in part, was due to persistent overcast and rain
that had caused the cancellation of one of McCain's B-17 searches and now
obscured the fleet during the approach.[2]

As dawn broke and the skies cleared on D-day, the seventh, the furious barrage from the ships of the American Expeditionary Force caught the
Japanese on Guadalcanal and Tulagi totally off guard. Marines from the
amphibious force first waded ashore at Tulagi, followed an hour or so later
by landings on Guadalcanal. For a time, the Marines met stiff resistance on

Tulagi, but there was next to no opposition on the ground at Guadalcanal. The air over the landings was a different matter. From Rabaul the Japanese retaliated with twin-engine land-attack aircraft, dive-bombers, and fighters. Fletcher's carrier planes blunted the assault but at the cost of sixteen American aircraft shot down or lost in operational accidents. Once again, bad weather to the north and west meant B-17s out of New Caledonia were not able to search McCain's sector 1, and a Fortress flying from Espíritu Santo failed to return from probing sector 2, which included Guadalcanal. The *Mackinac* sheltered in the waters of the Maramasike Estuary at Malaita on D-day, allowing its brood of VPs to extend searches in sector 4 a day earlier than McCain had planned. When McCain's aircraft completed nearly all their D-day searches without sighting any enemy ships or aircraft, it appeared by the end of the day that the Japanese fleet would not be a factor.[3]

★ ★ ★ ★

McCain's reconnaissance aircraft fanned out again at daybreak on the eighth following their D-plus one search patterns. The coverage was excellent in some of the sectors, with up to 95 percent of the areas searched. But sector 1 was still not reconnoitered due to the poor weather, which also prevented B-17s from probing the right half of sector 2 in the southern Solomons. Searches were negative in all the other sectors. Accidents claimed two more of McCain's precious PBYs during the day. At 2333 local time— that is, twenty-seven minutes before midnight—McCain forwarded a summary of the searches and their results to Turner, Fletcher, and Ghormley.[4]

While McCain's aircraft had come up empty in their searches on 8 August, earlier in the day Sowespac Hudsons had spied and reported on what appeared to be a Japanese force of cruisers, destroyers, and seaplane tenders headed for Guadalcanal. This was in fact Admiral Mikawa Gunichi's force of five heavy cruisers, two light cruisers, and a destroyer, which had sortied from Rabaul and was on course southeast toward the amphibious force at Guadalcanal and Tulagi. The Hudsons' reports did not get to Ghormley's task force commanders until later on the eighth. Late on the eighth, Turner concluded from the supposed presence of tenders that the Japanese would use Rekata Bay on Santa Isabel Island as a base from which to launch torpedo attacks on his transports, and he transmitted a message to McCain requesting a strike on the enemy ships early the next day. McCain agreed to have his VPs do so after his aircraft had verified that the Japanese were present at Santa Isabel and ordered the *Mackinac* to pull four of its PBYs from searching their eastern subsectors and redirect them to an attack on the night of the ninth. B-17s from Saunders' 11th group would strike during the day. The bombers found no enemy ships at Rekata Bay, and the rest of the *Mackinac*'s PBYs, combing 100 percent of their sector that day, reported negative results. In the meantime, though, Turner had decided that the threat of additional air attacks warranted his decision to remove his force from the landing area early on the ninth.[5]

On the evening of 8 August, erroneously assuming that all of Turner's forces had disembarked and that they had achieved all their objectives, Fletcher asked for permission from Ghormley to withdraw his carriers, after two days in support of the operation and a day earlier than the deadline he had committed to. This meant that only McCain's aircraft remained to provide searches and air cover in support of the amphibious force, which had not landed all the Marines and had not secured the vital Lunga airfield. Although Fletcher had been copied on Turner's message about the enemy cruiser-tender force, he had no independent confirmation from McCain's searchers about this force or any others that might be operating out of Rabaul. Fletcher's own searches on the eighth turned up nothing. Not until after Fletcher had made his recommendation did McCain inform him (as well as Turner) that not all of his sectors had been searched. Thus, having no direct evidence of an imminent Japanese threat, and in any event not having aviators trained to make nocturnal attacks on enemy ships, Fletcher could see no reason to keep his flattops in the vicinity of Guadalcanal once he received approval of his recommendation from Ghormley. Withdrawal also provided an opportunity for TF-61's ships to replenish their depleted oil bunkers.[6]

Like Fletcher, although more than a week later, Turner discovered another flaw in McCain's search plan, this time in an area to the north and west of sector 4 (the responsibility of the *Mackinac*'s PBYs out of Malaita). He informed McCain of the problem on 7 August and asked him "to consider [a] morning search" in that area. "There is no contemporary evidence," according to historian John Lundstrom, "that [Turner's] message ever reached McCain in time" and there was therefore no reason for McCain either to reply or to comply. Lundstrom concluded that McCain never received Turner's message due to incompatibilities in radio frequencies among the disparate commands. Had he received Turner's dispatch, McCain might in any case have used his discretion and declined to commit more of the *Mackinac*'s aircraft to the west of sector 4, especially because he assumed that some of the tender's PBYs would be diverted to a night torpedo strike on the Japanese ships thought to be assembled at Rekata Bay. Further-more, the area in question was to be reconnoitered by aircraft from Sowes-pac, and it would have been more appropriate for Turner to have queried MacArthur (through Ghormley) about coverage in that sector. In fact, the Hudson from that command had spotted Mikawa's ships, although Turner misinterpreted the report to mean a possible seaplane attack.[7] It is impor-tant to note that McCain's tactical doctrine and the timing of his searches were intended to detect an enemy carrier force, which would launch a strike at first light, not a surface force cloaked in darkness, which Turner's screen-ing force presumably could counter.

With boldness leavened by good fortune, Mikawa exploited the gaps in Allied reconnaissance and skillfully threaded his cruisers southeast through the island chain until by midnight on the eighth his strike group was in position to deliver a devastating blow to the cruisers and destroyers screen-ing Turner's landing force. A little after 0130 on the ninth, the Japanese col-umn rounded Savo Island and fell in among the Allied warships lying to the east and south. Well drilled in night tactics, the Japanese loosed torpedoes and rained shells on the surprised screening force. In less than an hour three American cruisers and one Australian cruiser were on fire and sinking, with heavy casualties. Without following up with an assault on Turner's ships off Lunga, the Japanese withdrew as swiftly as they had attacked, suffering minor damage to their own ships and leaving in their wake confusion and consternation among the American task force commanders. The Battle of Savo Island, as it became known, was one of the worst defeats in American naval history, a debacle for which, it was clear, there would be ample blame to share.[8]

Four months after the battle, Adm. Arthur J. Hepburn, former com-mander in chief, U.S. Fleet and chairman of the General Board, began an "informal" investigation of the Savo disaster. Hepburn's charge was to determine the causes of the defeat and to assess "whether or not culpabil-ity attaches to any individual engaged in the operation." He did not solicit accounts from either Fletcher or McCain and relied heavily on Turner's observations and conclusions. In a secret report issued in May 1943, Hep-burn stressed that McCain's aircraft had not searched sector 1 and only half of sector 2 on the eighth and that Turner did not receive this vital infor-mation until sometime later. If Mikawa's force had averaged twenty knots, it would have been within 140 miles of Savo by nightfall on the eighth. Returning searchers from Espíritu would have missed the Japanese, but had McCain complied with Turner's request, *Mackinac* planes might have spotted them. Hepburn determined that "it is not unreasonable to suppose that timely information of the failure of the search plan might at least have resulted in a precautionary order to the Screening Force to maintain the highest condition of readiness."[9]

In his conclusions Hepburn tacked a middle course between "culpable inefficiency on the one hand and more or less excusable error of judgment on the other." He determined that the devastating losses at Savo were the result of inexperience in combat operations, near total dependence on air reconnaissance for tactical intelligence, poor communications, lack of battle readiness on the ships themselves, and surprise by the Japanese. Indirectly indicting McCain, Hepburn concluded that "there had been practically no effective reconnaissance covering enemy approach during the day of August 8." In his endorsement of the report, Nimitz concurred that one of the reasons for the catastrophe was the "failure of either carrier or land-based air to conduct effective search and lack of coordination of searches." Capt. George L. Russell in King's office reviewed the Hepburn report at the end of July 1943. He commented that McCain had failed to probe the area where the Japanese approached Savo, even "after Rear Admiral Turner, in effect, asked him to do so." Yet he agreed with Hepburn that he did not believe McCain "should be called to account for it." In the end, King accepted the report, filed it, and recommended it remain secret until after the end of the war.[10]

McCain's decision to report on the results of searches after all his aircraft had returned introduced unnecessary and potentially dangerous delays in warning of approaching enemy ships and aircraft. For example, when Turner finally received McCain's summary message well after 2300, he surmised that there was no threat from a Japanese surface force that night. In 1960, he concluded that "I failed to assume that McCain wouldn't keep me informed of what his pilots were or weren't doing. . . . It was a masterful failure of air reconnaissance and my fellow aviators." As for Fletcher, there was not much he could have done to augment searches to the northwest from his carriers' position southeast of Guadalcanal had he known earlier on the eighth that McCain's aircraft had not covered all of their assigned sectors. McCain may have concluded that it made sense to issue single, inclusive reports instead of adding another score of messages to the traffic on an already overburdened radio net; and the reports from McCain's searchers on the seventh and eighth were negative. One might reasonably infer that had any of McCain's aircraft spotted Mikawa's warships they would have reported the contact and that McCain would have had the initiative and common sense to sound the alarm immediately. And the sector not searched and through which Mikawa's force stole on the seventh and the eighth was Sowespac's responsibility, not Sopac's. Yet as late as 22 August McCain persisted in consolidating search reports and dispatching them at or a little past midnight.[11] Information of any sort, whether by radio or any other means of transmission, was hard to come by at that juncture of the war. Why McCain did not issue individual sighting reports and do so more quickly, which he had promised Fletcher at the end of July, remains an inexplicable and inexcusable administrative and judgmental oversight on his part.

By the end of the day on the ninth, Turner had pulled his ships out of Guadalcanal, retiring toward Nouméa. He took with him troops he had not had time to get ashore and had left the Marines to fend for themselves without any immediate logistical support. Fletcher, meanwhile, continued on course for a refueling rendezvous southwest of Espíritu Santo, where he arrived on the afternoon of the tenth. It took two days to top off his ships, after which TF-61 headed back north and on the fifteenth took up a cruising position south of the Solomons. Fletcher hoped this would allow him to support the Marines in a crisis while still giving him the flexibility to deal with a Japanese carrier force should it appear.[12]

Fletcher's withdrawal left the Marines on Guadalcanal temporarily without fighter defense. Because the airfield at Lunga was not complete, Fletcher could not dispatch any of his depleted fighter force there, as McCain had suggested he might do as he withdrew his carriers. None of McCain's other ideas was feasible under the circumstances either, so he and the Marines on Guadalcanal would have to wait for the arrival of the air group on the *Long Island*, which would be further delayed because Ghormley had ordered the carrier to Suva. Fletcher and Ghormley both understood from Cincpac intelligence that they could expect the Japanese to respond to the Allied landings with a massive counteroffensive to retake the southern Solomons, nearly certain to involve a substantial carrier force. They also realized that they had to keep secure the lines of communication from New Caledonia through Espíritu Santo to Guadalcanal and Tulagi. For some time—certainly exceeding two or three days—only McCain's air forces were available to provide cover for the Marines ashore. McCain later wondered what the consequences would have been had the Japanese intervened in force at that critical moment: "I don't see how they could have lost. . . . God was

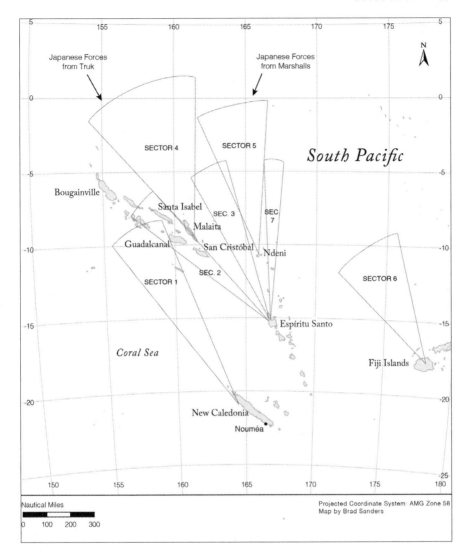

Map 1. Airsopac Searches, 7–8 August 1942 (Comairsopac Op Plan 1-42, NARA II)

with us." The pressure was on to get the Lunga field and others in shape as quickly as possible.[13]

In the aftermath of the Savo catastrophe and the departure of TF-61 and TF-62, Ghormley determined that it was too risky to keep the *Mackinac*, *McFarland*, and McCain's VPs forward positioned at Malaita and Ndeni. On the evening of the ninth, McCain received orders from Ghormley to pull the *Mackinac* and its PBYs out of Malaita and for the *McFarland* to withdraw from Ndeni; both ships and their aircraft were to resume operations at Espíritu Santo. *Mackinac's* aircraft in sector 4 got in one last search on the tenth before returning to Espíritu, although their flights were limited to about the half the distance they had planned to fly. Sector 2 was not searched that day because the bombers out of Espíritu had been sent on the wild goose chase to Rekata Bay.[14]

The unwelcome retirement from Malaita and Ndeni left McCain and his staff scrambling to revise their search plans now that nearly all Airsopac patrol aircraft were operating from Espíritu Santo. The withdrawal of the *Mackinac* and *McFarland*, coupled with vile weather in sector 1, limited flights on the tenth, but they picked up again on the eleventh and succeeding days. Surveillance was thorough in all sectors except 5, formerly the *McFarland's* responsibility, where either there were no searches or no reports for the better part of a week. In the aftermath of Savo, McCain had instituted early morning searches, yet the problem of tardy reports persisted, especially vexing to Fletcher, who signaled McCain on 11 August that "as soon as possible after completion [of] searches" he needed both "negative and positive information and percentage of coverage." Worried about enemy submarines near Guadalcanal and Tulagi, McCain ordered extra PBY patrols starting on 15 August. He also wanted his aircraft to fly a daily "offensive sweep" of the area looking for enemy surface ships as the Japanese geared up for a counteroffensive in the islands.[15]

They got immediate results. On 15 August, 11th Bombardment Group B-17s out of New Caledonia spotted and attacked a surfaced submarine in sector 2 near Tulagi. Two days later B-17s found a light cruiser and destroyer at Gizo Harbor on New Georgia Island, in addition to an attack transport and an oiler steaming in that direction. The bombers returned the next day to attack the cruiser and other ships at Gizo, with "telling effect." On the morning of the nineteenth, McCain's B-17s reported three destroyers and a submarine just two miles south of Tulagi as the Japanese ships positioned themselves to bombard American positions on Tulagi and Guadalcanal. Striking back within hours, two of the heavies hit the destroyer *Hagikaze* with 500-pound bombs, destroying a gun turret, damaging the rudder, and setting the ship on fire. Encouraged by Ghormley to "hit em again," McCain dispatched eight B-17s the next morning "to attack targets of opportunity." They had no further luck against Japanese warships but did shoot down an enemy patrol plane.[16]

Such successes notwithstanding, McCain's already demanding mission did not become any easier, especially given the dearth of forward bases and the attrition gnawing into TF-63's aircraft inventory. On 10 August, McCain informed Nimitz that he had lost twenty-six PBYs since he had taken over as Comairsopac and that he needed replacement aircraft as soon as possible. They were slow in coming. By the end of August, only eight new PBYs had arrived at Espíritu Santo, far short of what McCain recommended. B-17s and other aircraft were also being lost at rates McCain considered unsustainable. To make matters even worse, Ghormley suggested that six American squadrons be dispatched to the Royal New Zealand Air Force, possibly in exchange for an equivalent number of New Zealand units. McCain was incensed. With his Navy, Marine, and Army aircraft and crews stretched to the limit, it was incomprehensible that he would trade any of them for New Zealanders, who were unlikely to be better equipped or more experienced than the Americans. He was "unqualifiedly opposed to [the] proposal which is not only swapping horses but swapping streams," and Ghormley wisely dropped the idea.[17]

There was also the matter of fighter support for Guadalcanal, which in the absence of Fletcher's carriers depended on how fast the airstrip at Lunga (named Henderson Field in memory of Maj. Lofton R. Henderson, a Marine aviator killed during the Battle of Midway) could be completed. By 12 August, the field was in good enough shape for General Vandegrift to tell Ghormley that it was "ready for fighters and dive bombers. The sooner they arrive the better." That morning a PBY-5A amphibian flown by McCain's aide, Lt. William S. Simpson, landed at Henderson; on the return leg the Catalina flew out two Marine casualties. The following day, the *Long Island* finally arrived at Suva, but the ship's captain concluded that the inexperienced Marine aviators of VMF-223 could not safely fly from the flattop direct to Henderson. Following McCain's recommendation, the *Long Island* diverted to Efate on 17 August to drop off the VMF-223 fliers and pick up some aviators from VMF-212 who had been attached to VMF-223 and had the necessary qualifications to fly off the carrier. The *McFarland* ferried the *Long Island* air group's men, equipment, and aviation gasoline from Efate to Guadalcanal on the twenty-first. Covered by McCain's Airsopac aircraft and those from Fletcher's TF-61, the Marine F4F and SBD squadrons winged in to Henderson early in the afternoon on 20 August, forming the nucleus of a mixed Navy, Marine, and Army contingent under McCain's command that became known as the "Cactus Air Force." Two days later, five AAF P-400s landed at Henderson. The Marines now had the fighter protection they so badly needed, and McCain gained another forward base not only for Navy and Marine aircraft but also for staging Army B-17s, the first of which landed at Henderson on the twenty-second.[18]

Meanwhile, the Japanese determined to dislodge the Americans from Guadalcanal by transporting troops and supplies in small increments at night when detection was nearly impossible. They also reconstituted their Combined Fleet to support troop movements into the southern Solomons and to engage and defeat the American carrier force. Nimitz alerted Ghormley and MacArthur on 11 August that a Japanese carrier striking force could be expected to intervene in the South Pacific, although the best Cincpac intelligence could estimate was that it would be sometime in the "near future." Ghormley's Op Order 2-42 of 20 August relied on Fletcher to counter the Japanese flattops and called on McCain to cover reinforcements to Guadalcanal, re-establish his position at Ndeni, and attack enemy air bases and shipping with his VPs and land-based air. On his own initiative, McCain sought ways to advance as many AAF forces as possible by eliminating long-range searches from Fiji, augmenting the Army's aircraft in New Caledonia with more Lockheed Hudsons, and recommending that torpedo-equipped B-26s operate from Espíritu Santo. He believed that the Japanese were preparing to launch a major offensive operation and "I propose to have a fresh striking force ready for him."[19]

In compliance with Ghormley's directive, McCain dispatched the *Mackinac* to Ndeni, where the tender arrived on 20 August, accompanied by the minelayer *Breese* (DM 18). He also revised his 19 August operational order to rotate four of his search sectors 6 degrees to the right to provide more coverage to the north and east. It was none too soon, for, as Cincpac predicted, Japanese sea and air movements had dramatically increased. McCain anticipated "the enemy's big push in the next two or three days" and wanted to make sure he could "meet it with a fresh striking force" of PBYs, B-17s, and the aircraft on hand at Cactus. On the twenty-first, *Mackinac*'s Catalinas flying searches out of Ndeni in sector 5 to the north and northwest of the island spotted a Japanese patrol plane, and VP-23 PBYs prowling sector 3 reported four heavy cruisers and two destroyers steaming north away from Guadalcanal. In a "friendly fire" incident resulting from a breakdown in communications, two SBDs from Capt. Forrest P. Sherman's *Wasp* attacked the *Mackinac* at Ndeni, destroying a Vought OS2U floatplane and injuring thirteen of the ship's crewmembers. The twenty-second was also busy. McCain's searchers found another Japanese cruiser, a PBY attacked and damaged a submarine, and, based on a report that a Japanese cruiser was headed toward Ndeni, McCain ordered the *Mackinac* and the *Breese* to withdraw temporarily as a precaution.[20]

The Japanese, as Cincpac intelligence had anticipated, were on the move. They had divided their forces into two powerful fleets: the mobile force, or *Kidō Butai*, under veteran Admiral Nagumo Chuichi, included the big carriers *Shōkaku* and *Zuikaku* and the light carrier *Ryūjō*, along with two battleships and two heavy cruisers; and the advance force, consisting mostly of heavy cruisers under Vice Admiral Kondo Nobutake. The two forces were nominally to support a convoy commanded by Rear Admiral Tanaka Raizo bringing major reinforcements into Guadalcanal, but their primary objective was understood to be the destruction of the American carrier force. Cincpac was vague about the exact Japanese ship movements after 16 August, and accurate cryptographic intelligence was unavailable after the Japanese had updated their naval codes. As late as 22 August there was no indication from Pearl Harbor that the enemy was any closer to Guadalcanal than Truk, easily a thousand miles away. As a result, the Americans did not know when the Japanese had left port and had no idea even of their approximate location. Adequate warning would have to come from McCain's reconnaissance aircraft or from Fletcher's carrier-borne scouts.[21]

When the *Mackinac* pulled out of Ndeni, it left behind some of the VP-23 Catalinas to continue their searches. A little before 1000 on the twenty-third, Lt. (jg) Francis C. Riley, piloting one of the PBYs scouring sector 3, reported sighting two enemy heavy cruisers, three destroyers, and four transports north of Santa Isabel. Riley also spied a floatplane, presumably a scout from one of the cruisers. Although McCain did not know it at the time, Riley had found Tanaka's invasion group (actually comprising a light cruiser, eight destroyers, and three transports) on course south toward Guadalcanal. That evening five PBYs from Espíritu loaded with bombs and torpedoes took off to attack the Japanese ships but failed to find them. Nor could a strike group from Cactus or a *Saratoga* attack force, which on its return diverted to Lunga and remained overnight before landing back on the flattop the next morning. The reason why they missed the Japanese became obvious later in the day when aircraft from the *Mackinac*, now back at Ndeni with the *Breese*, reported that Tanaka's ships had reversed course and that subsequently the *Mackinac*'s searchers had lost contact. Because of another communications delay, neither Cactus nor Fletcher learned about these developments until after midnight on the twenty-fourth. Concluding from the information he had from Cincpac and from his own and

McCain's searches that Japanese carriers were still somewhere far to the north, Fletcher released the *Wasp* to refuel.[22]

The next day, 24 August, McCain's PBYs were out again at first light. Within a few hours, the *Mackinac*'s VP-23 fliers spotted the enemy. At 0905, the Catalina flown by Ens. James A. Spraggins reported sighting a Japanese cruiser; thirty minutes later Ens. Gale C. Burkey radioed that he had observed and was tracking a carrier, two cruisers, and a destroyer. The contact turned out to be the carrier *Ryūjō* steaming south in support of Tanaka's Guadalcanal invasion force. Other VP-23 aircraft reported that they had seen elements of Tanaka's convoy. Three of the VPs signaled that they had been spotted and attacked by enemy aircraft. As these sightings filtered in, Ghormley felt it necessary to admonish McCain to "impress pilots search planes vital importance prompt report of contacts enemy forces and necessity frequent subsequent amplifying reports." In contrast to the night of 8–9 August, McCain quickly circulated the reports, yet a mixup at TF-61 kept Fletcher in the dark about the Japanese carrier until after 1100, when he finally received a copy of Burkey's message.[23]

McCain's airmen had done exactly what had been expected of them in providing timely warning of the advancing Japanese forces, but the sequence of reports, coupled with confusion over VP-23 call signs, meant that Fletcher could not be certain where the carrier (or carriers) were. One of the VP-23 PBYs came tantalizingly close to Nagumo's mobile force but never spotted it, and another VP sighted elements of the advance force that afternoon, yet missed Nagumo's flattops. Thus, while McCain's VPs found the *Ryūjō* and Tanaka's force, they did not sight Nagumo's *Kidō Butai*, which presented the biggest threat to Fletcher's carriers and, ultimately, to the entire Guadalcanal operation.[24]

Late that morning, Fletcher, hoping to ascertain the position of the Japanese mobile force, launched a search from the *Enterprise* while preparing the *Saratoga*'s aircraft to hit the Japanese carriers once they were located. Coincidentally, an hour or so later, bombers and fighters from the *Ryūjō* took off to raid Cactus. When the *Saratoga*'s radar detected what appeared to be the *Ryūjō* strike, Fletcher decided that he could wait no longer and ordered the *Saratoga*'s air group aloft at 1338 to attack the Japanese carrier, whose position he knew only from Burkey's now-four-hour-old report. Just then, one of the Japanese cruiser floatplanes radioed the Americans' position to Nagumo, and the *Shōkaku* and *Zuikaku* quickly sent off their own combined strike force. Both sides were now committed to battle, but only

Nagumo had accurate and up-to-date information on the enemy's where-abouts. That balance partially evened out thanks to another of McCain's searchers. At 1400 a VP-23 PBY from Ndeni flown by Lt. Joseph M. Kellam spotted the *Ryūjō*, and Fletcher forwarded the Japanese flattop's position to the *Saratoga*'s strike group. On his way back to Ndeni, Kellam confirmed his earlier report by visual signal to the *Enterprise* and McCain followed up with a series of updates to Fletcher on the Japanese positions.[25]

McCain's aircraft never discovered the Japanese mobile force. That dis-tinction went to SBDs from the *Enterprise*, which found and attacked the *Shōkaku* at about 1500. They inflicted no damage, and worse, neither the *Sara-toga* nor the *Enterprise* accurately copied the dive-bombers' reports. Fletcher's TF-61 thus missed an opportunity to deliver a major blow to Nagumo's *Kidō Butai*. About half an hour later, the *Saratoga*'s planes located and attacked the *Ryūjō* and its escorts, leaving the flattop burning, out of control, and sinking. Minutes after the *Saratoga* strike group left the scene of destruction, Nagumo's first wave of attackers bombed and severely damaged the *Enterprise*. Fortu-nately, the *Saratoga* and other ships in the task force came through unscathed, and a second wave of Japanese aircraft missed the Americans altogether before darkness fell. After the *Enterprise* was temporarily patched up and both carriers had recovered most of their aircraft, the task force withdrew south to refuel. Some of the *Enterprise*'s SBDs found refuge at Henderson Field. Con-fident that he had destroyed two big American carriers despite heavy losses of aircraft from his first strike, Nagumo landed his second strike group and turned north, widening the distance between him and Fletcher and losing any remaining chance he had of achieving a decisive victory.[26]

Other than the abortive efforts from Espíritu Santo and Cactus on the twenty-third, McCain's strike forces played a minimal role in what became known as the Battle of the Eastern Solomons. At 1305 on the twenty-fourth, Maj. Ernest Manierre led a flight of seven 11th Bombardment Group B-17s from Espíritu to hit the Japanese. Dividing up, three of the heavies found the *Ryūjō* at 1725 already mortally wounded by bombs and torpedoes from the *Saratoga*'s strike. The Americans claimed they scored at least two hits, but subsequent information proved that that was not the case. Returning after dark, a badly shot up Fortress crash-landed on Espíritu, killing five of its crew. The other four B-17s landed safely at Efate.[27]

On the night of 24–25 August, two *Mackinac* PBYs reported finding Jap-anese ships north of Malaita, which McCain passed on as "an enemy carrier group" whose heading and speed seemed to indicate that they intended to overtake Fletcher's force. PBYs out on morning patrols encountered what they thought were carrier aircraft, presumably from the *Kidō Butai*, as well as various other "suspicious vessels." Grasping the opportunity to eliminate the Japanese flattops, Marine and Navy dive-bombers and fighters took off from Henderson before first light; instead of Nagumo's force they found Tanaka's convoy and succeeded in sinking one of the transports and damaging another. About two hours later, the destroyer *Mutsuki* fell prey to three B-17s from the 11th Bombardment Group. These losses led Tanaka to give up and withdraw, his retreat verified by a *Mackinac* PBY a little before 1100. Seeing that the Japanese retreat had ended the immediate threat to the Americans on Guadalcanal, Ghormley had nothing but praise for McCain's forces. "Your rugged and hard working search and striking groups have done a grand job," he communicated on the twenty-sixth.[28]

Routine operations kept McCain's TF-63 aircraft and crews busy in the aftermath of the battle. On the twenty-fifth and twenty-sixth, VP-23 Catalinas spotted submarines lurking in the waters between Espíritu Santo and Guadalcanal, at least one of them cruising on the surface. The undersea craft were a real threat to Fletcher's task force (now minus the damaged *Enterprise*, but with the *Wasp* back after an unsuccessful independent effort to find the Japanese carriers) as it continued to support operations ashore and cover convoys resupplying the Marines on Cactus. A *Mackinac* PBY attacked and damaged a surfaced sub with depth charges on the twenty-seventh. Another of the VP-23 flying boats from the *Mackinac* searched in vain for a Catalina out of Espíritu Santo that was thought to have been shot down the day before somewhere east of Guadalcanal. The same day one of McCain's aircraft rescued the crew of an *Enterprise* torpedo bomber from the Stewart Islands northeast of Malaita.[29]

Much like the Battle of the Coral Sea, the Eastern Solomons clash was a tactical draw, and like the Coral Sea it had positive strategic implications for the Allies. The Japanese, while still believing they had destroyed two American carriers, were generally aware that there would not be a quick victory in the Solomons and determined to fight and win a protracted campaign. They began sending a steady stream of reinforcements and supplies down "the Slot," the nickname for the confined artery bisecting the major islands in the archipelago—mostly using destroyers at night—and stepped up the air pressure on Guadalcanal with daily raids on Henderson. For their part, the Americans gained some breathing space. With a major Japanese counterstroke now unlikely, the Marines had time to secure their

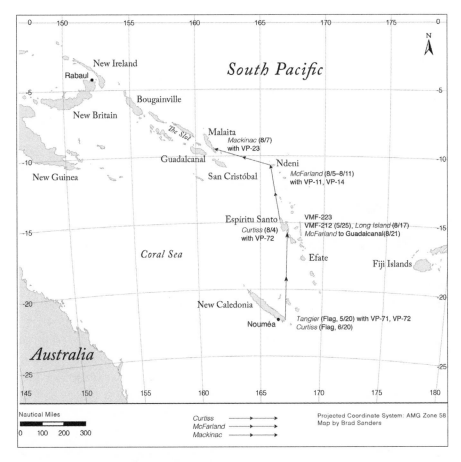

Map 2. South Pacific and Solomons Ship and Air Movements, May–August 1942 (Comairsopac, *Curtiss, Mackinac, McFarland, Tangier* War Diaries, RG 38, NARA II)

position on Guadalcanal and McCain a chance to strengthen the Cactus Air Force. Ghormley emphasized the importance of building up shore- and tender-based air and, considering the attrition TF-63 had suffered so far in the campaign, placed a priority on bolstering McCain's resources as much as possible. McCain enjoyed a windfall with the *Enterprise* dive-bombers left stranded at Henderson, and on the twenty-eighth he heard he would receive nineteen more F4Fs with VMF-224 and twelve SBDs with VMSB-231. The Marines flew into Espíritu Santo the next day en route to Cactus. Adding to McCain's inventory, too, were nine more P-400s at Cactus, and four more PBYs, which arrived at Espíritu Santo from Fiji on the twenty-eighth. McCain's forces were also well situated more or less permanently forward where they could maintain extended patrols and carry out both offensive and defensive operations.[30]

Nevertheless, TF-63 aircraft had little luck detecting Japanese ships transiting the Slot, primarily because they were hard-pressed to maintain their virtually round-the-clock searches, the latter of which McCain still considered necessary to guard against the possibility of a sudden reappearance of the Japanese carriers. On the other hand, Marine SBDs scored a major triumph on the night of 28 August when they sank the Japanese destroyer *Asagiri* bringing in reinforcements to Guadalcanal. And McCain's VPs enjoyed a rare success in air-to-air combat on 5 September. A little past 1300 that day, one of the *Mackinac*'s PBYs, flown by Lieutenant Riley and patrolling sector 3 east of the Solomons, tangled with and shot down a four-engine Kawanishi Type 97 ("Mavis") flying boat. As the historian Samuel Eliot Morison put it in his chronicle of American naval operations in World War II: "The two cumbersome craft circled each other like a pair of flying elephants, spitting fire until the Kawanishi fell in flames." "Well done to Lieutenant Riley and his straight shooting crew," Ghormley signaled the next day.[31]

TF-61 was back up to its former three-carrier strength with the addition of the *Hornet* on 29 August, and Fletcher released the *Wasp* and its air group to Nouméa for rest and repairs on the thirtieth. In retrospect, given TF-61's operations in the relatively confined waters south and east of Guadalcanal what happened next should not have been a surprise. Early on the morning of the thirty-first, the Japanese submarine *I-26* penetrated the defensive screen around the task force and loosed a torpedo into the *Saratoga*, which temporarily went dead in the water. With minimal power restored and under tow, the carrier flew off its dive-bombers and torpedo planes for Espíritu and most of its fighters to Efate while McCain ordered the *McFarland*'s PBYs to provide cover for the crippled ship. Fletcher accompanied the *Saratoga* to Tongatabu for temporary repairs before proceeding to Pearl Harbor, where he learned he would go to Washington on temporary duty, ending his tour in the South Pacific on a sour note. Again, Fletcher's ill luck was a blessing for McCain, who now enjoyed another transfusion of badly needed Navy aircraft for his depleted units ashore.[32]

As the *Saratoga* calamity unfolded, McCain was on Guadalcanal consulting with Vandegrift about the situation at Cactus. He flew in on the thirtieth in a B-17 out of Espíritu Santo, met with Vandegrift and his staff, and that evening retired with the general to have a few drinks. He was privileged to have a ringside seat as a Japanese cruiser lobbed a few rounds into the Marine perimeter that night, and early the next morning he witnessed one of the frustratingly routine enemy air raids on Henderson. In his typical manner, McCain boosted morale by talking to as many airmen and ground crews as he could, assuring them that he would do all he could to back them up in what he understood to be a pivotal fight destined to determine the outcome of the Pacific War.[33]

Guadalcanal quickly devolved into a costly attrition campaign. A day after getting back to the *Curtiss*, McCain told Nimitz that the Japanese were "making [a] major effort to recapture" Guadalcanal and that "daily bombings" were taking a toll on the defenders. Of nineteen F4Fs that had flown in on the twentieth, fourteen had been damaged or destroyed, leaving only five in serviceable condition. Worse, the "pilots in Cactus [were] very tired" from nearly constant combat. The Wildcats could more than hold their own against Japanese fighters, but the AAF P-400s were "no good at altitude and disheartening to brave men who fly them." He understood that "no help can or should be expected of carrier VF unless based ashore" and recommended that two full squadrons of F4Fs or twin-engine Army Lockheed P-38 Lightnings be sent "with no delay." McCain concluded that Guadalcanal "as a major base" was "admirably located." "With substantially the reinforcement requested," he continued, "Cactus can be a sinkhole for enemy air power and can be consolidated, expanded and exploited to [the] enemy's mortal hurt. The reverse is true if we lose Cactus. If the reinforcement requested is not made available Cactus cannot be supplied and hence cannot be held."[34]

Nimitz understood the situation. In a message to King on 2 September he repeated McCain's assessment that due to the loss of the *Enterprise* and the *Saratoga* and the "present shortage of trained carrier air groups" the only solution to the immediate needs was more land-based air in the Solomons. The aircraft released from the two stricken flattops helped, but the cupboard was nearly bare in Hawaii and on the West Coast, where there were shortages of F4Fs. He hoped King would intercede with the Army to provide P-38s, which he and McCain deemed far superior to the P-400s as interceptors. "Let's give GUADALCANAL the wherewithal to live up to its name. Something for the Japs to remember forever," Nimitz told King. Undersecretary of the Navy James V. Forrestal, on an inspection trip to the South Pacific, concurred that more aircraft, "especially fighters," were "imperative if [the] position is to be held." King passed on the request for P-38s to General Marshall and the Joint Chiefs of Staff. Advised by the Army Air Forces commanding general and member of the Joint Chiefs of

Staff, Gen. Henry H. Arnold, that the European theater lacked fighters, Marshall rejected King's appeal.[35] As if they needed reminding that the Solomons effort was on a shoestring, McCain and the Navy knew they were on their own to provide aircraft for Cactus.

Bad weather prevented McCain from doing anything to beef up air assets on Guadalcanal for the next several days. Rain interrupted round-the-clock work on Henderson, temporarily rendering the field unusable. "If it isn't one thing it seems to be another!" McCain wrote to Ghormley in frustration. On the sixth, he asked Ghormley for permission to fly "spare" F4Fs from Espíritu to Efate, where some of the Wildcats from the Saratoga's VF-5 squadron had settled on the thirty-first. Five days later, McCain ordered the entire Saratoga unit to Cactus, injecting an additional twenty-four fighters just in time to provide relief for the beleaguered bastion.[36]

Alerted by Ghormley that another major Japanese effort to retake the island was imminent, McCain wanted to get back to Guadalcanal to see for himself what the conditions were like for the beleaguered Marines and get a feel for how well his forces were prepared to deal with an enemy offensive. He took a B-17 from Espíritu Santo to Henderson on the evening of the eleventh, getting there not long after the Saratoga fighters had landed and joining Turner, who flew in on a PBY5A amphibian. He and Turner met with Vandegrift and the new commander of what was now designated the First Marine Air Wing at Cactus, Maj. Gen. Roy S. Geiger. McCain and Turner relayed Ghormley's doubts about whether the island could be held without massive reinforcements, which were not likely to arrive anytime soon.[37]

The next day, McCain experienced firsthand what the Guadalcanal defenders were up against. Marine and Navy fighters, including the recently arrived VF-5, downed six Japanese bombers during a noon air raid. That night the Marines held off a fierce Japanese attack on a rise above the Lunga River, forever preserved in Guadalcanal lore as Edson's Ridge, named for Marine Lt. Col. Merritt A. Edson. And, getting a taste of combat, McCain had to endure shelling of the American positions around the airfield by four Japanese warships. At 0645 on the thirteenth, McCain and Turner departed from Henderson to return to Espíritu. When he got back he reported optimistically to Ghormley that "material situation Cactus okay," but he did concede that the "personnel [were] very tired—no rest at night [on] account bombardment by surface craft or by day [on] account air alerts."[38]

While McCain was on Cactus the threat Ghormley had most feared materialized in the form of a reconstituted fleet under Admiral Kondo that included Nagumo's *Shōkaku* and *Zuikaku*, plus the light carrier *Zuihō*. Believing they had sufficiently worn down the Americans, the Japanese planned to have bombers and fighters from Rabaul wipe out the remaining air defenses on Guadalcanal in preparation for an all-out amphibious assault to recapture the island. Leaving Truk on the ninth, Kondo's force would provide additional cover for the landings and eliminate the American flattops should they try to intervene. On the tenth, Cincpac informed Comsopac that the *Shōkaku* and *Zuikaku* were most likely headed toward Guadalcanal and that Cactus could expect attacks within a matter of a few days.[39]

Late on the morning of the eleventh, one of McCain's PBYs patrolling north of Malaita radioed that it had sighted and attacked a destroyer and a cargo ship, the first contact the Americans had with the Japanese force. That afternoon a coast watcher reported that a "huge ship possibly aircraft carrier" and two cruisers had transited the Buka Passage and were headed south toward Guadalcanal. After midnight, a Japanese submarine shelled the *Mackinac* at Ndeni. Although there was no damage, as a precaution early on the twelfth McCain directed the *Mackinac* and the *Ballard* (AVD 10), a sister ship of the *McFarland* that had also been converted into a seaplane tender, to vacate Ndeni. There were more sightings later on the twelfth, culminating in a Catalina's report at 1328 of a Japanese carrier and its cruiser escort apparently maneuvering to launch aircraft. An hour later, as the PBY continued to shadow the enemy ships, McCain ordered a strike force of fifteen B-17s into the air from Espíritu. Another PBY spotted the same group that evening, only to lose contact a short while later. Nor could the B-17s find their targets; even worse, three of the bombers were forced down at sea, their crews lucky to survive until rescued days later.[40]

More reports of Japanese ships came in to Airsopac on the afternoon of the thirteenth, followed at 1140 the next morning when one of McCain's PBYs, flown by Lt. (jg) Baxter E. Moore, found a carrier and its escorts north of Guadalcanal, which turned out to be part of Nagumo's force. Within minutes fighters from the *Shōkaku* shot down Moore's plane. As soon as he verified Moore's report, McCain dispatched another B-17 strike from Espíritu. This time the bombers found and attacked the Japanese, scoring what they believed were three hits on the enemy ships, but managing only a near miss that slightly damaged a heavy cruiser. Meanwhile, that day, TF-61, now under the command of Rear Adm. Leigh Noyes in the *Wasp*, with Sherman serving as flag captain and de facto chief of staff, was supporting Turner's convoy bringing in reinforcements to Guadalcanal from Espíritu Santo. As soon as Noyes received word of the Japanese carrier group, he launched a combined search-strike from the *Wasp* and the *Hornet*, which just missed finding Nagumo's ships. They failed because the Japanese, having not spotted the American ships, gave up and reversed course to refuel. It was, as the historian John Lundstrom concluded, one of the "great 'almosts' of the Guadalcanal campaign," very likely a reprise of the Battle of the Eastern Solomons.[41]

Reassured that the immediate threat to his convoy was over, Turner pressed on to Guadalcanal on the fifteenth, while Noyes and TF-61 closed on the islands from the southeast to provide air cover for Turner's ships. TF-61's course led straight into another area patrolled by Japanese submarines and resulted in another shock to the American carrier forces. Early that afternoon, the *I-19* spotted the *Wasp* and discharged a spread of six torpedoes, two of which struck the flattop and set the ship ablaze. Almost unbelievably, two more of the tin fish sped past the *Wasp* and her escorts to hit and badly damage the battleship *North Carolina* (BB 55) and sink the destroyer *O'Brien* (DD 415), both screening the *Hornet*. John Lundstrom wrote that it was "the single most devastating salvo of the war." Abandoned and wracked by explosions and fires, the *Wasp* sank that evening, while the *Hornet* and its escorts pulled back to safer waters farther to the southeast. The only saving grace in what was otherwise a black day that cost the Navy nearly two hundred dead and left it with only one carrier in the theater was that Turner's convoy made it safely through to deliver the supplies and men so badly needed on Guadalcanal.[42]

Despite this latest setback to the American fortunes, McCain was generally upbeat about the prospects of the Guadalcanal campaign, although he made it clear that victory hinged on adequate resources. From the start of the Guadalcanal operation through the middle of September, McCain's VP units had been in the air almost continually, flying an average of twelve patrols per day—even more during the initial phases of the landings and during the Battle of the Eastern Solomons—and logging more than six thousand hours in the air. They had paid a price. Eleven PBYs had been lost, either to enemy action or due to accidents and other operational incidents, and twenty-seven officers and men had died. PBY losses amounted to 23 percent during August; B-17s had suffered a 26 percent loss rate that month. But most alarming, Cactus was hemorrhaging airplanes, losing 26 percent of its fighter strength per week during the same period. On 29 August, McCain pleaded with Ghormley that a "regular replacement program must be initiated immediately as one of the essentials necessary in order that present positions may be maintained and preparations made for a further advance." He suggested that the "present tempo of operations" demanded at least one PBY replacement squadron per month.[43]

There were also steps that McCain thought the Marines could take to improve Guadalcanal's defenses against further attacks by either surface ships or carriers. McCain wrote to Vandegrift and Geiger suggesting that a strike force of Avengers and Dauntlesses could be organized to carry out night attacks on Japanese shipping. Henderson would have to be illuminated, much like carrier flight decks, morning and afternoon reconnaissance was essential, and communications needed to be further improved. All of this was risky, he admitted, but "the chance *must* be taken if you are to stop raids." A Catalina lingering over Henderson could provide early warning of air and surface attacks. "Your whole existence up there," he added, "depends on hitting those Jap ships consistently *before* they get there, while they are there, or during departure." He also believed that Turner might be able to organize a force to raid the Japanese at night, although the success of such attacks depended on timely intelligence of the location and movement of enemy ships. "You have the striking force to do it now," he concluded. "May the God of the Presbyterians keep away the rain, and keep you and your command in health and good spirits."[44]

Admiral Nimitz in Pearl Harbor and Admiral King in Washington considered McCain's appraisal of the circumstances affecting his command along with other estimates of the situation as they made critical decisions regarding the command structure in the Pacific. A step in that direction occurred on 1 September, when Nimitz consolidated carrier and VP aviation under the commander, Aircraft, Pacific Fleet (Comairpac). Nimitz had intended to hand the new administrative billet to Halsey, thinking that he had not fully recovered from the skin disorder that had beached him before the Battle of Midway. But he changed his mind when he met Halsey and determined that he was fully up to the rigors of combat command. Jake Fitch was available to slot in as Comairpac, at least temporarily. As for Fletcher, Nimitz believed he would return before the end of the year to take the repaired *Saratoga* back to the South Pacific. Nimitz weighed further changes when he received Forrestal's inspection report, which raised questions about Ghormley's and McCain's mental and physical abilities to carry on with what now appeared to be a desperate, grinding war of attrition in the Solomons. Already dissatisfied with McCain's handling of his air searches at the Battle of Savo Island, Nimitz now began thinking that he might have to relieve him from command.[45]

King decided to remove Rear Adm. John Towers as chief of the Bureau of Aeronautics by promoting him to vice admiral and giving him the Comairpac job in Pearl Harbor. Halsey would get the carrier command, and McCain would come back to Washington to replace Towers as BuAer chief. Nimitz and King hammered out the arrangements at a meeting in San Francisco on 6–7 September, where they also concurred that Fitch would succeed McCain as Comairsopac when Towers took over as Comairpac. Halsey as a vice admiral would assume responsibilities as the senior carrier task force commander and be "subordinate to Ghormley." Ghormley got an inkling that changes were in the offing when he received a message from Nimitz on the ninth requesting that he confirm the names of the flag officers under his command and list the combatant naval forces for which they were responsible.[46]

Towers learned of the command shakeup from Secretary of the Navy Frank Knox on the twelfth. Pleased to go out to Pearl as Comairpac, he was much less delighted to hear that McCain would take over BuAer, a job for which Towers believed he was unsuited due to his lack of experience in planning and procurement. Towers may also have opposed McCain because McCain was one of the "Johnny-Come-Latelys," whom Towers judged had blocked early aviators from achieving higher commands. Towers trusted, though, that McCain would have the good sense to retain and delegate responsibilities to the experienced administrative team that Towers had put together at the bureau. He also anticipated that McCain in his new billet would continue the cordial relations he had forged with the Army's air arm. To AAF chief Hap Arnold, Towers wrote that "it is my sincere hope that my successor, surrounded as he will be with officers who know my views and understand your problems as well as ours, will slip right into the groove."[47]

Word reached McCain on the morning of the fifteenth that Aubrey Fitch was to be his relief as Comairsopac. Nimitz suggested that Fitch retain McCain's staff. Fitch agreed but insisted that he bring along one of the officers from his Comairpac staff to sort out the communications difficulties that had plagued the command for months. Coincidentally, McCain himself had determined that it was impossible to control all communications from the *Curtiss* and decided to transfer radio operations and personnel ashore at Espíritu starting on the fourteenth. In the meantime, McCain's searches revealed continued Japanese ship movements in and around the islands. On the sixteenth, a strike group of Cactus SBDs and TBFs attacked a Japanese force of three light cruisers and four destroyers off New Georgia, reporting a torpedo hit and a near miss by a bomb on one of the cruisers. B-17s followed with a raid on enemy ships at Gizo Harbor and shore installations at Rekata Bay on the seventeenth.[48]

After stopping on Guadalcanal to size up the situation there, Fitch flew to Espíritu Santo, where he officially relieved McCain as Comairsopac on the afternoon of the twenty-first. Fitch found his new command in relatively good shape, particularly compared to when McCain had taken over. As of the third week of September there were ninety-four F4F-4s in Sopac, thirty of which were at Henderson Field and another twenty-one en route to Nouméa aboard the aircraft transport *Hammondsport* (APV 2), sixty-eight SBDs, of which thirty-one were at Henderson, forty-one PBYs (including three full squadrons), and forty B-17s with the 11th Bombardment Group. Older models of the Wildcat were also in the inventory, but most were not available for front-line duty and were held in reserve in Espíritu, Efate, and Samoa. Fitch requested more fighters, dive-bombers, and torpedo planes, some of which were available and could arrive from the West Coast within a month, but like McCain he would never have enough.[49]

Not pleased with McCain's departure were the officers and enlisted Marines on Cactus, all of whom had acquired something transcending simple respect for the man. They believed that alone among the Navy's brass McCain understood what they had endured in the muck of Guadalcanal, understood their sacrifices in blood and material, and had become their principal advocate with other Sopac commanders. Above all, he was a fighter who did not run away, or "haul ass," as they perceived both Fletcher and Turner had done at critical junctures in the Guadalcanal campaign. Vandegrift lamented, "I can think of nothing worse than to be in Washington at this time. Your friends here will miss you, but we know we will have a friend in court who will render a sympathetic ear when told that we need more fighter planes." McCain confessed to Vandegrift that "I hate Washington thoroughly and all the stuff that goes on there nauseates me. However, I feel that I may be of some use to the boys on the front in my new detail. What I hate most is the breaking off of my close association with yourself and the tough eggs under you." To Geiger he wrote that "it is with sadness and regret that I go to other duty. Until the day I die I will take intense pride in my association with you brave and gallant men." Geiger replied, "All hands are sorry to see you leave us and appreciate your letter and all wish to let you know that we have had complete confidence in you as our commander."[50]

On 22 September, after passing a special physical exam mandated for senior officers in the South Pacific, McCain flew to Nouméa to confer with Ghormley about the situation in the South Pacific. He was there for two days before a Coronado picked him up early on the twenty-fourth to fly him to Suva on the first leg of the long journey back to Pearl Harbor. With him was Leigh Noyes, whom Nimitz had banished from carrier command after the loss of the *Wasp*. From Suva it was on to Canton and Palmyra, where the Coronado had to turn around to return to Nouméa. While waiting for two Marine Douglas R4D aircraft to ferry him and Noyes the rest of the way to Hawaii, McCain ran into Nimitz, who was on his way to New Caledonia to confer with Ghormley about matters in Sopac. Nimitz took McCain aside and asked him about Noyes and Fletcher. McCain thought that Noyes was fine, suffering only from minor injuries incurred during the explosions and fires on the *Wasp*. Fletcher was a different case. McCain agreed with Nimitz's decision "to give him a blow (rest) on the mainland." "I was going to write to you about him," McCain said, adding that "two or three of these [carrier] fights are enough for any one man. A rest will do him good."[51]

In the wake of McCain's relief, the *New York Times* cited "air experts" who were upset with the decision to appoint him as BuAer chief, apparently underscoring the Navy's conservative approach to promotion and unwillingness to elevate experienced air officers to high-ranking administrative and command posts. *Time* editorialized that the Navy had made a mistake in sending Towers, the "Navy's No. 1 airman," to Pearl Harbor and replacing him at BuAer with a "battleship admiral." The magazine acknowledged that McCain was a "good officer," but that "he got an airman's rating late, is not an airman by profession, but a battleship admiral with pay-and-a-half and a flying suit." "As a result," *Time*'s editors concluded, "there is now no airman in a position to participate in the strategic thinking of the Navy. At the time when airmen have practically won the battle over surface fleets at sea, they have lost the battle decisively in Washington."

McCain's son James Gordon leaped to his father's defense in a letter to *Time*'s editors two weeks later. He summarized McCain's peacetime aviation accomplishments, including a carrier command, and pointed out that he had had actual air combat experience while Comairsopac. Yes his father did wear a "flying suit," and "all the available evidence points most emphatically to the fact that he uses it for its intended purpose." An aviator who learned to fly with McCain at Pensacola wrote that he had been shown no favoritism, had "passed with flying colors the hardest part of the course—the criticism by [his] fellow students," and fully deserved his flight suit and flight pay.[52]

McCain himself might have agreed with the press opinions, although for entirely different reasons. It was frustrating to leave a job not nearly half done, especially at a time when the Guadalcanal campaign was at a crossroads and the next few months would decide its outcome. At a Cincpac conference in Pearl Harbor on the morning of 27 September, while waiting for air transport to the West Coast, McCain exuded optimism. He believed that the Marine and Navy fighter units would prevail in the struggle on Guadalcanal provided "sufficient fighter planes and pilots can be brought in to maintain present levels." The problem, though, was that those aircraft and aviators were not immediately available. Where McCain expressed cautious optimism, the constant Japanese air and sea pressure on Guadalcanal and the seemingly unremitting loss of ships and aircraft had a corrosive effect on Ghormley and his Sopac command at Nouméa. On 16 October, he informed Nimitz that his forces were "totally inadequate" to cope with anticipated Japanese offensives and that unless additional air reinforcements came to the South Pacific, it was not likely Guadalcanal could be held. Ghormley was correct about the dangers that lay ahead, but his pessimism contrasted with McCain's optimism and with the high morale level Nimitz had observed himself during his own visit to Guadalcanal. Nor was either he or King ready to dispatch additional resources to the South Pacific. Convinced that now was not the time for irresolution or timidity at Comsopac, Nimitz ordered Halsey to relieve Ghormley on 18 October.[53]

McCain as Comairsopac deserves credit for building and integrating a heterogeneous force of land-based and tender-based air, including Navy, Marine, AAF, and Allied aviation units in a remote area of the world under far less than optimum circumstances. His coordination and leadership of those forces in the South Pacific anticipated the "jointness" now valued and sought by military strategists and planners. The sea and air forces under McCain's command complemented the limited carrier resources so vital to consolidating the defenses in the South Pacific and in the first offensive in Guadalcanal and the Solomons. His fighting spirit and infectious enthusiasm resonated throughout his command, especially with the Marines fighting under the terrible hardships on Guadalcanal. More important, his optimistic and accurate assessment of the attrition that would eventually wear down Japanese air power and secure victory for the American and Allied forces in the Solomons counterbalanced the defeatism emanating from Admiral Ghormley and his staff.

At the same time, there were deficiencies in McCain's Airsopac command that he was unable to overcome or to address successfully. When the Allied and Japanese forces were more or less evenly matched in the first phase of the Guadalcanal campaign, superior organization, administration, training, and tactics were critical. Not surprisingly, neither adversary was able to gain a decisive advantage, and the struggle devolved into a bruising war of attrition where ultimately the sheer weight of American resources brought victory in February 1943. Under these circumstances, early in the operation when attention to detail and efficiency were paramount, McCain was not always up to the challenge, especially immediately after the Guadalcanal landings. Admittedly, the communications problems he had to contend with were real and not of his own making. As the historian Lisle Rose has pointed out, there were no high-speed data links or satellite communications in 1942. All McCain and other officers had to go on in the "crude context" of war in the South Pacific in the summer and fall of 1942 were sometimes confusing and tardy messages from Cincpac, vague signals and other intelligence about Japanese ship and aircraft movements, visual sightings from their own sea and air units, and sometimes garbled reports based largely on guesswork relayed through unreliable radio communications nets.[54]

Because even under the best of circumstances, command decisions must be made expeditiously based on inadequate and incomplete information, it was incumbent on McCain and vital to the mission of his command to provide that information as quickly and accurately as possible. He did not do so before and during the Battle of Savo Island. Although McCain hardly distinguished himself at the Battle of the Eastern Solomons, there were mitigating factors beyond his control, and he might have felt some sense of vindication in learning that Jake Fitch, his successor as Comairsopac, encountered some of the same structural problems with searches and timely reporting of contacts the night before the 26 October Battle of the Santa Cruz Islands. Moreover, at the Eastern Solomons, VP aircraft and crews accomplished the arduous and dangerous jobs of spotting, trailing, and reporting their contacts, and McCain ensured that all the task forces promptly received the updated intelligence.

The historian Douglas Smith has given McCain a grade of "D" for decision making at the Battle of the Eastern Solomons, based on the Naval War College's commander's analysis and "estimate of the situation." Considering that McCain and other commanders were groping through the uncertainties caused by Clausewitz's "friction" and "fog of war," McCain's overall mark should be elevated because of his awareness of the strategic situation in the Solomons, because of the improvements he made in communication and control after the unmitigated disaster at Savo on the night of 8–9 August, and because of his capacity for dealing with the inherent complexities of a multiservice and multinational command.[55] Despite McCain's failures, there is no reason to doubt that as Comairsopac he demonstrated innovative thinking, initiative, resourcefulness, and commitment, all of which are vital to operational command. In other words, McCain—by a narrow margin and after a steep learning curve—passed his first test in combat leadership. Now lying in wait was an entirely different dimension of modern war, which he would fight not in the tropical heat and fetid air of the South Pacific but in the volatile political and administrative pressure cooker of the Navy Department in Washington.

CHAPTER 5

The War in Washington
The Bureau of Aeronautics

On the afternoon of 27 September 1942, John McCain and Frank Jack Fletcher boarded one of Pan Am's Boeing 314 Clippers at Pearl Harbor for the fifteen-hour overnight flight to San Francisco, during which they had ample time to discuss their mutual experiences in the South Pacific. McCain underscored his earlier evaluation of Fletcher's general well-being in a letter to Nimitz he drafted during a layover in San Diego on the thirtieth. Fletcher had admitted that he was "very concerned and very apprehensive" about how his task group was doing in his absence. McCain thought Fletcher was in "good shape," though "very tired," which was to be expected of anyone who had endured the rigors of three carrier battles. He had recommended that his friend "not ask to go on another detail until he felt at his best; that he owed that both to himself and to the job." Fletcher replied, "You are right, I will take as long a leave as I can get, and if I feel my best will ask to go again and I am sure I will." McCain told Nimitz, "I feel he should be taken at his word." Partly as a result of McCain's personal assessment, Nimitz concluded that he needed to allow top officers time off to recharge their batteries and not completely wear them out. But Fletcher would never return to carrier command in the Pacific. King had decided, unfairly, that Fletcher had not demonstrated sufficient aggressiveness in the South Pacific and had lost four carriers either sunk or badly damaged. He had to go. Fletcher's next assignment saw him off to Alaska as commander, Northwest Sea Frontier.[1]

Like Fletcher, McCain was drained after his South Pacific tour, but at age fifty-eight he had for the most part come though the experience in good health. He had gained eight pounds since taking command as Comairsopac, in part due to what his medical records called "vitamin therapy," most likely B supplements to stimulate his appetite. He also kept to a regimen that included a "nap every afternoon down there, battle or no battle." After only a brief visit with Kate at their new place in Coronado, McCain left on a Navy twin-engine Douglas R3D-1 on the morning of 1 October for

Washington. The Navy plane broke down in El Paso, where McCain picked up a Marine R3D that evening for the rest of the journey. At 1000 the next day, he reported to the Navy Department for temporary duty pending his appointment a week later as chief of the Bureau of Aeronautics. Kate followed him to Washington on the twenty-seventh, and within a month the couple had settled into an apartment at 1870 Wyoming Avenue, NW.[2]

The Bureau of Aeronautics that McCain took over in October 1942 sprawled over three floors (or "decks") in three wings of the Main Navy building between the south side of Constitution Avenue and the Mall. Main Navy was a "temporary" structure built to accommodate the Navy's emergency space needs during World War I, which over the ensuing decades had remained to provide accommodations for virtually the entire Navy bureaucratic establishment. By the fall of 1942, however, the service was out of room, not just in Main Navy but in the entire District of Columbia. BuAer alone numbered 1,098 officers by the end of 1942, compared to only 58 in the fall of 1939. For McCain and everyone else in the Navy, finding experienced and knowledgeable personnel and enough office space for them would be an unremitting struggle.[3]

Big as it was, BuAer was also unique within the Navy's bureau system. It had been created in 1921 as a result of an existential crisis during which naval aviation sought to preserve its integrity in the face of an assault by Brig. Gen. William ("Billy") Mitchell, who had led a two-year propaganda and political campaign to subsume all of military aviation into a unified air service. Key aviation officers with political connections in Congress joined with Assistant Secretary of the Navy Franklin D. Roosevelt to respond to the threat. They proposed consolidating all the technical and administrative functions of naval aviation—then diluted among the Bureaus of Construction and Repair, Steam Engineering, Ordnance, and Navigation, as well as the office of the Chief of Naval Operations—into a single bureau. In July 1921, Congress approved and the president signed a naval appropriations bill providing for the establishment of the bureau. Rear Adm. William A. Moffett, the director of naval aviation in the office of the CNO, became the bureau's first chief.[4]

Through the 1920s and up to his death in the crash of the Navy airship *Akron* (ZRS 4) in April 1933, Moffett crafted BuAer into what some have called a "superbureau." He astutely parlayed his political connections and his innate sense of public relations to build the bureau into a bastion against Mitchell and his allies as well as to make naval aviation an integral arm of the fleet. After some resistance, he won the loyalty of the Navy's aviators, the "true believers" who had agitated for a separate corps, akin to that of the Marines. Eventually BuAer took on all policy, planning, and procurement functions for naval aviation and made inroads against the powerful Bureau of Navigation on personnel matters. Careful not to impinge on the prerogatives of the Bureau of Navigation, Moffett took his time, patiently chipping away at BuNav's responsibility (or "cognizance" in Navy jargon) for aviation officer assignments, building up a reserve force of aviators, securing exemption from sea duty for engineering officers, and otherwise winning nearly total control over personnel.[5]

A few days after McCain officially took the helm as BuAer chief on the ninth, Frank Knox defended McCain's appointment in a letter to Nimitz. He insisted that "unwise and ill-informed friends of Towers" were behind the negative press coverage, adding that "McCain will have to break down some unfriendliness" in the Navy Department. He was sure that "the Bureau itself will gain by the change" and opined that "Towers, while able, is not a good administrator or coordinator. I think McCain is both."[6]

McCain joined Knox at a press conference on 13 October, where he elaborated on official Navy reports highlighting recent developments in the Solomons. Although the Navy and Marines had suffered setbacks, including the three American cruisers sunk at Savo Island, the Japanese had paid dearly in ships and aircraft over the previous two months. McCain saluted American and Allied airmen for their hard work and sacrifice and asserted that the Japanese were being worn down by combined Navy, Marine, and Army air power. He admitted that the enemy had succeeded in sending reinforcements to Guadalcanal, but they had not been able to land the heavy equipment needed to sustain an offensive sufficient to dislodge the Marines. In presenting estimates of the numbers of Japanese versus American aircraft destroyed during the campaign, McCain was not entirely candid, painting a rosier picture of the situation than he had in his assessment of VP and fighter losses at the end of August. Yet he was consistent in his conviction that the Allies had the wherewithal to "hold the place" against continued Japanese efforts to retake the island. Coming from a fighting admiral and recipient of the Navy's Distinguished Service Medal for his singular role in "the occupation of the Guadalcanal-Tulagi area by our forces and the destruction and serious damaging of numerous aircraft and vessels of the enemy," it was exactly the publicity the Navy needed as the campaign in the Solomons dragged on through the fall.[7]

Upon assuming his new billet, McCain found in BuAer an organization that had under wartime exigencies seen major changes, all of which had occurred on the watch of his predecessor, John Towers. Towers had played a key role in the design of big new aircraft carriers, successfully resisting calls by McCain and others for small ships. After the war in Europe began and the United States expanded its armament programs, Towers ensured that the Navy got the best aircraft designs and in sufficient numbers, despite pressures on manufacturers to meet demands from the Allies. Roosevelt's 1940 50,000-plane program, of which the Navy would get 13,500, placed additional pressure on BuAer to meet aircraft procurement demands, while in the wake of the fall of France, Georgia congressman Carl Vinson increased the number to 15,000, along with an exponential increase in the number of airmen. Lend-Lease in 1941 threatened to disrupt BuAer's planning and procurement, as did an agreement to train thousands of British pilots in the United States.[8]

Budget and staff increases reflected the new priorities and challenges. BuAer had received about $36 million per year through the 1930s; now the bureau anticipated spending a mind-boggling $1 billion in fiscal year 1942 alone, starting on 1 July 1941. By the middle of 1941, the number of BuAer officers in Washington had gone up 76 percent over the previous year, and 326 civilians had been added to the payroll. When it became clear that reorganization was needed, Knox hired the consulting firm of Booz, Fry, Allen and Hamilton to survey all of the Navy's bureaus. It took six months to examine BuAer alone.[9]

Knox and Towers received the Booz report on 16 August. Basically, Booz found that at the planning level BuAer was doing well, but that there were shortcomings in the divisions responsible for carrying out the plans. The firm criticized the bureau for not moving away from the peacetime Navy culture, where officers had been rotated in and out of its divisions regardless of their experience or competency. Needed, the report concluded, were experts who knew how to run large organizations, more often than not executives recruited from the business world. Knox took the first steps in that direction in September when he brought in Artemus L. Gates as the new Assistant Secretary of the Navy for Air. "Di" Gates, a member of the famed First Yale Unit, the group of Ivy League aviators who volunteered to go overseas in 1917, went on after the war to become president of New York Trust, one of Wall Street's most prominent financial houses.[10]

Towers wasted no time implementing a major reorganization that addressed most, if not all, of the Booz recommendations. Principally, he cut the number of divisions from a dozen to five (Planning, Maintenance, Material, Personnel and Training, and Flight, with most of the former divisions relegated to branches within the divisions) and increased the responsibilities of their directors. This limited the number of officers with direct access to the bureau chief and freed Towers and his assistant bureau chief, Capt. DeWitt C. ("Duke") Ramsey, to concentrate on policy and planning. Towers also set up offices for three assistants, recruited from the business world, to handle contracts, production, and labor. Towers agitated for, but was unable to achieve, complete control over aviation training, with the result that that responsibility remained awkwardly divided between BuAer and Nimitz's BuNav.[11]

The BuAer McCain inherited from Towers in October 1942 underwent few organizational changes over the next ten months. In January 1943, the bureau began to remove some of its personnel and functions from Washington due to the limited availability of space in the capital, which since Pearl Harbor had been inundated with thousands of newcomers each month. All records and contract files were centralized in the Records and Distribution Section of the Material Division's Procurement Branch in January, and in July 1943 the Technical Data Group was established in the Material Division to consolidate aircraft specifications and other technical information. At the end of February, Program Planning was promoted to branch status within the Planning Division. These changes, while mostly of a peripheral nature, helped streamline BuAer's administrative structure to deal with the enormous scope of the bureau's responsibilities in 1943.[12]

Only two weeks after taking over as bureau chief, McCain provided King with his ideas about gauging the numbers and types of aircraft needed to meet operational demands. In the aftermath of Pearl Harbor, Roosevelt had approved Towers' recommendation for 27,500 aircraft. Congress followed this with an appropriation of $7 billion for naval aviation in fiscal year 1942 and another $4 billion in fiscal year 1943. Within these parameters and extrapolating from his recent experience of losses at Cactus and among his VP units in the Solomons, McCain estimated that fifty-four F4Fs, fifty-four SBDs, and thirty TBFs were needed at Guadalcanal as replacements each month. He thought that BuAer could manage getting the fighters, but acquiring the other aircraft would not be so easy. He suggested that the production of SBDs should be increased and that the numbers would have to be supplemented with aircraft previously assigned to training or to the Army. The Army was not likely to be pleased and "will likely reject vigorously and might attempt retaliation."[13]

In another memo to King two days later, McCain indicated that additional aircraft were needed in the rear echelons to support the offensive in the South Pacific. At minimum, two squadrons (twenty-four) of B-24s were necessary, along with a squadron (twenty-seven) of long-range fighters (preferably P-38s), a squadron of eighteen new Curtiss SB2C Helldiver dive-bombers, and another squadron of eighteen torpedo planes. "One or more" escort carriers would also be required for aircraft transport. These were minimal requests, which even if met in total, would amount to only a "somewhat meager" addition to the forces available in the South Pacific.[14]

On 31 October, McCain received BuAer's revised "Summary of Objectives," which provided guidelines for aircraft production based on calculations of requirements, estimates of numbers of aircraft, personnel, and rates of training to meet the Navy's Operating Force Plan through the end of calendar year 1944. For 1943, the president agreed to the War Production Board's goal of 107,000 aircraft, of which the Navy was expected to receive 24,116 (later reduced to 22,341). BuAer's Material Division estimated, correctly, in January 1943 that the best the Navy could do was to meet 80 percent of that goal, in other words, about 17,000 aircraft, which was still more than twice what had been delivered in 1942.[15]

The 1943 estimates included more than 6,000 fighters, about a third of which were the high-performance, gull-winged Vought F4U Corsair and a handful were the Grumman F6F Hellcat then just entering production; 4,200 dive-bombers, most of which were the venerable SBD, but which also included the troubled Curtiss SB2C; 2,700 TBFs, two-thirds coming from Grumman and a third produced as TBMs by the General Motors Eastern Aircraft Division in Trenton, New Jersey; and 2,400 flying boats, about half of them the reliable PBY but also including the twin-engine Martin PBM and the other half the twin-engine Lockheed PV-1 Ventura and Consolidated PB4Y, the Navy version of the AAF B-24.[16]

Exponential increases in aircraft procurement and appropriations brought changes in the bureau's budgeting and contractual procedures. A potential bottleneck arose in the fall of 1942 because the Bureau of Supplies and Accounts (BuS&A) had to draft all aircraft requisitions and approve all contracts negotiated by BuAer. On 9 December 1942, Undersecretary of the Navy James Forrestal called a meeting in his office to discuss ways of expediting the contracting process. The outcome was Forrestal's recommendation, subsequently approved by the Secretary of the Navy, to give BuAer wide discretionary authority to draw up and execute its own contracts. BuS&A was not happy with the change, which it believed undermined much of its control over fiscal matters and further arrogated power to the Bureau of Aeronautics.[17]

Reporting to Forrestal on 18 December, McCain explained the new responsibilities of the Bureau of Aeronautics in a way he hoped would allay some of the anxiety in BuS&A. BuAer intended only to "procure those items which, because of their technical aeronautical nature, are such that . . . the Bureau alone can best choose the contractor and determine and negotiate the specifications, the contract terms and the price." He added that "the responsibility for these items can not be delegated, and to delegate any part of the procurement process invites inefficiency and delay. . . . Conversely, where other agencies have primary responsibility for the items, or where the items are such that other agencies can better effect the procurement, the Bureau not only should make use of these agencies, but should if possible delegate to them all of the procurement process." McCain concluded that BuAer planned to expand the Aviation Supply Office (ASO) at the Naval Aircraft Factory to take on the new contracting tasks and assumed that the ASO would allow BuS&A to handle contracts for items not strictly aeronautical in nature. The rapidly expanding ASO separated from the Naval Aircraft Factory to become part of the new Naval Aviation Supply Depot in Philadelphia in February 1943.[18]

In a reorganization a short while later, McCain brought in Rear Adm. Ralph E. Davison, Rear Adm. Ernest M. Pace Jr., and Capt. Arthur C. Miles as contracting officers and formed the Contracts, Contracts Administration, and Records and Distribution sections within the Procurement Branch of BuAer's Material Division. Writing to the subcommittee of the House Naval Affairs Committee on 10 April 1943, McCain said that he could not with certainty determine how much time had been saved in negotiating each contract, but that it was most likely on the order of two to three weeks. "Less tangible" gains had been accomplished in clarifying the wording of contracts and lessening potentially litigious misunderstandings with vendors.[19]

Aircraft design and production were central to BuAer's planning, execution, prioritization, and coordination of the acquisition process. A dauntingly complex undertaking, especially under the stresses of global

conflict, aircraft design and production called for the assessment of requirements (constantly shifting in light of information from the combat theaters), determining aircraft characteristics, design changes, estimates of the
number of aircraft and the types needed based in part on operational circumstances and attrition rates, and supervision of aircraft and spare parts
production, inspection, and delivery. McCain followed the outline of the
27,500-plane objective of early 1942 that broadly determined the aircraft
industry's expansion. BuAer had to cooperate with manufacturers, as well
as with the Army Air Forces and the Aircraft Division of the civilian War
Production Board. All the while, Congress and the Bureau of the Budget
constantly looked over everyone's shoulders to ensure that costs remained
reasonable and that there was no collusion among manufacturers or wartime profiteering. Responsibility for procurement within the bureau rested
primarily in the Planning and Material divisions, although other divisions,
branches, and sections were also affected.[20]

Trips to the West Coast and the Pacific took McCain away from his
desk in late 1942 and early 1943. On 27 November, McCain took off from
Washington on a ten-day tour to gather information about aircraft production and determine operational requirements in San Diego, Los Angeles, San Francisco, and Seattle. A longer inspection trip came early in the
new year, 1943. Leaving Ralph Davison behind as acting bureau chief,
McCain flew out of Anacostia on 7 January on a Lockheed twin-engine
R5O transport to visit the new aviation training center in Corpus Christi,
Texas. From Texas he continued to San Diego to inspect Consolidated's
work on Navy contracts, followed by visits to Douglas and Northrop in
El Segundo and Lockheed in Burbank. He flew to Alameda on the tenth
and spent two days in the Bay Area before joining Secretary of the Navy
Knox on a Pan Am Clipper for the flight to Hawaii, arriving there on the
morning of the twelfth.[21]

In Pearl, McCain conferred for two days with Nimitz and Towers, dis-
cussing, among other things, aircraft production and the introduction of the
new Hellcat. On the fourteenth, he was off to the South Pacific by PB2Y
via Midway, Johnston, Canton, and Suva. He arrived at Espíritu Santo on
the afternoon of 20 January and joined Jake Fitch on the flagship *Curtiss*.
After delays due to mechanical problems and minor accidents with their
aircraft, Nimitz and Knox flew in from Pearl Harbor later on the twentieth, joined by Halsey fresh in from an inspection visit to New Zealand.
During McCain's overnight stay, a lone Japanese airplane bombed Espíritu,

the first time that had occurred during the war. Although the attack caused no damage or casualties, it made everyone nervous that somehow an intelligence leak had let the enemy know about their presence. The next morning McCain and the others in the party flew to Cactus on a PBY-5A amphibian escorted by Marine Wildcats.[22]

McCain found the situation on Guadalcanal much improved in the four months since he had left. The Marines were in far better shape, nourished at last by ample infusions of food, medical supplies, and ammunition, and backed up by fresh Army units. The Japanese, on the other hand, were on the verge of starvation and defeat. Henderson Field was now a fully functional air base, with auxiliary strips packed with Marine and Navy fighters and bombers. Victories at sea and in the air, while costly to both sides, had tipped the scales in favor of the Americans, yet there was still more fighting before the campaign could advance up the Solomons. As if to remind McCain and his fellow officers that the war in the South Pacific was not over, Japanese bombers struck Lunga that evening and continued the aerial assault throughout the night. McCain, Halsey, and Knox sought refuge in the Marines' trenches, while Nimitz, fearing mosquitoes and malaria more than Japanese ordnance, remained in the relative comfort of his hut. Family lore, unsubstantiated by the record, has an unfortunate McCain spending the night not in a trench or foxhole, but in a recently abandoned but still uncovered latrine.[23]

After a night that even the most battle-hardened leathernecks would have found unpleasant, McCain and his party boarded the Catalina amphibian early the next morning to inspect the seaplane base and other facilities at Efate. They stayed overnight there before leaving the next morning, the twenty-third, by Coronado for Nouméa, where they arrived at 1100. That afternoon McCain, Nimitz, Halsey, Marine general DeWitt Peck, and their staffs met for nearly two hours to discuss the situation in the South Pacific. Nimitz believed that if all went well the Guadalcanal campaign could be wrapped up by 1 April, provided there were enough aircraft. McCain assured Nimitz that naval aircraft production was sufficient to meet the needs and suggested that Halsey go through channels and send a dispatch to King asking for the planes; King would then pass on the request to BuAer for approval and action. No decisions were reached at the conference, although it was generally understood that once Guadalcanal was secured it would be used as a base for further operations in the Solomons by Halsey and his command. While he was in Nouméa, McCain met Towers, who was nearing the end of his own South Pacific inspection tour and was gratified to learn that the F6F program was progressing well.[24]

The Coronado picked up McCain, Nimitz, and Knox on the morning of the twenty-fourth for the flight to Suva on the first leg of the trek back to Pearl Harbor, which included overnight stays at Pago Pago, Canton, and Palmyra. The party reached Pearl on the afternoon of the twenty-eighth. Bad weather kept McCain and Knox in Hawaii an extra day before they left by Pan Am Clipper for San Francisco on the afternoon of the thirtieth. McCain returned to Washington by Navy R5O via San Diego, El Paso, and Memphis, getting in to Anacostia on the afternoon of 1 February and completing a grueling journey that took him away from the office for no fewer than twenty-six days. Only a little more than a week later, word reached Washington that the Japanese had evacuated their troops from Guadalcanal and the bloody struggle for that previously obscure island was finally over.[25]

McCain's South Pacific tour provided evidence that the aircraft shortages that had confounded him and others during the initial stages of the Solomons campaign were a thing of the past. In turn, this revelation underscored problems McCain and BuAer faced in determining aircraft attrition rates. With no guidelines or precedents, BuAer's Planning Division had devised a complex formula in 1942 based on banking compound-interest theory that factored in production rates, estimated monthly aircraft losses, the ages and types of aircraft, and their expected service lifetimes. The calculations were heavily dependent on reports from the combat theaters and accurate computations of the resulting data. Before the war, the bureau had relied on card files for each airplane, but it was obvious by the middle of 1942 that the system was totally inadequate to keep track of the tens of thousands of aircraft in the pipeline. The Planning Division therefore instituted an automated system to crunch the numbers using IBM punch cards and calculating machines. Implemented in August 1942 and fully operational by early 1943, the system provided up-to-date comparisons of requirements and aircraft availability and allowed BuAer planners to gauge requirements more accurately and fine-tune aircraft production accordingly. By early 1943, it was evident that the numbers of aircraft lost in combat were considerably lower than what had been projected a year before, with the result that BuAer had to bring its aircraft production rates in line with the new attrition estimates.[26]

Armed with more reliable data, McCain presented a multiyear aircraft program to Vice Adm. Frederick J. Horne Jr., the Vice Chief of Naval

Operations (VCNO), in March 1943. BuAer called for increasing the Navy's production total from 27,500 to 33,056 airplanes. The revised figure was based on the need to equip the new flattops coming into the fleet (eleven more fast carriers and no fewer than seventy more escort carriers than previously estimated); adjustments to the carriers' air groups reflecting combat experience and allowing more flexibility in offensive and defensive operations (two fighter squadrons instead of one, one dive-bomber squadron, and one torpedo bomber squadron); additional long-range landplanes for antisubmarine warfare in the Atlantic; and about a thousand more training aircraft to meet the demand for 2,500 pilots per month. After the Joint Chiefs of Staff reduced the size of the program to 31,447 aircraft, the Secretary of the Navy and president approved it on 19 June.[27]

That aircraft design and production in the middle of a war was far from an exact science became painfully evident with the Curtiss SB2C Helldiver. In an attempt to get a replacement for the obsolescent SBD dive-bomber as soon as possible, the Navy rushed ahead in July 1940 with a production contract for the SB2C before the prototype had been tested and accepted. In February 1941, the first experimental model crashed during a test flight, setting the program back for more than a year while Curtiss made extensive modifications to the production version, the first of which was not delivered until June 1942. Further delays in the program occurred in getting an entirely new factory in Columbus, Ohio, up and running. Not until December 1942 did the first airplanes reach operating units, and nearly another year passed before the airplane got into combat. Even then, aviators scorned the SB2C (nicknamed the "Beast") for its evil handling characteristics, and carrier commanders found the dive-bomber difficult to maintain, although the much-maligned airplane went on to have a sound operational record.[28]

Even Grumman, one of the Navy's most experienced and trusted manufacturers, ran into production difficulties, though different than the ones afflicting Curtiss. McCain was typical in the praise the company received for its contributions to the war; at one point he declared that Grumman Wildcats and Avengers had "prevented the invasion of Australia; stopped the enemy at Guadalcanal and helped drive him off at Midway and thus prevented the invasion of the Hawaiian Islands." The company had committed to produce 175 of the new F6Fs per month, along with the spare parts needed to keep the airplanes flying after delivery. Yet in May 1943, despite efforts to expand its Bethpage, Long Island, plant and open new factories, Grumman fell behind in the delivery of spares. Desperate operators

in the field resorted to cannibalizing crippled aircraft to keep the others flying, not an acceptable solution to the problem. Cdr. Herbert D. Riley, who
had been McCain's aide in San Diego in 1941, was in the Materials and
Resources section of BuAer's Material Division when the problem reached
a crisis point. He recalled that with McCain's full support he had to issue
an ultimatum to Grumman's management: the Navy would refuse to take
delivery of any more Hellcats unless and until the company caught up with
spares production. Grumman had no choice but to cut back monthly F6F
production until the Navy was satisfied that it had enough spares to support
the operating aircraft. In a 1 June dispatch to operators on the West Coast,
McCain noted that "the example of Grumman having been brought into
line . . . has unquestionably had a great psychological effect on other contractors." "This was our greatest battle at Grumman," Riley later recounted,
but "we got the spares, and we never had similar trouble again. It worked."[29]

The Navy needed Grumman to achieve its goals both for production
of existing aircraft and for development of new designs. One such project
was a night fighter, which McCain called for in October 1942 shortly after
taking over as BuAer chief. From his experience in the Solomons, McCain
realized that it was unacceptable to let the Japanese rule the night skies, if
only to bedevil the Navy and Marines with nuisance (or "heckling") raids
over Guadalcanal. Grumman had received a contract in 1941 for a twin-
engine fighter, which flew for the first time in December 1943 as the XF7F-1
Tigercat. McCain realized that the big, heavily armed airplane, which the
Marines wanted for close air support, could be used as a night fighter. Recon-
figured as a two-seater, with a radar set operated by the second crewmember,
the airplane flew as XF7F-2N, but due to delays and production problems it
was too late to see service during the war.[30]

Providing spare parts and instituting efficient aircraft and engine maintenance procedures were problems McCain inherited from Towers' tour as
bureau chief. On 27 August 1942, Harvey C. Emery, a civilian working for
Gates in the office of the Secretary of the Navy, had submitted a scath-
ing report identifying multiple problems in the ways BuAer's Maintenance
Division had dealt with planning, finances, coordination with other divisions and agencies, and bottlenecks in the flow of spares and other essential
materials. Many of the shortcomings were due to the rapid acceleration of
aircraft procurement and lack of oversight from senior officers in the bureau.
The appointment of Capt. Frederick W. Pennoyer Jr., an engineering officer, as director of the division was a step in the right direction. Pennoyer

reported to McCain in January 1943 that he had reassigned personnel, reorganized some of the unit's functions, and transferred some of those responsibilities to the Aviation Supply Office.[31]

These were necessary correctives, but they were not enough to solve the bureau's persistent aircraft and engine maintenance and repair problems. Ironically, it was now Towers as Comairpac who complained most loudly about the spares problem that he had not been able to solve as BuAer chief. In November 1942, he pronounced the logistics and spare parts situation "catastrophic," especially in the South Pacific, where at least one squadron had been left with only a single operational airplane due to the dearth of parts. Later he remarked to McCain that "the situation in the South Pacific with regard to spares is really critical—repeat critical." In May 1943, McCain identified the scheduling of aircraft and aircraft engine overhauls as the major obstacle. He believed the problem could be addressed by centralizing authority in BuAer and assigning work schedules on specific aircraft and engines to bases in each of the five major operational and training commands. For instance, Comairpac stations on the West Coast and Hawaii were given primary responsibility for combat aircraft overhaul and repair, while work on transport, utility, and training aircraft went mostly to training commands. BuAer would provide "overall coordination" of scheduling and "arrange for transfer of work between commands when so requested" by the individual commanders. In August, each of the commands submitted schedules for bureau approval. A solution to the problem remained elusive, and meanwhile hundreds of aircraft remained on the ground and unavailable for use for many months to come.[32]

Still another problem during the war was the need to effect modifications to aircraft revealed by operational experience without shutting down or otherwise disrupting assembly lines. The answer was to continue production of basic models with only minor changes to the standard specification, then dispatch the completed airplanes (usually in "blocks" of twenty-five or so) to modification centers where they received updates to armament, avionics, and other equipment. The first modification centers in late 1942 were a Navy-operated facility at Roosevelt Field on Long Island and one operated by Consolidated Aircraft at Elizabeth City, North Carolina, where carrier and patrol aircraft, respectively, were modified for delivery to the British. In the spring of 1943, Consolidated opened centers at San Diego and Norfolk, where PB4Ys built for the Army Air Forces but allotted to the Navy underwent extensive upgrades. An expedient that maintained the necessary balance between quantity and quality of aircraft, the Navy's aircraft modification program remained relatively small through 1943, but rapidly accelerated in 1944.[33]

For McCain, a further complication in aircraft procurement and planning in 1943 was meeting commitments that had been made to supply aircraft to the Allies. Britain was the chief beneficiary, followed by the Soviet Union. In July 1942, the British and Americans reached an agreement whereby the total aircraft allocation to the British out of U.S. production was reduced from more than 10,000 airplanes that year to a little more than 6,000. The Navy's commitment to the British through April 1943 was trimmed by 718 aircraft, most of them PBYs. Responding to a British request in December 1942 to increase the allocation, McCain agreed to send an additional 437 aircraft to the Royal Air Force and 1,901 to the Royal Navy. Then, in July 1943, as aircraft production began to catch up with requirements, he assented to sending another 1,778 aircraft to the Royal Navy. By September 1943, 2,382 aircraft had been transferred to the British. For their part, the Russians were recipients of the PBN-1 Nomad, the Naval Aircraft Factory's improved version of the PBY. With Navy patrol squadrons transitioning to landplanes like the PB4Y and the British declining to take the new flying boats, McCain negotiated an agreement with the Russians to acquire PBNs. According to Herbert Riley, McCain did not want "a couple hundred Russians on a snooping job" in Philadelphia, where the NAF was involved in numerous confidential projects, so the decision was to have the airplanes flown to Elizabeth City for delivery. Altogether, 137 Nomads went to the Soviet Union by March 1945.[34]

Not only did McCain have to do a juggling act to adapt aircraft production to constantly evolving combat requirements, but he also had to make decisions about an entirely new weapon system that, while promising, could divert much-needed resources and personnel from existing programs. After years of research and development at the Naval Aircraft Factory and successful tests in April 1942, BuAer was ready to go ahead with limited production of what were known as assault drones. Designated TDN-1s, these remotely piloted twin-engine aircraft, equipped with radio control and television for guidance, could deliver bombs or torpedoes against land targets and shipping without risking the lives of aviators. The program had evolved from Delmar Fahrney's prewar target drone program and had received the endorsement of Admiral King as Project Option, under the command of Capt. Oscar Smith, a messianic convert to what were in effect the Navy's first guided missiles. BuAer and the NAF had misgivings about the sudden enthusiasm for the program in the office of the CNO, fearing that moving ahead too quickly would strain the production capability of the factory and might invite failure that would jeopardize long-term prospects for the new technology. Towers, in particular, wanted the program pared down, and he succeeded in getting the office of the CNO to reduce it from one thousand aircraft to five hundred, with a concomitant reduction in the number of badly needed aviation personnel.[35]

★ ★ ★ ★

McCain, who liked to think "outside the box," was more amenable to the assault drone program than was his predecessor and strongly backed the NAF's efforts to transition the TDN-1 from the prototype stage into limited production. He was also enthusiastic about ways to move forward with the operational variant of the weapon, designated as the TDR-1 and manufactured by the Interstate Aircraft and Engineering Company, a small firm located in El Segundo. As the NAF completed the first batch of TDNs in December 1942, McCain congratulated the NAF's manager, Capt. Walter W. Webster, for his efforts, which "had contributed in a large measure to the potentiality of radio controlled aircraft as a weapon of war. No stone should remain unturned which might contribute to the realization of this potentiality." In March 1943, after discussions with McCain, VCNO Horne presented an ambitious plan for employing three combat units consisting of nearly 900 drone and control aircraft and more than 3,600 officers and men, supported by a training organization with another 45 aircraft and 2,500 officers and men. King signed off on the program on 23 March, and Horne immediately informed McCain that he wanted a total of 3,000 drones, starting in June 1944.[36]

With Horne's proposal in hand, McCain began to have second thoughts about the potentially adverse effects that a program of such magnitude would have on BuAer's production requirements. He wrote to Horne on 12 April that he thought the assault drone plan would cost $200 million and would interfere with existing aircraft production while straining BuAer's efforts to train pilots and technical specialists. After more meetings, Horne agreed to a compromise whereby 1,500 drones would be acquired on top of the 500 already authorized. On 1 May, McCain estimated that the cost would be $101,500,000, in addition to the $41 million for the 500 aircraft already authorized. King and Gates agreed to what became known as the

"50% Project," and on 7 May McCain notified Horne that BuAer would carry out the program as directed. Interstate was to produce 1,100 of the TDRs; in order not to disrupt existing programs, the remaining 400 were divided among two other companies that were not among the established aircraft manufacturers.[37] How well the weapons performed in combat would not be resolved until 1944 at the earliest.

Along with the problems concomitant to the introduction of new weapons and the expansion of aircraft production was a huge increase in Navy pilot training. In 1941, Towers had brought in Cdr. (later Capt.) Arthur W. Radford, another early aviator, to oversee flight training for BuAer, which "advised" the Bureau of Navigation on matters regarding aviation personnel but essentially exercised authority over assignments and instruction of officers and enlisted men. Initially set at 7,200 aviators per year, the program went up to 30,000 Navy and Marine aviators annually in the immediate aftermath of Pearl Harbor. Towers proposed bringing all training together under Radford, but resistance from Vice Adm. Randall Jacobs, chief of the new Bureau of Naval Personnel (BuPers), delayed centralization of instruction until September 1942. It was also necessary to add more training facilities. Existing bases at Pensacola, Corpus Christi, Key West, Jacksonville, Miami, and Banana River, Florida, had to be expanded, new bases established, and naval flight preparatory and preflight schools set up at colleges and universities to recruit and train potential aviators. Wisely, McCain kept the capable and experienced Radford on to handle aviation training.[38]

McCain wanted "enough damn planes for the United States Navy, and enough damn pilots to fly them," yet he understood that training programs had to be balanced with aircraft production. On 26 December, responding to a request from Admiral Jacobs through Admiral Horne, McCain explained that the demands for pilots would level off in 1943 and that "a point will be reached in 1944 where aircraft and personnel begin to exceed presently approved requirements." He speculated that the surplus in people and equipment could be taken up by new shore establishments or that "the rate of training pilots may be reduced" from its current levels to 19,500 per year. Because of the long lead time (roughly eighteen months) in training aviators and aviation specialists, the Navy had to decide soon. Horne disagreed, believing that if there were any changes in requirements they would be for more and not fewer aviation personnel. As a consequence, the annual training rate remained unchanged through the early part of 1943.[39]

McCain compiled statistics that highlighted the rates of combat and operational attrition as well as the requirements for carrier- and shore-based replacement squadrons before providing Horne with new personnel figures on 8 April 1943. BuAer estimated that 35,495 pilots would be needed in 1943 and only 30,500 would be available. In 1944, the requirement went up to 52,445, but the number of pilots—53,500—would be sufficient to meet estimated needs. McCain explained that BuAer's revised estimates were due to raising the number of operating units, fewer carriers lost in combat than had previously been considered, an increase in the size of the Naval Air Transport Service (NATS), and augmenting the number of pilots assigned to each airplane to mitigate the fatigue anticipated from accelerated offensive operations. Because the instruction program could not be cut back immediately, 28,000 new aviators would be trained in 1944, followed by 19,500 per year through 1946.[40]

★ ★ ★ ★

Another personnel problem McCain faced was a shortage of officers in Washington. Following a survey of estimated requirements, McCain reported to the Secretary of the Navy in December that he needed 1,126 officers by the end of 1942, and 1,473 by the end of June 1943. A total of 189 enlisted personnel were needed by the end of 1942, increasing to 304 by 30 June 1943. It was not clear where the people would come from, given demands elsewhere in the Navy. McCain suggested that some of the shortfall could be made up by bringing in WAVES (Women Accepted for Voluntary Emergency Service), 600 of whom might replace officers and enlisted men in the bureau by the middle of 1943. For some time, the bureau had been among the Navy's most enlightened organizations in attracting and employing women, yet in this case there was a proviso: more than 200 of the WAVE officers would have to be trained in or have experience in aeronautical engineering, which was not likely to happen soon.[41]

A related issue was the employment of civilian personnel, which under McCain attained crisis proportions in the spring of 1943. The Booz report had recommended centralizing oversight of civilian employees, but it was not until 31 December 1942 that the Civilian Personnel Section was set up in the Administration Division, with responsibility for recruiting and supervising all civilians in the bureau. At the time, nearly 1,500 civilians worked at BuAer, with another 400 estimated to be hired by the middle of 1943. In November, BuAer had requested authorization to employ 2,520 civilians for the fiscal year 1944 (to begin in July 1943), but the Bureau of the Budget insisted on no more than 1,470. As workloads increased, pressure mounted to make more efficient use of civilian employees, while BuAer's need for technical specialists, salary limits, and military demands created a general labor shortage. Women took up some of the slack, but they did not provide a solution to the problem. By the end of September 1943, BuAer counted 134 WAVE officers and 93 enlisted women in Washington, most of whom worked in clerical jobs and as replacements for men and did not add much to the number of personnel needed in the bureau.[42]

It was apparent to McCain that unless more civilians could be hired there would not be enough people to handle BuAer's increased clerical demands. McCain sent a letter to Assistant Secretary of the Navy Ralph A. Bard on 29 April 1943 in which he explained that "the existing workload is not being performed adequately by the present staff. . . . It will be impossible to perform the expanding functions of the Bureau unless exception is made to limitations on civilian employment by the Bureau of the Budget." Bard, a member of the War Manpower Commission, intervened with the Bureau of the Budget to obtain a slight increase in the number of civilian workers, but still not enough to meet BuAer's needs. The dilemma was never completely solved and remained one of the many headaches bothering McCain during his tour as BuAer chief.[43]

Intelligence was another area where BuAer's responsibilities collided with those of other Navy agencies and bureaus. Before Pearl Harbor, Towers had implemented a program for recruiting and training Air Combat Intelligence Officers. Many of them older college graduates and all of them commissioned as reserve officers, these ACIOs, as they were known, served on carriers where they tracked enemy air activities, debriefed aviators, and compiled and circulated action reports. They also were assigned to naval air stations and to the Atlantic and Pacific area commanders in chief. The first ACIOs, many from Ivy League schools, were ready in time to participate in the Guadalcanal campaign. BuAer's Aviation Intelligence Branch collected and analyzed ACIO reports, technical information on enemy aircraft, and other data from a network of sources. The branch then disseminated the information to the rest of the bureau, the naval aviation establishment, and the operating forces in various publications, reports, and briefs. King specifically viewed the ACIO program as another example of Towers' empire building, and the Office of Naval Intelligence (ONI) regarded the work of the Aviation Intelligence Branch as a needless duplication and usurpation of its authority.[44]

Rear Adm. Harry C. Train, the director of naval intelligence, reviewed the situation in October 1942. He believed that technical information remained within the purview of BuAer, but that it should be categorized as "research" rather than intelligence. Information on foreign aircraft and combat intelligence from the ACIOs should be made "subject to all directives emanating from the Director of Naval Intelligence through the office of the Vice Chief of Naval Operations, as a regular part of the Intelligence service." In response, McCain explained that King had authorized creation of the foreign intelligence section specifically to analyze technical information "primarily to meet the needs of this bureau" and that BuAer "does not catalogue information which is needed and is used by the Commander-in-Chief for fleet and air operations." ACIOs, McCain continued, were "not intelligence officers in the usual sense of the word; in reality they are assistant operations officers" whose "work is operational in nature." "It is felt that it would be a serious mistake," McCain concluded, "to make them subject to Naval Intelligence directives as a regular part of the Intelligence Service."[45]

At least for the short term, McCain succeeded in preserving BuAer's ACIO and other intelligence activities. To ameliorate ONI's concerns, he changed the name of the Air Intelligence Branch to the Air Information Branch, redesignated ACIOs as Air Combat Information Officers, transferred some personnel to ONI, and pledged closer liaison with ONI on technical matters. In January 1943, he reorganized and expanded the branch to separate its information gathering and processing functions from its administrative and distribution activities. Foreign intelligence became Special Foreign Projects to indicate more clearly its emphasis on technical information, and the ACIOs were placed directly under the new Administration Section, which coordinated liaison with ONI and the CNO.[46]

Intelligence was only one of the overlapping administrative and bureaucratic problems McCain faced as BuAer chief. Another manifested itself in the course of enlarging existing and creating new shore establishments. In 1943, eighty-seven bases were built or expanded, many of them inland in order to minimize disruption of operations on the coasts. The strains were especially acute at naval air stations, where the influx of new airplanes created serious congestion by the end of 1942. McCain announced in November that while $600 million per year had been committed to the expansion of shore bases, it was not enough to relieve overcrowding, which was fast becoming an operational and safety problem. Material and personnel shortages compounded matters, as did the necessity of coordinating construction projects with the Bureau of Yards and Docks. All projects had to be fully justified in their necessity with supporting information and data before the responsible agencies signed off on them. It was necessary, too, that BuAer coordinate its base projects with the plans of the operating forces to avoid working at cross purposes. McCain, frustrated by inadequately or inaccurately documented proposals from the field, guessed that half of BuAer's correspondence concerning new construction involved rejecting requests or calling for more evidence of need. He believed that "many hours of valuable time both in the Bureau and on the station" could be saved simply by submitting applications that had been more "carefully examined" beforehand.[47]

McCain found the tendency to add superfluous, nonaviation functions to bases especially burdensome. North Island, for example, housed at least twenty units, among them two Army Air Forces squadrons, a Marine service group, and schools for radio operators, cooks, and bakers. With little or no notification, North Island and other facilities had also become impromptu staging locations for advance base personnel, straining housing and training facilities. The reasons were always due to "emergencies," accompanied by sincere assurances that the situations were only temporary, yet the disruptions lingered long afterward.[48]

Organizational changes initiated by McCain helped make more efficient use of existing facilities, yet ultimately only base construction and expansion eased the problems. Some naval air stations, including Hampton Roads, North Island, and Seattle, were designated Naval Air Centers, and Pensacola and Corpus Christi became Naval Air Training Centers in December 1942. Their establishment incorporated the addition of at least two and as many as eight auxiliary air stations, with the original naval air station becoming the organizational nucleus of facilities spread over wide areas. With the establishment of the centers, BuAer no longer had to deal with each of the auxiliary units separately and consequently realized a significant reduction in its administrative workload. Planned or built during McCain's watch were large new stations in Beaufort, South Carolina, and smaller ones in Maine; Quonset Point, Rhode Island, and Norfolk saw major expansions; naval reserve bases at Willow Grove, Pennsylvania, and Atlanta were redesignated as naval air stations and expanded; and new lighter-than-air bases sprang up on both the East and West Coasts. Big stations were built at Ottumwa, Iowa; Olathe, Kansas; and Livermore, California, mostly to provide for primary training.[49]

Speaking at the commissioning of NAS Patuxent River on 1 April 1943, McCain remarked that it was "the most needed station in the Navy." He was not far off the mark, since the Navy had for some time needed a new aircraft experimental facility. Since 1918, NAS Anacostia had been responsible for testing the Navy's latest aircraft. Across from Washington, Anacostia had the advantage of propinquity to the Navy Department, but by late 1941 it was totally inadequate for evaluating the numbers and types of aircraft coming through the development and prototype cycle. After considering alternative sites, a board appointed by BuAer Chief Towers recommended a location in St. Mary's County, Maryland, where the Patuxent River flows into Chesapeake Bay. The first construction contracts went out in February 1942. Isolated and spacious at 6,500 acres, NAS Patuxent River was still easily accessible from Washington, only about sixty miles north, and relatively close to Hampton, Virginia, where the National Advisory Committee for Aeronautics operated its Langley Memorial Aeronautical Laboratory. By the middle of July 1943, "Pax River" as it became known, had taken over flight-testing responsibilities from Anacostia as well as some of the experimental and training operations that had been carried out at Norfolk.[50]

BuAer was responsible for liaison and coordination with the Army on a variety of matters, some of which generated controversy and not all of which resulted in amicable solutions. For the most part, McCain exercised diplomacy and got along well with his Army counterparts, but air transport became a problem that tried his patience to the limit. Under Towers all transport activities had been centralized within the Naval Air Transport Service, administered by an aviator—none other than the Navy's first fighter ace David Ingalls—through the office of the CNO. The issue seemed to have been resolved, but it arose again in the late spring of 1943 during an investigation into the two services' air transport operations by the Joint Administrative Committee, which had been set up by the Joint Chiefs of Staff to address Army-Navy logistics and administrative problems. Sensing that the probe was really an Army attack on NATS, McCain sent a memo to King on 5 June. He could not have been more direct: "The Navy would be stupid indeed to turn over its swift, front line transport to another agency which is in every sense a competitor for space in air transport."[51]

Air transport proved to be just the tip of an interservice iceberg that loomed that spring. For at least a generation, the Army and Navy had jousted over control of land-based aviation, which the AAF believed intersected with and threatened its strategic mission. The problem lay mostly dormant until the German U-boat offensive in the winter and spring of 1942 led the Navy to increase its demands for big, long-range aircraft for antisubmarine warfare (ASW). Those requirements alone were enough to agitate Army airmen, but they also believed the Navy had mishandled the ASW effort, especially planning, intelligence, allocation of resources, and liaison with the Army, resulting in the loss of valuable shipping and even more indispensable lives. Navy officers, on the other hand, feared that the AAF would exploit the ASW problem to take over all land-based aviation and ultimately subsume naval aviation into a single unified air force. Worrisome, too, was the AAF's Antisubmarine Command, created in October 1942 with nominal responsibility for sharing the protection of shipping with the Navy.[52]

Aircraft procurement and administrative reorganization brought things to a head in the spring of 1943. For some time, cooperative acquisition had worked reasonably well, with the Navy procuring and turning aircraft over to the AAF and vice versa. Yet when the Navy, as part of its 27,500-aircraft program, asked for 400 B-24s by July 1944, the AAF dug in its heels. Army Air Forces Gen. Hap Arnold protested that the AAF needed the big bombers for its strategic missions and that his organization was fully prepared to assist the Navy as required. Further exacerbating the situation were Army officers' suspicions that the Navy would divert the bombers from the European theater to the Pacific, where they would be used for long-range strike missions. Marshall suggested a possible solution to the impasse in April when he proposed setting up under the JCS a joint Army-Navy command to control all antisubmarine air resources. The Navy's response was the establishment on 20 May 1943 of Tenth Fleet, consolidating all ASW in an administrative entity directly under King's command. Among other things, Tenth Fleet included responsibility for all long-range shore-based aircraft, which appeared to preclude or at least circumscribe any role for the AAF in ASW.[53]

In a brief meeting with King at the White House on 21 May, Arnold suggested a compromise whereby a general officer would command all Army long-range land-based aircraft and that command would be fully integrated into Tenth Fleet. King liked the idea. In a follow-up memo to Marshall he proposed that "my concept is that the functions of the Commanding General will be administration, material readiness, and training of Army A/S aviation. For operations, wings, groups or squadrons under their proper commanders would be allocated, temporarily and to the best advantage, to Sea Frontier, the Atlantic Fleet, or to special task forces (some of them under Army Air Command). . . . If there is any further clarification desired, will you set a time and place for you and me to get together to talk the matter over?" In the meantime, McCain, in a memo on 5 June, informed King that in addition to misunderstandings about air transport there was likely to be disagreement about the Navy's concept of "striking forces." Fleet air wings, Marine air units, and night fighters operating from island bases against "enemy shipping, enemy air, and enemy installations," he insisted, were "a true and irreplaceable part of the Naval combat arm for amphibious warfare and *must* be Navy manned."[54]

Further exchanges between Marshall and King tended to complicate the problem more than simplify it. In another memo to Marshall on 5 June, King pointed out that Army deputy chief of staff Lt. Gen. Joseph T. McNarney, in a meeting with Vice Adm. Richard S. Edwards, Deputy Chief of Naval Operations, had implied that the AAF would control all long-range land-based aircraft in the ASW role, which would in turn mean fundamental changes to the Navy's command structure. King objected to any such arrangement, underscoring his earlier insistence that any AAF forces engaged in ASW had to be under Navy command. Marshall tried to calm the waters in a memo to King three days later. He wrote that the JCS had agreed that in determining the "tactics and technique" involved in any joint operation, the "force concerned" had principal responsibility consonant with accomplishing the mission. He assured King that McNarney, in his conversation with Edwards, had not intended any reorganization or other changes in the Navy's command structure.[55] It was clear that the Army and Navy were overdue for a face-to-face conference to discuss and resolve these and other pressing interservice questions.

McCain and his chief of staff Matt Gardner, now a captain, met with Arnold and McNarney on the afternoon of 10 June. Arnold and McNarney conceded that the Navy needed its own "striking forces" but that the two services should confer from time to time on the number of aircraft to ensure that there was no duplication of AAF requirements and that the Navy should consider redesignating its shore-based fleet air wings to conform more closely to their missions, especially ASW. They also agreed with Gardner's proposal that the AAF hand over to the Navy all of its ASW B-24s; in return, the Navy would provide an equivalent number of normally equipped B-24s from its inventory. He estimated that seventy-seven aircraft were involved in the trade and that King and Marshall could work out a schedule of deliveries. Arnold said that he had never been pleased about the "antisubmarine business in the first place and that he would be very glad to get out of it at any time that he could." Finally, assured by McCain that there were no overlapping facilities or duplication of functions, Arnold and McNarney agreed that the Navy should continue as before with its separate air transport operations.[56]

Four days later, in a memo to Marshall, King followed up with specifics about the B-24 swap. The Navy would take over all ASW before 1 September, by which time the AAF will have relinquished its ASW responsibilities; starting in July and continuing through September, the Navy would acquire all seventy-seven of the Army's ASW-modified B-24s in exchange for the same number of unmodified aircraft. In his reply, Marshall agreed that what King offered was a "practical solution" to the problem. He added, though, that he believed the McCain-Arnold-McNarney meeting included an agreement that the Navy would not operate its fleet air wings as "striking forces," that the units would be limited to ASW only, and that all long-range bomber aircraft in the Western Hemisphere would be controlled by the Army. King responded that there was nothing in the B-24 exchange that involved fundamental changes in Army-Navy roles and missions and that there was no immediate need to deal with the question of "striking forces." Marshall held his ground. He maintained that "the question of responsibility for offensive operations against submarines and that of responsibility for long-range air striking forces are so closely related that a proper solution of one, in my opinion, involves consideration of the other." Further, he warned that Secretary of War Henry Stimson wanted the Navy immediately to accept the McCain-Arnold-McNarney agreement or he would be "unwilling to consent to the transfer of Army anti-submarine airplanes to the Navy" and that it might be necessary to take the matter to the president. While conceding Marshall's argument about the close relationship between the ASW and long-range strike missions and agreeing that fleet air wings operating heavy bombing aircraft would constrain their operations to ASW alone, King insisted that nothing in the agreement was intended "to limit or restrict a commander in the field, Army or Navy, in his use of all available aircraft as weapons of opportunity or necessity."[57]

The exchange of B-24s went ahead as scheduled, yet the ASW argument revealed deep fissures between the Army and Navy over strategic responsibilities that had been temporarily shelved but not fully resolved. They would again come up as the services and Congress addressed the question of a unified air force in 1944 and 1945.[58] McCain had gotten on well with his AAF counterparts in his South Pacific command, and as far as he knew they had enthusiastically reciprocated. His 10 June understanding with Arnold and McNarney appeared to guarantee that those close relationships would continue, especially at the administrative and operational levels. Yet, ironically, he could not help but see in the ensuing communications between King and Marshall that the agreement presaged an effort to remove the Navy's air arm and incorporate it into an independent service dominated by the Army. To McCain and other naval aviators, surrendering their air arm was totally unacceptable.

Interservice controversies aside, McCain and the Bureau of Aeronautics by the summer of 1943 had largely come to grips with a wide variety of issues associated with planning, procurement, production, and personnel. Matt Gardner, Ralph Davison, Arthur Radford, and Frederick Pennoyer, among others, formed the core of an experienced and capable staff that ensured that key matters came to McCain's attention, and they handled many of the day-to-day administrative responsibilities at Main Navy. There had been no major organizational changes in the bureau, which on the whole was beneficial considering the plethora of immediate wartime adjustments and problems that McCain needed to address and implement. Vexing dilemmas remained. Jurisdictional disputes with other bureaus and agencies were muted but unsolved; aircraft maintenance and repair were still troublesome; so was the persistent shortage of Navy and civilian office personnel in Washington, which hampered the efficient flow of information through the bureau. Still not fully settled—although steps had been taken toward a solution—was achieving a balance between operational requirements and the procurement of aircraft, engines, and spares. McCain was far from a hands-on manager and had been more than happy to leave many of these problems to his subordinates. At the same time, he was not hesitant to tackle the most urgent matters personally, and on most questions had King's explicit support. He may not have known it, but that summer King would take steps leading to the most fundamental changes in the administration of naval aviation since 1921.

CHAPTER 6

Washington and the Pacific
DCNO (Air)

J ohn McCain knew the CNO, Adm. Ernest King, well enough to understand that his boss was used to getting his way, sometimes by cajoling and often by bullying. Well before McCain took over as chief of the Bureau of Aeronautics, King had been thinking about sweeping administrative reforms, part of which involved centralizing authority for many of the functions that since the creation of the office of the CNO had been distributed among the various bureaus. More specifically, he believed that BuAer was too big and not nimble enough to address the immediate and long-range planning necessary to coordinate logistical and operational demands and that no internal reforms or reorganization within BuAer were sufficient to bring about the efficiency and control needed to fight a global war. Now was the time, with the cooperation of McCain and others, to effect major changes that would remove operations planning, policy-making, and logistics responsibilities from the bureau and to centralize those functions in the office of the CNO.[1] This meant relegating BuAer to a technical and material organization, which like other bureaus would be limited to promulgating and executing the decisions handed down from the CNO. Moreover, the change would take BuAer out of the direct chain of command to the Secretary of the Navy and signify its demise as the "superbureau" that King himself had led from 1933 to 1936.

King had already tried and failed to reorganize the Bureau of Aeronautics. When he was on the General Board in 1939, he had been part of discussions about ways to integrate the Navy's diverse aviation functions and responsibilities within the CNO's office and the service as a whole. Moreover, King had never been keen on how close Towers had been to Undersecretary Forrestal and Assistant Secretary Gates, and he disliked how bureau chiefs bypassed the CNO's office to gain direct access to the secretary. On 17 March 1942, only five days after he had been appointed CNO, King suggested consolidating the Navy Department's principal functions within four "grand divisions": material, personnel, readiness, and operations. Of those functional organizations, only material remained outside the authority of the CNO, residing primarily within the purview of the Secretary of the Navy and his assistant and undersecretaries. After conferring with Towers, King issued a directive on 15 May creating an assistant CNO for air, which many assumed would be filled by Towers. Instead, Towers and Gates proposed that a new assistant chief of BuAer be established with explicit authority for aviation personnel and training, thereby alienating both King and BuPers chief Vice Adm. Randall Jacobs. Weary of the internecine bickering and opposed to undermining the civilian authority within the Navy, Roosevelt informed Secretary Knox on the twenty-fifth that he thought the CNO should concentrate on operations and not "take on all the other responsibilities of getting the Navy ready to fight."[2]

Where most would retreat in the face of presidential opposition, King doggedly continued his offensive. On 28 May, he set up assistant CNOs for personnel and material. A few days later, Vice Admiral Horne, the VCNO, acting under King's orders, removed BuAer's responsibility for personnel and awarded it to BuPers chief, Jacobs, who would become the new assistant CNO for personnel. Finally, Roosevelt had had enough. He reminded King that he and not the CNO or Cominch was "Commander-in-Chief of the Navy" and directed King to cease all reorganization efforts. On 13 June, King rescinded his previous orders, abolished the assistant CNOs, and assured Knox that he would not undertake any further organizational changes. Nevertheless, a vestige of the abortive reorganization plan remained as the Aviation Division (Op-40) in the office of the CNO, which retained some planning activities and liaison authority with other bureaus and agencies.[3]

King was chastened, but he still believed his only offense had been that he had "neglected to consult the President and the Secretary" before proceeding with his administrative reforms. He bided his time. A year passed before he got another opportunity. With Towers out of the way in Pearl Harbor as Comairpac, McCain in Washington as BuAer chief, and public opinion favoring more emphasis on aviation in the highest echelons of the Navy, King judged he stood a better chance of getting what he wanted. On 8 May 1943, King's flag secretary, Capt. George L. Russell, circulated a draft reorganization order that included four deputy chiefs of naval operations: operations, material, personnel, and aviation. The duties of the Deputy Chief of Naval Operations (Aviation) included aircraft development and procurement, logistics, aviation training facilities, personnel, and, most significant, "the correlation of appropriate and necessary policies relating thereto." King's proposal generated almost immediate opposition from airmen, who believed it would jeopardize their hard-won autonomy in the naval establishment and remove them from important planning and logistics functions that they had exercised in BuAer.[4]

Four days later, McCain injected himself into the controversy. Most critically he did not want the aviators' agitation to gain further momentum and sought a middle course that would satisfy King's desires for change while assuaging the airmen's concerns. In comments on Russell's draft, he suggested that the title be changed to Deputy Chief of Naval Operations (Air) (DCNO [Air]) to align it with that of the Assistant Secretary of the Navy for Air and that the new official be a naval aviator. He added that "this officer is charged with the coordination of these activities, the supervision of programs for procurement of aircraft, for logistics requirements, for air training and *shore operating* facilities, for personnel requirements, *including their aviation training*, for aircraft development, and with the correlation of appropriate and necessary policies relating thereto."[5] If McCain had his way, at least the contentious question of aviator training would be resolved by removing those responsibilities from the Bureau of Naval Personnel.

King followed Russell's draft and McCain's comments with a memo to Knox on 17 June recommending that the office of the Deputy Chief of Naval Operations (Air) be created as part of a wider reorganization scheme. At the same time, he advised that the DCNO (Air) be established first, without waiting for approval of the entire plan. Knox forwarded King's memo to Roosevelt two days later, recommending that the president approve it and adding that King wanted McCain to fill the new billet. Again there was resistance from aviators, as well as from those who worried that the aggregation of more authority within the office of the CNO would upset the military-civilian balance of power. By stipulating that the proposed DCNO (Air) would not be part of a general reorganization and that the new officer would "correlate and coordinate" with BuAer, King hoped to defuse the opposition. Furthermore, he believed that McCain, a respected figure in the Washington naval establishment, would engender the trust needed to bring about the changes, in part through a harmonious relationship with Artemus Gates and civilian specialists in the office of the Secretary of the Navy. Nearly a month of political maneuvering passed before Knox received Roosevelt's approval, along with the president's understanding that DeWitt Ramsey, now a rear admiral, would succeed McCain as BuAer chief.[6]

Another month went by before Knox announced in an 18 August letter to all department bureaus and offices that "there shall be established in the Office of the Chief of Naval Operations a Deputy Chief of Naval Operations (Air) whose function is to correlate and coordinate all military aspects including policy, plans, [and] logistics of naval aviation." Specifically, the DCNO (Air) "shall be charged with the preparation, readiness, and logistics support of the naval aeronautic operating forces included within the several fleets, seagoing forces and sea frontier forces of the United States Navy, and with the coordination and direction of the effort to this end of the bureaus and offices of the Navy Department."[7]

Knox elaborated on the reorganization in a second letter on the same day. BuAer would lose its Planning, Personnel, Training, and Flight Divisions and its Air Information Branch. Each would become similarly named divisions within the office of the CNO. The CNO's Aviation Division would be dissolved, its previous functions taken over by the newly created divisions. BuAer would sever connections with the Naval Air Transport Service, which remained in the CNO's office but which would now operate directly under the DCNO (Air). The director of Marine Corps aviation and other Marine aviation offices were also to be administered by the DCNO (Air). A joint memo from Ramsey and McCain, also on the eighteenth, stated that all of BuAer's civilian employees would remain in the same jobs, at least "for the time being," and all correspondence would continue to be handled temporarily by BuAer until the details of the reorganization were finalized. According to the official administrative history, BuAer thus reverted to its "hard-core engineering and development mission" and was reborn as the "material agency for naval aviation." King, Knox, and McCain agreed that for the immediate future it was best not to be too specific about the functions of DCNO (Air) and allow them to evolve over time.[8]

★ ★ ★ ★

McCain consented to the scheme in part because he concluded that BuAer had become so swamped by planning, policy, operational, logistics, and other problems that it was impossible to fulfill its material and development responsibilities. Other reasons are more open to conjecture. His accession to the change might have been out of sheer loyalty to King, who had always been one of his champions. He might also have thought that currying favor with King would allow him to have a voice in high-level planning, strategy, and operations and open avenues to a combat command that might have been closed had he stayed on as BuAer chief. McCain could also count on Matt Gardner, his former BuAer chief of staff and now an aviation planning officer on King's staff, to enhance his credibility in policy and planning decisions. More cynically, the move might simultaneously shut the door for Towers to have a voice in strategic planning and prevent him from having the major combat command he so eagerly coveted. One senior officer who chafed under King's near absolute authority over combat billets wryly adapted a quotation from Gilbert and Sullivan: "Just stay at your desk and never go to sea, and you will be ruler of the King's Navee." McCain himself never confided to anyone his reasons, and the official record is unclear. As for King, he later admitted that McCain "was not very much in the way of brains . . . but he was a fighter." He also embraced McCain as a team player with experience in Washington and an officer who held the confidence of most—but certainly not all—aviators.[9]

★ ★ ★ ★

Upon assuming the new DCNO (Air) billet, McCain was elevated to vice admiral. King anticipated that the additional star would enhance the credibility of the new office with the airmen and allay at least some of their concerns about the status of naval aviation. McCain was pleased to accept the promotion, official notification of which came from Knox on 6 August, with the new rank to date from 28 July. King was increasingly aware that the vicissitudes of command had taken their toll on the health of his flag officers, and he made sure that the promotion was contingent on McCain's passing a physical exam, which he did on 6 August. McCain, who struggled to put on weight, got the good news after a more rigorous physical in March 1944 that he had gained six pounds in the last six months. Yet the exam revealed something new and potentially troubling, especially considering McCain's habit of smoking at least twenty cigarettes a day: hypertension, or high blood pressure. Doctors, however, deemed the condition "mild," despite its potential for cardiovascular disease, and cleared him for "all his duties at sea."[10]

Far from laying to rest grievances that aviators had long held within the naval establishment, King's organizational innovations fanned the flames of controversy. He had hoped that the creation of DCNO (Air) would mollify aviators who still imagined they were being systematically ignored by hidebound senior officers and perpetually marginalized within the Navy's power structure. Although the DCNO (Air) gave aviators direct access to the CNO's office and more influence in air operations without having their ideas and policies filtered through the BuAer chief and the Secretary of the Navy, some were still not satisfied. They were especially concerned that at this critical juncture in 1943, when the Navy was going over to the offensive in the Pacific and new carriers were coming on line, they might not receive the commands they deserved unless they were better represented at the top operational level. Some even advocated the creation of an entirely separate air corps, with autonomy similar to that enjoyed by the Army Air Forces and with their own representation on the Joint Chiefs of Staff. Others were so alienated that they were willing to succumb to the damnable heresy of a unified air service incorporating both Army and Navy air arms. Telling the press that "there is no clamor in the Navy for a separate air arm," Knox tried his best to head off the separatist faction and tamp down speculation about intraservice dissension.[11]

To get a better understanding of aviation's current and future status, Adm. Harry E. Yarnell, whom King had brought out of retirement in June to advise him on aviation, circulated a questionnaire to airmen and fleet officers in August. The survey revealed more than King and Yarnell wanted to hear about the depth and breadth of the fault lines separating naval aviators from high-ranking officers whom they believed did not fully comprehend the significance or accomplishments of aviation. There was general consensus that the service had mishandled aviation, had failed to exploit the full offensive potential of the aircraft carrier, and had systematically excluded aviators from senior commands. Only thorough, top-to-bottom changes could salvage the situation; King's changes were nothing more than a Band-Aid on a festering wound. To make matters worse, Nimitz objected that in soliciting the opinions of the aviators, Yarnell and King had undercut his authority, and he ordered senior officers to route their replies to Yarnell through his office.[12]

Towers, too, weighed in on the subject of administrative reform and its implications for aviators and naval aviation. In a letter to Horne he stressed that "there is great discontent with aviation out here" and that "they do not repose trust and confidence in [the] current Chief of Bureau." Only a few days after he learned of McCain's new job as DCNO (Air), Towers sent a memo to Nimitz in which he again pointed out that aviators resented policies that had blocked their avenues to command. The DCNO (Air) organization appeared to have been cobbled together at the last minute and in his estimation was "unsound, probably is illegal, and is confusing and overlapping." Rather than enhancing the aviators' influence, the new office undermined it. As if that were not enough, Towers was unwavering in his belief that McCain lacked the administrative ability to be effective in either his old or his new assignments.[13]

McCain knew that a top priority was to regain the confidence of the airmen if he were to have any chance of success in his new job. He sent out his own questionnaire and summarized the results in a judiciously worded report to King in early October. Emancipation was not an option. The naval aviator, he assured King, "can not be separated from the Navy or made disloyal thereto with a hammer and a chisel." He acknowledged, though, that the aviator, "treated with consideration as a specialist, does not receive the consideration he should have as a Naval officer better rounded, they think, than most others, in planning and in intermediate commands. They seem to feel that the Naval aviator as a well-rounded Naval officer is qualified to, and should, in due order, speak for the Navy as a whole on various planning committees and planning subcommittees." In other words, McCain asserted, aviators "feel that Aviation in the Navy has become of age, that the airplane is the hardest hitting unit, and that, as such aviators should no longer be advisers but should in due order, be the advised."[14]

Not only had airmen been excluded from high-level policy and planning decisions, but they had also been shut out of key operational commands. Aviators, McCain observed, "feel strongly that in task forces where the major purpose is air, such task force should be commanded by an aviator. When mixed forces are involved, the commander, if a non-aviator, should have an aviator as chief of staff, and vice versa." Promotions were a "sensitive nerve" for the aviators. McCain urged that junior aviation officers be elevated as quickly as possible so that they could take major task group commands and staff positions. Yet promotions that gave the appearance of expediency were "harmful rather than helpful," and "the only course is to go Presbyterian and do what the job demands." "Large increases in flag ranks in the Aeronautical Organization," he determined, were an absolute necessity.[15]

McCain followed up by elaborating on one of his ideas that he thought would guarantee aviators greater access to positions in the Navy's operational command structure. In January 1944, he recommended, and King agreed, that all commanders of surface forces had to appoint aviators as their chiefs of staff. Concomitantly, aviators in command of carrier task forces would have to choose surface officers to head up their staffs. Even though the scheme guaranteed a net gain for aviators as high-ranking nonaviators in fleet commands brought aviators into important advisory jobs at the same time as aviators gained seniority on their own, not all the fliers were pleased. Many true believers in the cause complained, with some justification, that they were still being excluded from key flag billets.[16]

How effective McCain was in maintaining the confidence of the aviators and reassuring them that he was committed to their cause remained problematic. With McCain's and Yarnell's reports in hand, King waited until January 1944 to respond. He emphatically disagreed with those who sought independence for aviation: "naval operations must be carried out *under one command* by officers trained in the use of all arms." But, in what he hoped would assuage the extremists, he added that aviation had to be infused in all levels of command and operations. As for the specific functions and responsibilities of the DCNO (Air), King stressed that they did not supersede the authority of the Secretary of the Navy or mean a "separate air command." Rather, he concluded, "it is to be expected that the functions of the DCNO (A) will be modified from time to time in light of experience, but it is not intended and is not contemplated that this office become a military *command*."[17]

It was also essential to inform the public that aviation was important to the Navy and deter political efforts to consolidate all military and naval aviation. Some in the news media had commented that in comparison to the Army, the Navy was not committed to aviation. McCain cited an incident where a reporter for a major magazine got the runaround from Nimitz's staff when he asked for their help in getting back to the states from Hawaii. In contrast, Lt. Gen. Robert C. Richardson, the senior Army commander in the Central Pacific, and his staff had bent over backward to arrange for the newsman's transportation and had him on his way home within a matter of hours. According to McCain, friends of the Navy in the press, among them Hanson Baldwin of the *New York Times* and former naval aviator Frank W. ("Spig") Wead, "all state that all the Navy has to do in order firmly to intrench its case against any united or combined air force is a simple recital of facts."[18]

McCain took the initiative on publicity, which he hoped would bolster naval aviation's popular image while assuring the aviators of his commitment to their cause. A cover piece in the illustrated magazine *Collier's* credited him for much of the success of Navy planes and men in the Solomons and assessed him as a "man of authority" who knew how to bring the "full weight of American force" to defeat the Japanese. An article in the *New York Times* on the occasion of the thirtieth anniversary of the General Board's decision to create a Navy aeronautical establishment quoted McCain at length. "Huge task forces, spearheaded by carrier-based aircraft," he said, "are poising for pile-driver blows against the enemy. . . . Naval aviation has become an extremely powerful weapon, possibly the most powerful. Let every officer and man in Naval Aviation resolve, on this anniversary of the formal beginning of this branch, to continue and intensify the unrelenting punishment we have given to the enemy from the air until he is utterly defeated." In just a year, naval aviation had expanded threefold: new *Essex*-class fleet carriers were being commissioned, as were "baby flattops" (the escort carriers used for a variety of convoy, ferrying, and combat missions); the number of aircraft had tripled since 1942; and training programs were churning out 30,000 pilots annually. It was all, McCain said, a tribute to the pioneer aviators whose "unshakable faith in the military utility of the airplane" had made the momentous transformation possible.[19]

He conveyed much the same message on 15 May 1944 in testimony before a congressional select committee on postwar military policy. Arguing that the Navy's air arm was crucial to winning the war as quickly as possible, McCain pointed out that naval aircraft carried out specialized strike, reconnaissance, scouting, close air support, and antisubmarine warfare missions that were beyond the usual capabilities of the Army Air Forces. He went on to describe the typical carrier task force and the mix of aircraft it embarked "to deliver in one blow a synchronized and coordinated attack" against the enemy. Fast carriers had their own scouting and fleet air defense capability and would soon be capable of night air operations. Working in small groups with destroyers, escort carriers were effective in protecting convoys and tracking down and killing enemy submarines. To concerns that the Navy's shore-based forces duplicated those of the Army Air Forces, McCain replied that the production of PB4Ys constituted only one-third of one month of bomber production. James Forrestal, for one, was much impressed with how well McCain articulated the Navy's position to the public and Congress, especially "at a time when the Army-Navy merger question was apparently about to become very active."[20]

Within the service, McCain sought to clarify the functions of the DCNO (Air) in ways he hoped would reassure skeptical naval aviators. In a March 1944 memo to Admiral Horne, he recommended that important billets in his office be held by aviators and that the DCNO (Air) have "cognizance" for aviation logistics and for the characteristics and allocation of aircraft and aircraft carriers in consonance with operational requirements. Naval aviators may have been pleased that they had a presence in the office of the CNO, but neither they nor McCain were happy with Horne's insistence that all aviation matters be directed through his office. Horne, who had in effect taken over most of King's CNO responsibilities, freeing King to concentrate on his job as Cominch, objected to any changes that would undermine the principle of unified command or that would allow McCain parallel access to King. Horne persuaded King to determine that "the duties of the Deputy Chief of Naval Operations (Air) will be performed under the direction of the Vice Chief of Naval Operations." McCain had to report to Horne and not directly to King. It was now clear that there would be no autonomy for aviation and that DCNO (Air) would have a limited presence in the decision-making hierarchy in Washington. Much like BuAer, DCNO (Air) was for the most part relegated to the "nuts and bolts" of running naval aviation, which was as frustrating for McCain as it was for the aviators.[21]

Although there had been progress, King's administrative reforms of 1943 and 1944 left many aviators even more distressed about their status within the service than they had been before. If the Navy airmen remained dubious about McCain and the commitment of the service to aviation, Marine aviators were not. Although for some time they had been involved in policy making and planning, they believed that working with and through the DCNO (Air) would increase their role in operational decision making. As part of his reorganization agenda, King had recommended the possible merger of Marine and Navy aviation. McCain as BuAer chief had appointed a board, chaired by Capt. Harold B. ("Slats") Sallada, which studied the matter and concluded that there already was considerable coordination between the two aviation branches and that amalgamation would not enhance efficiency. Marines had not forgotten how McCain had stood with them at Guadalcanal, and they saw McCain as one of their own who would preserve their independence. With Maj. Gen. Roy Geiger, who had worked with McCain at Guadalcanal, as head of Marine aviation and acting as liaison with the DCNO (Air), they were assured of a loud voice in the highest echelons of the Navy's command.[22]

In his new job McCain wanted to gain an understanding of operations and aviation requirements in the Pacific. On 12 October, he had flown out of Washington on the first leg of long inspection trip that took him to the West Coast and Hawaii. After a stop in Greenwood to visit family members, he proceeded to San Diego, Burbank, and Seattle to inspect aircraft plants before boarding one of Pan Am's Clippers for the flight from San Francisco to Honolulu, where he arrived on the twenty-third. He reported to Admiral Nimitz at Pearl later on that day. In conferences with Nimitz, his chief of staff, Rear Adm. Charles H. ("Soc") McMorris, Vice Adm. Raymond Spruance, commander of the Central Pacific Force, Towers, and others, McCain broached his ideas about future operations in the Central Pacific. His plans, which had been hatched over the previous two months, were nothing if not ambitious, calling for a rapid advance through the Marshalls and carrier raids against the Japanese home islands as early as June 1944. Spruance and his staff, aware of the logistics involved in such an audacious undertaking, dismissed McCain's scheme as unrealistic. On the other hand, Towers and other aviation planners at Pearl Harbor saw merit in McCain's proposal, which while not immediately feasible might be "attractive and desirable at some future date."[23]

It is likely that McCain knew his proposal was premature and not something that would be wholeheartedly embraced by the planners at Pearl Harbor. Rather he saw it as an opportunity to demonstrate to Nimitz and King that he was thinking about the future of carrier warfare and about the speed and direction of the rapidly evolving offensive in the Central Pacific. McCain was out of Washington again at the end of January, once more to gather information on aircraft manufacturing in San Diego and Los Angeles. On 2 February, his peregrinations took him to San Diego, where he caught up with Towers, who had hoped to talk with McCain about ways of expediting the flow of aircraft into the theater. Instead, to his frustration all Towers heard was another iteration of McCain's ideas for a carrier assault on Japan. Afterward, on 5 February, McCain met with Nimitz in Pearl Harbor before spending three days in the Gilberts to see how air base development was progressing in the recently seized islands. Returning to Hawaii, he discussed aircraft supply and logistics with Nimitz, Towers, and their staffs. He agreed with Towers that the rapid influx of new aircraft in the Pacific had caused bottlenecks and told him that he wanted to recruit his chief of staff, Rear Adm. Arthur Radford, to chair a panel to address the aircraft procurement situation, which had taken on a new and vexing twist by the end of 1943.[24]

Increased output from aircraft manufacturers, the production limit set in June, and lower-than-anticipated attrition rates had coalesced to create the unusual problem of too many airplanes. Although it was comforting to know that there would be sufficient aircraft for the planned 1944 offensives, it was apparent that the fleet needed a policy to remove or return damaged, worn out, or obsolescent aircraft to make room for the new planes coming through the pipeline. It would also be necessary to ensure that supply, maintenance, and repairs were done efficiently and in concert with production and logistic support, especially in the Pacific. Repair priorities had to take into account that the fleet was not interested in the return of aged or obsolescent aircraft and preferred instead to have crashed or damaged current models back in service as soon as possible. Before they needed costly and time-consuming repairs, worn-out airplanes had to be stricken from the Navy lists. Finally, it was necessary to alleviate or eliminate the growing backlog of airplanes and engines awaiting overhaul and repair.[25]

Radford had McCain's complete confidence as head of the board convened to tackle these questions. Before taking over as Towers' chief of staff in December 1943, Radford had performed well in administering aviation training, had ably commanded the first light carrier division in the Pacific, and had led a task group during the November 1943 Gilberts operation. Reluctant to give up Radford, Towers proposed Capt. John J. Ballentine, a highly capable carrier skipper, as an alternative, but McCain would not budge on his decision, and Towers gave in. Members of Radford's board included the assistant chief of BuAer, Rear Adm. Lawrence B. Richardson, the assistant director of Marine Corps aviation, Col. Albert D. Cooley, and Capt. Charles W. Fox from the Bureau of Supplies and Accounts.[26]

The Radford board met for the first time on 12 April. The panel followed two primary "theses": that production requirements should be aligned with the "maximum output of aircraft facilities"; and that "the Navy should procure only enough new aircraft to meet attrition and to outfit new units and activities that were being formed." McCain charged the board with examining how combat conditions affected aircraft service life, the capacity of aircraft assembly and repair (A&R) units to maintain old airplanes in service, balancing new aircraft production with overhauling and repairing existing aircraft, creating an aircraft retirement policy, and the logistics of taking old planes out of service and repairing or replacing them. Over the next three weeks, the board met fifteen times, at which forty-seven officers from BuAer, the Bureau of Supplies and Accounts, the commander, Air Force Atlantic Fleet, and Comairpac testified. Among the many considerations, the board had to determine the service life of an airplane, keeping in mind that its useful life was usually longer than its combat life, which in turn depended on military conditions. The removal of old airplanes from the lists was another major topic. Scrapping airplanes made room for new ones and put used parts in the pipeline, but the Navy had in place a bureaucratic apparatus and sets of rules that had to be followed to the letter before aircraft could be stricken. Moreover, the number of airplanes removed had to be adjusted in accordance with the number of new planes arriving in the combat areas. As usable parts were salvaged, manufacturers of new spares would have to cut back production to avoid oversupply problems. A&R stations had to schedule their work to coincide with the return of aircraft from the theater and with the requirements of operating and training units. It helped that aircraft modification had been removed from the A&R shops and given over to specialized modification facilities. Centralized coordination and control of the entire process was essential, which itself depended on accurate and up-to-date record keeping.[27]

The board completed its hearings and reported to McCain on 4 May. Two days later, McCain accepted the report and sent copies to Vice Admiral Horne and Assistant Secretary of the Navy Gates for their consideration and approval. Forrestal, who succeeded Knox as Secretary of the Navy upon Knox's death in late April, put his imprimatur on the report by the end of June. Essentially a synthesis resulting from a series of compromises, the Radford board report formed the basis of what became known as the Integrated Aeronautic Program (IAP). The IAP covered four particulars according to the official BuAer administrative history: "(a) the assignment of new aircraft to combat units; (b) the return of aircraft to the U.S. for reconditioning and further assignment after specified combat tours; (c) the retirement of second-tour aircraft before maintenance became costly and time-consuming; and (d) the support of the aeronautical organization through the use of the allowances for pools, pipelines and reconditioning that were kept realistic by frequent reappraisals."[28]

A major part of the Radford board's recommendations sought to ensure that combat units had the most up-to-date aircraft. Rapid technological developments caused an airplane to become obsolete, and modifications in the field were not likely to improve combat effectiveness. Accordingly, the board insisted that a "steady flow of new aircraft was essential." The board set ceilings for the military usefulness of various categories of planes. For example, the board projected eight months for fighters, dive-bombers, and torpedo planes operating in both the Pacific and the Atlantic; eight months for patrol planes in the Pacific; and twelve months for similar aircraft in service in the Atlantic. The report recommended that after a thorough review of the aircraft lists, all obsolete aircraft be stricken and that they be scrapped as quickly as possible. The board estimated that more than 1,500 new carrier aircraft would be needed each month, balanced by removing a similar number from the lists, not an easy logistical or administrative undertaking.[29]

Among the multitude of recommendations put forward by the Radford board, one of the most controversial was a proposal to expand the work of Carrier Aircraft Service Units (CASUs) to include preparing returned aircraft for dispatch to assembly and repair shops. Shore-based CASUs and their carrier-based counterparts, Carrier Aircraft Service Divisions, had been brought together administratively under Comairpac in September 1943 as part of the effort to centralize aviation logistics in the Pacific. Self-contained mobile supply and maintenance units serving the operating squadrons, CASUs were considered by the historian Clark Reynolds to be "an open secret weapon" that contributed to the extraordinary mobility of the fast carrier task forces. To bring more centralization to aircraft maintenance and repair, the Radford board assumed that consolidation would return aircraft to the fleet quicker and in better condition than if the work had been done by A&Rs at naval air stations. The proposal met immediate and strenuous opposition from A&R units on the West Coast, which protested that the CASUs did not have the personnel or equipment to take on the extra work. Further study resulted in a new recommendation, approved by the CNO, to keep the work at the A&Rs.[30]

On 9 September, the Radford board reconvened with its original members to review progress on the IAP. After hearing from more than 130 witnesses, the board issued its reports and recommendations on 2 October. In general, the board found that the program was accomplishing its purposes and that the results had "been definitely beneficial." At the same time, the panel recommended that aircraft attrition rates be revised based on experience, that the size of carrier aircraft pools in the Pacific be increased, and that due to their size and the extent of their activities A&R units be consolidated in commands separate from those of the naval air stations. Furthermore, the board agreed with a request from Comairpac to convert four tank landing ships into dedicated aircraft repair ships, and that private contractors take over the repair and reconditioning of Navy transport aircraft. Finally, the board recommended that DCNO (Air) appoint a committee on maintenance, material, and supply "to oversee the integrated program" and make further adjustments to the IAP as needed. The board also submitted a supplemental report specifically addressing planning and logistics procedures and policies that came under the responsibility of the DCNO (Air). King approved the report in his endorsement of 13 November.[31]

Lost in most narratives of the naval air war, the Integrated Aeronautic Program was an organizational and administrative triumph initiated by McCain that helped bring victory in the Pacific. The Radford board and the IAP created the foundation of a rational plan that became the framework for managing aircraft acquisition through the remainder of the war. It was not perfect, and it demanded, as the BuAer administrative history concluded, "a substantial amount of coordination and control" and "smooth flows" of aircraft and equipment. Accurate records and record keeping by the administrative bureaus and operating forces were also essential to the success of the program. Generally the scheme met the objective of ensuring that only new airplanes went to combat units. Reconditioned planes taken out of combat went to training and other units in the United States, where pilots and crews gained familiarity with the same types of aircraft they would use and maintain in the field.[32]

By the end of 1943, large numbers of modern aircraft embarked on new fast carriers were arriving at Pearl Harbor, ready to spearhead the American drive in the Central Pacific. With the *Essex* (CV 9), the first in a class of new heavy carriers, the smaller but speedy *Independence* (CVL 22)-class light carriers, and a constellation of fast battleships, cruisers, and destroyers, Nimitz finally had the ships needed to organize task forces for the naval air campaign. It was also evident that despite the continued unrest among aviation officers, new ships needed new skippers and that sheer necessity would open important carrier commands. Towers and Nimitz identified key officers for combat assignments, and McCain in Washington concurred with their recommendations. Among the rising stars in the aviation establishment were Alfred E. Montgomery, John W. Reeves Jr., William K. Harrill, Arthur C. Davis, Samuel P. Ginder, Gerald F. Bogan, and Frederick C. ("Ted") Sherman.[33]

At the highest command levels, only a handful of senior admirals were acceptable to both King and Nimitz to take charge of the fleets and carrier task forces. Bill Halsey was one of them, respected for his experience by his peers and glorified by the public as a heroic fighting seadog. Halsey's flattops, under the commands of Rear Adms. Frederick Sherman and Alfred Montgomery, had attacked Rabaul in November 1943, forcing the Japanese to withdraw their remaining aircraft to Truk. With Rabaul neutralized, Halsey's force, constituted as the Third Fleet, provided support for the successful invasion of Bougainville, the last big island in the Solomons. Once major operations on Bougainville ended in April, the long South Pacific campaign ended, and Halsey became available to Nimitz for operations in the Central Pacific.[34]

At the same time, this was a contingent moment for Nimitz, because Spruance was his favorite and also deserved consideration for a major command. Compared to Halsey's brashness and hunger for publicity, Spruance projected a modest, thoughtful, and deliberate presence. In command of the Central Pacific Force (later renamed the Fifth Fleet), Spruance had been responsible for Operation Galvanic, the invasion of Tarawa and Makin in the Gilbert Islands. Partial to Halsey, Comairpac Towers was not pleased that Nimitz had chosen Spruance, a nonaviator, for the job, and he was critical of how Spruance had employed the carriers defensively, tying them to the invasion force in anticipation of an engagement with the main Japanese fleet that never materialized. In February, Spruance was in overall command of Operation Flintlock, the much less bloody invasion of Kwajalein and Eniwetok in the Marshalls.[35]

At the next echelon of the leadership hierarchy were the officers commanding the carrier task forces. Like Towers one of the cohort of early naval aviators, Marc Mitscher had commanded the *Hornet* during the Halsey-Doolittle raid and at the Battle of Midway, where he made a sequence of potentially career-ending poor decisions. He redeemed himself as a rear admiral and air commander, Solomon Islands (Comairsols), taking charge of land-based air in the latter stages of that campaign. Under Mitscher, Task Force 58, as a component of Spruance's Fifth Fleet, devastated Japanese shipping and air power at Truk, thus contributing to the relative ease with which the Marshalls were seized. Mitscher's successes with TF-58 led to his promotion in March to vice admiral and commander of the Fast Carrier Forces Pacific Fleet. According to the historian Clark Reynolds, the Marshalls and Truk operations "changed the complexion of the war in the Central Pacific," whereby the fast carrier task forces allowed Japanese island strongholds to be bypassed and accelerated the timetable for the offensive farther to the west.[36]

The next objective in the Central Pacific offensive was the Marianas, Operation Forager, planning for which began in April. Halsey, Spruance, and Mitscher were the team Nimitz intended to rely on to prosecute this phase of the war. Neither Nimitz nor Towers, who had been promoted to deputy Cincpac-Cincpoa under Nimitz, were friends of McCain, who lay as a wild card in the deck of potential task force commanders and itched to get back to the Pacific. McCain had been biding his time in Washington, staying close to King as BuAer chief and DCNO (Air), while not generating waves that would sweep him off the short list for senior carrier command. Sometime in early March—the exact date is unclear—King chose McCain to lead a carrier task force. According to Clark Reynolds, King's ulterior motive for awarding McCain a task force command was that he wanted him "out of Washington because he was ineffective in his job" as DCNO (Air), although he cites no direct evidence that that was King's primary reason for the change. Forrestal questioned King's decision, not because he thought McCain had been ineffective in Washington but because "there are other men with more recent sea and air experience who might be better than he for a task of major importance." In fact, Forrestal admired McCain for his administrative and political experience and for standing up for the Navy and naval aviation.[37] Regardless of King's rationale, the bottom line was that McCain had earned his aviator's wings, was capable, personable, popular with the press and enlisted personnel, and had a reputation as an aggressive combat officer. Agree with him or not, King had the final say in such high-level personnel decisions; his wishes always superseded the wants and objections of others. He did not have to explain himself to anyone.

Adding McCain to the team in the Pacific was part of the rotation of fleet and task force commanders and staffs that had been suggested by Towers when he was BuAer chief and later by Adm. Charles M. ("Savvy") Cooke Jr., King's chief planning officer. At a meeting in San Francisco in May, Nimitz and King agreed that Halsey and his Third Fleet would at intervals spell Spruance and his Fifth Fleet. When Spruance completed an operation (in this instance Forager) he and his staff would return to Pearl Harbor to plan the Navy's next moves in the Central Pacific; in their absence, Halsey would take over command of the air and surface forces constituting the "Big Blue Fleet," as it was popularly known. Task Force 58 under Mitscher therefore became Task Force 38 with McCain as the fleets changed designations and commanders. Remaining in place through the end of the war, this "two-platoon" system provided relief from the rigors of combat while speeding up the Central Pacific offensive.[38]

It is likely McCain learned of King's decision to hand him a task force command sometime during the second week of March, not long before he took off on a five-day inspection trip of naval aviation facilities in the South. On the fourteenth McCain flew from Washington to Jacksonville, Florida, where he met Cdr. John S. ("Jimmie") Thach, who had been assigned to

NAS Jacksonville as an instructor. An Arkansas native, Thach was a 1927 Academy graduate and combat aviator who as commander of VF-3 had downed four Japanese aircraft at Midway. In that battle he had employed the so-called Thach Weave, a defensive-offensive tactic where a section of two fighters cut across one another's paths when either one was attacked. When the adversary closed on one of the planes in Thach's formation, he was forced into the gunsight of the other, the predator in effect becoming the prey. At Jacksonville, Thach indoctrinated neophyte combat pilots in the teamwork needed for the maneuver and other fighter tactics that helped ensure that American naval aviators surpassed their Japanese opponents in the battles of 1944 and 1945.[39]

Before he left Jacksonville, McCain asked Thach, "How would you like to work for me? I'd like for you to be my operations officer." Thach readily accepted: "I'm delighted. I can think of no better job that I could have." Then he asked why McCain had singled him out for the duty. McCain answered, "I'll tell you one reason. I've heard that you're not a yes man, and I don't want any yes men on my staff." After McCain cleared it with the chief of naval air operational training to have Thach released from his current duties, Thach followed McCain to Washington, where McCain had worked with Halsey to arrange top priority for Thach to go out to the Pacific to put together a staff and observe carrier organization and operations. McCain told Thach before he left that "I want to get you out there as soon as I can, then you watch and see everything they do and be sure and make a note on any mistakes they make."[40]

Like Thach, McCain needed to see carrier task force operations in person. On 11 May, he received orders to report to Nimitz for temporary duty beginning on the twenty-fifth. Rather than fly or take the train, McCain packed up and drove the family's 1939 Chevrolet sedan to the West Coast, intending to leave it in San Diego for Kate when she came out from Washington. From San Francisco he flew to Pearl Harbor, arriving there on the morning of the twenty-fourth. He conferred with Nimitz the next day and received a copy of plans for the Marianas operation. McCain asked Nimitz if he could observe the Marianas operations from the *Enterprise*, skippered by his former chief of staff Matt Gardner. Instead, Nimitz told him that he would first go to Spruance's flagship, the heavy cruiser *Indianapolis* (CA 35), after which he would be reassigned to the *Lexington* (CV 16), on which Mitscher flew his flag as TF-58 commander. Thach would go out with McCain on the *Indianapolis*, then join the *Lexington*, where he would collaborate with Capt. Arleigh A. Burke, Mitscher's able chief of staff. At a meeting with Towers later on the twenty-fifth, McCain raised specific objections to the Marianas operational plan, which Towers believed revealed McCain's lack of understanding of its strategic and logistical context. Nevertheless, Towers ultimately agreed that some of McCain's ideas, especially those about using Marine instead of Army aircraft to hold down the islands after they had been seized, were worth consideration.[41]

The *Indianapolis*, top-heavy with the brass and their staffs, stood out from Pearl on the afternoon of the twenty-sixth, making up a little task group with the destroyers *Selfridge* (DD 357) and *Ellet* (DD 398) bound for Majuro in the eastern Marshalls, about halfway between Pearl Harbor and the Marianas. En route McCain shared the cruiser's flag bridge with Spruance and studied the plans and organizational details of the Marianas operation with Spruance and his staff. When the *Indianapolis* threaded the north channel into Majuro's deep and spacious lagoon on the morning of 2 June, McCain could not help but feel a sense of awe. Compared to the "shoestring" he and Fletcher had had to work with in the South Pacific less than two years before, the armada of gray steel McCain beheld in the anchorage looked more like an entire navy than anything else. At Majuro, Spruance's force numbered no fewer than 111 warships, the majority of them constructed since Pearl Harbor, out of a total of 535 ships and amphibious craft, brought together to deliver more than 127,000 Marines and soldiers onto the beaches.[42]

The major units under Spruance were Mitscher's Fast Carrier Forces (TF-58), the Joint Expeditionary Force (TF-51) under Vice Adm. Kelly Turner, and land-based aircraft (TF-57) under Vice Adm. John H. Hoover. TF-58 alone comprised 93 ships, more than 900 aircraft, and nearly 100,000 men. There were no fewer than fifteen fast carriers, split into four roughly equal task groups: TG-58.1, Rear Adm. Joseph J. ("Jocko") Clark; TG-58.2, Rear Admiral Montgomery; TG-58.3, Rear Admiral Reeves; and TG-58.4, Rear Admiral Harrill. The *Indianapolis* was part of a support unit attached to TG-58.3, which also included the *Lexington* and Gardner's *Enterprise*.[43]

The *Indianapolis* cleared Majuro on the third, bound for Eniwetok, about six hundred miles to the northwest, where the cruiser linked up with Turner's amphibious force. Thach, meanwhile, was McCain's eyes and ears on the *Lexington*, working with Burke while running back and forth from the carrier's bridge to the Combat Information Center (CIC). The nerve center, or "brain," of the ship, the CIC—located first in the island, but later in a more protected space on the gallery deck below the flight deck—collected, evaluated, and disseminated tactical information from a wide variety of sources, including radar, radio nets, intelligence reports, aerology, and visual observations from the carrier, aircraft, and other ships. By the end of 1943, all Pacific Fleet carriers had received the new installations. A task force fighter director officer (FDO) in the CIC analyzed radar plots from the flagship and other CICs and coordinated individual carrier FDOs and those on surface ships. The FDOs relied on improved air search radars and multichannel VHF radio, which allowed them to maintain near continuous contact with their fighters, and on an aircraft recognition system known as Identification Friend-or-Foe (IFF), which used coded transponders that helped distinguish friendly from hostile aircraft. CICs simultaneously controlled strike and patrol aircraft and communicated with other CICs in the task force and with the task force fighter director officer. Both Thach and McCain understood the importance of the CIC as a wartime innovation in command and control vital to the operations of the fast carrier task force.[44]

Mitscher's TF-58 left Majuro in a gray drizzle on the sixth and three days later caught up with Spruance and the amphibious force northwest of Eniwetok. The Japanese had correctly surmised the American objectives and understood the necessity of preventing the seizure of the Marianas, deemed crucial to Japan's inner defensive perimeter. Operation A-Go mobilized the Imperial Navy's offensive strength to engage and defeat the American forces in what Admiral Toyoda Soemu, commander in chief of the Combined Fleet, believed would be the decisive battle of the Pacific War. Under Vice Admiral Ozawa Jisaburo, the Mobile Fleet, with nine carriers and nearly 440 aircraft, sortied from Tawi-Tawi in the southwestern Philippines on 13 June. In the meantime, TF-58 strikes virtually wiped out Japanese air power in the Marianas in preparation for the 15 June landing of two Marine divisions on Saipan's west coast.[45]

Spruance enjoyed superb intelligence on the eve of what became known as the Battle of the Philippine Sea. From Pearl Harbor came synopses of Japanese fleet movements through radio traffic analysis, and in his flagship *Indianapolis* was a mobile radio intercept unit led by Cdr. Gilven M. Slonim, a talented Japanese-language expert. Slonim forwarded reports to Burke on Mitscher's *Lexington*, who shared the intelligence with Thach. Later, as a task group commander, McCain gained operational intelligence from a personal arrangement with Slonim to receive messages containing information from Slonim's radio intercepts and other sources.[46]

From Slonim and other intelligence, Spruance knew the Japanese were on the move, and he could visualize the size and composition of the enemy carrier forces. But where were they, exactly? On 14 June, submarines reported that the Mobile Fleet had sortied from Tawi-Tawi and subsequently had passed into the Philippine Sea. Three days later, Spruance received a report that coast watchers had sighted Ozawa's force transiting San Bernardino Strait. Nimitz believed a confrontation was imminent. On the sixteenth, he sent a dispatch to Spruance: "On the eve of a possible fleet action you and the officers and men under your command have the confidence of the naval service and the country. We count on you to make the victory decisive."[47]

Spruance was still in the dark about the precise location of Ozawa's ships, but like Nimitz he was now sure there would be a major fleet action. He finally got the information he wanted late on the seventeenth when the submarine *Cavalla* (SS 244) radioed that it was shadowing the Mobile Fleet about 350 nautical miles east of the Philippines and more than 800 miles west of TF-58. Mitscher guessed that if the Japanese held course to the east and TF-58 steamed west, the task force might find Ozawa within range of TF-58's aircraft late in the afternoon of the eighteenth. Yet the Americans could do nothing until TF-58 searchers found the Mobile Fleet. Before they did so, Ozawa's aircraft, enjoying their range advantage, made contact first, locating elements of TF-58 on the afternoon of the eighteenth.[48]

Once he realized that the Japanese were committing to battle, but still not having all the information he needed, Spruance made a critical decision. While he did not know where the Mobile Fleet was, he did know that the Japanese could remain out of range, shuttling attackers from their carriers into airfields on Guam. Furthermore, a separate element of the Japanese force might employ an "end run" to outflank TF-58 and disrupt the invasion. Spruance decided to have Turner withdraw most of the vulnerable transports a "safe" distance east of Saipan as TF-58 remained in its covering position just west of the Marianas. Mitscher was furious when he got the word. Burke, too, was livid. He and Thach hoped to convince Spruance to change his mind and release the carriers to surge west during the night and strike the Japanese at first light on the nineteenth. Yet when Mitscher asked for permission from Spruance to do so, Spruance remained adamantly opposed to the idea. He had decided: Mitscher's carriers would stay close to the Marianas in a purely defensive posture.[49]

Armed with accurate reports about the location of TF-58 from his long-range scouts, Ozawa launched his strike aircraft early on the nineteenth, while still beyond Mitscher's reach. Prevailing winds from the east allowed the Japanese carriers to remain on course toward the Marianas when conducting air operations, whereas Mitscher's carriers had to reverse direction from a westerly heading to gain enough wind over the deck for launches and recoveries. As unidentified aircraft ("bogeys") appeared on TF-58 radar screens about 0950, FDOs vectored defending Hellcats to intercept the attackers. The Japanese followed their initial attack with three more, the last of which ended about 1500. During the air battle, American submarines torpedoed and sank Ozawa's flagship, the new carrier *Taiho*, and the veteran *Shōkaku*. No TF-58 flattops suffered direct hits, although some were damaged by near misses. Altogether, fighters and antiaircraft fire downed 261 Japanese aircraft, the most ever in a single day of aerial combat; the Americans lost only 31. Even worse for the Japanese were the irreplaceable carrier pilots and aircrew who lost their lives that day. One of the *Lexington*'s fighter pilots thought the battle resembled an "old-time turkey shoot," not realizing at the time that he had experienced an American victory that heralded the end of Japanese carrier-based air power.[50]

Ozawa had lost two big carriers and hundreds of aircraft and crews, yet he anticipated getting back into the fray after his ships refueled and regrouped. Spruance, still not certain of the location of the Mobile Fleet and worried that a detached element of the Japanese force might pounce from an unexpected direction, hesitated in granting Mitscher permission to pursue. He was also mindful that Mitscher's carriers were more than three hundred miles from Ozawa; they would have to make good time to the west to bring the Japanese within range, all while backtracking to conduct air operations. Nevertheless, Spruance authorized Mitscher to steam westward in hopes of contacting the Japanese, while releasing one of TF-58's task groups to refuel and stay close to Saipan. Mitscher's searchers did not sight Ozawa's carriers until after 1530. Mitscher knew that if he did not act quickly the enemy would disappear into the gloom. At 1600, realizing that he would have to recover aircraft after dark, he ordered his three carrier task groups to launch full deckload strikes.[51]

Within a half-hour, fighters, dive-bombers, and torpedo planes roared off from the American carriers, the airmen justifiably anxious about whether they would have enough fuel to return to their ships. About two hours later and just thirty minutes before sunset, they found and attacked the Japanese Mobile Fleet, hitting the big *Zuikaku*, the light carriers *Junyō* and *Chiyoda*, and the *Hiyō*, which exploded in a fireball and sank. The battleship *Haruna* was struck by bombs, as were three oilers, two of which went down. Up to sixty aircraft were most likely lost defending the remnants of the Mobile Fleet as it withdrew out of range. TF-58 aviators, low on fuel and shrouded by darkness, had to find their way back to their carriers, which had closed some of the distance after they had launched. The flattops illuminated their flight decks, and other ships turned on searchlights to guide the fliers to safety. Some officers were concerned that illumination would attract the attention of enemy subs, but Thach preferred that the carriers light their decks "like an airport runway." Pilots who had not ditched alighted on any carrier they could find, sometimes jumping the arresting gear, crashing or colliding with the steel wire barriers protecting planes parked forward. Nevertheless, 140 aircraft were recovered, although 86 planes and their pilots and crews went missing, most of whom were plucked from the water by TF-58 destroyers and floatplanes, submarines, and "Dumbo" flying boats out of Saipan.[52]

There remained a chance on the morning of the twenty-first that TF-58 could still catch the Mobile Fleet. Mitscher launched a strike shortly after dawn, but his aircraft failed to contact the Japanese, now more than 350 miles distant. Later that morning, the destroyer *Dortch* (DD 670) transferred McCain from the *Indianapolis* to the *Lexington*, where he joined Thach, Mitscher, and Reeves. Finally realizing that pursuit of the Japanese was a forlorn hope, Spruance abandoned offensive air operations on the evening of the twenty-first, and the weary ships and sailors headed back toward Saipan, refueling along the way. Three days later, on the twenty-fourth, McCain reported to Admiral Clark on the *Hornet* (CV 12) for TG-58.1's strike against Japanese air power in the Bonins. Operation Jocko, as Mitscher called it, counted another sixty-six enemy aircraft destroyed. On the twenty-seventh, Clark's group entered the big lagoon at Eniwetok, the new advance base in the Marshalls, where they reunited with other elements of the task force. Eager to have his observers back from temporary duty with the Fifth Fleet, Halsey told Spruance on the twenty-fourth that he "would greatly appreciate" their "early return to Pearl" so that they could begin planning for the next phase of operations in the Central Pacific. He had to wait until the thirtieth, when McCain and his staff arrived at Pearl Harbor. After meetings with Halsey and others, McCain flew to the mainland on 3 July and was back at his desk in Washington on the sixth.[53]

Critiques of the Battle of the Philippine Sea were not long in coming. Towers remarked that he was "terribly disappointed about recent naval actions west of the Marianas" and later charged that Spruance's "ultra-conservatism" had allowed most of Ozawa's carriers to escape. Thach thought that the TF-58 losses incurred during the night of the twentieth would not have happened "if we'd done the right thing" and gone after the Japanese the day before. Mitscher's action report reflected sentiments that Spruance had blundered in not ordering TF-58 to pursue the Japanese on the night of 18–19 June: "The enemy had escaped. He had been badly hurt by one aggressive carrier air strike, at the one time he was within range. His fleet was not sunk." Clark and other aviators refuted those who believed that Spruance had been right to keep Mitscher close to Saipan to cover the invasion force, arguing that a far superior defense would have been to take the battle directly to the Japanese Mobile Fleet.[54] McCain was silent. Like King, who praised Spruance during a visit to Saipan in July, he prudently avoided criticizing Spruance or saying anything that might have generated more friction at the top levels of command.

In the analysis of the battle McCain sent to Mitscher, he lauded the accuracy of the fleet's antiaircraft fire, recommended better coordination of combat air patrol (CAP) radio frequencies to improve early warning of enemy attacks, and urged that ships and aircraft share similar markings for rapid identification. Although he did not say so, we can safely infer that he agreed with Thach, Towers, and others that Spruance had made a mistake by keeping TF-58 close to Saipan and that he had erred in not allowing Mitscher to proceed westward to engage Ozawa's Mobile Fleet. Spruance's caution had led to a costly missed opportunity. On the other hand, McCain may have appreciated that Spruance, as fleet commander, was responsible for an entire operation involving a complex amalgam of air, sea, and amphibious resources and that, like his own experience at Guadalcanal, part of Spruance's mission was to ensure that American forces were not surprised by the Japanese. He might also have sympathized with the communication problems that still plagued the Navy almost two years after Guadalcanal. At 0105 on the nineteenth, a PBM flying boat signaled that it had picked up elements of the Japanese fleet, yet the VP's message did not get to Spruance until more than eight hours later. The inexplicably long delay in getting the PBM sighting report to Spruance would have resonated with McCain, whose own VP search reports, much to Fletcher's dismay, had been notoriously tardy. He also noted that among the task group commanders, Clark and Reeves shared his own fighting spirit and penchant for aggressiveness. Harrill, relieved of his task group command on 29 June due to an acute case of appendicitis, proved indecisive in battle. He would not have been on McCain's short list for continuing in command even if he had been in good health.[55]

McCain and Thach stressed the effectiveness of TF-58 in suppressing if not totally neutralizing Japanese air power in the Marianas and Bonins. Three days of intensive fighter sweeps established air superiority before the Saipan landings, while night fighters added a twenty-four-hour dimension to fleet air power. Equipping F6F-3 Hellcats with 500-pound bombs made them into flexible fighter-bombers, deadly against both land targets and shipping. TF-58's air defense also left a generally positive impression. The disposition of the task force, its individual groups, radar early warning, fighter direction, CAP, and the sophisticated layers of antiaircraft fire devastated the Japanese attackers on the nineteenth. As well as fighter direction and air defense worked for TF-58 while it was tied to Saipan, both men wondered if an equally effective approach might have been achieved by going after Japanese aircraft more aggressively at the source, either on the ground or on their carriers.[56]

One cannot overstate the significance of the Battle of the Philippine Sea. It was a decisive victory, the great fleet engagement in the western Pacific that both adversaries had planned to fight for almost fifty years. This battle, and not Midway two years before, was the pivotal battle of the Pacific War. Neither McCain nor anyone else at the time knew that they had been part of the greatest carrier battle of all time and that there would never be another encounter of this type or scale. Nor were they aware that Japan's carriers had been effectively eliminated as a fighting force. As far as they knew, the Japanese still had at least six operational carriers, that their land-based air forces remained mostly intact, and that the fast carriers still had a major role in projecting naval sea and air power from the Marianas to Japan's inner defenses.

McCain's month with the Fifth Fleet and Task Force 58 yielded invaluable firsthand experience and a wealth of knowledge about carrier and amphibious operations that he and his able staff drew on when they assumed their responsibilities in carrier task force command. For better or worse, McCain's performance in the months that lay ahead would determine his reputation and legacy among the leaders of the new air navy.

CHAPTER 7

Task Force Command

O rders to assume the Pacific carrier task force command arrived at McCain's desk in Main Navy on 25 July. While McCain had been with Task Force 58 in the Marianas, Forrestal had determined that Vice Adm. Aubrey Fitch would replace him as DCNO (Air), beginning on 1 August. Leaving Rear Adm. Arthur Radford to fill in briefly as acting DCNO (Air), McCain and Thach were off to San Francisco, and from there took the overnight hop to Hawaii in one of Nimitz's flag planes, landing at Pearl Harbor on 8 August. McCain had understood that he would take over as commander, Fast Carrier Task Force Pacific, Mitscher's official billet with the Fifth Fleet, when Fifth Fleet transitioned to Third Fleet under Halsey, but that changed while he was on his way out to Pearl Harbor. On the tenth, two days after he reported for duty at Pearl, he learned that King had divided the carrier task force command: Mitscher would stay on as the new commander, First Fast Carrier Task Force Pacific, and McCain became commander, Second Fast Carrier Task Force Pacific, both serving in what was now Task Force 38 in Halsey's Third Fleet. McCain would get more hands-on experience, temporarily commanding TG-38.1 under Mitscher in a "makee-learn" orientation role.[1]

That McCain was uncomfortable with the arrangement is an understatement. As the senior of the two officers, he would now be subordinate to Mitscher, if only for a time. He suspected that Mitscher had maneuvered behind the scenes to get King and Nimitz to agree to the divided command and was incensed that Mitscher had decided to stay on for several more months instead of rotating out with Spruance when Halsey took over the Third Fleet. Nor was he placated by King's assurances that he "was to carry on in the same manner as Vice Admiral Mitscher; that is, he would act as a Carrier Task Force Commander, which would enable Cincpac to alternate McCain and Mitscher in the same manner as it planned to rotate Admiral Spruance and Admiral Halsey." Moreover, Mitscher obstinately refused to lend any of his staff to McCain. Feeling doubly slighted, McCain appealed

to Towers, who backed Mitscher but conceded that McCain might temporarily use some of Jocko Clark's former TG-58.1 staff. Following subsequent
meetings with McCain, Towers, and Halsey, Nimitz rejected McCain's pleas
that it was his turn to take over the fast carriers.[2]

It was now a fait accompli; Mitscher would hold on to the carrier task
force command through the completion of the Marianas campaign and the
beginning of the next stage of the Pacific offensive. The JCS proposed that
Nimitz's and MacArthur's forces converge on the southern Philippines,
from which they could advance on Luzon or Formosa, assault Okinawa in
the Ryukyus, and jump from there to Kyushu in the home islands. Mindanao was the first objective, with the invasion tentatively set for 15
November, followed by Leyte. Airfields on Peleliu in the Palaus and on
Morotai in the Halmaheras would have to be established first, and Yap and
Ulithi in the western Carolines either occupied or neutralized. Nimitz and
MacArthur agreed about Mindanao and Leyte, but Nimitz wanted to bypass
Luzon, the largest island and home of the capital Manila, which MacAr-
thur had pledged to liberate, in favor of Formosa, allowing Allied forces to
link up with the Chinese on the mainland and augment Army Air Forces
B-29 bases in the Marianas. After MacArthur and Nimitz met with Roos-
evelt in Hawaii in late July, MacArthur seemed to have made his case for
Luzon. The Joint Chiefs decided to wait until after the Leyte landings on
20 December before making a firm decision about either Luzon or Formosa.[3]

Meanwhile, a few days after McCain had packed up to leave Washington for the Pacific, Kate took a train to San Diego and the family's small
two-story house at 625 A Avenue in Coronado. John and Kate had bought
the house in 1942, one of three designed in the Spanish Moderne style
by the renowned naval architect Charles Frederick Herreshoff. While on
active duty with the Navy, the president's youngest son John lived in the
second Herreshoff house facing the street; coincidentally Franklin, Eleanor,
and son James stopped there for lunch on 19 July. Two days later, after visiting the naval hospital and the amphibious training center in San Diego,
Roosevelt boarded the heavy cruiser *Baltimore* (CA 68) for Honolulu and
his showdown with Nimitz and MacArthur.[4]

At Pearl, McCain and Thach spent a week in meetings with Nimitz, Halsey, McMorris, and Towers, during which McCain was brought up
to date on the new command arrangements and with the strategic decisions that had been made about the future campaigns in the Pacific. In
the interim, with little time to spare and without guidance from Mitscher,

McCain had been busy assembling his staff and drafting plans for his task group. Following his own policy, his chief of staff had to be a nonaviator. He and Thach agreed that Rear Adm. Wilder D. Baker was the right man for the job. A 1914 Academy graduate, Baker had been a trailblazer in introducing operations research to the administration of antisubmarine warfare in the Atlantic, had commanded a cruiser division in Harrill's TG-58.4, and, when Harrill had fallen ill, temporarily relieved him in command of the carrier task group. Baker had the necessary knowledge and experience, and, like Thach, was not a "yes man" who would be reluctant to share uncomfortable realities with his boss.[5]

Rounding out McCain's brain trust were Lt. Cdr. Gordon D. Cady, former commanding officer of VF-11, who came on board as assistant operations officer; Lt. Cdr. J. N. MacInnes as the group's fighter director officer; Lt. William T. Longstreth, an experienced ACIO, as the flag intelligence officer; and Cdr. James H. Hean as navigation and gunnery officer. Paperwork—routine and otherwise—fell to a reserve lieutenant, Charles A. Sisson, as McCain's flag secretary. Thach's air operations officer was Cdr. Noel A. M. Gayler, who had served with Thach in VF-3. Gayler later recounted that McCain "made no pretense of being a great technician of any kind, but he was a fighter and a good leader" who "had great shrewdness in appraising people and knew how to get people to work for him." Gayler understood that McCain preferred to delegate responsibility to his staff, which he recounted was "essentially run" by Thach.[6]

McCain arrived at the fleet anchorage in Eniwetok on 18 August and hoisted his flag in the *Wasp* (CV 18), wearing two hats as commander of TG-58.1 and commander, Second Fast Carrier Task Force. That afternoon McCain went over to the *Lexington* to confer with Mitscher and his staff about the new task group arrangement and other matters pertinent to the forthcoming operations. His motive may also have been to persuade Mitscher to promise to turn the task force over to him as soon as possible and before the next phase of the Pacific offensive. If that was the agenda, he got nowhere. In fact, Mitscher, apparently dismissing McCain as another of the despised "Johnny-Come-Lately" usurpers, holed up in his sea cabin and refused even to greet McCain when he arrived on board. Mitscher's petulance was supremely unprofessional and demeaning to both him and his command. A short meeting finally did ensue, but it changed nothing, although Clark shifted to the *Hornet* in the task group for the time being to assist McCain and his staff. McCain had nothing more to say about the incident than "Pete [Mitscher] thought he still had plenty of work to do."[7]

In addition to the *Wasp* and the *Hornet*, McCain's newly constituted task group included the light carriers *Cowpens* (CVL 25) and *Belleau Wood* (CVL 24), from Rear Adm. Ralph Davison's TG-58.4, replacing the *Monterey* (CVL 26), as well as the heavy cruisers *Boston* (CA 69) and *Canberra* (CA 70), and five destroyers. At 0623 on 21 August, McCain's ships got under way for two days of flight and gunnery drills in the vicinity of Eniwetok. On the twenty-sixth, McCain's task group became TF-38.1 as Task Force 58 mutated into Task Force 38, Halsey relieved Spruance, and Fifth Fleet became Third Fleet. TG-38.1 was now the largest of four task groups. It included the carriers *Wasp*, *Hornet*, *Cowpens*, and *Belleau Wood*; heavy cruisers *Boston*, *Canberra*, and *Wichita* (CA 45); a screen of eleven destroyers; and a surface strike unit consisting of the three cruisers and three destroyers. According to Cincpac's operations plan (Op Plan 6-44 of 21 July) and Halsey's Op Plan 14-44 of 1 August, the task force was to support amphibious landings at Peleliu, Morotai, and Ulithi, a circlet of sand and coral that Halsey coveted as an advance fleet anchorage, together with air strikes in the southern Philippines in preparation for the Mindanao invasion. Both plans added wording that reflected Nimitz's dismay that Japanese units had escaped after the Battle of the Philippine Sea: Halsey's "primary task" was to engage a "major portion of the enemy fleet" should it make an appearance.[8]

About 0500 on the twenty-ninth, McCain's task group stood out from Eniwetok, followed at roughly one-hour intervals by Rear Adm. Gerald Bogan's TG-38.2 and Rear Adm. Frederick Sherman's TG-38.3. Davison's group had sortied a day earlier to attack the Bonins before covering the Peleliu operation. There were no fewer than sixteen fast carriers in the task force, including seven of the new *Essex* class. Halsey, in the fast battleship *New Jersey* (BB 62), outfitted as a flagship with staterooms, conference room, communications spaces, and air conditioning, had left Pearl Harbor on the twenty-fourth and did not rendezvous with TF-38 until 11 September. On the thirty-first, Halsey had informed McCain that after hitting the Palaus on 6–8 September, TG-38.1 was to break off from TF-38 to support Vice Adm. Thomas Kinkaid's South West Pacific Seventh Fleet operations at Morotai on 15 and 16 September (code-named Tradewind). McCain's voluminous 26 August operation order (Op Order 1-44), prepared by Wilder Baker, specified strikes against aircraft, airfields, shipping, and ground targets in support of the Palaus and Morotai operations; Ulithi and Yap were also objectives. Although the group's principal job was supporting amphibious operations, McCain's plan added that "in case opportunity for the destruction of major portion of the Japanese fleet offers or can be created, such destruction will become the primary task." The wording of McCain's order almost exactly followed that of Nimitz's and Halsey's earlier plans.[9]

Only one day out and south of Eniwetok, McCain's group experienced the loss of Thach's assistant operations officer, Gordon Cady, who crash landed on the *Belleau Wood*. The arresting hook on his Hellcat sheared off, and the airplane flipped on its back and collided with the crash barrier. Cady suffered a fractured skull and died two hours after the accident. He was buried at sea the following day. Not until November did Thach bring in as Cady's replacement Lt. Cdr. William Leonard, another VF-11 veteran who had also been his VF-3 executive officer at Midway.[10]

McCain's group refueled northeast of Manus on 2 September, before heading northwest to a point about 150 miles south of the Palaus. On the afternoon of the sixth, fighters from McCain's group assaulted airfields on Ngesbus, Angaur, and Babelthaup islands. More strikes followed on the seventh and eighth, concentrating on enemy antiaircraft installations, warehouses, and fuel dumps, as well as Saipan Town and a phosphate plant on Angaur. McCain's aircraft dropped napalm bombs, the first time this jellied-gasoline incendiary weapon had been used by carrier planes, although it may have been employed earlier on Saipan. All told, the group launched more than four hundred sorties over three days before withdrawing on the eighth with TG-38.2 and TG-38.3 for an overnight twenty-five-knot dash into Mindanao.[11]

At 0555 on the ninth, TG-38.1 launched a fighter sweep against airfields and shipping in southern Mindanao, the first strikes against the Philippines by carrier aircraft. The Japanese offered only minor resistance in the air and on the ground, although the *Hornet*'s radar picked up a formation of bogeys that closed to within ninety miles of the task group before they turned back. Later, the group's CAP shot down two Japanese aircraft, one of them within twenty-five miles of the flattops. The group flew 183 sorties against targets on Mindanao the following day before pulling away about noon to rendezvous with the refueling group about three hundred miles east of the islands. Given the paucity of targets on Mindanao, Mitscher directed the three task groups to concentrate on Cebu and Negros Islands in the Visayas. On the twelfth and thirteenth, aircraft from McCain's group flew more than 570 offensive missions, claiming forty-eight enemy planes destroyed in the air and twenty-eight on the ground, along with one large and five small cargo ships sunk. Hangars, docks, and barracks were also struck. CAP fighters intercepted and shot down two Japanese intruders. At 1830 on the thirteenth, McCain's group swung away from the task force to join the Seventh Fleet for the Morotai operation.[12]

On 14 September, TG-38.1 bombed Japanese aircraft, ground installations, and shipping in the northern Celebes while en route to Morotai. According to the group's war diary, the strikes demonstrated the extraordinary mobility and offensive power of the fast carriers, which were capable of "picking a different target daily and moving during the night to distances from 200 to 250 miles to a new area for attacks." On the fifteenth, McCain's force cruised about fifty miles due north of Morotai, providing cover for the landings by Kinkaid's Task Force 77. Fighters strafed airfields on Morotai and hit aircraft on the ground at Langoan in the Celebes. Facing no opposition either in the air or on the ground, Kinkaid released McCain's group on the afternoon of the sixteenth. Wishing them "good luck," he thanked TG-38.1 for its "excellent assistance and cooperation" during one of the least costly amphibious operations of the Pacific War. In contrast, the simultaneous invasion of Peleliu in the Palaus, supported by TG-38.4, met stiff resistance and turned out to be much longer and more bloody than anticipated.[13]

Evidence of the weakness of Japanese air power in Mindanao, coupled with a report from a *Hornet* aviator who had been shot down off Leyte and rescued by friendly Filipinos, caused Halsey to reconsider the entire Philippines operation. He advised Nimitz on 13 September that Leyte was "wide open" and suggested that he consider canceling the Mindanao invasion and send an invasion force directly into Leyte. Other than Ulithi, it was not necessary to seize Yap or any other islands in the western Carolines; unfortunately, it was too late to cancel the invasion of Peleliu. Nimitz liked the idea of diverting forces assigned to taking Yap and Mindanao to Leyte and quickly informed King, who in turn broached the idea with Marshall and the Joint Chiefs, then meeting with Roosevelt, Churchill, and the Combined Chiefs of Staff in Quebec. On the fifteenth, the JCS authorized the Leyte operation (code-named King-II) to begin on 20 October, exactly two months sooner than previously planned.[14]

TF-38 now turned its attention to the destruction of Japanese aircraft and shipping in and around Luzon, while still fulfilling its commitment to support the Marines struggling to secure Peleliu. From Morotai, McCain's carriers steamed northeast, refueling and receiving aircraft replacements on the seventeenth; that day the *Monterey* joined McCain's group, relieving the *Belleau Wood*, which rejoined Davison's TG-38.4. TG-38.1 reunited with TGs 38.2 and 38.3 at noon on the eighteenth about 120 miles west of the Palaus. McCain's ships topped off with fuel on the morning of the nineteenth, then at 1330 turned northwest with the task force to attack targets on Luzon at daybreak on 21 September.[15]

Hidden under cloud cover and enforcing radio silence, TG-38.1, in conjunction with Mitscher's other two groups, closed the east coast of Luzon overnight; by radio McCain warned his aviators to anticipate "hot fighting over land and water" the next morning. In position about ninety miles off Polillo Island by 0600 on the twenty-first, McCain's task group detected enemy reconnaissance aircraft ("snoopers") almost immediately, but winds gusting to thirty-five knots and rain squalls caused a delay of more than an hour in launching the group's CAP and other patrols. At 0734, and only thirty miles from the task group, *Hornet* fighters on CAP shot down a Yokosuka D4Y ("Judy") dive-bomber that had been snooping the American ships. McCain's group did not get off its first strikes, aimed at shipping in Manila Bay, until 0758. In much improved weather, fighters and bombers found "abundant" targets, sinking fifteen cargo ships, four oilers, a destroyer, a frigate, and a repair vessel. Upwards of twenty-five aircraft were thought to be destroyed in the air or on the ground. Back at Pearl, Towers crowed that the task force had enjoyed "wonderful success" in the raids and that the Japanese had "no effective defense against these heavy carrier strikes."[16]

Severe weather again interfered with flight operations on the twenty-second. Before daylight, radar picked up a bogey approaching at low altitude, and the *Hornet* catapulted four fighters to intercept it. The snooper penetrated Sherman's TG-38.3 screen and circled the task group for an hour as the ships' antiaircraft guns blazed away without effect. The *Hornet*'s interceptors finally shot it down, although McCain believed the plane's "beautiful job of shadowing" had alerted the Japanese to the position of the task force. Sure enough, shortly after McCain's group launched its first strikes of the day, between six and eight Japanese fighters sneaked in under the clouds to attack McCain's group. Three dropped bombs—all of which missed the flattops as they maneuvered independently at twenty-five knots—and heavy antiaircraft fire brought down two of the enemy. Yet two *Hornet* crewmembers were killed by Japanese strafing. The threat of a typhoon forming east of the task force caused Mitscher to cancel further offensive operations, and that evening the carriers withdrew at high speed to the south and east. In two raids that day, TG-38.1 sank four tankers and a cargo ship while claiming damage to a dry dock, two more cargo ships, and another tanker. Warehouses and dock facilities were also extensively damaged or destroyed. Six more enemy planes were shot down or destroyed on the ground.[17]

Japanese shipping and aircraft in the Visayas were the next priority for McCain's group. About noon on 23 September, TG-38.1 refueled from three oilers about 250 miles east of Leyte and took on replacement aircraft and pilots from the escort carrier *Nassau* (CVE 16). That evening Mitscher's three TF-38 carrier groups broke off from the refueling group and sprinted northwest at twenty-one knots overnight, pulling up by dawn about sixty miles off San Bernardino Strait, the passage separating Luzon from the island of Samar. McCain's group flew strikes all day, concentrating on airfields and shipping on and around Negros, Cebu, and Panay, with good results. Four cargo ships and transports, destroyers or destroyer escorts, and a host of small craft were either damaged or sunk. Twenty planes were destroyed or damaged on the ground. After recovering aircraft, McCain's group separated from the task force and withdrew south and east, skirting north of the Palaus and arriving at Manus on the afternoon of the twenty-eighth. Bogan's TG-38.2 and Sherman's TG-38.3 followed McCain's group out of the combat area a few days later, putting in at Ulithi, which had been seized on 23 September.[18]

When the ships of McCain's Task Group 38.1 dropped anchor in spacious Seeadler Harbor on the eastern extremity of Manus, they had been at sea for nearly thirty-one days. As the group provisioned and rearmed and its officers and men enjoyed a well-earned respite from the war, McCain and his staff assessed the results of the previous month's operations. By their estimates, the group's aircraft had downed 77 enemy planes and destroyed another 125 on the ground. Antiaircraft fire from ships in the task group splashed 15 Japanese planes. As the historian Barrett Tillman has pointed out, claims for aircraft destroyed in aerial combat were notoriously exaggerated, sometimes by up to 100 percent. For the Battle of the Philippine Sea, Tillman determined that the claims of Japanese aircraft shot down exceeded reality by 57 percent, and a Naval War College study of the Battle of Leyte Gulf found that Japanese aircraft losses were 64 percent of Allied claims. If we assume 64 percent of claims was also the case for TG-38.1 in its September operations, the actual results were perhaps 50 enemy planes shot down by the group's aircraft and maybe 80 more destroyed on the ground. Estimates that 37 ships had been sunk and 61 damaged were also most likely similarly exaggerated, as was the destruction to airfields, barracks, warehouses, docks, and industrial plants. In his action report of 7 October, McCain acknowledged that the damage estimates were primarily based on pilots' accounts and could not always be verified by before-and-after photos of the targets. Inevitably, there had been a cost, both human and material. Twenty-one pilots and crew had been killed and 27 aircraft lost due to enemy action or operational accidents.[19]

McCain and his staff were confident that TG-38.1—and carrier air power in general—had delivered devastating blows to Japanese air and sea power in and around the Philippines. On the other hand, they cautioned that "there is a great deal of room for improvement" in nearly all areas of task group organization and operations. They found, for example, that the group's Helldivers had suffered both total and percentage losses higher than those of other aircraft (six of nineteen, or more than 31 percent of combat losses) and recommended that they be removed from the carrier air groups "immediately" and that Hellcats and F4U Corsairs replace them in the dive-bombing capacity. "Both the Hellcat and the Corsair have been proven time and again in combat and by carefully measured tests in practice to be more accurate in DIVE bombing than any other aircraft and least likely to be shot down," McCain's report concluded. As the carriers closed on the Japanese home islands, "where there are large numbers of enemy land based planes," the report stressed that "it is common sense of the plainest and most ordinary garden variety that our carriers should be considered and used only as fighter strips." Night fighters proved useful against snoopers invading task group air space before dawn and immediately after nightfall, as well as in bad weather. The report recommended that a separate night fighter task group be organized when more aircraft and crews became available. Fighter direction, on the whole, was good, although the performance of search radars could have been better, and there were difficulties tracking antisnooper and antisubmarine patrols simultaneously.[20]

Communications shortcomings, McCain reported, stemmed from inadequate equipment and a dearth of trained personnel, as well as interference among VHF radio nets and direction finders. Intelligence was generally good. Nevertheless, at times McCain found himself inundated with multiple copies of captured enemy documents that had "little interest or bearing on our immediate or future operations." Much of that information could be eliminated or condensed for flag use. Flag plot itself was too small to accommodate the ACIO, other personnel, charts, and materials needed for complex carrier task force operations. He preferred that flag plot be located close to the flattop's Combat Information Center, which was not going to happen after the CIC had been removed from all *Essex*-class carrier islands to more protected locations on the gallery decks below the flight decks. Finally, he indicated that there was an urgent need for better photography of ground targets, since pilot reports were sometimes 100 percent wrong about numbers of aircraft damaged or destroyed. McCain's report recommended that the task group receive an additional F6F photo plane and that carrier photo labs be expanded to handle the anticipated volume of photographs.[21]

Whereas communications and intelligence needed attention, logistics did not. McCain's task group relied on the Third Fleet's at-sea logistics group, TG-30.8, under the command of Capt. Jasper T. Acuff. By the fall of 1944, the group consisted of thirty-four oilers, eleven escort carriers, and more than fifty destroyers and destroyer escorts, rotating in support of the fast carriers and other elements of the fleet. TG-30.8 escort carriers provided air cover and antisubmarine defense for the logistics force and transferred replacement aircraft and personnel. Acuff coordinated with Halsey in scheduling fuelings for the task group from his oilers, while McCain topped off destroyers from his flattops at intervals between rendezvous with the replenishment group. McCain remarked that "all fueling proceeded smoothly due to the efficiency and cooperation of the Tanker Group," with some of the evolutions taking only a little more than six hours as the ships maintained speeds of up to twelve knots.[22] He did not state it in his report, but it is safe to conclude that McCain understood how critical the at-sea logistics group was to the mobility and flexibility of the fast carriers and the success of their operations in and around the Philippines.

While elements of TF-38 laid over at Ulithi and Manus, King, Nimitz, Spruance, and their staffs met in San Francisco to formulate plans for the next phases of the Pacific War. At the close of the three-day meeting on 1 October, King finally conceded that Luzon was preferable to Formosa as the next objective, to be followed by a two-stage assault on Japan along two axes. Tentatively planned for 20 January 1945, Iwo Jima in the Bonins, roughly midway between the Marianas and Tokyo, would be a target for Nimitz's Pacific Fleet forces. Closely following Iwo Jima would be a more ambitious operation, set for 1 March, aimed at the Ryukyus, or the Nansei Shoto, where a combined Army and Marine force would seize the big island of Okinawa, which in turn would serve as a springboard for the invasion of Japan itself. The plan and timetable received approval from the Joint Chiefs two days later.[23]

Of more immediate urgency, with less than three weeks to spare, was planning for the Leyte invasion. Under MacArthur's South West Pacific command, Kinkaid's Central Philippines Attack Force, organized as Task Force 77, was to carry out the amphibious landing, covered by Seventh Fleet escort carriers. Mitscher's TF-38 would provide the principal air support. According to Nimitz's King-II operation plan (Op Plan 8-44 of 27 September) Halsey's flattops were to neutralize enemy air and shipping in Formosa, Luzon, the Visayas, and Mindanao starting nine days before the landings. TF-38 would be responsible for air support for the ground forces during and for as long as necessary after the landings. Nimitz directed Halsey that "in case opportunity for destruction of major portion of the enemy fleet is offered or can be created, such destruction becomes the primary task." Halsey reciprocated: "My goal is the same as yours—to completely annihilate the Jap fleet if the opportunity offers." Halsey's plan (Op Order 21-44) of 3 October called for raids on Okinawa, Formosa, Luzon, and northern Leyte starting on 10 October, followed by attacks on Leyte and the Visayas on the sixteenth and seventeenth, and operations in direct support of the amphibious operation on the twentieth. Thereafter, Third Fleet would offer "strategic support" by strikes against enemy air and sea forces that might menace the operation. A sentence echoed Nimitz's directive: "If opportunity exists or can be created to destroy a major portion of enemy fleet, this becomes primary task." A potential problem was that the divided command responsibility precluded any direct communication between Halsey and Kinkaid and that all messages had to be routed through Nimitz and MacArthur.[24]

At this point, as planning proceeded for the Leyte operation, McCain might have believed—or even pleaded—that he had proved himself sufficiently to assume command of the fast carriers from Mitscher. Yet Halsey, as Third Fleet commander, after discussions with Nimitz, had the "strong impression" that McCain still needed more "operative experience as a Task Group commander, before taking over the Carrier Task Force." In his estimation Mitscher's performance had been "so uniformly superb, that I have been loathe to let him go." So, as before, and at least through the end of October, Mitscher remained as commander, First Fast Carrier Task Force and commander, Task Force 38 riding in the *Lexington*, while McCain in the *Wasp* continued as commander, Second Fast Carrier Task Force and commander, Task Group 38.1, still reporting to Mitscher. Bogan stayed with TG-38.2, which included Halsey's flagship *New Jersey*, Sherman commanded TG-38.3, and Davison led TG-38.4. Vice Adm. Willis A. Lee's fast battleships, usually distributed among the task groups, constituted Task Force 34, an administrative unit that could be brought together as the tactical situation demanded. The most dramatic addition was the *Essex*-class *Hancock* (CV 19) to Bogan's task group, giving it five carriers instead of four. Mitscher's task force now totaled seventeen fast carriers with nearly 1,100 aircraft.[25]

McCain's plan for the Philippines campaign (Op Order 2-44 of 8 October) paralleled Halsey's operation order, including a paraphrasing of Nimitz's and Halsey's anticipation of a fleet action: "If an opportunity occurs, or can be created, to destroy enemy Naval forces this will become the primary mission." In addition to the carriers *Hornet*, *Wasp*, *Cowpens*, and *Monterey*, McCain's task group included the heavy cruisers *Wichita*, *Boston*, and *Canberra* and a screen of fifteen destroyers. As before, the cruisers, along with three destroyers, could be constituted if necessary as a surface striking unit. The scheme detailed three days of strikes against Japanese airfields in southern Okinawa and Formosa beginning on A-minus ten, after which, starting on 17 October, the task group would conduct fighter sweeps and strikes against targets on Luzon, the Visayas, and Leyte. For the most part, fighters and bombers from the big carriers would fly strike missions, while fighters from the *Cowpens* and *Monterey* would be responsible for CAP.[26]

It was no secret to the Japanese that after the conquest of the Marianas the Allies intended to take all or part of the Philippines, from which aircraft and ships would seriously compromise Japan's inner defense perimeter and sever lines of communication south to the strategically vital Netherlands East Indies. Admiral Toyoda Soemu's plan, known as *Shō-Gō*, included the sequential defense of the Philippines, Formosa, the Ryukyus, and finally Kyushu and the home islands. *Shō-1* proposed reinforcing the numbers of troops and aircraft in the Philippines and using shore-based aircraft from Luzon and Formosa as well as Admiral Ozawa Jisaburo's Mobile Fleet carriers. Yet, in contrast to earlier Japanese planning that focused on enemy naval—especially carrier—forces, the primary objective now was the destruction of landing craft, transports, and auxiliaries engaged in amphibious operations. Foundational to the strategy was the basic principle of interior lines of communication, which theoretically allowed the Japanese to shift forces quickly from one defensive position to another. The Japanese also reckoned that even though they faced a superior enemy, they still had sufficient capability to concentrate their land, sea, and air forces at the Philippines to fight and win a battle that would determine the outcome of the conflict.[27]

By 1117 on 2 October, McCain's group was under way from Manus, shaping a course north and west while conducting air exercises west of Yap. Adverse weather on the periphery of a typhoon that delayed the departure of TGs 38.2 and 38.3 from Ulithi caused the task force to cancel air operations for two days. In McCain's group the *Cowpens* suffered the loss of a torpedo plane and three fighters that had been wrecked on the hangar deck as the carrier rolled in the heavy seas. On the evening of the seventh, McCain's, Bogan's, and Sherman's groups linked up with Davison's TG-38.4, which had been providing cover for the Peleliu operation. Together the task force refueled the next day in preparation for the run in to Okinawa. At 0600 on the tenth, about 130 miles southeast of Okinawa, TG-38.1 launched a fighter sweep to gain control of the air over Naha, followed by four strikes against the airfield that destroyed up to twenty aircraft on the ground, battered field installations, and sank seventeen small and medium-size vessels. Japanese antiaircraft fire caused the loss of four of McCain's aircraft. Shrugging off a perfunctory Japanese air attack on the task force that afternoon and evening, McCain's CAP claimed two enemy aircraft shot down.[28]

After the Okinawa strikes, the task force withdrew on a southwesterly course to meet the refueling group about three hundred miles northeast of Luzon early on the morning of the eleventh. That afternoon, McCain's and Davison's groups dispatched fighters to strike the Japanese airfield at Aparri on northern Luzon. Halsey conceived of the raid as a diversion, meant to deceive the Japanese into thinking that the carriers would continue the assault on Luzon and divert defenders from Formosa. The strike was a success insofar as it caught and destroyed fifteen aircraft on the ground, but it was a failure in its original intent. Within hours, Vice Admiral Fukudome Shigeru began preparations to meet the American attack on Formosa, with more than 230 Army and Navy fighters ready for battle, among them most of Ozawa's precious carrier aircraft and aviators.[29]

That the Big Blue Fleet was not going to achieve surprise was evident overnight on 11–12 October, when Japanese planes tracked Mitscher's flattops on their high-speed run to Formosa. Before sunrise the task force reached a point about one hundred miles east of the island, Bogan's and Sherman's groups in formation to the north, and McCain's and Davison's arrayed to the south. TG-38.1 launched its first strikes starting at 0605, aimed at targets in and around the major naval and air base at Takao (now Kaohsiung) on Formosa's southwestern coast. In the first strike (Strike Able) McCain's flagship *Wasp* sent out forty aircraft, half of which were F6F fighters and fighter-bombers and the rest evenly divided among TBMs and SB2Cs. They bombed, rocketed, and strafed an aluminum plant and docks and warehouses in and around Takao. This was only the first of three attacks by 325 planes from McCain's group, whose warplanes also rained bombs and rockets on an aircraft factory east of the city at Heito and on airfields at Toshien and Reygaro. An estimated sixty-eight aircraft were destroyed on the ground and another thirteen in the air. Airmen from the *Wasp*'s VF-14 alone shot down ten enemy fighters. Admiral Fukudome watched in dismay as nearly a third of his fighter defenses were annihilated: "Our fighters were nothing but so many eggs thrown at the stone wall of the indomitable enemy formation. In a brief one-sided encounter, the combat terminated in our total defeat." Nevertheless, intense antiaircraft fire brought down seven of McCain's fighters, including two Hellcat photo planes, along with a torpedo plane and a bomber; the *Wasp*'s VF-14 lost two of its number but both aviators were picked up by a rescue sub. Like a wounded animal, the Japanese lashed out that evening with an attack on the task force, primarily aimed at TGs 38.2 and 38.4, antiaircraft fire from which shot down eleven planes.[30]

McCain's group flung three strikes against Takao starting at 0621 on Friday the thirteenth. Fighters and bombers again targeted Heito, an airfield at Tainan, an aircraft repair and supply facility at Okayama, and another airfield on the island of Batan midway between Formosa and Luzon. The group claimed more than thirty aircraft destroyed on the ground, although poor visibility due to deteriorating weather and smoke from brushfires set by the Japanese made it virtually impossible to verify the count. Meanwhile, the Japanese reconnoitered the task force almost continuously and harassed the American ships with nearly fifty raids, none of which penetrated the screen.[31]

If McCain and Mitscher thought they would escape from Formosa without further losses, they soon found out otherwise. Late in the afternoon of the thirteenth, radar screens throughout the task force lit up with multiple bogeys, leading Mitscher to cancel a planned fourth strike in favor of beefing up the carriers' CAPs in anticipation of trouble. At 1823 in the growing darkness, sharp-eyed lookouts on the *Wichita* in McCain's group spotted ten or twelve twin-engine torpedo planes (probably a mix of Yokosuka P1Y "Franceses" and Mitsubishi G4M "Bettys") approaching low and fast from the east. McCain ordered an emergency turn to port away from the attackers and called for an increase in fleet speed to twenty-five knots. Five of the enemy aimed at the *Wasp*, whose antiaircraft fire splashed four. The *Hornet* got another. One of the Japanese aircraft loosed a torpedo intended for the *Hornet*, but it struck the *Canberra* instead. Badly hurt, the cruiser slowed to a stop when its engine and boiler rooms flooded, but it did not seem to be in imminent danger of sinking. McCain ordered the *Wichita* to take the vessel under tow, covered by two of his own destroyers and three cruisers and four destroyers from Sherman's group. Halsey and Mitscher concurred in McCain's decision to have his task group cover the salvage operation and ordered Bogan's and Sherman's groups to help too. By midnight, the *Wichita* and *Canberra* were making slow progress to the southeast.[32]

The decision to save the *Canberra* precipitated a change in plans for the Formosa operation. Originally there were to have been two days of attacks, but now that three of Mitscher's task groups would remain in the vicinity of Formosa covering the salvage effort, Halsey saw an opportunity to hit the Japanese again. He ordered McCain's, Bogan's, and Sherman's groups to launch strikes on the morning of the fourteenth, while Davison's would bomb Aparri again. Then Bogan's and Sherman's groups were to withdraw to refuel as previously scheduled on the fifteenth. TG-38.1, reinforced by the light cruiser *Houston* (CL 81), would stay behind for a day to assist the salvage group. Warned by Cincpac that more Japanese attacks were likely, McCain signaled Mitscher and Halsey on the morning of the fourteenth that "Task Group 38.1 cannot protect the CANBERRA this evening during twilight." He received no reply to his message. Halsey reasoned that the Japanese aircraft losses, plus those expected from the additional TF-38 attacks on the fourteenth, made the risk acceptable.[33]

At 0600 on the fourteenth, McCain's, Bogan's, and Sherman's groups launched fighter sweeps and strikes against airfields and other targets on Formosa. Seventy TG-38.1 aircraft swarmed over Takao, Tainan, Heito, and Okayama, causing extensive damage to facilities and destroying thirty-two planes on the ground. Fighters from the *Hornet* tangled with Japanese planes flying into Formosa from Luzon, bringing down eleven of the enemy, and the group's CAP parried a thrust by Japanese dive-bombers and fighters, adding another nineteen kills. Lt. Charles L. Stimpson of the *Hornet*'s VF-11 bagged five of the enemy himself, along with another pair probably destroyed. After TGs 38.2 and 38.3 left to rendezvous with the fueling group and after recovering his strike aircraft by 1100, McCain repositioned his formation forty miles to the northeast of the crippled *Canberra*. He guessed that the Japanese, as they had the night before, were most likely to approach from that direction, where his ships would be delineated against the setting sun.[34]

McCain was correct. As many as sixteen Japanese torpedo planes (again most likely Franceses and Bettys) swept in from the east about 1830, just as he had anticipated. Destroyers in the screen splashed five of the enemy within minutes of their appearance, and heavy antiaircraft fire downed another three, but others seeped through the task group's defenses. Although sharp, high-speed maneuvers allowed the carriers to fend off most of the attackers, the *Houston*, positioned off the *Wasp*'s port bow, was not so fortunate. At about 1845, a torpedo slammed into the cruiser, ripping open the ship's starboard side and flooding the forward engine room. Almost immediately, the ship went dead in the water and began listing to starboard. McCain ordered the *Boston* and three destroyers to assist, then advised its skipper, Capt. William W. Behrens, to abandon the vessel when it appeared likely it would break up and sink. After some of the ship's complement were taken off, Behrens decided that the cruiser could be saved, and the *Boston* took the *Houston* in tow before midnight. Radar tracked numerous bogeys, but fortunately there were no further Japanese raids that night. Halsey sent the light cruisers *San Diego* (CL 53) and *Oakland* (CL 95) and two destroyers from Bogan's group to replace the *Boston* and the three destroyers detached to assist the stricken *Houston*.[35]

Throughout the night and the next day, 15 October, the salvage group, now designated Task Group 30.3 (and half-jokingly referred to as Cripdiv 1) with the two damaged cruisers shepherded by another three cruisers and eight destroyers, gradually made its way clear of Formosa. Meanwhile, starting about two hours after sunrise, McCain's group came under relentless assault from the Japanese. There were eleven raids in all, totaling nearly eighty aircraft. The group's CAP shot down fifty-three planes and antiaircraft fire got one more before things cooled down that evening. Before retiring east-southeast to refuel with the rest of TF-38, McCain detached the *Cowpens* and the *Wichita* to help with protecting the *Canberra* and *Houston* group.[36]

When it became obvious that the Japanese had mistakenly concluded that the crippled ships and their escort were the remnants of TF-38, Halsey grasped an opportunity to turn a liability into an asset. If the Japanese dispatched elements of their fleet to "mop up" what they believed was left of the American forces, Halsey could surprise them and thus achieve their destruction in the fleet engagement he so wholeheartedly desired. Late on the fifteenth, he ordered TGs 38.2 and 38.3 to position themselves to launch searches the next morning in preparation for a possible fleet action. To deceive the Japanese further, TG-30.3 sent out radio messages describing the dire situation of the entire task force. For a while the trick seemed to work. The Japanese went after TG-30.3 again on the sixteenth and scored another torpedo hit on the unlucky *Houston*, which due to heroic damage control still managed to remain afloat. The Japanese also sent out a cruiser force, which Halsey hoped would presage a major fleet commitment, but it quickly withdrew on the sixteenth after encountering planes from Bogan's group. In company with TGs 38.2 and 38.3, McCain's carrier force took the extra time to refuel and replace aircraft and aircrew while waiting for the Japanese fleet that never came. The salvage group, in the meantime, staggered eastward toward Ulithi, where it arrived safely on the twenty-seventh. On Halsey's recommendation, McCain received the Navy Cross for his role in saving the two cruisers in the face of unremitting Japanese air assaults. The citation specifically noted how McCain had "skillfully interposed his task group between the two crippled ships and the hostile air formations" and lauded him for "inspiring leadership, brilliant tactics and initiative" in "conducting a smashing defense against the powerful attackers [that] succeeded in repulsing all efforts by the Japanese to sink the stricken vessels."[37]

A savage spectacle of naval air power, the ferocious engagement over Okinawa and Formosa was comparable to the climactic moments of the Battle of Britain and the epic Battle of the Philippine Sea. "For a time," chronicled the historian Clark Reynolds, the air combat was nothing short of "titanic." Japanese aircraft losses from 10 October to 17 October totaled more than 580, a terrible disaster that made it virtually impossible for them to support their carrier and surface forces in the defense of the Philippines. McCain reported that his group alone destroyed 325 aircraft either in the air or on the ground through 17 October, which, considering the usual inflated claim rate, equals 208, or 36 percent of the total destroyed by the task force. At the same time, TF-38 lost 89 aircraft and 64 pilots and aircrew, of which McCain's group lost 26 aircraft in combat and operationally. Twenty-two of McCain's pilots and aircrew died or were declared missing.[38]

In the aftermath of the Formosa air battle and the agonizing *Canberra/ Houston* rescue, McCain's task group looked like this on the morning of 16

October: carriers *Wasp*, *Hornet*, and *Monterey*; heavy cruisers *Chester* (CA 27), *Salt Lake City* (CA 25), *Pensacola* (CA 24); light cruisers *San Diego* and *Oakland*; and a screen of twelve destroyers. Bunkers brim full and pilots and crew at least slightly refreshed, TG-38.1 turned toward Luzon that evening. At 0558 the next day, the *Wasp* launched a search to the west and north of the task force and got a CAP into the air over the group. The *Wasp*'s search and a similar one by TG-38.2 revealed that no enemy surface forces were within three hundred miles of TF-38 and that if the Japanese were to intervene against the Leyte landings it would most likely be with small ships shuttling reinforcements and supplies in and out, much like the "Tokyo Express" used in the Solomons. Halsey sent out orders detailing plans for the next three days of operations. McCain's group would forgo attacks on the Visayas and join Davison's group for strikes on central Luzon on 18 and 19 October, while the other two carrier groups refueled and stood by to provide air support for the landings on the twentieth. As the senior commander, McCain would coordinate the operations of both task groups.[39]

On 17 October, once he had confirmed that the first advance forces were landing at Leyte, Admiral Toyoda signaled the beginning of *Shō-1*. Constituting what the Americans called the Northern Force, Ozawa's four carriers (*Zuikaku*, *Zuihō*, *Chitose*, and *Chiyoda*), augmented by two hybrid battleship-carriers (*Ise* and *Hyuga*), were to contact TF-38 and lure it away from the amphibious forces at Leyte. Ozawa's flattops had been stripped of most of their air groups and consumed in the air defense of Formosa. Moreover, many Mobile Fleet cruisers and destroyers had been transferred to the other Japanese forces. Ozawa's Mobile Fleet would thus be sacrificed so that battleships and cruisers commanded by Admiral Kurita Takeo, constituting the First Striking Force (the Center Force in American parlance), could cut through the central Philippines and emerge from San Bernardino Strait to pounce on the transports and covering ships in Leyte Gulf. A third group of old battleships and newer cruisers under Vice Admiral Nishimura Shoji (the Southern Force) would simultaneously advance through the Surigao Strait toward Leyte, later supported by still another group of cruisers and destroyers commanded by Vice Admiral Shima Kiyohide. They, too, would sacrifice themselves but would divert Kinkaid's heavy ships and escort carriers from the beachhead and leave the landing force uncovered and vulnerable to Kurita's superior firepower. There was one more element to the plan. Toyoda had in reserve to be used only if necessary the *shimpu* or Special Attack Corps, suicide pilots (known to the Americans as kamikazes) assembled by Vice Admiral Onishi Takajiro, whose planes would in effect function as deadly guided missiles. In sum, Toyoda's plan was a colossal, almost hopeless, roll of the dice that was almost sure to end in the loss of the Imperial Fleet and most, if not all, of the Japanese air forces.[40]

Beginning at dawn on the eighteenth from a position about a hundred miles east of Luzon, McCain's group launched fighter sweeps and a strike against targets in and around Manila. Japanese fighters rose in defense, thirty of which McCain's airmen reported shooting down in the ensuing battles over the capital. Lt. Edward B. Turner with the *Wasp*'s VF-14 claimed five kills alone that day. Another thirty Japanese aircraft were wiped out on the ground at Clark Field and Mabalacat. On the other hand, a search-and-strike mission against Legaspi and shipping in nearby San Bernardino Strait failed to turn up any targets at all. The next day, McCain's fighters encountered no resistance in the air, but antiaircraft fire got three bombers and one fighter. On the other side of the equation, three strikes destroyed twenty-three aircraft on the ground and tore up barracks, hangars, fuel storage tanks, and other buildings at Clark, Nielson, and Nichols Fields. Considering the usual rate of overclaims, TG-38.1 destroyed fifty-three aircraft in the air and on the ground on the eighteenth and nineteenth.[41]

McCain's and Davison's groups, now off the island of Samar in the pre-dawn hours of the twentieth—A-day—launched fighter sweeps of airfields at Batuan and Surigao and two strikes against Japanese defensive positions to provide cover for the Leyte landings. As the first of four Army divisions crossed the beaches at H-hour, 1000, the Navy fliers found no air opposition, and the Japanese did little initially to oppose MacArthur's troops. For the next two days, McCain's group stood by to provide air support, conducted routine air operations, refueled, and took on replacement aircraft, equipment, and pilots. The *Cowpens* rejoined the group on the morning of the twenty-first, and the *Hancock* on the afternoon of the twenty-second, which brought the group up to five fast carriers and demanded modifications in the cruising formation to ensure the carriers' optimum positions for air operations and antiaircraft defense.[42]

Because Japanese surface forces had retreated without attacking the wounded *Canberra* and *Houston*, and there was no specific intelligence about the location and movement of major Japanese units, there was nothing on 22 October to indicate a major fleet engagement was imminent. After nearly three weeks of continuous operations, Halsey decided that TF-38's groups needed to rotate one-by-one to Ulithi for replenishment. He wanted an "all out effort" to accomplish a twenty-four-hour turnaround, so Ulithi would not be much of a breather for the weary ships, sailors, and airmen. McCain received Halsey's orders and at 2230 on the twenty-second began withdrawing toward the east, striking Yap on the morning of 24 October as his flattops passed north of the island en route to Ulithi.[43]

Retiring to Ulithi with a third of TF-38's air power, McCain sent a message to King that inadvertently caused Nimitz to question his future as a carrier task force commander. The controversy emerged as a result of his candid assessment of the SB2C Helldiver. McCain stressed that because his task group had been "subjected to incessant attack" off Formosa, he had to conduct nearly constant fighter operations. "In this kind of war," he continued, the SB2C was more of a liability than an asset: it "complicates plane handling, and occupies vital space which should go to invaluable VF." By "flat order," if need be, all the Helldivers needed to be replaced by fighters, including the new Vought Corsairs, and that now was the time, and "not in the future" to effect the change. Carrier air groups were already in transition as a result of Nimitz's decision on 23 July that the Essex-class ships would have their air complements beefed up from thirty-six to fifty-four fighters, with a corresponding reduction in the number of dive-bombers. Yet Nimitz not only disapproved of McCain's proposal, but he subsequently warned him that his recommendation could be misconstrued as a blanket malediction against an airplane that could raise the ire of Washington politicos and such vital and long-time aircraft manufacturers as the Curtiss company. More troublesome potentially were Nimitz's worries that the stress of combat had caused McCain to become "over-wrought mentally." He sought and received assurances from Halsey that McCain was "fit in all respects to go, and he will relieve Mitscher" during the agreed-upon task force rotation.[44]

At this juncture, no one at Cincpac or Third Fleet knew that Toyoda's Shō-1 had begun. Ozawa's carriers had slipped out of the Inland Sea on the twentieth, followed the next day by Shima's group from the Pescadores and Kurita's and Nishimura's heavy ships from Brunei in Borneo on the twenty-second, with all the forces converging on the Philippines. American submarines and not naval aircraft were the first to sound the alarm and to draw blood, just as they had at the Battle of the Philippine Sea in June. On the morning of 23 October, Halsey received word that submarines had located Kurita's force at the southwestern entrance to the Palawan Passage. Even better news came later after the subs torpedoed and sank two heavy cruisers and badly damaged another. Halsey already had an inkling that something big

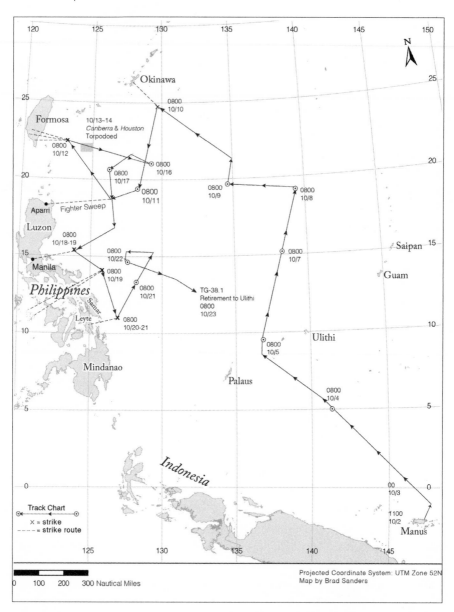

Map 3. Task Group 38.1 Operations, 2–23 October 1944; USS *Wasp* Track Chart, October 1944 (USS *Wasp* Action Report, Oct. 2–27, 1944, www.Fold3.com, accessed Feb. 20, 2013)

was brewing and had alerted Mitscher's three task groups to prepare for dawn searches to the west the next day, which they did. It did not take long before they found Kurita's ships at about 0800 on the twenty-fourth just south of Mindoro. Shortly after 0830, Halsey ordered Sherman and Bogan to launch strikes against the Japanese force; Davison's group had sent out a "reinforced" search and had to wait until they were recovered before dispatching its aircraft. At the same time, Halsey was worried about the possibility that a Japanese carrier force might ambush his three task groups from somewhere to the north. Thus, at 0846, he radioed McCain to cancel the Yap strike, recalling TG-38.1 with orders to rendezvous with Acuff's TG-30.8 oilers and to send out dawn searches to the north and northwest on the twenty-fifth. Within the hour, McCain's task group pirouetted left and doubled back on a roughly reciprocal course northwest at twenty-five knots.[45]

Throughout the morning of 24 October, McCain closely monitored the developing tactical situation at Leyte. Repeated strikes by Bogan's and Davison's groups on Kurita's Center Force as it transited the Sibuyan Sea resulted in sinking the superbattleship *Musashi* and badly damaging a heavy cruiser, but other ships were mostly unscathed. In what became known as the Battle of the Sibuyan Sea, the Americans believed they had inflicted much more damage than they actually had, and when Kurita reversed course to the west it appeared as if the Japanese had given up. TF-38 suffered too. Attacks by Japanese land-based aircraft on Sherman's TG-38.3 that morning resulted in severe bomb damage to the light carrier *Princeton* (CVL 23), which had to be sunk following a massive internal explosion. The reported losses in the Sibuyan Sea and Kurita's apparent withdrawal appeared to indicate a major Japanese defeat, thus guaranteeing the security of Kinkaid's forces at Leyte from intervention by surface ships. Any remaining Japanese ships that did manage to get through San Bernardino, Halsey reasoned, would be easily repelled by Lee's battleships. That afternoon he signaled Lee that his TF-34, with four battleships, five cruisers, and a large destroyer screen, would be consolidated upon receipt of subsequent messages. Kinkaid picked up the dispatch, but not the succeeding order Halsey sent by TBS (Talk Between Ships, a short-range, high-frequency radio transceiver). The upshot was that Kinkaid wrongly assumed that TF-34 had already been organized to cover the exit of San Bernardino Strait.[46]

For his part, Halsey concluded that Kinkaid's heavy ships and aircraft from his escort carriers could deal with Nishimura's Southern Force, which entered Surigao Strait that evening. And he was right. In a night gunnery match that ended about 0400 on the twenty-fifth, Seventh Fleet battleships under the command of Rear Adm. Jesse B. Oldendorf defeated the Japanese force, then pursued the stragglers out of the strait and away from the gulf, with help from aircraft from Kinkaid's "baby flattops." Halsey was also correct in thinking that Oldendorf had more than enough ships and Kinkaid sufficient aircraft to counter the weakened Japanese Center Force, which, according to scouting reports on the evening of the twenty-fourth, had turned around to the east. Finally locating Ozawa's carriers late that afternoon, Halsey made the critical decision to bring TF-38 together, with Lee's battleships assembled in TF-34, for an overnight run north for a dawn strike on the Japanese Northern Force. The upshot was that by daybreak Kinkaid lacked any heavy ships or fast carriers to defend his amphibious force at just the moment when Kurita issued from San Bernardino and charged down the east coast of the island of Samar.[47]

McCain's TG-38.1 reached the designated fueling point about dawn on the twenty-fifth and launched its search, CAP, and other patrols at 0600. At 0724, about an hour after his ships began taking on fuel, McCain received a dispatch from Mitscher that TF-38 was on course north toward two large groups of warships: Ozawa's carriers. Mitscher reminded McCain to "report any positive result [of] your searches immediately." A confusing series of events then began to unfold rapidly. Only one minute after receipt of Mitscher's message, McCain intercepted a report from Kinkaid to Halsey that TF-77's escort carriers and their destroyer screens were under attack by Kurita's force off Samar and that he needed an "immediate air strike" from Mitscher's carriers. This was impossible because Mitscher at 0800 signaled that he was well to the north engaging Ozawa's force. At 0910, a search plane from the *Wasp* reported that it had found two of Ozawa's carriers; within minutes, McCain relayed the report to Mitscher, who told him to cancel his searches to the north and prepare for strikes against the Japanese carriers. At 0934, McCain received Halsey's signal: "Strike as practicable."[48]

Following an ever-rising torrent of urgent messages from Kinkaid to Halsey demanding assistance, McCain shifted his attention from Ozawa's flattops to Kurita's Center Force. At 0848, Halsey radioed a dispatch to McCain telling him to "proceed at best possible speed" to attack the Japanese heavy ships then assailing Kinkaid's force off Samar. McCain did not receive the message until 1001. Meanwhile, he took the initiative to help Kinkaid. At 0858, he told Halsey and Mitscher that he would complete refueling within a half-hour and turn toward Samar at twenty-five knots. After recovering the group's CAP, increasing speed to thirty knots, and doing some quick range calculations, McCain ordered his torpedo planes to be rearmed with bombs instead of the heavier torpedoes. He also signaled Kinkaid to see if his aircraft could land and refuel at the field recently taken from the Japanese at Tacloban. When he received no response, McCain consulted Baker and Bogan, who assured him that Tacloban, although wet and muddy, was usable in an emergency. Yet, out of caution, McCain stayed with his decision to have the torpedo planes take off loaded with 500-pound bombs and not the ship-killing tin fish.[49]

With the prevailing wind out of the northeast and the group on course to the west/southwest, normal doctrine would have the carriers break out of the task group and head into the wind as they launched and recovered aircraft. This so-called modified Baker maneuver took expert seamanship on the part of all the ships' captains and disrupted the formation while the carriers launched and recovered large numbers of aircraft during a battle. Familiar with the dilemma, Thach proposed and McCain agreed to have the carriers sprint to thirty-three knots, "bulging" but not breaking out of the formation, then wheel around to land and launch a half dozen or so aircraft at a time without having to leave the screen or slow the speed of advance. It was a totally unorthodox and potentially high-risk evolution as the five flattops and their screens maneuvered at high speed within the formation, but the time-saving trick came off brilliantly. While the *Cowpens* and the *Monterey* took over CAP and antisnooper patrols for the task group, the *Wasp*, *Hornet*, and *Hancock* got off deckload strikes beginning at 1030. The flattops were still 340 miles from the Philippines and at the extreme range limit of many of their aircraft, especially the big, thirsty SB2Cs.[50]

Halsey still believed that Kinkaid's forces would have no problems dealing with whatever Kurita's depleted Center Force could bring to bear on them, and that he had done more than enough by committing McCain's task group to assist TF-77. He was perplexed by reports of the dire predicament off Samar, where Kinkaid's escort carriers, desperately fleeing south, launched strikes on Kurita's ships while destroyers and destroyer escorts made suicidal torpedo attacks. Halsey had signaled Kinkaid at 0855 that he was sending McCain to help and told McCain to advise Kinkaid of the "earliest time of strike." He did not know that due to problems relaying messages through MacArthur's communication net that Kinkaid had no knowledge of his actions. About an hour later, at 1000, Halsey got two communications: one from Kinkaid reporting that "my situation is critical" and another from Pearl, where Nimitz had been closely monitoring developments. The latter, "Where is rept Where is Task Force Thirty-Four RR The World Wonders," has gone down as one of the most famous messages in naval history. When Halsey read Nimitz's dispatch he was irate. He interpreted it as an unprofessional gratuitous insult until he realized that the last sentence was leftover cryptological padding. Still he believed he had no choice other than to order Bogan's and Lee's groups to end the pursuit of Ozawa. After Lee's force slowed to refuel, Halsey broke off two battleships, including the *New Jersey*, as a separate task group to run south to succor Kinkaid.[51]

By 1102, forty-eight Hellcats, thirty-three Helldivers, and nineteen Avengers from McCain's group had joined up and were dodging storms as they hurried southwest at 10,500 feet toward the Japanese Center Force, then estimated to be 335 miles distant. Lt. Cdr. Howard S. Roberts, commanding the *Wasp*'s VT-14, ordered each of his TBMs to jettison one of their four bombs to lighten their ordnance loads and extend their range. Aviators in the first strike group swooped in on Kurita's ships at 1316, after Kurita had broken off his assault on the escort carriers and was forming up to reverse course north toward San Bernardino Strait. Roberts' squadron encountered "heavy but ineffective" antiaircraft fire as they dove on Kurita's rapidly maneuvering formation. Flash reports coming into flag plot on the *Wasp* at 1455 were wildly off the mark. *Wasp* airmen claimed bomb hits on a battleship and hits and near misses on what they thought were *Nachi*-class heavy cruisers before Kurita's formation hid under a dense cloud formation. In reality, only one bomb hit the heavy cruiser *Tone*, and it did not explode. The *Hornet*'s bombers reported that they had seriously damaged the superbattleship *Yamato* as well as hitting two other battleships and three heavy cruisers. The *Wasp* lost a Hellcat and two Avengers in the attacks, and the *Hornet* three SB2Cs. One *Hornet* Helldiver returned to the carrier with a gallon and a half of gas after a nearly six-hour mission. Nine SB2Cs from the *Hancock* did not make it back to the carrier; four of them exhausted their fuel and had to land on Seventh Fleet escort carriers, while another pair put down at Tacloban.[52]

At 1245, McCain followed his group's first strike with a second, less robust one consisting of thirty-five fighters, twenty bombers, and twenty-one torpedo planes from the *Hornet* and *Hancock*. SB2Cs from the *Hornet* reported they bombed two enemy battleships and two heavy cruisers, although they scored no hits. The carrier's torpedo planes claimed hits on two cruisers and a destroyer. Eight Helldivers from the *Hornet* were missing when the second strike was recovered by 1845, but all but two safely landed at Tacloban and eventually made their way back to Ulithi. Destroyers rescued pilots and crewmen from several aircraft that ran out of gas and ditched in the water ahead of the task group. Mostly because there had not been time to swap the Helldivers' general-purpose bombs (intended for use against carriers) for armor-piercing weapons, the attacks on the twenty-fifth did nothing to damage or even slow down Kurita's ships. Worse, the strikes resulted in the loss of six Helldivers, along with a Hellcat and two Avengers; ten pilots and crewmen were either killed or missing.[53]

It was obvious that McCain suspected the strikes had not accomplished as much as reported when he signaled the carriers at 0205 on the twenty-sixth to prepare for another attack. A little more than an hour later and about a hundred miles off the northeast coast of Samar, night fighters from the *Hancock* took off to search for Kurita's force, which had cleared San Bernardino and was expected to be off the east coast of Mindoro about dawn. About the same time, Bogan, back from the attacks on Ozawa's force, joined McCain, with McCain now having tactical control over both task groups.[54]

TG-38.1's first strike (twelve Hellcats, twelve Helldivers, and fourteen Avengers), launched at 0558 from a position northeast of Samar. The Avengers were loaded with torpedoes to, as McCain said, "kick the hell out of those ships." A second, heavier strike followed at 0810 with forty-four fighters, twenty-one dive-bombers, and fifteen torpedo bombers. The third and last strike launched at 1245 with forty-eight fighters, fifteen bombers, and twenty-three torpedo planes. At 0810, McCain's first planes rolled in against Kurita's ships, steaming under cloud cover in the Tablas Strait northwest of Panay, with those from the other two strikes following in succession. Kurita's battleships were irresistible targets. Lieutenant Commander Roberts of the *Wasp's* VT-14 exclaimed that his TBMs and the carrier's VB-14 Helldivers made a "beautifully coordinated attack" on the *Yamato*, which he observed suffered two bomb hits and one torpedo strike. Two bombs struck the smaller and slower *Nagato*. Torpedo planes sank the light cruiser *Noshiro* and bombers damaged the heavy cruiser *Kumano*, while three destroyers were targeted, one of which was sunk. This time the pilots' estimates were generally accurate, although they reported more torpedo hits than actually occurred. Twelve Japanese aircraft also were reported shot down during the day. McCain's group lost four fighters, two dive-bombers, and two torpedo bombers to antiaircraft fire. Eleven pilots and aircrew were killed or missing in combat and another three in operational accidents.[55]

★ ★ ★ ★

By 1745 on 26 October, after the *Wasp* had recovered its aircraft from the third TG-38.1 strike on Kurita's rapidly retreating force, Halsey determined from McCain's reports that it was unlikely TF-38 could do much more against the Japanese. The Battle of Leyte Gulf was over. Halsey ordered McCain's and Bogan's groups to withdraw for refueling early on the twenty-seventh. TG-38.1 would then continue to Ulithi for the replenishment the group had missed when it had been recalled on the twenty-fourth. Bogan's group and Mitscher's other two groups lingered off Samar for another two days, providing fighter cover and delivering strikes in support of the forces at Leyte. Kinkaid's already beleaguered escort carriers needed the help. On the twenty-fifth and twenty-sixth they came under attack from Onishi's kamikaze suicide corps. Four of the baby flattops were victims, one of which, the *St. Lo* (CVE 63), took a direct hit on the flight deck, exploded, and sank with heavy casualties.[56]

After recovering its aircraft, McCain's group withdrew at fifteen knots on the evening of the twenty-sixth for the planned rendezvous and refueling scheduled for early the next morning. That evening the *Hancock* and two destroyers left to rejoin Bogan's group. About 0600 on 27 October, McCain's TG-38.1 met Bogan's TG-38.2, TG-34.5 (including the *New Jersey*), and the refueling group about two hundred miles east of Samar. Later that morning, a destroyer took McCain, Baker, Thach, Longstreth, and others over to the *New Jersey* for more than two hours of meetings with Halsey and his staff. That afternoon, fifty-one planes and twenty-six pilots transferred from McCain's carriers to Bogan's, and the six Helldivers that had landed at Tacloban finally made their way back to the *Hornet*. On course to Ulithi the next day, McCain dispatched preliminary reports of the operations on the twenty-fifth and twenty-sixth to Halsey. He also congratulated the officers and men under him for having "fought and won" the fierce air battle of Formosa, stressing that he was "glad to have been with you." TG-38.1 arrived off Ulithi about 0600 on 29 October and was safely within the anchorage less than three hours later.[57]

★ ★ ★ ★

McCain's action report for the October operations, circulated in the middle of December, mostly stressed the obvious. The task group demonstrated vulnerability to evening torpedo plane attacks, evidenced by the success the Japanese had on 13–14 October. McCain believed that deploying destroyers as pickets in sectors where the attacks were most likely to occur offered a partial solution. Night fighter operations extended the carriers' usual dawn-to-dusk schedule and caused carriers to maneuver in ways that violated the integrity of the group and curtailed antiaircraft fire when bogeys were in the area. McCain believed a partial answer was for each group in the task force to keep one deck clear to launch and land night fighters without disrupting the entire formation. Communications continued to plague the fast carriers, especially on the twenty-fifth and twenty-sixth, when a thousand stations clogged the circuits, resulting in delays of up to six hours in getting messages through. Not hearing from Kinkaid about the condition of the Tacloban field, for example, was a factor in McCain's decision on the twenty-fifth to load planes with bombs rather than torpedoes, which might have "been much more successful and effective" against Kurita's ships. McCain saw the Japanese suicide planes as "the latest and most threatening problem that has yet confronted the U.S. Navy," reflecting the "fanatical mind" of the Japanese, and demanding "the application by the pilots and operations personnel of a complete understanding of radar and complexities of air defense and air control." Small groups, or individual attackers, approaching at high speeds and low altitudes were especially difficult to detect and defend against. McCain suggested that "exercises" to simulate Japanese suicide tactics might offer solutions.[58]

Controversy set in not long after the Battle of Leyte Gulf, not unlike following the Battle of the Philippine Sea. Apparent in hindsight was the divided command caused by the convergence of MacArthur's South West Pacific and Nimitz's Central Pacific forces in the Philippines. Confusion resulting from the lack of any direct communication between the Third and Seventh Fleets made mutual support and cooperation virtually impossible during the crisis TF-77 encountered on the morning of 25 October. Yet politics and the tensions between MacArthur's and Nimitz's overlapping commands limited the alternatives. If anything, Nimitz and MacArthur deserve at least some share of the blame.[59]

Halsey's routine habit of issuing orders directly to the task groups, bypassing Mitscher in the process, added to the muddled command situation at Leyte. For example, Halsey ignored Mitscher in sending McCain a vague dispatch on the evening of 16 October to conduct a dawn search for enemy surface forces in sectors to the west and north of the task force off Luzon, then attempting by dispatch to clarify the order so that the sectors of McCain's search did not overlap those of Bogan's TG-38.2. McCain did not receive the revised orders. Halsey also skipped over

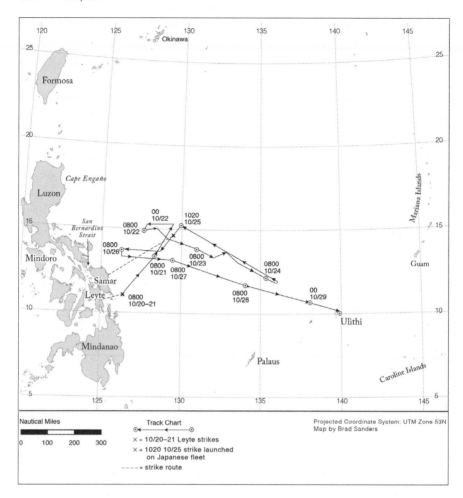

Map 4. Task Group 38.1 Operations, 20–29 October 1944; Battle of Leyte Gulf (USS *Wasp* Action Report, Oct. 2–27, 1944, www.Fold3.com, accessed Feb. 20, 2013)

Mitscher on the morning of the twenty-fourth in ordering an attack by TF-38 on Kurita's force.[60]

Halsey knew that Nimitz's 1000 dispatch on the twenty-fifth was all he needed to understand that there was displeasure in Pearl Harbor about his decision to pursue Ozawa's carriers. He transmitted a long message to Nimitz on the twenty-fifth in which he explained that it was not reasonable to keep Mitscher's carriers "statically" off Samar and why Ozawa's force and not Kurita's endangered Kinkaid. The dispatch had a decidedly defensive tone. In his opinion the carriers were not, as some argued, "bait," or a "secondary force."

To the end of his life, and in denial of the verdict of history and historians, he refused to acknowledge his mistake, insisting that if he had erred it was in ordering Bogan's flattops and Lee's battlewagons south, which precluded the destruction of Ozawa's remaining heavy ships, in particular the hybrid carrier/battleships *Ise* and *Hyuga*. Towers liked Halsey's aggressiveness and blamed Kinkaid's failure to provide adequate air searches north of Leyte as the reason for the near-disaster off Samar. Nimitz was circumspect in his criticism of Halsey, while King was more direct, although later he was more even-handed and concluded that both Halsey and Kinkaid shared the blame.[61]

In making sense of the Battle of Leyte Gulf, most historians have tried to carve out a middle ground. To Clark Reynolds, mistakes all around at Leyte contributed to what he concluded was another incomplete victory. Halsey was "proud" and "stubborn" and failed to understand how his subordinates, especially Mitscher, whose role in the battle was virtually non-existent, could provide valuable advice. Thomas Hughes, Halsey's most recent biographer, identified communication problems within the divided command for the failures at Leyte, but also blamed Halsey for slavishly adhering to the principle of concentration when he could have divided his forces to provide Kinkaid with additional support. Kinkaid, for his part, lacked details about Halsey's movements or those of the Japanese and "took too much for granted," particularly in assuming that TF-34 had been formed to guard San Bernardino. Many factors were beyond his control, but it is clear he lost sight of the tactical situation as events moved rapidly on 24–25 October. Kinkaid's biographer, the historian Gerald Wheeler, asserted that Kinkaid paid more "attention to the mission" than did Halsey, meaning that the pair had primary responsibility for ensuring the success of the amphibious operation and protecting troops ashore. Pursuing Ozawa while not determining whether Kurita's Center Force had been taken care of was proof that Halsey had not performed his part of the overall mission.[62]

McCain, on the other hand, received nothing but praise for his actions, especially in the battle off Formosa. In that engagement he skillfully disposed and maneuvered TG-38.1 to place it in the optimum position to launch strikes on Japanese airfields and other targets and to thwart ferocious Japanese aerial counterattacks against his carriers. His group was a major factor in virtually wiping out Japanese air power on Formosa and Luzon before the landings at Leyte. At key points he acted with commendable initiative, both in protecting the damaged *Canberra* and *Houston* and in responding to Kinkaid's pleas for help off Samar before he received orders from Halsey. He shared the disappointment that Kurita's Center Force managed to escape total destruction, but no one at the time believed he could have done more under the circumstances on 25–26 October. We do not know what he thought about Halsey's decision to go north, although he might have agreed with Thach that Halsey "certainly should have gone after those carriers."[63] We do know that McCain had gained experience in handling fast carrier task groups in combat and that with Baker, Thach, and others, he had a competent and experienced staff he could count on to plan and execute future operations. He understood that few endeavors were more unpredictable and dangerous than warfare at sea, yet as October drifted into November he was fully confident of the readiness of his ships and men to take the fast carrier force to ultimate victory in the western Pacific.

CHAPTER 8

Task Force 38

M cCain's task group had been at sea for nearly two exhausting months of intense operations when it arrived at Ulithi on the morning of 29 October. At 1100 the next day, only hours after TG-38.3 had arrived at Ulithi, Mitscher briefly met with McCain in his flag quarters on the *Lexington* and relinquished command of TF-38. Rather than moving to the *Lexington* with his staff, McCain decided to retain the *Wasp* as his flagship and stay with TG-38.1, at least for the time being. Mitscher, Burke, and the rest of Mitscher's staff left for Pearl Harbor on the thirtyfirst. It was obvious to nearly everyone that Mitscher was worn out and that in retrospect he would have been better off rotating out with Spruance instead of staying on with Halsey, under whom he had functioned more like a high-ranking observer than a task force commander. On the other hand, McCain's experience at the task group level was invaluable and preferable to having him take over full responsibility for the task force at the outset of the Philippines campaign.[1]

Keeping with Halsey's makeshift task group rotation in the aftermath of the Battle of Leyte Gulf, Sherman's TG-38.3 pulled into the anchorage a day after McCain's, while Bogan's TG-38.2 and Davison's TG-38.4 stayed behind to continue air coverage in the Philippines. MacArthur sorely needed their help, since dreadful weather and sodden airfields limited the deployment of AAF fighters and bombers to Leyte. Standing in, the fast carriers paid a heavy price. In Davison's group, his flagship *Franklin* (CV 13) and the *Belleau Wood* took hard hits from the kamikazes, which also struck the *Intrepid* (CV 11), Bogan's flagship. Task Force 38 air groups were run down and tired, too, from nearly constant combat operations.[2]

On 31 October, Rear Adm. Alfred Montgomery, an aviator and one of the most experienced fast carrier officers available at the time, broke his flag in the *Hornet*, relieving McCain as commander of TG-38.1. Montgomery had led a big carrier raid on Wake Island in October 1943, and a month later commanded carrier groups in Halsey's attack on Rabaul and Spruance's operation against the Gilberts. Competent, bright, and battle-tested, "Monty" Montgomery had innovated multicarrier formations that provided a model for the independent task groups employed by Spruance, Mitscher, Halsey, and McCain in 1944. McCain knew him well from his time as his exec on the *Ranger* and had the utmost confidence in his ability to handle TG-38.1.[3]

Halsey had hoped the tactical situation in the Philippines would be stabilized sufficiently to give the fast carriers and aircrews some rest before undertaking future operations. One, outlined by Halsey on 12 October, delayed on 26 October, and subsequently canceled, was Operation Hotfoot, an ambitious plan to strike strategic targets in the Japanese home islands of Kyushu and Honshu that McCain had anticipated with "a good deal of satisfaction." It also grated on Halsey that many of the Japanese heavy ships had escaped destruction in the Battle of Leyte Gulf, and he worried that Japan might still find a way to use its surviving carriers to disrupt operations around the Philippines and in the South China Sea. It was apparent, too, that while TF-38 strikes had been effective in the short term, the Japanese had recovered enough to funnel additional air power into the Philippines from Formosa. Finally, it was clear that due to persistent rain that held up airfield construction, the forces on the ground in the Philippines were not going to get much help from Army Maj. Gen. George Kenney's Fifth Air Force. It is an understatement to say that Halsey was displeased, but neither he nor McCain anticipated they faced two months of brutal attrition warfare in and around the Philippines.[4]

So, TF-38 again visited Leyte and the Philippines. On 1 November, Halsey directed McCain to speed up reprovisioning and rearming of Montgomery's TG-38.1 and ordered him to have that group rendezvous with TGs 38.2 (Bogan) and 38.3 (Sherman) on 3 November at a refueling point about two hundred miles due east of Leyte. There TF-38 would join Halsey and the *New Jersey* to begin Operation Pulverize against enemy targets on Luzon. Halsey sortied from Ulithi with Bogan's group on 1 November, followed by TG-38.1 with McCain and the *Wasp* on the afternoon of the second. Davison's TG-38.4 had to steam back to Ulithi with the badly damaged *Franklin* and *Belleau Wood*. After rearming and picking up the *Yorktown* (CV 10) and its escorts, Davison's group was to return to sea on 5 November.[5]

★ ★ ★ ★

McCain's three carrier groups came together as scheduled early on the morning of the third. Refueling and transfer of aircraft from Jasper Acuff's

TG-30.8 oilers and escort carriers went smoothly during the day, but that evening McCain got a harsh reminder that there were threats to his force under the sea as well as above it. At 2325, as the task force was zigzagging north at fifteen knots, the Japanese submarine *I-41* stole past the screen into Sherman's group and loosed a torpedo into the light cruiser *Reno* (CL 96). McCain immediately ordered an emergency turn and increased the speed of the task force to twenty-five knots to clear the area. Torn apart by explosions and quickly flooding aft, the *Reno* survived as a result of heroic damage-control efforts, and under destroyer escort it was towed back to Ulithi. The next day, destroyers in the screen contacted another submarine, although they were unable to chase it down, and before dawn on the fifth, the *Boyd* (DD 544) in Montgomery's group was the target of another subma-rine, whose fish ran wide of their target.[6]

McCain's carriers began launching at 0615 on 5 November about eighty miles off Polillo Island. The Americans swept over Luzon like a tsunami. In 1,407 offensive sorties over two days, fighters claimed 105 enemy aircraft shot down, most of them over Clark Field. Taking into account more accu-rate reporting and the 70 percent rate of overclaims, the aviators actually got more than 73 aerial kills, still an impressive performance. More than 320 aircraft were destroyed on the ground at Clark, Mabalacat, and Aparri airfields. In his action report, McCain boasted that the total of enemy air-craft destroyed or damaged over the two days was "the greatest number of planes destroyed in any one operation by any air force in history." In what McCain later called "a savage body blow to the Jap system of reinforcement and supply," the raids also pounded radio stations, hangars, runways, rail-ways, docks, oil storage tanks, and fuel dumps. A transport and destroyer escort were reported sunk in Manila Bay, another transport at Subic Bay, and an oiler and small cargo ship off the Bataan Peninsula. McCain's air-men exacted a toll on the Imperial Navy too. In Manila Bay they sank the heavy cruiser *Nachi* with torpedoes and bombs and claimed hits on an unnamed light cruiser and seven destroyers. Thirty-seven task force aircraft, more than half of which were fighters, were lost in the attacks, as well as eighteen airmen.[7]

McCain's CAP defeated the inevitable Japanese counterattacks, down-ing eight enemy planes over the fleet, while another four fell to antiair-craft fire. Yet on the afternoon of the fifth, a kamikaze penetrated the force defenses and plunged into the starboard side of the *Lexington*'s island, igniting fires, knocking out some of the ship's controls, and causing many casualties, although the carrier continued flight operations.[8] Even though the strikes on the fifth and sixth came at a cost, and considering that the airmen exaggerated some of the results, the aerial assault by McCain's task force helped mitigate the immediate threat to MacArthur's and Kinkaid's forces at Leyte and diminished the Japanese ability to retaliate against the task force.

Following strikes on the sixth, the three task groups withdrew to rendezvous with oilers at noon on the seventh about three hundred miles east of Samar. Montgomery's and Sherman's groups refueled during the day, while Bogan's continued to Ulithi to reprovision and rearm, its place in the task force taken by Davison's reconstituted TG-38.4. At 1600 the next day, 8 November, the *Wasp*, along with three destroyers, left the force for Guam to exchange Air Group 14 for fresh Air Group 81. Capt. Oscar A. Weller, the *Wasp*'s commanding officer, had reported to McCain that since the Battle of Leyte Gulf he had become "gravely concerned about the abnormal physical and mental condition" of the officers and men in the air group and that the unit had deteriorated to the point where it was "no longer ready for active service." Totally worn out, the unit had lost seventy-two aviators and aircrew and ninety-seven aircraft in nearly continuous action since the middle of May. Halsey concurred that under the circumstances there was no choice but to have the air group replaced as soon as possible.[9]

Caught in the middle of the crisis that enveloped the *Wasp* and its air complement, McCain decided to stay with the carrier and assigned Sherman as officer in tactical command (OTC) of the task force pending his return from Guam. At the same time, Admiral Montgomery transferred his flag from the *Hornet* to the *Yorktown*. On reaching Apra Harbor on Guam at 0655 on the tenth, McCain expressed his gratitude to the *Wasp*'s aviators and anticipated the departing unit would soon enjoy "plenty of luck, liquor, and ladies." The carrier then embarked Air Group 81 and took on ammunition, aviation gasoline, and provisions. Yet because storage facilities for bunker oil were unavailable at Guam, the *Wasp* and its escorts departed from Apra at dawn on 11 November to rendezvous and refuel on the thirteenth with TGs 38.1, 38.3, and 38.4 about two hundred miles east of Luzon. Bogan's TG-38.2, meanwhile, remained at Ulithi with orders to link up with the task force on the sixteenth.[10]

The disruption caused by the breakdown of Air Group 14 and the diversion to Guam frustrated McCain. He reported that such "side trips for special purposes cannot be tolerated" and that air group exchanges had to be made at Ulithi or some other point closer to the carriers' operational areas. In a letter to Halsey he pointed out that because the efficiency of air groups deteriorated in direct proportion to their length of time at sea, the airmen had to have adequate time ashore to restore morale and undergo training, underscoring the need for more replacement units at forward areas. Nimitz recognized that carrier air groups needed to be "relieved as early as possible," and he reassured Halsey and McCain that "steps are being taken to accelerate carrier air group replacements and to provide more opportunity for rest and recuperation." Things improved as spare air groups were brought forward as needed and exchanges took place during periods of rest and replenishment. Yet the exigencies of war meant that the new groups did not always have opportunities to train with the ships' crews and there was no time for permanent revisions to be made in Cincpac's air group replacement schedules.[11]

These and other operational problems paled in comparison to the existential threat the kamikazes presented to McCain's fast carriers in the waters off the Philippines. On board the *Wasp* en route from Guam to rejoin TF-38, McCain circulated an order to his task groups outlining potential procedures to defend the carriers against Japanese suicide attacks. He had hinted about the need to do something about the kamikazes in his action report summarizing operations in October and during the Battle of Leyte Gulf, and over the ensuing weeks he and Thach had discussed possible solutions. They agreed that downing 80 to 90 percent of the suiciders was not good enough. From recent experience they understood that if even one got through it could sink a carrier or at least take the ship out of action. "Now 100 percent destruction of the attackers is necessary to preserve the safety of the Task Force," McCain concluded. Furthermore, he now knew that although ships' CICs had been adequate for picking up relatively large formations of enemy aircraft attacking from one or two directions, they were less capable of detecting single aircraft approaching from a variety of directions and altitudes, as had been revealed by Japanese suicide tactics at Leyte Gulf.[12]

Thach suggested, and McCain concurred, that the task force initiate new defensive tactics and formations, which McCain outlined in a directive to his task groups on 11 November. He noted that "the most successful football teams obtain the formations and trick plays used by their opponents and duplicate them against the first team in practice until a satisfactory defense is perfected." Dubbed "Moose-trap," the practice exercises had one or two fighter or dive-bomber units play the role of suiciders while the task force devised methods of concentrating defenses to counter them. Another tactic, borrowed from Jocko Clark, was to position radar picket destroyers (called "Tomcats") fifty to sixty miles in front of the task force, where they could provide early warning of attackers and vector their CAP ("RapCap") to intercept them. Friendly aircraft were required to orbit the destroyers, thus separating them from enemy planes that might hide themselves in the formation and isolating them to be shot down by antiaircraft fire or by the carriers' CAP scouting ahead of the task force ("ScoCap"). The tactic of exterminating the returning aircraft of Japanese "parasites" became known as "delousing." In addition to the ScoCap, so-called Jack patrols were to go out at dusk to intercept Japanese planes approaching at low altitude in the darkness. "DadCap" fighters covered the force during daylight, and "Bat-Cap" aircraft took over at nightfall. McCain ordered task groups to begin Moose-trap exercises as soon as possible so that he and his staff could evaluate the results and implement new defensive measures without delay.[13]

On 15 November, the *Enterprise*, in Davison's group, was among the first carriers to conduct and report on Moose-trap exercises. The ship launched eight Helldivers and its regular CAP of sixteen Hellcats. The bombers turned off their IFF radar transponders and from 25,000 feet and 125 miles from the carrier began their run-in to the target. Radar detected the bombers almost immediately, and fighter direction sent out eight Hellcats to intercept. As the "attackers" descended to make a high-speed, low-altitude approach from about 35 miles out, the fighters closed in and "shot down" seven of them. The bombers that eluded the fighters managed to get within visual range of the carrier. The *Enterprise* fighter director officer considered the drill a success. His sole recommendation was that radar operators get "frequent practice" and be specially trained to pick up individual aircraft approaching at low altitudes, the tactic most often used by kamikazes.[14] Moose-trap looked promising, but it remained to be seen how effective the new tactics and procedures would be in real-world combat, and no one at the time anticipated that the Tomcat destroyers would ultimately be the targets of a disproportionate share of kamikaze attacks.

Meanwhile, in McCain's absence, the task force, under Sherman's tactical command, had ambushed a Japanese convoy transiting the Camotes Sea to deliver reinforcements to Ormoc Bay on the west side of Leyte. The attacks on the morning of 11 November sank four transports, four destroyers and a minesweeper; only one destroyer managed to escape the carnage. TF-38 fighters claimed thirteen enemy aircraft shot down during the strikes on the convoy. Still under Sherman, TF-38 launched more than 750 offensive sorties on the thirteenth against shipping in Manila Bay, where fighters and bombers sank the light cruiser *Kiso* and four more destroyers, as well as sixteen cargo ships and three tankers. But the strikes came at the cost of twenty-three aircraft and thirty-two aircrew, most of them victims of heavy antiaircraft fire over Manila.[15]

According to the Japanese, TF-38 aircraft deliberately attacked and sank the 1,600-ton hospital ship *Muro Maru* on the thirteenth, killing thirty-two of the vessel's crewmembers. It was not the first such incident. The 1,700-ton *Tachibana Maru* had been damaged on 5 November when it was accidentally strafed by McCain's airmen west of Manila Bay. The Japanese lodged a formal protest, alleging that the *Muro Maru* was outside Manila harbor and no closer than one thousand yards from the nearest warship or military installation. They further threatened that "such unlawful conduct will lead to [a] grave situation" and that the United States must "admit unlawfulness of past conduct . . . punish those responsible [and] give absolute guarantee to prevent repetition of unlawful attacks in future." By January, the complaint had found its way to King, who passed it on to Nimitz for him to investigate. Nimitz replied that the only information he had was from the *Yorktown*'s VB-3 and VF-3 aircraft action reports, which indicated that a transport had been bombed and damaged outside Manila Bay. The VB-3 flight leader believed he saw a red cross on the ship, but the vessel was not painted white, had no markings on its deck, and was believed to have fired on the aircraft in his squadron. King passed the details of the incident on to the State Department, which informed the Japanese through the Spanish Embassy that American armed forces respected the immunity of hospital ships.[16]

Just before midnight on the thirteenth, the task force, now back under McCain's tactical command and constituting Montgomery's, Sherman's, and Davison's groups, turned west to close at high speed on the Philippines in anticipation of early morning strikes against more targets in and around Manila. At 0620 on the fourteenth, about ninety miles east of Luzon, TF-38 launched the first of two fighter sweeps and strikes aimed again at the Clark Field complex, as well as Batangas and a newly discovered airstrip at Nasugbu south of Manila. By now the Japanese had learned to disperse and camouflage their aircraft, which made them hard for McCain's aviators to spot and attack. Eight enemy fighters were reported shot down and only twenty destroyed on the ground. Despite exaggerated reports of shipping sunk or badly damaged that day, the Japanese lost only two tankers. McCain's carrier bombers also wrought destruction at the former U.S. navy yard at Cavite in Manila. McCain's force lost eleven aircraft in combat and four operationally. Altogether, TF-38 flew 601 offensive sorties that day.[17]

Halsey had hoped to initiate a regular rotation of the carrier task groups off Luzon, but his plans never fully coalesced due to the demands of the protracted air campaign. Shortly after midnight on 15 November, TF-38 retired eastward to meet Acuff's oiler group and Bogan's TG-38.2, which had sortied from Ulithi in company with Halsey and the *New Jersey*. Montgomery's and Davison's groups were to refuel at the rendezvous point while Sherman's TG-38.3 had orders to Ulithi for rearming and reprovisioning. The three groups came together about four hundred miles east of Samar on the morning of the sixteenth. At 0940, a destroyer took McCain and his staff over to the *New Jersey* for three hours of meetings to discuss further plans with Halsey and his subordinates. That afternoon, the three carrier groups were reshuffled, with the *Hornet* and two destroyers detached from Montgomery's TG-38.1 to join Davison's group. At 1600 the next day (17 November), McCain transferred his flag from the *Wasp* to the *Hancock* in Bogan's group, which brought Halsey and McCain together in the same tactical formation.[18]

McCain's force refueled on the eighteenth as it proceeded west to carry out more strikes against the Japanese in Luzon. Starting before 0630 on the nineteenth, the carriers launched fighter sweeps and the first of four strikes against airfields and other targets in the Manila area. Airmen claimed numerous enemy planes destroyed in the air and on the ground, in addition to shipping in Manila Bay, San Fernando, and Subic Bay. Moose-trap training helped defend the task force from Japanese retaliation. Before dawn, night fighters from the *Independence* in Bogan's group tangled with and knocked down a four-engine Kawanishi ("Emily") flying boat snooping the fleet. Later the task force CAP splashed ten aircraft, including four Frances torpedo bombers and a Betty, that were part of a ten-plane formation that threatened the ships that evening. Antiaircraft fire from Tomcat destroyers brought down another three enemy planes before the task force withdrew.[19]

Leslie Nichols, a correspondent with the Mutual Broadcasting System, interviewed McCain that day as pilots returned to the *Hancock* after the attacks on Luzon. Asked why the Japanese had seemingly not done more to defend their positions in the Philippines, McCain responded, "They have been fairly aggressive, probably in accordance with the strength they have been able to muster. Our attacks, particularly those on the 5th and 6th of November, when hundreds of planes were destroyed, have been very destructive." Training deficiencies also limited what the enemy was able to do. "There are some good pilots and some well trained units left in the Japanese air force," McCain explained. "However," he went on, "their training and ability is below the standards shown in the early days of the war. They realize this as well as we do and it is emphasized by the stupid desperation of some of their attacks as a substitute for skill and brains." In comparison, the American naval aviator was smarter and "remains the best trained pilot for his purposes in the world." Nichols suggested that the Japanese might be holding some of their air power in reserve to defend the home islands and offered that "greater caution should be adopted in possible future operations." McCain countered, "It is difficult to conceive that Japan can muster sufficient force to stop the carrier forces anywhere. . . . It is impossible for me to foresee any manner of warfare adjacent to the sea in which the highly mobile airfields which constitute the carrier task forces, will not play a useful or even a decisive part" in winning the war.[20]

TF-38 spent the next four days about three hundred miles east of Samar refueling, taking on replacement aircraft and aircrew, and carrying out gunnery and Moose-trap exercises. McCain again went aboard the *New Jersey* on the twenty-first to meet with Halsey and his staff to plan more strikes on Luzon. He told Halsey that he admired his "bold moves," which had caught the Japanese with their "pants down," and he liked his ideas for further strikes on Luzon by the Big Blue Fleet. Davison's group, from which the *Bunker Hill* (CV 17) had been detached to Ulithi on the sixteenth and which now included only the *Enterprise* and the *San Jacinto* (CVL 30), left at midnight on the twentieth for Ulithi, with orders to bomb Yap with napalm on the twenty-second. Montgomery's TG-38.1 was dispatched to Ulithi on the twenty-third, Thanksgiving Day. McCain now had only two task groups—Bogan's and Sherman's—for the next operation, aimed at Japanese shipping in and around Manila.[21]

Bogeys began closing on the task force well before it reached the launching point about sixty miles off Luzon at sunrise on the twenty-fifth. *Independence* night fighters took off to intercept, but the intruders eluded them and continued to do so all morning as they shadowed the carriers. The first of three strikes went out at 0620, with the others following at roughly three-hour intervals into the early afternoon. Attackers from the *Ticonderoga* (CV 14) in Sherman's TG-38.3 sank the heavy cruiser *Kumano*, which had previously been torpedoed by submarines off Luzon and had taken refuge in Santa Cruz harbor. Among other Japanese ships sunk or damaged during the day were three landing ships, a frigate, seven transports, nine medium cargo ships, and a medium oiler. Fighters claimed twenty-five enemy planes shot down over the targets and another twenty-eight destroyed on the ground. Compared to previous strikes, the American losses were minimal: four planes and eight pilots and aircrew in combat and nine aircraft and three pilots in operational accidents.[22]

The Japanese responded with the heaviest attacks on TF-38's carriers since the battle of Formosa: six raids that gashed the task force despite the Tomcat pickets and enhanced CAP tactics. In the first of the assaults, at 1231, a Zero dove through the screen around Bogan's group, was hit by AA fire, and broke apart. The plane's bomb missed the *Hancock*, which was launching the third strike of the day. Fragments of the fuselage and a wing hit the port side of the carrier's flight deck and struck near the island, starting a fire that damage-control crews quickly extinguished. Within a half-hour, two kamikazes evaded antiaircraft fire and crashed the *Intrepid*, also in Bogan's group, starting fires that took more than two hours to get under control. A suicide plane also struck the light carrier *Cabot* (CVL 28), penetrating the flight deck, and another just missed, its bomb detonating close aboard. The hits on the ship caused serious damage and killed or injured fifty-two of the crew. Sherman's flagship, the *Essex*, was also the victim of a kamikaze, which tore up the flight and hangar decks and left nearly sixty personnel killed or wounded. Suiciders aiming at the *Iowa* (BB 61) and the light cruiser *Miami* (CL 89) fell to antiaircraft guns. McCain wrote that "there were those of us that day who discovered what it was like to watch an undamaged Jap plane, its engine screaming crazily, come hurtling straight for our ship, only to veer into the sea close overside because the pilot had been killed in the last split second of his death dive." By 1305, the worst was over, although enemy aircraft continued to threaten the task force throughout the rest of the afternoon. CAP fighters and antiaircraft fire downed a total of thirty-two enemy planes before the task force retired east from the area at 1830.[23]

As far as Halsey was concerned, the strikes on the twenty-fifth fulfilled his obligation to shield Kinkaid and the forces at Leyte. Furthermore, he stressed that he was unwilling to expose his carriers to the risk of kamikazes in "casual strikes" and would only continue to do so for more "valuable stakes or at vital times." And now was not that time. To give TF-38's carriers and crews a breather from combat, he ordered Bogan's group (with McCain in the *Hancock*) to head directly to Ulithi and told Sherman to refuel and then follow TG-38.2 to Ulithi. The *Enterprise* and the *San Jacinto*, remnants of Davison's TG-38.4, dropped anchor at Ulithi on the afternoon of 22 November. Three days later, on the twenty-fifth, Davison handed over the task group to Jocko Clark and on the twenty-seventh rode back to Pearl with the *Enterprise* for a much-needed rest. The *Hancock* and TG-38.2 arrived at the anchorage on the afternoon of the twenty-seventh; Sherman's group planned to reach the fleet base on 2 December. The *Intrepid*'s damage was so severe that repairs were impossible at Ulithi, and the flattop had to return to the West Coast, along with the *Franklin* and the *Belleau Wood*, for work in major shipyards. Henceforth, Kenney's Fifth Air Force, Seventh Fleet escort carriers, and Marine Hellcats and Corsairs flown in from Peleliu and the Solomons would take on the burden of air support for the troops at Leyte.[24]

There was little time for relaxation at Ulithi. MacArthur's next objective was Mindoro, the island south of Luzon that he needed to provide additional bases from which the Fifth Air Force could operate in support of the big invasion of Luzon. Because aircraft on the ground at Leyte could not be spared, MacArthur wanted the fast carriers to provide cover for Mindoro. Code-named L-3 (or Love-3), Mindoro was scheduled for 5 December, only two weeks before the Luzon operation. To give the AAF time to build up strength in Leyte and for TF-38 to recover from the crisis of the twenty-fifth, Nimitz and Halsey urged a delay, but MacArthur refused, believing that to do so would give the Japanese more time to bolster their forces in Luzon. On 29 November, Nimitz sent a diplomatically worded dispatch to MacArthur explaining that after weeks of intense combat the carriers needed time for repairs, replenishment, and aircrew replacement. In a separate dispatch to MacArthur, Halsey underscored the points Nimitz had made and stressed that TF-38 needed more time to prepare for the Mindoro landings. Late on the thirtieth, MacArthur agreed to the ten-day delay.[25]

Because Halsey did not hear immediately about MacArthur's decision, he ordered two of McCain's task groups—38.1 and 38.2—out of Ulithi to join Sherman's group, still at sea, in preparation for the Mindoro operation. Not long after McCain's carriers left the anchorage at 0820 on the first, they learned of the postponement, and all three task groups headed back to

Ulithi. Just in case the fast carriers were needed for an emergency, a temporary task group centered on the *Lexington* and *San Jacinto* and commanded by Bogan patrolled north of the atoll for the next week.[26]

The interlude at Ulithi allowed McCain to assess the previous month's operations and plan for the next phases of the war. He chafed under circumstances off Leyte that had obviated the carriers' chief tactical advantages of mobility and surprise. "In all our operations," he noted, "the task force had faced conditions which minimized the defensive value of surprise. Here for the first time we were striking large land masses and networks of airfields dispersed across hundreds of miles. It meant that our every launching position was dictated within fairly narrow limits by the geography of the objective, with the result that the mere appearance of our planes over a target announced to the Japs very nearly where they would be able to find the carriers." Cdr. James Hean on McCain's staff asked wryly, "Admiral, why in hell don't we make it easy for everybody and just put down a buoy out here as an aid to navigation?"[27]

Moose-trap exercises had mitigated the kamikaze threat, although a good deal more training and experience were necessary to perfect the new tactics. McCain and Thach recognized, also, that a corollary to the defensive measures they had implemented were offensive efforts to deal with the menace at the source, especially when the task force was confined to a support position close to shore. The solution: "blanket the threatening enemy air opposition day and night with the most air power available." They proposed throwing this "blanket" over the enemy's airfields to smother air opposition and allow carrier planes to pursue secondary objectives while simultaneously reducing the threat of air assault on the fleet. McCain and Thach reasoned that it was possible to achieve "more spectacular results" against the enemy by increasing offensive sorties, but that those effects would likely limit the carriers' defenses and result in more damage to the task force. The "balance" between the two was "delicate." "The enemy must never be permitted to lift even one corner of the 'blanket' over his airfields, or the safety of the entire Task Force is jeopardized. Regardless of the attractiveness of other targets, responsible commanders must not be lulled into diverting so much of their air strength from the 'blanket' that the enemy's air is no longer thoroughly held helpless while it is being systematically destroyed." "The stake is too high," they concluded, "to risk this contingency."[28]

Thach acknowledged that it was impossible to suppress Japanese air power entirely. He envisioned a "holey blanket" spread over the largest enemy airfields that eliminated most, but not all, of the threat. Kamikazes that survived and managed to get through to the task force could then be dealt with by the Tomcat pickets and CAP using Moose-trap-derived tactics. To enhance the coverage of McCain's "blanket," Thach called for a "three-strike" system. Previously, carriers had launched half their aircraft in the first strike of the day, then waited until the first strike was about to land before launching a second deckload. The interval sometimes allowed the Japanese time to get their planes in the air to attack the task force. Thach wanted the carriers to launch two-thirds of their aircraft with half of the planes carrying bombs ("Strike A"), and the other half, consisting of fighters ("Strike B"), lacking bombs but loaded with more fuel. The bombers returned to the carriers after their strikes, while the fighters lingered over the targets to pick off any remaining enemy aircraft. By the time the fighters returned to the carriers, a third strike (Strike "C") had been launched and was over the targets, adhering to the same pattern as the first. The arrangement resulted in near-continuous coverage of the enemy airfields, but the innovative system demanded accelerated launch and recovery cycles and carefully choreographed maneuvers by the carrier skippers.[29]

The execution of what became known as the "Big Blue Blanket," a reference to Halsey's Big Blue Fleet, hinged on having adequate numbers of first-line aircraft and fresh, well-trained pilots and aircrews for the carriers. From his experience in Washington, McCain knew how the aircraft procurement and pilot training systems worked and had a realistic picture of how they affected operations with the fleet. In a dispatch to TF-38 carrier groups, he emphasized that the CNO and Comairpac dictated the makeup and size of carrier aircraft complements, and that he, as commander, TF-38 (CTF-38), could under some "special" circumstances also determine the composition of air groups. Within those parameters, pilots and aircrew ideally needed to be sustained at 150 percent of the carrier's aircraft complements but that they still had combat effectiveness at 125 percent; below that level "active replacement measures need to be taken" using "combat replacement teams" that had trained together. McCain warned his task group commanders not to break up those teams or to exchange individual aircrew and squadrons among the task groups, unless there was "grave inequality" or a dire need to meet an immediate combat emergency. He delegated responsibility for handling replacements to the task group commanders, making sure that they copied him on their requirements and that they did so well before the next replenishment cycle.[30]

McCain saw the achievement of "air supremacy in the absolute" over
Luzon as "a job for fighters." On 20 November he repeated his earlier recommendation about transitioning air groups to mostly fighters and fighter-
bombers, discarding all SB2Cs, and keeping a squadron of eighteen TBMs.
Sherman was in complete agreement that the heavy carrier air groups include
ninety-two fighters and fighter-bombers (preferably Corsairs), together with
eighteen TBM torpedo bombers. Clark wanted "more and faster fighters."
Bogan preferred eighty fighters and twenty-four dive-bombers. Davison
agreed with McCain that more fighters were essential to counter increasing
numbers of enemy aircraft, particularly as the carriers closed in on Japan,
but he did not want to see the air groups lose their "punch" against shipping and land targets. Differing with McCain, Davison believed that the
newest model of the Helldiver, the SB2C-3, with a more powerful engine
and four-blade propeller, "has been performing well," and could deliver torpedoes as well as bombs. He insisted on a varied complement of sixty-two
fighters (including a fighter-bomber squadron), eighteen dive-bombers, and
eighteen torpedo planes. Montgomery agreed with Davison that the carriers needed balanced air groups consisting of sixty-two fighters, eighteen
dive-bombers, and eighteen torpedo planes, but he thought they should
gradually eliminate the dive-bombers and increase the number of fighters to
seventy-eight. Radford, now commander of Carrier Division Six, cautioned
that rapidly enlarging the fighter complement of the air groups meant introducing replacement aviators and aircrews who had no operational training
and were not ready for combat. He recommended against expanding the
number of fighters in those groups "until training catches up." "Quality and
not quantity is the fundamental," he concluded, as the fast carriers prepared
for the next round of operations.[31]

King rendered the final decision on 23 December: a compromise of sorts
whereby for at least the next cycle of operations the carriers' air groups would
have seventy-two fighters and fighter-bombers, fifteen dive-bombers, and fifteen torpedo planes. McCain, Thach, and their new assistant operations
officer, Bill Leonard, remained convinced that Hellcat and Corsair fighter-
bombers were more than adequate replacements for the Helldivers. Leonard
recalled that when McCain heard of King's decision to keep the SB2Cs, he
"exploded." "I thought he was going to stomp me." But "he smiled sweetly in
a minute and told me to get with Jim Thach and write some blue dispatches
for him to vent his ire and get the program back on track."[32] McCain was not
about to give up on his opposition to the SB2C.

Another consideration for McCain while the task force lay over at Ulithi was coordinating ship movements to maximize antiaircraft gunfire. He understood that fighters normally broke off their pursuit of attackers when they came within range of the ships' antiaircraft batteries, allowing gunners free fields of fire without the need to distinguish between friendly and hostile aircraft. Within that context, task group commanders had to understand how best to maneuver their ships to achieve the greatest volume of gunfire. Much depended on the direction of the wind and whether the threat came from aircraft making diving attacks or coming in low over the water. For example, a ship on course into the wind meant that a dive-bomber had to steepen its dive, whereas a downwind course resulted in a shallower trajectory, both of which affected the accuracy of AA fire. Torpedo planes preferred to attack from ahead or just off the bow to minimize the deflection problem; a downwind course eased the problem and an upwind course made it more difficult. Ships achieved the greatest volume of fire off their beams due to the symmetrical layout of their antiaircraft batteries. As a result of his analysis, McCain concluded that "high speed into the wind or changes of course through the wind will contribute to our safety and not necessarily interfere with gunfire." To provide the best defense against low-level torpedo planes, he recommended that ships should first present their beams to the attacker, maximizing gunfire, then quickly maneuver upwind when the planes came within torpedo range to make the attacker's deflection problem more difficult.[33] McCain's ideas were based on sophisticated analysis and careful observations, but they were not necessarily easily accomplished by task groups under aerial assault from multiple directions while maneuvering at high speed and still maintaining the integrity of the carrier group.

McCain and his staff decided that a major reorganization of the task force was necessary to solve the antiaircraft fire problem and maximize the protection of the fleet. Instead of four task groups, they decided to concentrate the carriers into three larger and more cohesive assemblages. The groups would be closer together, allowing more effective command and control, coordination of fighter direction among task groups, as well as concentration of combat air patrols and the carriers' protective surface screens. In part, the change was an expedient, the result of the attrition from the intense two months of operations, which had worn down the units, but it proved effective in augmenting fleet defense in subsequent operations.[34]

While McCain, his staff, and the task group commanders planned for the Mindoro operation, TF-38 aircrew had more than a week of badly needed rest and relaxation. McCain emphasized that aviators had to have time off. He wrote to Halsey on 12 November that "after the protracted operations such as recently encountered in the PHILIPPINE campaign, [air] groups occasionally lose tone to such an extent as to make an immediate shift practically mandatory for assured effectiveness." At least three weeks ashore during each six-month combat tour was essential both for morale and for the training needed to maintain the "offensive qualities of our fast carrier forces." Ulithi was not yet fully prepared to accommodate all of McCain's weary sailors, many of whom had to put in long hours and days loading provisions and ammunition and doing essential repairs and maintenance to ships and aircraft. Some recreation facilities were ready at Mogmog and Sorlen, islands at the northern extremity of the atoll. Sorlen had a palm-shaded white sand beach, lapped by the lagoon's gentle waters, and Mogmog featured basketball courts, baseball diamonds, and a football field. Soft drinks and beer (sometimes cold, but most often warm Iron City imported from Pittsburgh) were available to enlisted personnel, while thirsty officers, true to the Navy's social structure, could also imbibe whiskey and other hard liquor. Within another month, Mogmog and Sorlen had the capacity to entertain eight thousand enlisted personnel and a thousand officers daily.[35]

To cover the Mindoro landings, TF-38, rather than standing immobilized off the central Philippines, would now range north and east of Luzon, hammering airfields and shipping in and around the big island and interdicting Japanese naval and air forces staging from Formosa and the Ryukyus. Halsey envisioned Operation Obliteration as a "strategic" support mission that provided mobility for the fast carriers and protection from kamikazes while preventing the Japanese from using airfields in Luzon to menace the Mindoro operation and softening up Luzon in preparation for the 9 January invasion. Carrier operations were to be coordinated with searches by land-based aircraft out of the Marianas, submarine patrols, and Army Air Forces strikes on targets in Formosa and Japan. Halsey had earlier suggested to Nimitz that as part of his operation the carriers make a foray into the South China Sea to strike remaining elements of the Japanese fleet, airfields, and industrial targets. Nimitz scuttled the idea, although he did leave the door open for Halsey to take the task force there at a later date.[36]

McCain's plan, framed in his Op Order 4-44 of 7 December, amplified Halsey's. TF-38 would be organized into three task groups: Montgomery's TG-38.1, Bogan's TG-38.2, and Sherman's TG-38.3. Davison's group was temporarily dissolved. The task force would exit Ulithi starting on 10 December, fuel on the twelfth, and launch its first strikes at first light on the fourteenth, a day before the Mindoro operation. Additional strikes would follow on the fifteenth and sixteenth, after which the carriers would withdraw to refuel in preparation for three more days of strikes on 19, 20, and 21 December if needed. To "induce a certain degree of paralysis" in Japanese air power, McCain wanted fighters to unfold the "blanket" over as many airfields as possible and avoid chasing escaping aircraft, leaving them to be picked off by other fighters positioned overhead nearby. Employing the three-strike system, six strikes per day would rotate in and out of the target areas. Fighters armed with rockets and bombs would go in on the first day's strikes, with dive-bombers and torpedo planes following after enemy air opposition had been eliminated or suppressed. So-called heckling missions would be flown at night by low-flying night fighters to harass the enemy. Montgomery had responsibility for southern and southwestern Luzon, including Manila, Bogan was assigned to Clark and other airfields north of Manila, and Sherman's group targeted Lingayen Gulf and objectives farther north on Luzon.[37]

Clouds and scattered rain showers obscured the horizon when the *Hancock*, McCain's flagship commanded by Capt. Robert F. Hickey, along with the *Hornet* and four destroyers, weighed anchor at Ulithi on the morning of 10 December for exercises north of the atoll. Montgomery's TG-38.1 had sortied about two hours earlier. The rest of Bogan's TG-38.2 sailed at dawn on the eleventh and joined up with McCain's group outside the anchorage; Sherman's TG-38.3, the last of the units, followed Bogan an hour later. When all three task groups rendezvoused north and west of Ulithi at noon on the twelfth, TF-38 had thirteen fast carriers divided among the three reconstituted task groups. Montgomery's group included the *Essex*-class carriers *Yorktown* and *Wasp* and the light carriers *Cowpens* and *Monterey*, supported by the battleships *Massachusetts* (BB 59) and *Alabama* (BB 60), four heavy cruisers and one light cruiser, and a screen of fifteen destroyers. Bogan's TG-38.2 was a five-carrier group with three *Essexes* (the *Lexington*, *Hancock*, and *Hornet*), plus the *Cabot* and *Independence* and the *New Jersey* (Halsey's flagship), *Iowa*, and *Wisconsin* (BB 64) in the support force, along with five light cruisers and a screen of twenty destroyers. Sherman commanded the *Essex* and *Ticonderoga* and the light carriers *Langley* (CVL 27) and *San Jacinto* in TG-38.3, with the battleships *Washington* (BB 56), *South Dakota* (BB 57), and *North Carolina* and four light cruisers in the support force and eighteen destroyers in the screen.[38]

After more exercises on the twelfth and five hours refueling from TG-30.8 oilers on the thirteenth, the task force formed up for the over-night twenty-two-knot run into Luzon. The first of a succession of fighter sweeps launched at 0630 on the fourteenth from about ninety miles east of the island, blanketing airfields and suppressing Japanese air power before the Mindoro landings the next day. In 614 sorties McCain's rocket- and bomb-armed fighters hit forty-six Japanese air bases, primarily in the vicin-ity of Manila, reporting the destruction of 40 enemy planes in the air and another 139 on the ground, despite the Japanese efforts at dispersal and concealment. Four Japanese tankers and transports of varying size were sent to the bottom, and four destroyers and a destroyer escort were damaged and probably sunk. Runways, oil storage facilities, ammunition dumps, and a radar site also came under attack. Heavy antiaircraft fire accounted for most of the ten combat losses suffered by the force; another seventeen fighters fell in operational accidents. Seventeen pilots were either killed or missing, although two of those shot down might have found their way into the hands of friendly Filipinos.[39]

Task Force 38 kept up the pressure on the fifteenth. With no immediate threats to the flattops and needing to make up for some of the aircraft lost the previous day, McCain granted Bogan permission to divert some of his group's CAP fighters to augment the fighter sweeps, adding to the total of 638 offensive missions that netted fifty-four planes destroyed, all but seven on the ground. Once the opposition had been all but eliminated in the skies over Luzon, the Helldivers and Avengers swooped in. Along with the fighters, they battered enemy shipping, mostly in Manila and Subic Bays, sinking an amphibious ship, a small frigate, a cargo vessel, and the transport *Oryoku Maru*, killing hundreds of American POWs. Other targets included hangars, warehouses, docks, an oil tank, an ammunition dump, and railroad locomotives. Four fighters, a dive-bomber, and a torpedo plane went down in combat, and another eleven fighters and three torpedo planes were lost in operations; seven pilots were dead or missing.[40]

Generally, TF-38's efforts on the fourteenth and fifteenth paid off. Sup-ported by Seventh Fleet escort carriers, the Mindoro landings went off on the fifteenth mostly according to plan. Yet the operation was not without its cost to the Navy. On the thirteenth, kamikazes had heavily damaged the light cruiser *Nashville* (CL 43) and crashed a destroyer as they escorted the invasion force off Negros. Army troops encountered minimal enemy opposition on shore and quickly secured the airfield at San Jose and other objectives on the southwest side of the island. That day the invasion force met only occasional and mostly ineffectual interference from Japanese aircraft, although kamikazes sank two LSTs and damaged another destroyer.[41]

In the middle of the first strikes of the day on the morning the sixteenth, fighters from the *Hancock* and *Lexington* encountered eleven Japanese planes on a heading for the task force. In short order, all the enemy aircraft—Bettys and Nakajima Ki-44 ("Tojo") fighters—were shot down, ending the threat to the task force even before it began. The toll for the rest of the day indicated how badly Japanese air power had been hurt: four more planes were destroyed in the air and only twenty-two on the ground. Enemy ships sunk included two transports and an assortment of lesser vessels. With fewer air and shipping targets, TF-38 concentrated on ground objectives. Fighters and bombers tore up a truck convoy, a train, an ammunition dump, a hangar, a storehouse, and damaged various other structures and railroad equipment. The Navy fliers even managed to bring down a railroad bridge, a particularly difficult target for aircraft. Eleven fighters and three dive-bombers were lost, along with seven pilots and crewmen. With the war devolving into a succession of bloody attrition campaigns designed to wear the Japanese down in stages, statistics mattered. Over three days and more than 1,900 sorties, TF-38 claimed 62 enemy aircraft shot down and 208 destroyed on the ground (adjusted for overclaims, roughly 43 in the air and 146 on the ground), at the cost of 61 aircraft and 31 men. Nearly 86,000 tons of warships and merchant vessels were reported sunk or damaged. As the task force withdrew to its designated refueling point about three hundred miles east of Samar, Halsey congratulated the officers and men for "a brilliantly planned and executed operation." What was more, McCain's and Thach's Big Blue Blanket had been a resounding success.[42]

Growing concerns about the deteriorating weather tempered any euphoria in the task force as it approached the rendezvous with Jasper Acuff's TG-30.8's oilers on the morning of the seventeenth. Acuff had split his group into three units, roughly aligned north to south, each to refuel one of the task groups. The *Hancock* and other ships began fueling at 1025, but heavy seas caused steering problems. After several instances where vessels nearly collided, McCain ordered an increase in speed from eight to ten knots in an effort to maintain the ships' steerage way. Finally, at 1251 Halsey canceled all refueling. Forty minutes later, TF-38 broke away from the replenishment group and altered course to the north and west to rendezvous again at dawn the next day. McCain ordered three of the destroyers, deemed most critically low on fuel from three days of screening the task force, to stay with the oilers, from which they hoped to gulp down enough oil to tide them over until everyone reached the new refueling point.[43]

No one, least of all McCain, knew that the heavy weather on the seventeenth was the result of a major storm that had been brewing for days in the eastern Philippine Sea. Only two days before, on the fifteenth, Pacific Fleet Weather Central at Pearl Harbor had begun to dispatch weather map analyses twice daily. Other meteorological information came from weather stations on Kwajalein and Manus. In addition, starting in early November, aerographers attached to seaplanes patrolling from Kossol Passage, Palau, had been reporting on local weather conditions. As early as the fourteenth, the first day of TF-38's Luzon strikes, Fleet Weather Central had reported that a tropical disturbance had been detected southeast of Guam. Far removed from TF-38's operating area, and in fact totally unrelated to another disturbance building up undetected closer to the fleet, the nascent storm did not alarm any of Halsey's or McCain's aerological staff. On the *New Jersey*, Cdr. George F. Kosco was Third Fleet's chief aerological officer. A Naval Academy graduate with an MS degree in aerology from MIT, he had served on carriers and had studied hurricanes in the Caribbean. As a seasoned weather warrior, he knew the potential dangers of operating in the western Pacific during the typhoon season, which generally ran from June to December. Nothing he observed on the fourteenth or fifteenth seemed out of the ordinary or inconsistent with the wind and sea conditions emanating from a weak cold front approaching the task force from the northwest.[44]

On the sixteenth, Kosco had informed Halsey that he thought a storm was making up far to the southeast between Ulithi and Guam and that reports from Fleet Weather Central appeared to verify that location. He believed that even if it was not snuffed out by the cold front, the storm was likely to follow the path of other tropical disturbances and track (or "recurve") safely to the north. At about 1000 on the seventeenth, the seaplane tender *Chandeleur* (AV 10), operating out of Kossol Passage, passed the word that one of its Martin PBM-3D Mariner flying boats on routine patrol had detected a storm with sixty-knot winds at 13 degrees north and 132 degrees east. Meanwhile, the *Hornet's* aerologist noted that by noon that day the cloud formations and a stiffening northeasterly wind backing to the north left "little doubt as to the approach of a cyclonic storm from the southeast," but he did not specify how far it was from the task force. That afternoon Kosco estimated that the storm was strengthening and was about

200 miles closer to the task force than he had originally thought. Yet it was still almost 250 miles away and likely to move northeast as it bumped into the cold front. Sometime after 1400, Kosco saw the *Chandeleur*'s report, which placed the storm even closer to the southeast. At 1540, McCain ordered a course change to bring the fleet to a new (third) refueling point farther to the south and west, which Halsey and his staff believed would be well out of the way of the storm, even if it continued on its present track. Through the evening the task force kept ahead of the storm on a generally parallel course to the west-northwest.[45]

Seas mounted and the wind whipped up overnight. McCain cut the speed of the task force from seventeen to fourteen knots. Calculating that the fleet could not reach the new refueling point by dawn and that based on the *Chandeleur* report the ships might run directly into the path of the storm, Halsey changed his mind and identified still a fourth refueling rendezvous at 15 degrees 30 minutes north and 127 degrees 40 minutes east. Only about twenty-five miles northwest of the task force, the new refueling point was easily reachable by dawn. At midnight, McCain's ships changed course to 180 degrees—due south—then two hours later turned to the northwest, maneuvers that the historian Samuel Eliot Morison wrote were "in the hope of finding smoother water," presumably to effect refueling. At 0227 on 18 December, the task force contacted Acuff's fueling group bearing thirty miles to the northeast and already encountering heavy going at the leading edge of the storm.[46]

In the meantime, Kosco began to doubt his earlier predictions of the storm's intensity and location. He, like McCain and others, noted that local weather conditions continued to worsen through the evening. That, combined with a falling barometer on the fleet flagship, convinced Kosco that the storm was worse than he anticipated and now dangerously close. He now believed that the fleet should take a course to the south. At 0420, after conferring with Kosco, Halsey directed him to radio McCain by TBS to ascertain what information he had on the location of the storm. McCain responded ten minutes later that the weather had deteriorated to the point where it was unlikely his ships could refuel from the oilers and recommended that the big carriers refuel the destroyers as soon as possible. Kosco then radioed Bogan, who responded that he believed the storm was at 17 degrees north and 131 degrees east, or about 190 miles northeast of its actual position at the time. Belatedly realizing that he had not answered Kosco's question, McCain reported at 0555 that he thought the storm was a good distance southeast of the task force and moving northwest at twelve to fifteen knots.[47]

Based on the updated but still mostly opaque meteorological picture, Halsey rescinded orders to refuel at the previous (fourth) rendezvous point and ordered the fleet to head due south. McCain immediately complied, and the task force, along with TG-30.8, turned to 180 degrees. After alongside refueling proved impossible, McCain ordered the destroyers to attempt it over the oilers' sterns, a method intended to reduce the danger of collision. Acuff responded that he had tried to do so the day before and had failed due to the wind and sea conditions; with a nearly forty-knot wind from the north and following seas, astern refueling was not going to happen that morning either. At 0701, in one more effort to get oil into the destroyers, McCain ordered the task force to take a 060-degree heading at a speed of ten knots. Because the new course put the wind off the port bow, he thought the destroyers might be able to refuel from the lee, or starboard, side of the carriers and battleships, but the track took the ships to the north-northeast directly into the teeth of what had now become a vicious typhoon boiling just miles away. Finally, as towering waves and winds exceeding forty knots lashed the task force, McCain canceled all attempts to refuel the destroyers at 0802. At the same time, he received a TBS from Halsey to resume course south, and he did so at 0806.[48]

★ ★ ★ ★

By now it was too late to evade the deadly tempest as it crashed into the fleet. McCain, hearing that Acuff's CVEs were laboring in the huge waves, released them to take the best course and speed. McCain informed Halsey at 0830 that his destroyers were dangerously low on fuel, with some in his own group down to 10 percent reserve and others hovering around 15 percent. There were two problems: one was that some of the ships might run dry; the other was that they needed the oil to maintain a safe ballasted condition in heavy weather. The usual procedure under those circumstances was to pump seawater into the bunkers, but that took time. When fueling did become possible, the water had to be pumped back out, which was also time-consuming, and there was always the possibility of salt water contaminating both the new and the remaining fuel oil. With the fleet scattered and in danger more from the weather than from the Japanese, Halsey informed MacArthur that he would have to postpone further strikes on Luzon.[49]

The 1906 Naval Academy yearbook *Lucky Bag* praised passed
midshipman McCain for his humor
and facetiously congratulated
him as the "skeleton in the family
closet" who gained "1 3/8" ounces
during his time at the Academy.
McCain earned various nicknames,
among them "Mac," "Lentz," and
"Johnnie," but the one that stuck
was "Slew." Robert L. Ghormley,
Aubrey W. ("Jake") Fitch, John H.
Towers, Leigh H. Noyes, Isaac C.
Kidd, and Frank Jack Fletcher were
among his classmates who made
flag rank. Lucky Bag, *Naval History
and Heritage Command*

Ensign McCain served in the battleship *Connecticut* (BB 18), flagship of what was
known as the Great White Fleet. In early 1908, the fleet stopped in Colombo, Ceylon
(now Sri Lanka), allowing McCain and other officers to sample aspects of the local culture. *NHH41663, Naval History and Heritage Command*

McCain's first command was the ammunition ship *Nitro* (AE 2), outfitted to haul explosives for ships of the battle fleet. While McCain was in command from June 1931 to April 1933, the *Nitro* performed unexciting but necessary duty, delivering cargo, passengers, and ammunition to navy yards and depots on the East and West Coasts. NH68307, *Naval History and Heritage Command*

The *Ranger* (CV 4) was the Navy's first carrier built as such from the keel up. Captain McCain commanded the flattop from June 1937 to June 1939, during which time the ship participated in fleet exercises (or "problems") in the Pacific and Caribbean. This photo shows the carrier off Oahu in April 1938. 80-G-464155, *NARA II*

In September 1937, the *Ranger* was part of a Navy goodwill mission to Peru, where the United States was a participant in the Inter-American Technical Aviation Conference in the capital city of Lima. McCain served as master of ceremonies as the carrier crossed the equator on the thirteenth. As part of the occasion, McCain welcomed King Neptune and his court and ordered that "Neptune's flag" fly from the ship's yardarm. *80-GX-391531, NARA II*

McCain assumed command of Naval Air Station North Island in San Diego in July 1939. Over the next year and a half, he oversaw the expansion of North Island's training, material, and operational responsibilities. Here McCain confers with Secretary of the Navy Frank Knox on 16 September 1940 during one of Knox's inspection tours of Navy facilities on the West Coast. Still posted to North Island in January 1941, McCain as a rear admiral assumed new duties as commander, Patrol Wings (Compatwings), U.S. Fleet. *80-GX-318521, NARA II*

As the new commander, Aircraft South Pacific Force (Comairsopac), McCain hoisted his flag on the seaplane tender *Tangier* (AV 8) in the Great Road, Nouméa, New Caledonia, on 20 May 1942. McCain had responsibility for all land-based and tender-based aviation in the South Pacific theater. The *Tangier* is anchored at Nouméa on 11 May with some of its complement of Consolidated PBY-5 Catalina flying boats. *80-G-20751, NARA II*

McCain shifted his flag from the *Tangier* to the seaplane tender *Curtiss* (AV 4) on 20 June 1942. In this photo, the *Curtiss* is transferring supplies and equipment from the *Tangier* at Nouméa. *80-G-20783, NARA II*

In July 1942, McCain's ships and aircraft advanced to a new base at Espíritu Santo in the New Hebrides. Search-and-strike aircraft from Espíritu supported the Allied offensive in the Solomons that began with the Marines' invasion of Guadalcanal on 7 August. *80-G-36090, NARA II*

McCain's South Pacific command included Army Air Forces men and aircraft. As Comairsopac, McCain confers at Espíritu Santo in August 1942 with (*right*) Army Air Forces colonel LaVerne Saunders and Army major general Millard F. Harmon, commanding general, U.S. Army Forces, South Pacific. *80-GX-70587, NARA II*

On 12 August 1942, McCain's flag plane, a Consolidated PBY-5A Catalina amphibian, flew in to the captured airstrip on Guadalcanal, later named Henderson Field in memory of a Marine aviator killed during the Battle of Midway. *Hoover Institution Archives*

McCain visits with 1st Marine Division commander Maj. Gen. Alexander A. ("Archie") Vandegrift on Guadalcanal in late August 1942. *80-GX-12558, NARA II*

After an inspection trip to the South Pacific, McCain, now chief of the Bureau of Aeronautics, flew back to Pearl Harbor with Adm. Chester W. Nimitz, commander in chief, Pacific Fleet, on 24 January 1943. They are shown here during a stopover at Pago Pago. *80-GX-65315, NARA II*

McCain spoke at the commissioning of Naval Air Station Patuxent River on 1 April 1943. Pax River, as it was known, became the Navy's principal aircraft testing and development facility. *80-GX-208438, NARA II*

McCain chairs a conference on aviation training in Washington, 16–17 June 1943. Also present at the meeting were two rear admirals, Alfred E. Montgomery (*third from left*) and George D. Murray (*second from right*), both experienced fast-carrier commanders. *80-GX-41863, NARA II*

As a vice admiral, McCain became the new Deputy Chief of Naval Operations (Air) (DCNO [Air]) in Washington in July 1943. He joined his wife Kate at the launch of the new *Essex*-class carrier *Bon Homme Richard* (CV 31) at the New York (Brooklyn) Navy Yard on 29 April 1944. Kate was the ship's sponsor at the launching ceremonies. *80-GX-179319, NARA II*

DCNO (Air) McCain on the cover of the weekly magazine *Collier's*, 23 October 1943. *JTE Multimedia LLC*

Vice Adm. Aubrey Fitch, one of McCain's Academy classmates, succeeds McCain as DCNO (Air) on 1 August 1944. *80-GX-46196, NARA II*

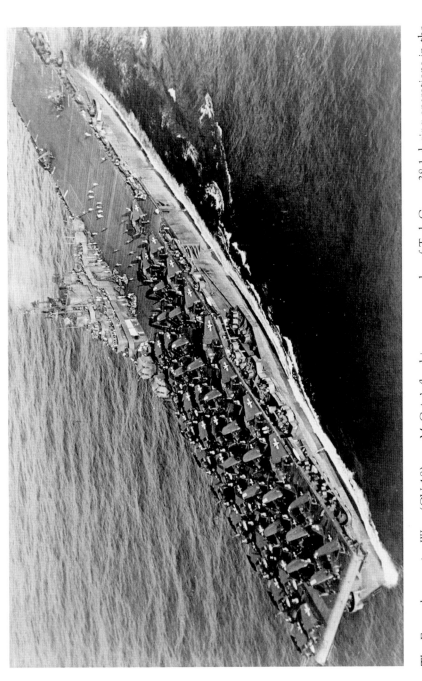

The *Essex*-class carrier *Wasp* (CV 18) was McCain's flagship as commander of Task Group 38.1 during operations in the Philippines and the Battle of Leyte Gulf in the fall of 1944. *80-G-261904, NARA II*

Vice Adm. William F. Halsey awards McCain the Navy Cross on McCain's flagship, the *Essex*-class carrier *Hancock* (CV 19). McCain was awarded the honor on 17 November 1944 for his role in saving the cruisers *Canberra* (CA 70) and *Houston* (CL 81) in the face of unremitting Japanese air assaults off Formosa. *80-GX-29062, NARA II*

Task Force 38 aircraft devastated Japanese shipping in Manila Bay on 13 November 1944. *80-G-272613, NARA II*

Task Force 38 carriers at anchor in the lagoon at Ulithi, Caroline Islands, 8 December 1944. The flattops are sometimes identified as "Murderers Row." 80-G-294131, NARA II

McCain on the *Hancock* in
December 1944. *80-GX-
294462, NARA II*

One of McCain's ships, the light carrier *Langley* (CVL 27), laboring during the typhoon of
17 December 1944. The storm resulted in 3 destroyers sunk, 9 ships heavily damaged, 146
aircraft destroyed, and 790 officers and men lost. *80-G-305484, NARA II*

McCain with his operations officer, Cdr. John S. ("Jimmie") Thach, in flag plot on the *Hancock* in December 1944 or early January 1945. *80-GX-308561, NARA II*

Aircraft from the *Hancock* assault a Japanese shipyard in Hong Kong on 16 January 1945. *80-G-300640, NARA II*

TBM Avenger torpedo bombers from the carrier *Essex*'s Air Group 4 return from strikes on Japanese targets in the Saigon area, 12 January 1945. *80-G-300666, NARA II*

McCain at Ulithi,
late January 1945.
80-GX-308316, NARA II

McCain confers with Rear Adm. Frederick C. Sherman, commander of Task Group 38.3 at Ulithi, in late January 1945 after the South China Sea and Formosa operations. *80-GX-308-305, NARA II*

A Japanese suicide plane strikes the carrier *Ticonderoga*'s (CV 14) island during Task Force 38 operations off Formosa on 21 January 1945. The flattop's skipper, Capt. Dixie Kiefer, and the ship's executive officer, Cdr. William O. Burch, were badly wounded. *80-G-273151, NARA II*

Minutes after the kamikaze hit on the *Ticonderoga*, McCain's flagship *Hancock* was badly damaged when a 500-pound bomb fell from the bomb bay of a TBM torpedo bomber and exploded on the flight deck. Fifty officers and enlisted men died and nearly eighty were injured, some critically. Yet the carrier was back in action only two hours later. *80-G-470287, NARA II*

McCain's new Task Force 38 flagship, the *Essex*-class carrier *Shangri-La* (CV 38), in wartime camouflage. UA 476.42, *Naval Historical Foundation Collection*

McCain assumed command of Task Force 38 and the fast carriers from Vice Adm. Marc A. Mitscher on 27 May 1945. McCain is with Mitscher on the *Shangri-La* off Okinawa during the transfer of command ceremonies. *80-GX-278752, NARA II*

McCain and Thach talk with John L. Sullivan on the *Shangri-La* following his swearing-in as the new Assistant Secretary of the Navy for Air, 2 July 1945. *80-GX-343854, NARA II*

A Japanese hybrid battleship/carrier (either the *Ise* or the *Hyuga*) under attack near the Japanese naval facility at Kure on 24 July 1945. 80-G-490153, NARA II

One of the Japanese rail ferries under attack from McCain's TF-38 aircraft in the waters between Hokkaido and Honshu. The rail ferry strikes on 14 July 1945 reduced coal shipments to 18 percent of their previous levels, crippling Japanese electric power production and other industries dependent on coal. *80-G-490113, NARA II*

McCain on the flag bridge of the *Shangri-La* in August 1945. *80-GX-469006, NARA II*

Victory in the Pacific. McCain's TF-38 carriers maneuver in close formation off Japan for Operation Snapshot on 16 August 1945. *80-G-278815, NARA II*

Halsey and McCain on the *Missouri* (BB 63) following the Japanese surrender ceremonies on 2 September 1945. *80-GX-354119, NARA II*

McCain's son, Cdr. John S. McCain Jr., had lunch with his father on the submarine tender *Proteus* (AS 19) at Yokosuka on 2 September 1945. *80-GX-360354, NARA II*

McCain stopped in Pearl Harbor on 4 September 1945, en route to San Diego. This may be the last official photograph of McCain before his death two days later at his home in Coronado. *80-GX-495611, NARA II*

Not only were the destroyers and escort carriers in peril that morning, so too were McCain's light carriers. Built on light cruiser hulls, with "blisters" extending below the waterlines to compensate for the added topside weight, the *Independence*-class CVLs had a reputation for instability. A 1945 study comparing them to the bigger carriers found that their "motion in a seaway . . . is sufficient, at times, to make [air] operations much more hazardous than in the larger vessels," and that "judicious choice of speed, course, and acceleration" was necessary for safety under certain conditions. That became obvious at 0916 when the *Monterey* in Montgomery's group signaled that fires had broken out on the hangar deck. After a particularly violent roll, aircraft had torn loose from their hold-downs and crashed into other planes, which caught fire even though their gas tanks had been emptied. When the carrier came around to a new course to lessen the rolling, McCain ordered the task force to follow, but the *Cowpens*, also laboring in the heavy seas, could not comply and remained on a heading of 140 degrees. McCain detached two destroyers to stay with the *Cowpens* and told Montgomery to operate his group independently, while the other two groups assumed a heading of 140 degrees. At 0932, Montgomery reported that the *Monterey* was dead in the water and that he had ordered a cruiser and two destroyers to stand by to assist. At 0944, the ship radioed that the conflagration was under control and at 1000 that it had been extinguished. The commanding officer hoped to have power restored soon, but it took another hour and a half before the carrier got under way.[50]

McCain tried a new course (200 degrees) and speed at 1043 that he anticipated would allow the task force to retain its integrity and permit the light carriers to ride easier. Seven minutes later, the *Cowpens* radioed that it, too, had a hangar fire and was having steering problems; the fire was swiftly brought under control and the ship had managed to swing left to lessen the rolling. In the meantime, the *San Jacinto* in Sherman's group reported that, like her sister ships, planes had broken loose on the hangar deck. Halsey released the task force at 1148 to "take the most comfortable course," and McCain turned left to 120 degrees, putting the wind on the port quarter, and advised Acuff of the new heading. But Acuff's ships were having their own problems. The escort carrier *Cape Esperance* (CVE 88) was fighting a fire on the flight deck, and Acuff's flagship, the destroyer *Aylwin* (DD 355), was without power and communications. Lookouts on the *Hancock* spotted three destroyers dead in the water four and a half miles off the carrier's port bow. By 1330, sixty-eight-knot winds from the northwest were punishing the task force with sheets of rain and zero visibility. The *New Jersey* recorded gusts of ninety-three knots. About that time SM (search) radars on the *Hornet*, *Wasp*, and *Yorktown* detected the center of what obviously was a typhoon north of the task force, one of the first times anyone had seen images of the eye of a storm. By 1400, when the *San Jacinto* reported that it also had a fire, caused when planes loose on the hangar deck severed an oil line, McCain came to the grim realization that he had lost control of his task force in the midst of a battle of a different sort in the Philippine Sea.[51]

More than anything else, survival was the priority for many that after-noon as the wind and waves hammered the fleet, and radios crackled with one emergency call after another. Possibly because he had a difficult time facing the reality that he had blundered into a storm he had tried so hard to avoid, Halsey did not report to Nimitz until 1345 that he was in the middle of a full-blown typhoon. Tales of heroism—and even some accusations of cowardice—attended the struggles of the ships and their crews. In Acuff's group, two *Farragut*-class destroyers, the *Monaghan* (DD 354) and the *Hull*, capsized and sank with heavy loss of life; the newer *Fletcher*-class destroyer *Spence* (DD 512) in Bogan's group rolled on its side, failed to recover, and was never seen again. The skipper of another *Farragut*-class ship, the *Dewey* (DD 349), saw the bridge inclinometer peg itself at 73 degrees; his vessel survived partly as the result of losing its forward funnel, which fortuitously reduced topside weight just when it looked like the ship would founder like its sisters.[52]

Winds and seas peaked in the early afternoon before gradually diminish-ing as the weather cleared and McCain's task force edged to the south toward still one more fueling rendezvous scheduled for early on the nineteenth. TF-38 met the logistics group at 0715, and McCain organized a comprehen-sive air-sea search for missing ships and sailors, now strewn over more than 2,500 square nautical miles. Destroyers and destroyer escorts pulled more than eighty survivors from the waters over the next three days. Later that morning, McCain went over to the *New Jersey* to confer with Halsey, assess the damage, and coordinate the rescue effort. It did not take long to realize that the losses were catastrophic: three destroyers sunk, nine ships heavily damaged, including three fast carriers (the *Monterey*, *San Jacinto*, and *Cow-pens*). Destroyed or damaged beyond repair were 146 aircraft, and 790 offi-cers and men were lost or dead; another 80 were injured. Halsey still held out hope to resume strikes on Luzon, but it quickly became apparent that in the aftermath of the typhoon, rescue planning took precedence and that further

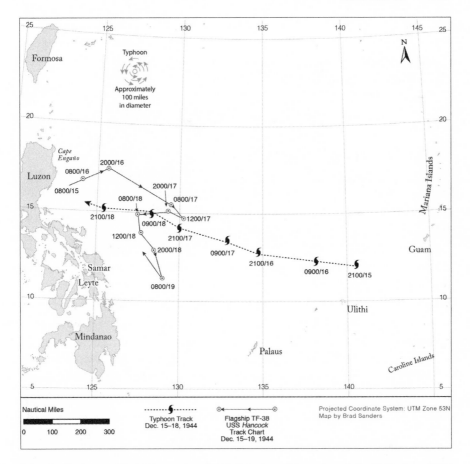

Map 5. Typhoon, 17–18 December 1944 (Morison, *Liberation of the Philippines*; USS *Hancock* War Diary, Dec. 1–31, 1944, www.Fold3.com, accessed April 24, 2013)

offensive operations were impossible. The reality sank in that the task force would have to retire for repairs and replenishment. After completing fueling on the afternoon of the twenty-second, the task force set course for Ulithi, staggering in to the atoll on the morning of the twenty-fourth.[53]

En route to Ulithi, McCain sent a personal letter to King. He guessed that King had supported him in October when Nimitz had speculated that in the aftermath of the Formosa campaign he was not up to the rigors of task force command. McCain knew that he was in the doghouse and that as a result of the typhoon there was a good chance he could lose King's confidence. A heartfelt expression of his appreciation was in order. "I needed, without modification or qualification, and of equal value,"

McCain wrote, "(1) Your assurance that you wished me well, and (2) your statement of confidence in my ability. So, I owe to you the maintenance of my self-respect, and such measure of success as I have had in the fighting, and thank you therefor."[54]

The day after Christmas, a court of inquiry convened at Ulithi on board the destroyer tender *Cascade* (AD 16) to investigate the context and consequences of the typhoon, which had now earned the nickname Cobra. Vice Adm. John H. Hoover, commander, Forward Areas, Central Pacific, presided, with Comairpac Rear Adm. George Murray and Rear Adm. Glenn B. Davis, a battleship division commander, on the panel. Capt. Herbert K. Gates, an engineering specialist, was the court's judge advocate, responsible for record keeping and for much of the questioning. Due to operational and planning priorities, the court called witnesses as they were available or when they were released from other duties. McCain came before the court at 1000 on the twenty-eighth. His testimony was brief. It was clear from his and previous officers' testimony that he had been the OTC and had made all decisions about the courses and speeds of TF-38 before, during, and after the storm. He admitted that as the weather worsened on the seventeenth he "did not appreciate at that time the oncoming speed of the gathering storm" and believed that "a movement of 100 or 200 miles would perhaps put us in the clear." Not until the morning of the eighteenth did he become "individually concerned" about the severity of the storm. A mitigating factor in deciding where to position the task force had been "the pressure of a commitment to strike Luzon, which I believe was uppermost in my mind and I'm sure uppermost in the minds of my staff." Court members asked if he had relied too much on "outside stations" and had ignored information from subordinate commanders who may have had more accurate information on the direction and strength of the typhoon. He simply replied, "I have no opinion of value on that." Nor was he willing without first conferring with TF-38's navigator to specify what course the task force had taken or should have taken immediately before encountering the typhoon.[55]

Whereas McCain was vague in his testimony, Halsey was not. He insisted that he did not have "timely warning" of the typhoon before correcting himself: "I'll put it another way. I had no warning." He was "under obligations" to strike Luzon, and his destroyers and other ships needed to refuel at the same time his fleet had to avoid a storm the intensity and direction of which he and Kosco had to ascertain based on a single outdated and incomplete weather report. From experience, he knew that the destroyers faced potential stability problems when they were in "light condition," as some of them were on the morning of the eighteenth. By that time, "there was no doubt in my mind" that the fleet was in store for a major storm but that it was "too late to do anything" either about refueling his ships or maneuvering to avoid the severe weather.[56]

More than fifty witnesses testified over more than a week before Hoover concluded the court's proceedings. In his report to Nimitz on 13 January, Hoover pointed the finger of blame squarely at Halsey, who bore the "preponderance of responsibility" for the disaster. Although Halsey's decisions about fleet movements had been "logical" under the circumstances, he had been responsible for "large errors in predicting the location and path" of the typhoon and had placed "too much reliance" on information from Fleet Weather Central. Moreover, Halsey was guilty of "wishful reasoning" and a "false sense of security" in attempting to continue offensive operations and ignoring the advice of subordinate commanders who had better knowledge of the local weather conditions. McCain shared Halsey's guilt. His decision to take course 060 degrees early on the eighteenth was an "error in judgment" that according to one historian "made a significant difference" at a critical juncture when the force still had time to avoid the typhoon. Nevertheless, while Halsey and McCain, as the officers in command, were responsible, the court concluded that the mistakes were made "under stress of war operations" and that "the extent of the blame as it applies to Commander Third Fleet or others, was impractical to assess."[57]

Among the court of inquiry's many recommendations were design studies by the Bureau of Ships aimed at improving the stability of light carriers and destroyers, especially under adverse weather conditions. Furthermore, the ships' commanding officers had to be fully aware of their vessels' stability characteristics and take all necessary precautions during storms. Officers also had to understand that they were likely to encounter typhoons and other tropical disturbances in the western Pacific. The court recommended that one or more weather ships be stationed in the Philippine Sea and that weather reconnaissance flights be scheduled at least twice daily. Aerological instruction needed improvement, as well, and more experienced aerological officers needed to be assigned to the Third and Fifth Fleets.[58]

Nimitz and King approved Hoover's report in their endorsements of 22 January and 21 February, respectively. King suggested minor changes in the wording of the court's findings that reflected his sentiment that Halsey and McCain had insufficient weather information and that their errors had been the result of their "firm determination" to carry out their mission. Nimitz used the typhoon as the cue for a letter to the fleet on 13 February in which he stressed the importance of sound seamanship. Even in the age of radio, radar, airborne reconnaissance, and sophisticated weather forecasting, a ship's master had to employ "ceaseless vigilance" in reading the wind and seas and understanding the basic laws of storms that had governed navigation for centuries. "Nothing is more dangerous than for a seaman to be grudging in taking precautions lest they turn out to have been unnecessary. Safety at sea for a thousand years has depended on exactly the opposite philosophy."[59]

In his oral history decades later, Thach recalled that McCain took the loss of ships and men "very personally" and that "it took a lot out of him." Thach had conferred with McCain on 16 and 17 December as information about the location of the typhoon filtered in to flag plot on the *Hancock*. The storm, Thach maintained, traced a "little loop" and as a result "it was very difficult to determine what track the typhoon was really on." He concluded that McCain's decision on the afternoon of the seventeenth to change course to the south and west might have taken the task force clear of the worst of the storm. Based on information he had from his aerologist and from Pearl Harbor, it was Halsey's "prerogative" as fleet commander to make the final decision about the best course.[60]

The historian Clark Reynolds was unequivocal in his condemnation of McCain for his part in taking the fast carriers into the typhoon. "Slew McCain played no positive role during the typhoon," Reynolds wrote, "and gave little evidence that he would have helped the situation." But Reynolds' contention that McCain "did not try to communicate with the task group commanders" during the storm is not true. There is no doubt that as the officer in tactical command of TF-38, McCain, after Halsey, bore responsibility for the disaster. He lost the crucial situational awareness that all officers in combat must exercise, and in his focus on accomplishing the mission, he could not visualize the bigger picture, of which the weather was a major component. Related was his insistence on maintaining the integrity of the task force when the safety of ships and men should have assumed priority. He could have, as another historian has suggested, refueled his destroyers from the carriers overnight on the fourteenth or fifteenth. But refueling at sea in daytime was a complex evolution; at night it would have involved excessive risk and upset the carriers' complex strike preparations and launch schedules.[61] Warfare, especially at sea, offers harsh lessons for even the most seasoned commanders, who must always assess risks and rewards in making decisions that literally involve life and death. Regardless of how much blame McCain deserved for his decisions before and during the typhoon, it was undeniable that mighty TF-38 had a lost a battle with the vast indifference of nature. McCain had blundered badly yet stayed in command of the fast carriers. It was now time to refocus on the job at hand: taking the naval air war even closer to the heart of the Japanese empire.

CHAPTER 9

Luzon and the South China Sea

It was not home. But for the officers and men of John McCain's TF-38 and for their weather-beaten and battle-scarred ships, Ulithi that Christmas Eve of 1944 was a welcome refuge. While the crews of his ships and aircraft unwound ashore at Sorlen's and Mogmog's bars and beaches, there was no rest for the fleet logistic support units. For the next week, the personnel of Service Squadron (Servron) 10 toiled twenty-four hours a day reprovisioning and rearming the task force in preparation for its return to action in the Philippines. Day and night, refrigerator ships, aviation store ships, ammunition ships, oilers, lighters, hospital ships, tugs, amphibious craft, and all manner of vessels great and small churned the waters of the deep blue lagoon. Just shuttling people around the vast atoll taxed the availability of launches and small boats. Heavy repair facilities were still not available at Ulithi, especially the big floating dry docks at Guam and Manus, yet repair ships with Servron 2 were able to deal with most of the storm-damaged ships, among them the *Essex*-class carriers *Hancock*, *Lexington*, *Wasp*, *Yorktown*, and *Ticonderoga*, and the light carriers *Independence*, *Cowpens*, *Langley*, and *Cabot*. The *Monterey* was an exception and had to retire to the West Coast for repairs.[1]

According to Halsey's plan to support the amphibious landings at Lingayen Gulf (code-named Mike-1), McCain's fast carriers would sortie from Ulithi ten days before the operation, which had been scheduled for 9 January. For two days TF-38 fighters and bombers would strike Formosa, then hit targets in Luzon on the sixth before returning to Formosa on the ninth. As opportunities arose, TF-38 fighters would carry out sweeps over Okinawa and other islands in the Ryukyus. Cincpac Nimitz concurred with Halsey that the Luzon operation was an opportunity to exploit the mobility of McCain's carriers to deliver potentially fatal blows to the Japanese while interdicting enemy naval and air forces staging through Formosa to Luzon. Halsey also wanted to pursue what remained of the Japanese Combined Fleet into the South China Sea, where intelligence indicated that the hybrid battleship-carriers *Ise* and *Hyuga* and other heavy units had fled after the defeat at Leyte Gulf. Japanese battleships and carriers remaining in the home islands were also potential threats to the Luzon and subsequent campaigns. Nimitz tentatively approved Halsey's proposal to go after Japanese bases, aircraft, and shipping in the littorals of the South China Sea—in Halsey's words "hitting them in the belly"—so long as he accomplished the primary task of covering the Lingayen landings.[2]

Meanwhile, only three days after anchoring at Ulithi, McCain and his staff had put the finishing touches on a plan that amplified Halsey's scheme to support the Luzon landings. McCain's operation order (Op Order 5-44) called for TF-38 to cover the amphibious landings by assaulting enemy naval and air forces in the Philippines and at their sources in Formosa and the Ryukyus, in addition to rooting out the vestiges of the Japanese fleet, thought to be hiding at Camranh Bay in Indochina. That enemy ships could disrupt the Luzon operations was evident from a hit-and-run raid on the Mindoro beachhead by Japanese cruisers and destroyers out of Camranh Bay on 26 December. McCain believed that while the Japanese had been badly hurt by recent losses in the Philippines, they would "commit [their] total available air strength in opposition to our landings on LUZON." The task force had to be fully prepared for enemy air attacks, many of them kamikazes, from bases in Luzon, Formosa, and the island of Hainan, although McCain estimated that the assaults would not quite have the intensity or frequency of those endured by the fleet in October and November. McCain's fighters, torpedo planes, and dive-bombers were to spread the "Big Blue Blanket" over airfields in Formosa, accompanied by fighter sweeps over Okinawa. Then, after refueling, the task force would turn its attention to Luzon three days before the landings, concentrating on targets roughly north of 17 degrees north, leaving most objectives south of the line to the AAF but reserving the right to cross the line if threats to the fleet materialized from bases in and around Manila. TF-38 would continue to hit Formosa and the southern Ryukyus while staying alert on "short notice to intercept an enemy Task Force or to attack concentrations of enemy ships and aircraft on the China coast."[3] McCain's plan was situational and contingent, reflecting the power and flexibility of the fast carrier task force.

McCain's carrier force was divided as before into three task groups— TG-38.1, TG-38.2, and TG-38.3—commanded, respectively, by Rear Adms. Arthur Radford, Gerald Bogan, and Frederick Sherman. Radford took over TG-38.1 on 29 December after Montgomery had been injured in a freak accident while transferring from a launch to an escort carrier in the anchorage. McCain's force included no fewer than eight heavy and four light carriers, along with six fast battleships, thirteen cruisers, and fifty-four destroyers. McCain flew his flag in the *Hancock*, attached to Bogan's group. To provide a round-the-clock dimension to the force, two carriers, the *Enterprise* and the *Independence*, formed TG-38.5, a night fighter group commanded by Rear Adm. Matt Gardner and operating as part of Bogan's group during the day and independently after dusk. Repaired after the kamikaze hit from 25 November, the *Essex*, in Sherman's TG-38.3, embarked two Marine fighter squadrons, VMF-124 and VMF-213, equipped with F4U Corsairs, the first time leathernecks flew from a TF-38 flattop.[4]

With the impending deployment of Marine air units, McCain saw another opportunity to lobby for strengthening the carriers' fighter groups while disposing of what he considered to be the troublesome SB2C Helldivers. On the twenty-fifth, he sent a message to Rear Adm. George Murray, Comairpac in Pearl Harbor, with his ideas. "In view of critical operation[s] in near future, the nature of which will require all possible VF strength in the Task Force for wide spread offensive missions," he recommended that "15 Helldivers be removed from both ESSEX and WASP to make room for the 36 Hellcats displaced by 36 Corsairs in ESSEX." By McCain's calculus the *Essex* would have thirty-six F4Us, fifty-five F6Fs, and fifteen TBMs, and the *Wasp's* new aircraft complement would be ninety-one F6Fs and fifteen TBMs. Removing the larger Helldivers left plenty of room for more of the smaller fighters. The former Helldiver aviators could remain in theater in case more bombers were needed or go back to the states to be retrained. McCain's persistence paid off, at least in part. On 3 January, Nimitz told him that unless there were extraordinary circumstances all large carriers would have seventy-three fighters (one more than King had decreed on 23 December), and would keep fifteen dive-bombers and fifteen torpedo planes.[5]

Capt. Jasper Acuff's TF-30.8 support group sortied from Ulithi on the morning of 29 December, followed by each of the carrier task groups in succession the following morning. The *Hancock* and TG-38.2 cleared the harbor at 0947, meeting up with the other groups that evening at a point about sixty miles northwest of the atoll and setting course northwest at a speed of twenty-two knots. The next morning the task force slowed, the carriers brushed up on their defensive tactics with more Moose-trap exercises, and the heavy screening ships broke off for separate gunnery, antiaircraft, and antisubmarine practice. At 1800, the force again came together in its cruising formation and resumed course slightly more to the west. The next day saw more drills, including simulated air attacks on the formation, with CAP and Jack patrols flown that evening before the force set course overnight for the fueling rendezvous with Acuff's group at daybreak the next morning, 2 January. Largely due to poor weather, refueling was not completed until 1545. A little more than an hour later, the task force turned west and began its overnight twenty-five-knot run in to the launch position about seventy-five miles east of Formosa.[6]

More foul weather early on the morning of the third held up the first strikes until 0724. A low ceiling obscured many of the targets, prompting McCain to call off further attacks early that afternoon. At 1408, after conferring with McCain, Halsey directed the force to retire overnight to a point off Cape Engaño southeast of Formosa. Despite improvements in photo intelligence and damage assessment, no one could be certain about the results of the attacks, although McCain estimated that twenty-seven enemy aircraft were splashed and another fifty-eight destroyed on the ground. Using the 70 percent overclaim rate, it is safe to assume that nineteen aircraft were shot down and more than forty were destroyed on the ground by TF-38 aircraft. In 527 offensive missions, 133 tons of bombs and 14 torpedoes were dropped. McCain's aviators claimed they sank two destroyer escorts and three cargo ships and damaged another fourteen ships, among them a large destroyer, but the 1947 assessment of Japanese records showed only two cargo ships and an aircraft ferry sunk that day. Hangars, docks, radar stations, locomotives, and railway bridges were targeted. The cost: fifteen TF-38 fighters and torpedo planes lost in combat, ten in operational accidents, and fifteen pilots and aircrew killed or missing. Considering the miserable weather conditions both at sea and over the targets, which disrupted the three-strike rotation, these were creditable results, although kamikazes crashed three Seventh Fleet escort carriers, one of which, the *Ommaney Bay* (CVE 79), burned and sank on 4 January.[7]

Back in launch position east of Formosa at 0700 on the fourth, TF-38 ran into the same bad weather that had curtailed operations on the third. Strikes got off mostly on schedule that morning, but conditions soured to the point that shortly after noon McCain canceled operations and recalled his aircraft, which were back on board by 1540. Bogeys appeared but did not threaten the task force. On the other hand, McCain's ships had to thread through a barrage of floating and moored mines throughout the day, luckily without any damage. TF-38 airmen claimed three Japanese aircraft shot down and twenty-three destroyed on the ground. In 471 strike sorties, the aviators reported that they had sunk two small transports and damaged a destroyer escort; warehouses, ammunition dumps, and an aircraft factory at Okayama were also bombed, strafed, and rocketed. Postwar analysis indicated that carrier aircraft sank no naval or merchant ships that day, but the records do show a destroyer escort sunk on the fifth near the Philippines. Seven task force fighters were lost in combat and operations, along with seven pilots and aircrew. One of the casualties, killed in a midair collision with his wingman over Heito, was the *Hancock*'s VF-7 skipper, Lt. Cdr. Leonard Check, with whom just seven weeks earlier McCain had discussed the results of raids on Luzon.[8]

Before sunrise on the fifth, McCain's ships rendezvoused with the oilers in Acuff's support group and began refueling at 0546. Later that morning, Matt Gardner arrived with the *Enterprise* from Pearl Harbor and flew over to the *Hancock* to brief McCain on his night carrier operations. As McCain had planned, the *Enterprise* joined the *Independence* and six destroyers in the new night group, TG-38.5, operating radar-equipped F6Fs and TBMs. Although their primary responsibilities were nocturnal strike, heckling, and CAP missions, the night carriers and their crews had to be on twenty-four-hour alert, augmenting the task force CAP as necessary and making their flight decks available for any emergencies that might arise. Following refueling operations, the task force wheeled around to the west and rang up twenty-one knots for the run in to Luzon.[9]

At 0610 on the sixth, about seventy miles off Luzon's east coast, TF-38's fighter and attack aircraft lifted off from the flattops for the first strikes in direct support of the Lingayen landings. Once more McCain and everyone else kept a close watch on the weather, which pushed the strike schedule back and obscured many of the targets in areas generally east of Lingayen Gulf and on the outskirts of Manila. Yet the results were better than might be expected under the circumstances. Fliers bagged fourteen enemy planes in the air and, despite Japanese efforts to scatter and camouflage them, another twenty-three on the ground, qualified by the standard overclaim deviations. Two enemy transports and two oilers went to the bottom, which accords closely with Japanese data that record four tankers sunk. Combat casualties were relatively light—five fighters—but operational losses, mostly due to weather, were worse. Nine fighters, two torpedo planes, and one bomber went down, but only six airmen were killed. The Marines flying from the

Essex encountered more than their share of problems due to the weather and unfamiliarity with the characteristics of the Corsair and inexperience in carrier operations. From 30 December to 9 January, they lost three aviators and eight airplanes in operational accidents, in addition to eleven airmen killed or missing in action.[10]

After softening up Luzon on the sixth, Halsey, convinced that most of the kamikaze threat originated on Formosa, wanted TF-38 to hit that island again the next day. But an urgent message from Adm. Thomas Kinkaid, Seventh Fleet commander and in charge of the Lingayen expeditionary force, surmised that the suiciders might be coming from small airfields on Luzon itself. Nimitz was not entirely convinced that was the case. Like Halsey, he did not want TF-38 tethered to Luzon any longer than necessary, but he decided to defer to MacArthur before directing McCain's force to spend another day in direct support of the landings. MacArthur considered Formosa the greater threat while acknowledging that TF-38 might be needed in case of an "emergency" in Luzon. In the end, Halsey concluded that before attacking Formosa the carriers needed to refuel, which in any case was necessary should he get final orders to attack enemy forces in the South China Sea. So McCain's force remained on station off Luzon for another day, although just to make sure Formosa was covered, McCain ordered Bogan to fly searches over the Luzon Strait.[11]

The decision made, McCain's TF-38 fliers revisited Luzon, getting strikes off as scheduled an hour before sunrise on the seventh. Over the coast and some distance inland lay a weather front, but farther to the west aircraft that penetrated the front met clear skies for the first time in more than a week. As the carriers launched and landed their strikes, McCain slowed the force so that the big ships could top off the destroyers in case there were any delays in meeting Acuff's refueling group the next morning. That day McCain's carriers flew 737 strike sorties, dropping 181 tons of bombs and expending more than a thousand rockets. TF-38 aircraft claimed four enemy planes shot down and seventy-five destroyed on the ground. Shipping reported destroyed included a midsized oiler, four small cargo vessels, and a host of lesser craft, although postwar studies did not indicate any Japanese losses. Trucks, fuel dumps, barracks, and antiaircraft positions were destroyed or damaged at Clark, Mabalacat, and other airfield complexes around Manila. In exchange, the human cost to the task force was fifteen pilots and aircrew killed or missing in action, while ten more were lost in operational accidents.[12]

Halsey's plan (code-named Gratitude) to take TF-38 into the South China Sea had the full support of Kinkaid and MacArthur, both of whom worried that the Japanese might initiate air and surface attacks on the Lingayen invasion force from Singapore and bases in China and Indochina. In early January, intelligence from Kinkaid estimated that Japan still had two carriers in operation, with possibly another six that might be ready for sea within the next several months. Four battleships had been repaired, two of which, including the big *Yamato* and its escorts, were thought to be steaming from the Inland Sea to Camranh Bay or Saigon. Intelligence believed the *Ise* and *Hyuga* had holed up at the Saint Jacques (now Vung Tau, Vietnam) anchorage near Saigon. The reality was considerably different. The Combined Fleet had four carriers in home waters, all with understrength air groups, and four battleships, some of which were still under repair; the *Ise* and *Hyuga* were at Singapore; and only light forces were left at Camranh Bay. But Nimitz and Halsey went ahead with their plans based on the information they had, however faulty or incomplete.[13]

For the first time, the American fast carrier force would assault a continent and not isolated islands or archipelagos. It was a fateful turn of events for the Japanese, whose carrier and land-based naval aviators had attacked targets on the mainland only eight years earlier in the early phases of the war with China. There were elements of risk in the operation. Tiny low-lying islands and submerged reefs dotted the South China Sea, placing a premium on pinpoint navigation. Weather was a factor, as it had been throughout the entire Philippines campaign. Once the Japanese learned that TF-38 was in the South China Sea, they might be able to surge air power through Formosa to block the carrier force from exiting through the Luzon Strait, in effect bottling it up off a hostile coast on the other side of the Philippines. The essential logistics train was stretched and more vulnerable than ever before. And intelligence, as we know, was far from perfect. From the AAF Nimitz learned that the *Ise* and *Hyuga* had left Saint Jacques, but he had no confirmation that they were headed to Singapore. They could be anywhere. To keep the Japanese in the dark as long as possible about his movements and objectives, Halsey ordered complete radio silence as soon as the Formosa strikes had been accomplished.[14]

Following the Luzon strikes on the seventh, McCain's ships retired overnight to a point about two hundred miles east of Cape Engaño where they joined Acuff's group at 0800 on the eighth. After refueling and taking on board replacement aircraft from TG-30.8 escort carriers, the task force set a new course to the northwest at twenty-one knots, intended to place the fast carriers off the east coast of Formosa for air operations before dawn on the ninth, the same day and about the same time Kinkaid's ships began bombarding the Japanese ashore at Lingayen Gulf. McCain ordered all carriers to recover their strikes before 1700, leaving Gardner's TG-38.5 to conduct dusk and night patrols. Thach recalled that one of their strikes specifically targeted "Pistol Pete," an antiaircraft installation on the southern tip of Formosa that he suspected used radar to provide early warning of the approach of carrier planes. Despite vile weather, TF-38 inflicted more losses on the Japanese, including an estimated forty-seven aircraft destroyed in the air and on the ground, two destroyer escorts and two oilers sunk and another four damaged. The actual Japanese losses were most likely a frigate and two subchasers, plus two large cargo ships and a big tanker. The cost to the task force was thirteen pilots and aircrew and nine airplanes. Meanwhile, TF-30.8 had broken off from the carriers on the afternoon of the eighth to cut through the Balintang Channel just north of Luzon and prepare to replenish the task force as soon as it entered the South China Sea.[15]

TF-38 raced overnight at twenty-three knots through the 100-mile-wide Bashi Channel between the south coast of Formosa and the Batanes Islands into the South China Sea. Shortly before 0500 on the tenth, *Independence* night fighters splashed a twin-engine plane heading north about sixty miles east of the task force, in addition to shooting down two more intruders much closer to the carriers at 0630. Because it was still dark and overcast, McCain was reasonably sure that the three planes did not locate or identify the task force. Later that morning, carrier search planes found a destroyer escort and a transport northwest of the task force, but they did not attack them out of concern that doing so might reveal the flattops' presence. Due to rough seas, Halsey postponed the refueling planned for the afternoon of the tenth until early the following day, and he canceled any further strikes on Formosa.[16]

It had been an inauspicious start to the operation, and things did not get much better the following day. As scheduled, TF-38 contacted Acuff's group about two hundred miles west of Luzon before dawn on the eleventh and began refueling at about 0700, but periodic rain squalls caused the process to drag out until well into the afternoon. Rather than put off the operation for another day, adding more risk of detection, Halsey ordered Bogan's TG-38.2 (with McCain's flagship *Hancock*) to advance to the planned launching point off the Indochina coast, leaving the remaining groups behind with

Sherman as officer in tactical command to complete refueling and provide CAP. Reinforced with the cruisers *Boston* and *Baltimore* and five destroyers from Radford's TG-38.1, Bogan's group broke off at 1500 and set course 245 degrees west-southwest at twenty-three knots.[17]

It was still dark on the twelfth when Bogan's group reached its launch position about fifty miles east of Camranh Bay on the Indochina coast, where Radford's and Sherman's groups caught up with them before sunrise. At 0700, McCain again took over tactical command of the task force. According to his operational plan, Halsey reorganized the heavy ships into Task Group 34.5, with the intention of bombarding enemy coastal positions and possibly engaging the *Ise* and *Hyuga* and any other vessels in the area. That detachment closed inshore just south of Camranh Bay but found no trace of the elusive Japanese capital ships before rejoining the task force. Promptly at 0731, McCain's aircraft roared aloft, formed up, and headed to their targets in and around Camranh Bay, Saigon, and Cape St. Jacques.[18]

McCain remarked that his force caught the enemy with "his guard down, unsuspecting, unprepared, wide open for a knockout." TF-38 aircraft flew 984 sorties, rained 245 tons of bombs on their targets, and launched 71 torpedoes, along with another thousand rockets. Action reports estimated that sixty-two vessels of all types were attacked, of which forty were sunk, totaling nearly 190,000 tons. Two convoys, with eleven transports and their nine escorts, were entirely wiped out, and the light cruiser *Kashii* succumbed to torpedoes and bombs. According to postwar estimates, twenty-one transports and cargo ships, twelve tankers, and thirteen warships, including the *Kashii*, were sunk, for a total of nearly 145,000 tons. McCain wrote off as "typhoon bait" those badly damaged Japanese ships that had been run aground to avoid being sunk in deep water. Ashore, tank farms went up in flames, refineries were heavily damaged, and wharves and warehouses set on fire in and around Saigon. Avengers torpedoed and destroyed the largest dock at Camranh Bay. McCain's airmen claimed fourteen enemy planes shot down and another seventy-seven destroyed on the ground, along with eighteen floatplanes and two flying boats sunk on the water. Fifty-three more aircraft were reported damaged. In return for what McCain wrote "had been a brutal blow" to the Japanese that day, the human and material cost to the task force was twenty-five pilots and aircrew and twenty-three aircraft.[19]

Following the strikes on the twelfth, the task force set course northeast at twenty knots to rendezvous with the refueling group at first light the next morning. The idea was to top off the ships while continuing north to a launching point for simultaneous strikes on Hong Kong, Canton, and, once more, Formosa. But the weather deteriorated overnight due to a tropical storm closing in from south and east of the task force. With the destroyers laboring in the heavy, gray swells, which occasionally broke over the carriers' flight decks, McCain cut the speed of the task force to eighteen and then to sixteen knots, yet still managed to meet Acuff's group on time at 0700. Fueling, though, did not begin until 0843 as the fleet crept east at ten knots, with the destroyers, naturally, having priority over the big ships. Continued poor visibility caused McCain to put off launching searches that morning. By noon, all hope of keeping to the original strike plans had evaporated. Reluctantly, at 1305 Halsey called off the China and Formosa strikes and ordered Acuff to keep his oilers with the task force until all ships had been replenished, which would not be possible until the next morning. Bogan's and Gardner's groups did manage to get off Jack patrols by 1530, but because of the bad weather they turned up nothing. At dusk fueling ceased, and TF-38 with the oilers turned again to the north at fifteen knots. Largely due to the weather—"our grimmest opponent," McCain acknowledged—it had not been a productive day for the fast carriers.[20]

By daybreak on the fourteenth at a position about two hundred miles west of Lingayen Gulf, the task force resumed replenishment operations on a ten-knot course to the northeast. Weather conditions had improved enough for the carriers to fly off searches, while radar picked up bogeys that may have spotted and radioed the location of the task force. Fueling took all day, following which, according to Halsey's contingency plan, the empty oilers shortcut through the Mindanao Sea and Surigao Strait to return to Ulithi. Their escorts were then to pick up a relief group of fully laden oilers at Leyte and return through Surigao Strait to meet the task force west of Luzon. Meanwhile, Cincpac intelligence had still been unable to pin down the location of the *Ise* and *Hyuga*. Worried that the heavy warships might be somewhere near Palawan, from which they might disrupt the Lingayen operations, Nimitz ordered TF-38 to remain in the South China Sea for the time being while searching for the big ships and to use "discretion" in deciding to carry out strikes against China.[21]

Once all the ships finally completed fueling, TF-38 steamed north at twenty knots, again being forced to slow due to the adverse weather, this time from the seasonal monsoon. Despite marginal visibility and a low overcast, McCain's carriers initiated fighter sweeps and bombing attacks at 0733 on the fifteenth from a position about 180 miles southeast of Hong Kong.

Throughout the morning, TF-38 aircraft ranged in an arc across the South China Sea from the island of Hainan in the south to Amoy in the north, while simultaneously hitting targets in Formosa and the Pescadores in the Formosa Strait. Reports of foul weather over many objectives and no prospects for improved conditions convinced McCain to suspend the strikes at 1137, although he maintained the fighter blanket over Formosa for most of the day. Compared to the 12 January strikes, those on the fifteenth were disappointing. TF-38 flew 499 offensive sorties, expending 170 tons of bombs and 625 rockets. McCain's airmen estimated they sank three large oilers and the destroyer *Hatakaze* in the Pescadores, and another eight ships damaged in Hong Kong and on Formosa, where the airfields near Takao were struck again. Generally in agreement, postwar records showed the enemy ships sunk other than the *Hatakaze* were a large tanker, a fast transport, and an old destroyer. TF-38 fliers claimed sixteen aircraft shot down, eighteen destroyed on the ground, and thirty-five more damaged. When intelligence revealed an enemy weather and radio station on Pratas Reef not far from the task force, aircraft from Gardner's group went in to "annihilate" it, together with a short runway and some small buildings. Seven TF-38 pilots and aircrew were lost, as well as twelve aircraft, during the day's operations.[22]

Early on the sixteenth, after an overnight run through rotten weather, McCain's task force was in position about 120 miles due south of Hong Kong for another round of strikes on enemy shipping and ground installations in China. Visibility was such that Gardner's TG-38.5 had to postpone its usual predawn searches, and the other carriers could not launch their searches and strikes until 0730. It was as if McCain's aviators entered the dragon's lair. Largely because they had lost the element of surprise, TF-38 aviators got a hot reception from AA installations around Hong Kong harbor, hardly the "moderate anti-aircraft fire" Nimitz had prematurely reported in a communique to the Secretary of the Navy. Concentrated along the tortuously narrow approaches to the harbor and possibly aided by new Japanese fire-control radars, the flak barrage resulted in the heaviest losses for McCain's task force since the 7 January strikes in and around Manila: forty pilots and aircrew, thirty-eight in combat. Twenty-two aircraft went down in battle and another twenty-seven operationally. The *Hancock*'s VB-7 recorded that the sixteenth was "the worst day in the Squadron's history." In the first two strikes the unit lost four Helldivers, followed by three F6F fighter-bombers from VF-7 downed in the third strike, and another VB-7 SB2C in the fourth attack. No pilots or aircrew from the *Hancock* were recovered.[23]

In 663 sorties, TF-38 dropped 214 tons of bombs and 13 torpedoes and fired 953 rockets. The results were meager, particularly considering the losses suffered by McCain's task force: ten enemy planes shot down and seven damaged or destroyed on the ground. TF-38 claimed three large cargo ships sunk, and four oilers, six cargo ships, five destroyer escorts, and one destroyer damaged in Hong Kong. Other vessels were damaged but not sunk at Canton, Yulin, and Hainan. Postwar records showed two cargo ships and three oilers sunk at Hong Kong and another oiler in Hainan. An attack on the former Pan American seaplane base in nearby Macau destroyed a hangar and other buildings, leading to a diplomatic protest and an embarrassing apology to the neutral Portuguese government.[24]

In subsequent dispatches McCain concluded that the Hong Kong strikes had yielded "small return for [the] effort." Of some 110,000 tons of shipping in the harbor, only 13,000 tons were sunk. "With good weather at Hong Kong and no air opposition," he concluded that "the results are cause for disappointment and concern." In his critique he pointed to "improved heavy enemy AA fire" both from the warships themselves and from shore installations; topography that caused the attacks to be funneled in one direction; "poor target selection" where buildings and other structures on shore were struck first, creating smoke that obscured more important targets; and torpedoes that failed in shallow water. The operation provided proof of McCain's contention that fighters—the F4U in particular—were superior dive-bombers compared to the SB2C. Most important, "as we close the main harbors of JAPAN" accurate intelligence and efficient target selection (preferably using experienced directors on the staffs of the task group commanders) were imperative. Even so, if Hong Kong were to be struck again, "knowing what we know now, we would sink every ship in the harbor inside of six hours, and burn the waterfront too."[25]

Following the second round of China strikes, the task force turned southeast to rendezvous with Acuff's replenishment group at the point west of Luzon where it had fueled on 14 January. The two forces met on schedule at 0800 on the seventeenth, but because of the weather, fueling did not begin for another hour and proceeded fitfully the rest of the day as the ships slowly steered a course to the east. At 1830, McCain ordered an end to the fueling operation, even though only some of the ships had been topped off. He followed with another order to steam north to reach a point where he hoped the weather would be better and refueling could be resumed. From twelve knots, initially, the fleet's speed was progressively reduced to eight knots as the warships bucked gale-force winds from the north-east. In Acuff's group a comber broke over the escort carrier *Nehenta Bay* (CVE 74), which lost fifteen feet of its flight deck. At one point, the destroyer *Cushing* (DD 797) reported a forty-degree roll; others saw fifty degrees. By midnight, as the monsoon intensified, it started to look like a repeat of the 18 December disaster.[26]

The next morning, 18 January, McCain, trying to keep the task force headed into the wind to reduce the risk to his and Acuff's vessels, ordered the task force to change course to the east, then southeast, and finally due south at 0910. When the wind suddenly swung around to smack the ships off the starboard bow, they had to turn more to the west, a course they kept for another two hours before having to turn left on a track south by south-east. Fueling was impossible. Only a handful of CAP flights and Jack patrols got off in the morning before all air operations had to be canceled.[27]

Now it was decision time. Following the 16 January raids, Halsey and McCain understood that continued offensive operations in the South China Sea were unlikely to yield results sufficient to offset TF-38 aircraft and personnel losses, the risk of land-based air attacks, and skirmishing with the monsoon. Halsey radioed Nimitz to that effect, adding that he wanted to move out of the South China Sea to a position east of the Philippines where he could continue to cover the Lingayen operation and if necessary strike Okinawa. He had plenty of ammunition and fuel. Nimitz signaled King that TF-38 "operations in South CHINA SEA are obtaining diminishing returns with increasing risk" and recommended that the carriers take up a position east of Luzon and strike targets in Formosa and Okinawa. Kinkaid's TF-77 would be reinforced with four battleships in case any enemy surface units showed up. Halsey replied that after the task force refueled it would pass through the Luzon Strait overnight on the eighteenth and nineteenth, hit Formosa on the morning of the nineteenth and Okinawa on 21 or 22 January.[28]

Given the snags with fueling and weather threats to the north, Halsey had second thoughts about exiting through the Luzon Strait. Late on 18 January, he suggested that TF-38 would continue south after refueling and exit through the Mindanao Sea and Surigao Strait. The historian Clark Reynolds has derided the plan as a "ridiculous idea [that] would have taken the fast carriers out of the war for a week." Yet Halsey's plan echoed an earlier dispatch copied to Nimitz. He admitted that the alternative route was a "compromise" but believed it meant the task force could provide additional air cover for reinforcements coming into Lingayen while keeping the carriers well south of the weather and allowing the ships to be replenished in relatively calm seas. The alternative route might have made the force more vulnerable to air attack, but Halsey thought McCain had plenty of fighters to deal with any threats and would benefit from additional coverage by Kinkaid's Seventh Fleet aircraft. Moreover, Halsey planned to refuel en route or at Leyte by 20 January, which would not have kept the carriers idle for the week Reynolds alleged.[29]

It all became moot when Halsey received a message from Nimitz early on the nineteenth strongly advising him to exit through the Luzon Strait, even if it meant spending a few more days in the South China Sea waiting for the weather to improve. Nimitz reminded Halsey of the threat of Japanese surface and air forces from the north and that passage of the task force through the Philippines to the south would potentially compromise its ability to safeguard the Luzon operations. Halsey signaled back that he would stay in the South China Sea and refuel on the nineteenth as conditions permitted, then exit through the Balintang Channel on the night of 20–21 January. He further informed Nimitz that the carriers would strike Formosa on the twenty-first and Okinawa on the twenty-third or twenty-fourth.[30]

For a change, the weather cooperated on the nineteenth, allowing servicing of McCain's force to begin as scheduled at 0730 at a point south of Scarborough Bank and about 150 miles west of Luzon. During the process, the task force reversed course 180 degrees from due south to due north, intended to position the carriers west of the Luzon Strait by the following morning. Two of the TG-30.8 oilers, now empty, broke away to scurry back to Ulithi through the Surigao Strait, shepherded by three CVEs; the rest of Acuff's group stayed with the flattops as they steamed north at fifteen knots.[31]

Throughout the day on the twentieth, as McCain's carriers drew closer to the strait, they began to attract the attention of the Japanese. Before noon, *Lexington* and *Essex* fighters shot down two enemy aircraft, with another twelve claimed by nightfall, most of them twin-engine fighters and bombers shuttling from Formosa to Luzon, and none of which directly threatened the task force. The flattops broke into the Balintang Channel at 1955 at twenty-five knots, with four destroyers leading the three task groups. On clearing the channel after midnight, the carriers turned to the north at twenty knots to close Formosa before dawn on the twenty-first. Halsey broke radio silence that morning to boast that TF-38 had "completed 3800 mile cruise in China

Sea with no battle damage and no enemy plane nearer than 20 miles" from the task force.[32]

The assault on Formosa began with fighter sweeps at 0650 from a position about 120 miles east of the island, with four more strikes following throughout the day, totaling nearly 800 sorties. More tons of bombs were delivered—289—than in any of the operations that month. At Takao, five large oilers and two transports were reported sunk, another oiler sent to the bottom at Toshien, and four other transports sunk elsewhere on the island. Three destroyers and three big oilers were thought to be damaged. All told, 53,100 tons of shipping were believed to have been sunk and another 61,000 tons damaged. Postwar analyses showed similar results: six oilers and four cargo ships sunk, plus two tank landing ships, for a total of 62,504 tons. Among the ground targets destroyed were docks, warehouses, and railroad shops and yards in or near Takao, and oil storage facilities at Toshien. Airfields, hangars, repair shops, and barracks also were targeted with success. TF-38 lost twenty aircraft and nineteen pilots and aircrew, making it the most costly operation since the 16 January raid on Hong Kong. In return, McCain's fliers claimed 39 enemy aircraft shot down and another 104 destroyed on the ground.[33]

Compared to the operations in the South China Sea, where McCain's ships had suffered no losses due to enemy action, 21 January offered a reminder that the Japanese were still a threat to the task force. Only two hours after the carriers launched the first of their strikes, task force radar screens picked up bogeys. A *Cabot* fighter shot one of them down about thirty-five miles from the carriers. McCain slowed and maneuvered his ships so that the destroyers could duck in and out of the screen to top off their bunkers from the battleships. About two hours into this process, Sherman's TG-38.3, the northernmost of the three task groups, reported that it was under air attack. One of the Japanese planes, identified as a Zero, eluded the ships' defenses and planted two bombs on the *Langley*, one of which struck the flight deck forward and exploded in the gallery deck immediately below. The damage was relatively minor, and the carrier was able to resume flight operations in a matter of a few hours, but three crewmen died. McCain quickly called off fueling operations, and the task group began maneuvering to counter the air threat. He also requested and received permission to shift the task force strikes from shipping to aircraft and aviation installations.[34]

Within moments of the attack on the *Langley*, a second Zero dove on the carrier. Juking through a fusillade of antiaircraft fire, the fighter veered left and struck the *Ticonderoga*, positioned off the *Langley*'s port bow. The airplane impacted amidship and its bomb passed through the flight deck, exploding between the gallery and hangar decks and igniting intense fires that quickly spread among the planes with their fuel-laden belly tanks. Bomb fragments and heat distorted and weakened major structural elements of the ship. Damage control personnel quickly confined the fires as plane handlers jettisoned burning aircraft over the side; the ship's aviation gasoline lines had previously been evacuated and filled with CO_2. Firefighters had made good progress over the next hour when at 1258 a second suicide plane hit the carrier's island, its ordnance showering the structure with lethal fragments and starting more fires. The flattop's skipper, Capt. Dixie Kiefer, and the ship's executive officer, Cdr. William O. Burch, were badly wounded, and the air officer was killed. Another 11 officers and 131 enlisted men died or went missing; 30 more officers and 170 enlisted men were injured. By 1437, the fires were under control. Injured badly, Kiefer remained on the bridge for another ten hours until he was sure that all the casualties had been attended to before relinquishing command to the ship's engineering officer, Cdr. Harmon V. Briner. Once it was certain that the *Ticonderoga* was no longer capable of air operations, McCain cleared the carrier to leave the task force and return to Ulithi for repairs, along with the destroyer *Maddox* (DD 731), which had also been struck and severely damaged by a kamikaze.[35]

A half-hour after the kamikaze hit the *Ticonderoga*, the *Hancock*, McCain's flagship, was recovering aircraft from the third strike of the day. After landing at 1328, a VT-7 TBM began taxiing forward. Moments later, as the torpedo plane was next to the carrier's island, a 500-pound bomb tumbled from the bomb bay and exploded on the deck. The results were catastrophic. The bomb detonated directly over the air office on the gallery deck, instantly demolishing that space and damaging adjacent offices and rooms. Burning gasoline from the Avenger poured through the gallery deck and ignited in the hangar deck below, consuming two Hellcats. The TBM's flight crew and nearby flight deck personnel died instantly, while smoke and flames trapped some men in the island, which had been peppered with shrapnel. On the port bridge wing watching landing operations, Thach had just ducked down behind some armor plate to light a cigarette when the explosion occurred. He escaped without injury. "The cigarette saved my life," he later recalled. Fifty officers and enlisted men died, and nearly eighty were injured, some critically. Hampered by broken water mains, emergency personnel fought the conflagrations on the flight and gallery decks, managing to extinguish them by 1405. It was a tribute to sophisticated damage-control procedures and heroic action by the crew that after temporary repairs the ship began landing aircraft again by 1520.[36]

McCain's ships sped northeast overnight to position themselves for attacks and photographic missions over Okinawa and other islands in the Ryukyus. Two hours after midnight on the twenty-second, Gardner's TG-38.5 carriers flew off radar-equipped Avengers on a long-range mission to strike shipping and military installations at Kiirun in northern Formosa. The idea was to create a diversion to make the Japanese think that island was the Americans' next target, which they may have done, but at the cost of three TBMs and nine aircrew. Well before first light about 120 miles south of Okinawa, the task force launched fighter sweeps, followed by strike and photo missions. In 682 strike sorties, TF-38 airmen damaged or destroyed hangars and port facilities in and around Naha on Okinawa and attacked the airfield on Ie Shima, just off the northwest coast of the big island. The Americans also claimed twenty-eight aircraft destroyed on the ground and three small transports sunk (postwar records show a single cargo ship sunk). Eleven TF-38 aircraft were lost, and six more pilots and flight crew were killed. Only optimists viewed the overall results as satisfactory, although the excellent photographs of airfields were useful in preparing for the invasion of Okinawa, scheduled for early spring. Planners suspected that hitting the Ryukyus, close as they were to the home islands, would stir up more opposition, but the Navy fliers encountered no enemy aircraft in the skies and there were no attacks on the task force. Nevertheless, as McCain's carriers retired to the south at twenty-five knots, they released decoy balloons tethered to sea anchors in hopes of masking their withdrawal from long-range radar-equipped enemy bombers.[37]

After daybreak on the twenty-third, McCain's ships met Acuff's refueling group about 230 miles northeast of Cape Engaño. The task force spent most of the day replenishing the ships' bunkers, each of the task groups maneuvering independently generally on a course to the east. That afternoon, McCain formed a new task group—TG-38.6—consisting of the damaged Hancock and Langley, along with Halsey's flagship New Jersey, two heavy cruisers, and six destroyers, to proceed directly to Ulithi, where they dropped anchor on the evening of 25 January. Mitscher came on board the Hancock the next day to debrief McCain and prepare to transfer his First Fast Carrier Task Force staff to the flagship. Meanwhile, McCain had left

Sherman in tactical command of TF-38, with orders to trail a day behind; Sherman and the rest of the task force pulled into Ulithi on the morning of the twenty-sixth.[38]

In accordance with the "two-platoon" system, Mitscher relieved McCain as commander of TF-38 at midnight on 27 January, and Task Force 38 became Task Force 58; at the same time, Adm. Raymond Spruance took over from Halsey, with Third Fleet now redesignated Fifth Fleet. Later on the twenty-seventh, McCain boarded a Curtiss R5C transport for the flight to Pearl Harbor, where he arrived just before midnight on the twenty-seventh, local time, after stopovers in Majuro and Johnston Island. Meanwhile, McCain's staff moved to the *Ticonderoga* on 28 January for the long journey back to Pearl.[39]

Nine days on the *Ticonderoga* gave McCain's staff time to assemble data and draft an action report for their boss when they arrived at Pearl Harbor on the morning of 7 February. Long and comprehensive, the report included a narrative of the operations, backed up by pages of statistics, analyses, and recommendations. McCain was pleased that his ships and men had accomplished their basic mission: support of the Philippines operations and the destruction or at least neutralization of Japanese naval and air strength with sustained and far-ranging carrier strikes on aircraft, airfields, shipping, and infrastructure. The statistics conveyed a sense of the intensity of the operations. From 30 October to 22 January, TF-38 flew no fewer than 13,616 strike sorties, sank or damaged an estimated 1.2 million tons of shipping, and destroyed or damaged 2,600 aircraft in the air and on the ground. As if that were not enough, McCain's airmen bombed, rocketed, strafed, and even torpedoed hundreds of airfields, harbor facilities, warehouses, fuel storage tanks, ammunition dumps, and radio and radar stations. Task Force 38 raids on railyards, freight cars, and locomotives played no small part in destroying Luzon's critical transportation and industrial infrastructure. Not surprisingly, the task force paid a high price. A total of 303 aviators died, 383 aircraft were lost, and 9 ships were damaged in combat, including 7 fast carriers.[40]

Verifying McCain's advocacy of a larger number of carriers in a smaller number of task groups, the report concluded that it was "feasible" to have four heavy carriers and one light carrier in a typical task group, allowing the battleships, cruisers, and destroyers to concentrate in the screen for more effective antiaircraft and antisubmarine protection. In fact, Bogan's TG-38.2 had included five carriers for strikes on Luzon in December. Careful

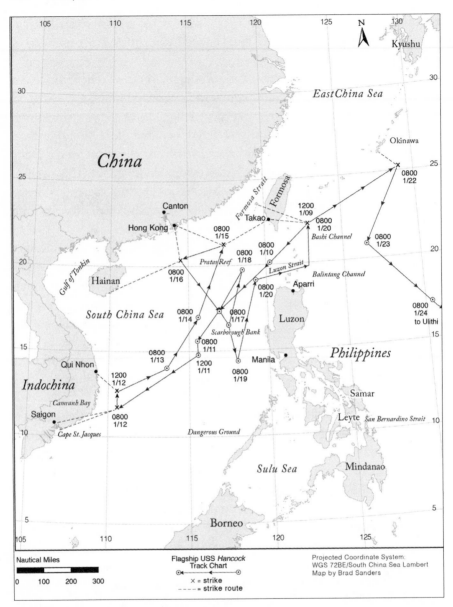

Map 6. Task Force 38 Operations in the South China Sea, January 1945; USS *Hancock* Track Chart, January 1945 (USS *Hancock* Action Report, Dec. 30–Jan. 25, 1945, www .Fold3.com, accessed Jan. 26, 2015)

management of the airspace around each group was possible as a result of improved communications and coordination among the task force and task group fighter directors. On the other hand, night carrier operations had caused problems. Gardner's two carriers stayed clear of the other groups during daylight operations, while still remaining within the task force CAP. After dark, the night group broke away to operate independently, sometimes not rejoining the task force until late the next morning. To resolve the awkward arrangement, which demanded creative planning and maneuvering, McCain recommended that the night carrier group have its own screening ships.[41]

As for task force air defense, especially from kamikazes, McCain's report concluded that the Japanese Special Attack Corps was not a "last ditch hysterical gesture" adopted by the Japanese in extremis. Rather, the suicide attacks demonstrated "a carefully studied change in the general plan of air attacks against ships" and that "unless some successful counter action could be taken we would lose the spearhead of our forces in the Pacific." McCain's Moose-trap exercises had been effective in demonstrating enemy attack methods and revealing weaknesses in the carriers' defenses. Jack patrols, Tomcat radar picket destroyers, revised CAP formations, and carefully positioned antiaircraft cruisers had been effective, but "the most successful method of beating the enemy land based air force" had been McCain's round-the-clock "Big Blue Blanket" over Japanese airfields. Yet "100% destruction of the attackers" was essential, and that was simply not possible due to the need for a "delicate balance" between the offensive and defensive assets and operations of the task force. To relieve the threat to the flattops, McCain recommended that the "blanket" have priority, with attacks on shipping and other targets ensuing in due course.[42]

Fighter direction, extended for the first time to encompass the entire task force, was a challenging proposition considering the number of carriers and the kamikaze threat. Interference within each task group and among the groups had been mitigated by the reduction in the number of groups, but fighter direction was still a formidable undertaking, and coordination had yet to be fully resolved. Accurate and timely data (from radar, radio direction finding, CAP reports, visual sightings, IFF, and destroyer pickets) had to be fed to the task group fighter directors before being passed on to the task force fighter director officer. He then processed the information and passed it back to the group officers to relay to the carriers and other ships in the group. This demanded dedicated radio circuits and often lower frequencies when radio silence was in effect. McCain's report recommended additional radio channels, which would expedite the flow of information through the carriers' CICs, and procedures to minimize delays in identifying threats, determining which threats had priority, and methods of handing off control of CAPs from one carrier or group to another.[43] It is no overstatement that fighter direction was complex, essential for both the offensive and defensive capabilities of the task force, and that even at this late stage of the war remained a work in progress.

McCain understood how important it was to publicize the Navy and its accomplishments in the Pacific War. As BuAer chief, he had put Hollywood high on BuAer's public relations agenda, and during a West Coast trip had met with Joan Leslie and Veronica Lake, costars in the 1943 musical *True to the Navy*. He also had a brief appearance in the documentary *The Fighting Lady*, an Oscar-winning 20th Century Fox film released late in 1944 recounting the story of the carrier *Yorktown* from 1943 through the fall of 1944. The press especially took to McCain's hard-bitten countenance, aggressive spirit, candidness, and his soft Mississippi accent, spiced with a dollop of profanity. His distinctive green cap, like Mitscher's long-billed lobsterman's hat and Jocko Clark's locomotive engineer's cap, always attracted public attention, as did his skill in rolling cigarettes with one hand. Halsey was less impressed. He remarked at one point that McCain's wretched-looking cap "was the most disreputable one I ever saw on an officer" and insisted that an orderly sweep up the loose Bull Durham tobacco McCain trailed when he visited his flagship.[44]

In compliance with orders from Nimitz, McCain had set up a "seagoing pressroom" for wire service newsmen on the *Hancock* shortly after departing from Ulithi, and reporters from various news agencies were distributed among the other carriers. McCain's report emphasized that "the psychological effect upon the correspondents, in feeling that they were included directly in the operating scheme of the Navy is not to be over-looked." Furthermore, the fleet devised a system whereby stories were immediately sent by radio and included in Nimitz's daily communiques, thus ensuring that the news was "still Page 1 material" and that operations received "a more adequate perspective in the minds of the American public than when the Navy news followed news of the ground forces and Army Air Corps by a considerable period." Nevertheless, opening up to the press could backfire, as Jimmie Thach found to his chagrin after a 7 January interview on the *Hancock* that Nimitz believed divulged confidential information that might "give aid and comfort to the enemy." For the same reason, Nimitz made it clear that no further information was to be made public about night carrier operations other than what Matt Gardner had revealed in an interview with Associated Press reporter Rembert James. McCain's report concluded that "a start in the right direction has been made in press coverage," but that still more needed to be done to speed up the process of getting the message out that "only the Navy could have done this."[45]

What did not appear in McCain's report is as revealing as what did appear. It was no surprise that he stressed that "the state of the weather actually placed the accomplishment of effective support [of the Philippine operations] by the Task Force in jeopardy." Yet there is no mention of the December typhoon, either in McCain's summary or in the staff's detailed analysis of task force aerology, possibly because there was nothing to add to the *Cascade* court of inquiry, and Nimitz and King had already rendered their verdicts. Nor does McCain's report say anything about rest and recuperation, possibly because he believed he had adequately addressed the problem in his 12 November communication to Halsey. Robert Hickey, the *Hancock*'s commanding officer, emphasized in his action report that the fast-paced tempo of operations and the seemingly endless cycles of four hours on watch and four hours off bred a mix of boredom and exhaustion with consequent "decrease in the alertness and efficiency" of ship and aircrews. Brief stays in Ulithi, where the ships' men were busy twenty-four hours a day with repairs, routine maintenance, and loading ammunition and other stores, were hardly relaxing. Pilots were also exhausted; the *Hancock*'s Air Group 7 had been going virtually nonstop for almost four months, and VF-7 had lost 65 percent of its original complement. Facing the prospect of even more intense operations, Hickey concluded that at least ten days to two weeks were needed at Ulithi between operations and that air groups be relieved after no more than four months of combat.[46] Hickey's report must have resonated with those higher up the chain of command, for the *Hancock* and other carriers got a well-deserved two weeks off at Ulithi before resuming operations with Mitscher and TF-58.

Halsey did not have much to say in his endorsement of McCain's report, other than to comment that the "Big Blue Blanket" had generally been effective in suppressing Japanese aircraft and airfields. He did, however, remind McCain that the "primarily offensive mission of the Fast Carrier Task Force must be constantly kept in mind" and that there may be occasions where "the importance of enemy targets will completely justify the increased risk of something less than the best defense for the force." In other words, strikes on enemy forces had priority over fleet air defense if and when such decisions had to be made. In contrast, Nimitz was almost effusive. Halsey's and McCain's operations had been "an outstanding example of the capabilities and versatility of the Fast Carrier Task Force" in providing both strategic and direct support for the Lingayen invasion. He especially liked TF-38's South China Sea incursion, which was "well-conceived and brilliantly executed."[47]

Not everyone agreed with Nimitz's assessment of the operation or believed that McCain had performed well in command of the fast carriers in the South China Sea. Gerry Bogan, TG-38.2 commander, much preferred working for Mitscher, whom he regarded as "a consummate master of naval air power, and when he ran Task Force 58 or 38 . . . it was a professional outfit, doing a professional job in a professional way." Under McCain, in contrast, "it was a goddamn circus," marred by slipshod administration and disruptive last-minute changes in operations plans. Sherman's chief of staff, Capt. Charles R. ("Cat") Brown, found McCain's sometimes informal leadership unprofessional and condescending. After receiving a saccharine message of encouragement from McCain during refueling on 8 January he handed Sherman a battle helmet to use "as a vomit bowl." Others believed that McCain never truly functioned as OTC of the task force, deferring to Halsey at critical junctures, particularly on 11 January, when he broke away with Bogan's TG-38.2 and left Sherman in tactical command of the task force. Amplifying this point, the historian Clark Reynolds maintained that Halsey had made the decision to divide the task force, "completely bypassing McCain."[48]

Thach and Halsey took exception to Reynolds' interpretation of the command relationship: "Halsey never took a task group away from McCain," recalled Thach, adding that the two had thoroughly discussed the tactical situation on the eleventh before Halsey issued his orders to separate Bogan's group. Thach insisted, moreover, that McCain "had tactical command *all* the time. The fleet commander had overall command but we (Admiral McCain) gave the tactical orders to the task force." He went on to explain that Reynolds did not understand how the fleet and task forces operated: "The tactical commander always when he puts out a signal or a dispatch for an operation he includes the fleet commander as one of the information addressees. In other words, he informs the fleet commander what he's planning, which direction he's going to go, and so forth. There's a continual exchange all the time between them." Halsey's chief of staff, Rear Adm. Robert B. Carney, was explicit that "it was Commander TF 38

. . . who issued the orders, not Commander 3rd Fleet." Halsey himself explained to his biographer Elmer B. Potter that he did not bypass his task force commanders: "I always assigned targets to hit, leaving details to group and task force commanders. . . . I always did this, and in doing it never felt that I was bypassing any junior echelon in my command. I have seen this statement made many times, presumably by people who did not understand the difference between strategical and tactical command." As close as they were to McCain, Thach and Halsey might not be entirely objective. On the other hand, a more disinterested third party was Cdr. Peter G. Molteni, TF-38's submarine liaison officer, who insisted that as far as he could recall McCain always exercised tactical command, although at times he might have wanted more specific input from Halsey on strike plans and targets.[49]

The controversy may never be resolved, either for the South China Sea or other incidents before and after involving Halsey and McCain. Yet we do know that the chain of command was (and is) fundamental to the Navy's (or any other military's) organizational and operational structure and that there was a clear understanding that a fleet commander's responsibility was broader in scope than that of a task force commander, just as an admiral's duty extends beyond those of the captain of the ship on which a flag officer might be assigned. We also know that Halsey relied on plans and held frequent meetings with his subordinates, to whom he delegated wide discretion and initiative for carrying out those plans in accord with generally understood operational doctrine. Moreover, Halsey's insistence that the fleet maintain radio silence underscored the need for his subordinates to function independently and to use their own initiative during operations.[50] For certain, at times and under extraordinary circumstances, those command responsibilities overlapped or became blurred. It remains, therefore, that from decades of experience in the Navy and months together with the fast carriers, Halsey and McCain shared a fundamental understanding of the basic elements of the Navy's command structure, and that, coupled with mutual respect, defined their professional relationship and the character of their operations in the Pacific.

TF-38's Luzon and South China Sea operations, though constrained by weather and unsatisfactory in that two of Japan's remaining capital ships had escaped destruction, nevertheless crippled Japan's tanker fleet and provided a barometer of the capability of the fast carrier force to deliver devastating blows against shipping and strategic infrastructure. The offensive also underscored the reality that Japan by the late winter of 1945 had effectively lost the Philippines and her vital lines of communication to the south, that with the Marianas in American hands the home islands were now open to sustained attack by long-range bombers, and that the empire's inner defenses were badly frayed. More specifically, TF-38 had again demonstrated its flexibility in long-range independent operations as well as close support of invasion forces in the Philippines. In addition, TF-38 had neutralized if not totally crushed Japanese air power in Luzon and Formosa and had helped reduce the proud Imperial Japanese Navy to little more than a reserve coast defense force. McCain was proud of the accomplishments of the officers on his staff who bore the burden of planning, of the air units that "made the amazing scores" against the enemy, and of the thousands of men "who put our planes into the skies."[51] He knew there was still much planning and preparation to do for the next, and most likely last, phases of the war, and he might have surmised that some reconciliation of the awkward command lines of authority had to be resolved as the top Navy brass weighed the options for the final defeat of Japan. He might also have guessed, correctly, that there would be command changes in the fast carrier forces, some of which might affect the part he would play as the Navy's air forces approached victory in the Pacific.

CHAPTER 10

Carriers against Japan

After a week in Pearl Harbor, John McCain, along with Wilder Baker, Jimmie Thach, and other members of his staff, boarded Nimitz's Coronado flag plane on the afternoon of 8 February 1945 for the flight back to the West Coast. As he flew on to Washington, with orders to report to Adm. Ernest King, McCain could not help but conclude, correctly, that King and others were less than delighted with the performance of TF-38 and that experienced aviators and flag officers like John Towers were champing at the bit to assume his Second Fast Carrier Force command. Most significant, he knew that he was deeply indebted to King for his support in the aftermath of the December typhoon and that his number one priority was to see his boss. With Thach in tow, McCain went over to Main Navy on 14 February to confer with King about plans for the next round of operations in the Pacific and, one can infer, receive assurances that he was still in line to relieve Mitscher in the next fast carrier command rotation.[1]

We know about the conference from Thach's recollections: "Mitscher and McCain were alternating and there was a lot of talk started such as 'wasn't it about time somebody else had a chance to do that.' And McCain didn't want [to give up the task force command]—because, you see, he'd had this experience and he was a good fighter. This was where he wanted to be and he felt that to give somebody else the job totally inexperienced in that sort of thing would be like changing to an inexperienced horse in the middle of a race—or in midstream, so to speak." Thach observed that "Admiral King indicated, not directly but by what he said concerning the future plans, that he wasn't about to relieve Admiral McCain." "It was," Thach concluded, "a very cordial visit."[2] McCain now knew he would be part of the next phase of operations in the Pacific, where the fast carriers were destined to play a starring role.

McCain spent a week in Washington working with his and Halsey's staffs on a broad spectrum of matters. Foremost were such fundamental problems as logistics, training, and aircraft procurement, but they also looked at how air cover had been handled in the European theater. No longer would the carriers roam over vast distances, engage Japanese air and sea forces, neutralize and bypass enemy island strongholds, or support amphibious operations against isolated islands. Rather, they now would operate off the Asian mainland in the face of massed enemy land-based air power, including thousands of kamikazes. As the historian Clark Reynolds pointed out, the fast carrier task force would be roughly analogous to the unsinkable British Isles, from which Allied strategic and tactical air power had been supporting operations in Europe. For Halsey's and McCain's planners there was the added complication of coordinating their operations with those of the Army Air Forces, particularly the long-range Boeing B-29s flying from new bases in the Marianas.[3]

For the present, however, it was Spruance's and Mitscher's turn. Fifth Fleet and TF-58 had responsibility for covering the Bonins and Ryukyus operations, both of which proved to be more bloody than anticipated. In the run-up to the invasion of Iwo Jima, Mitscher's TF-58 hit targets in and around Tokyo on 16 and 17 February, realizing a goal McCain had made soon after leaving the South Pacific in the fall of 1942 and had resurrected as Halsey's canceled Operation Hotfoot in October 1944. Starting the day before the Iwo Jima landings on the nineteenth and continuing until 1 March, TF-58 provided CAP and close air support for the Marines ashore as they fought a deadly battle of attrition on the island. Not until 26 March was the island finally reduced, at a cost of more than 20,000 Marine and Navy casualties. After covering Iwo Jima, TF-58 on 18 March launched strikes on airfields and other installations on Kyushu, followed by a week of attacks on positions in the Ryukyus leading up to the 1 April invasion. Over the next month, Mitscher's force endured fierce Japanese kamikaze and bombing attacks from the estimated three thousand Japanese aircraft mustered in Kyushu and the Ryukyus. At sea, ten fast carriers were damaged among the total of 368 ships and smaller craft sunk or damaged. Fifth Fleet lost more than 4,900 officers and men killed, while ashore the Marines and Army suffered more than 7,600 battle deaths in the bitter three-month campaign.[4]

If Iwo Jima and Okinawa were indicators, the final assault on Japan was likely to be equally costly if not more so, both in American and in Japanese lives. At least since the middle of 1944, planning for the defeat of Japan had hinged on the principle that nothing less than unconditional surrender would fulfill the American and Allied goals. At the Quebec conference in

September 1944, Roosevelt and Churchill had endorsed a strategy outlined by the Joint Chiefs of Staff that called for the destruction of Japanese naval and air power, followed by an intensifying sea and air blockade culminating in an invasion of the home islands. King believed that naval and air operations alone would so weaken and isolate Japan that surrender would ensue without the need for invasion, although he conceded that lodgment in the southern island of Kyushu might be necessary for advance bases to support the blockade and bombing campaign. Assuming that Kyushu would be the initial objective, the Joint Chiefs directed MacArthur and Nimitz to initiate detailed planning for the invasion, tentatively set for 1 December. On 25 May, the JCS formally approved the operation, code-named Olympic, with the new date of 1 November. Rather than divide the command as they had done with nearly disastrous results at Leyte, the Joint Chiefs assigned overall responsibility for the invasion and subsequent ground operations to MacArthur, with Nimitz's forces split for the first time into Spruance's Fifth Fleet, charged with the amphibious operation, and Halsey's Third Fleet, with the fast carrier support.[5]

Meanwhile, McCain observed with interest from the sidelines. He had flown out from Washington on 22 February, stopping as usual to visit family and friends in Greenwood on the way to San Diego and North Island. On leave for the next month at home in Coronado, he unwound as much as he could, although it was clear that the Pacific War was not far from his mind. McCain held a press conference at the stylish Hotel del Coronado on 2 March. Using the colorful language he was famed for, he declared that "I always have considered it a mark of inferiority to hate, but damn it all, I thoroughly hate the Japs!" He continued: "The Japs have been eliminated as a first class Naval power, as we rate them," and then he went on to discuss the success of the "blanket" operations in the Philippines in suppressing Japanese resistance in the air. "By keeping all fields under observation, our fighters could come in and knock down their planes as soon as they tried to take off," he remarked. "That's what we call 'putting the lid on them' and we're keeping it on them." He dismissed the typical Japanese aviator as a "dumbbell" who took far longer to train than the "American boy." In any case, "We kill them off so fast that they aren't getting a chance for training." As the carriers closed on the Japanese home islands, McCain predicted that given the weapons it needed the Navy would clamp down an airtight blockade and achieve victory "perhaps even sooner than has been estimated."[6]

McCain also took the opportunity during his time away from the war to write two long articles that appeared in the 14 and 21 July 1945 issues of the *Saturday Evening Post*. He emphasized how "carrier-based airpower for the first time in its history had stood up to land-based airpower and slugged it out, week after week, toe to toe" against the Japanese in the Philippines and the South China Sea in late 1944 and early 1945. In the face of persistent bad weather and the threat of Japanese suicide attacks, Task Force 38 had devastated enemy shipping and aircraft in Luzon and Formosa in support of the Leyte and Lingayen operations. At the same time, McCain was critical of decisions that kept the carriers close to the shore, negating the advantages of surprise and mobility. In contrast, the flattops had enjoyed the "fruits of tactical surprise" in the South China Sea, where they found Japanese land, sea, and air targets "ripe for the plucking." McCain wrote engagingly for a popular audience, providing readers with details about carrier operations and specifics obviously gleaned from task force action reports, although he tended to exaggerate the numbers of Japanese aircraft and ships destroyed while minimizing American aircraft and personnel losses. Secretary of the Navy James Forrestal congratulated McCain for the "interesting" articles and praised the Third Fleet, whose "strikes have thrilled the nation." Looking to the future, Forrestal believed the articles provided "good public information—of which we are going to need a lot more if we hope to combat the juggernaut that the Army and Air Forces are assembling in the drive for a single defense department and/or a separate air force."[7]

His leave over, McCain was off to San Francisco on 23 March, where he received a gold star to go along with the Distinguished Service Medal he had been awarded after his tour as Comairsopac in 1942. The accolade recognized McCain's aggressiveness and "brilliant tactical control" of the fast carrier forces during operations in the Philippines and South China Sea from September 1944 to January 1945. From San Francisco, McCain and (now Captain) Jimmie Thach flew in one of the Cincpac flag planes to Pearl Harbor, where they arrived on the morning of 4 April. That afternoon they met with Towers and Comairpac Vice Adm. George Murray, who briefed them on recent developments in the western Pacific. McCain and his staff, most of whom had come in from the West Coast by ship, spent the better part of the next month at Ford Island conferring with Halsey, Murray, Towers, and members of Nimitz's staff who had been left behind when Nimitz moved his Cincpac headquarters to Guam in January. In the midst of these planning sessions, Baker called McCain's staff together on the morning of

12 April to inform them that he had just learned that President Roosevelt had died at his retreat in Warm Springs, Georgia, and that Harry Truman was now the commander in chief. Better news arrived on the afternoon of 6 May: Germany had unconditionally surrendered and the war in Europe had at last come to an end.[8]

Nimitz's 15 May Op Plan 4-45 provided the basic framework for Third Fleet and TF-38 operations. Brief and to the point, the plan called for the unconditional surrender of Japan, to be achieved "at the earliest practicable date" with the destruction of Japanese naval and air defenses, an air and sea blockade, and finally an invasion of the "industrial heart" of the country. MacArthur's South West Pacific command would complete operations in the Philippines and support Nimitz's Pacific Ocean Area forces with reconnaissance in the South China Sea and neutralize the remaining Japanese air strength in Formosa. Nimitz's warships and aircraft bore primary responsibility for the blockade and reduction of Japanese naval and air assets, as well as the strategic mission of attacking the enemy's industrial fabric, which Nimitz believed would undermine the Japanese people's "will to resist." More specifically, Halsey's Third Fleet was to assault air forces, shipping, and shipyards while securing sea and air communications through the Central Pacific. After consulting with Nimitz in Guam, Halsey promulgated his own operations plan (Op Plan 3-45) on 20 May. The plan called for six task forces, including McCain's TF-38 and the recently organized British Task Force 37 under the command of Vice Admiral H. Bernard Rawlings, as well as a heavy surface striking force (TF-34) consisting of fast battleships under the command of Vice Adm. Willis Lee. TF-38 and TF-37 were to eliminate all potential Japanese naval and air threats and strike enemy shipping, shipyards, and strategic targets along the coasts to "effect maximum attrition" on Japanese forces in preparation "for the capture of additional positions as may be directed by CINCPOA."[9]

One of those "additional positions" was Kyushu. Yet even at this late date it was not out of the question that other objectives might be secured after Okinawa to support Olympic, or possibly as alternatives to invasion of the home islands. Nimitz and King liked a proposal from Spruance, code-named Longtom, for a landing on the Ningpo Peninsula–Chusan archipelago near Shanghai, where airfields could be established and an anchorage was available at Nimrod Sound. Nimitz's staff fleshed the idea out with a more detailed proposal for an invasion on 20 August, using fast carriers and land-based air in support, which King forwarded to the JCS. The Joint

Chiefs, though not enthusiastic but also not willing to drop Longtom alto-gether, relegated it to a back burner as they moved ahead with Olympic.[10] Until late in the game, Nimitz and other high-ranking Navy officers clung to Longtom or some variation of it in the hope that somehow events would preclude an invasion of Japan and that the sea and air blockade would be sufficient to effect Japan's capitulation.

On 9 May, most of McCain's staff left Hawaii aboard the light cruiser *Duluth* (CL 87) for the voyage to Ulithi, while McCain, Thach, Baker, and several other members of his staff followed by air, leaving Ford Island on the sixteenth. On the afternoon of 18 May, McCain broke flag on Capt. James D. Barner's new *Essex*-class carrier *Shangri-La* (CV 38) at the Ulithi anchorage. After more staff work and planning, the carrier got under way early on the morning of 24 May in company with Radford's TG-58.4, which had returned to Ulithi for routine upkeep and replenishment. About 190 miles south-east of Okinawa on the morning of the twenty-seventh, the *Shangri-La* and TG-58.4 rendezvoused with Ted Sherman's TG-58.3. While the *Shangri-La* refueled, Mitscher and members of his staff came over from the carrier *Randolph* (CV 15) for more than two hours of conferences with McCain and his subordinates. At midnight, Halsey relieved Spruance and once more Fifth Fleet became Third Fleet, for what proved to be the last rotation. Later that morning, the twenty-eighth, McCain met for nearly five hours with Mitscher and Halsey aboard Halsey's flagship *Missouri* (BB 63), which had just joined Radford's task group. Finally, that afternoon at 1500, McCain formally took command of TF-38, relieving Mitscher, who left the follow-ing morning in the *Randolph* for Guam and a badly needed rest stateside.[11]

Three task groups made up McCain's task force. Jocko Clark had TG-38.1 with the big carriers *Hornet* and *Bennington* (CV 20) and light carriers *Belleau Wood* and *San Jacinto*. Clark's screen included the battle-ships *Massachusetts* and *Indiana* (BB 58), heavy cruisers *Baltimore*, *Quincy* (CA 71), and *Pittsburgh* (CA 72), antiaircraft cruisers *Atlanta* (CLAA 104) and *San Juan* (CLAA 54), the light cruiser *Duluth*, and seventeen destroy-ers. Sherman commanded TG-38.3 with the *Essex* and *Randolph* and the light carriers *Bataan* (CVL 29) and *Monterey*, screened by the battle-ships *Washington* and *Alabama*, light cruisers *Pasadena* (CL 65), *Springfield* (CL 66), *Astoria* (CL 90), and *Wilkes-Barre* (CL 103), the antiaircraft cruiser *Oakland* (CLAA 95), and twenty-two destroyers. In addition to the *Shangri-La*, Radford's TG-38.4 included the *Essex*-class *Yorktown* and *Ticonderoga*, along with the *Independence*, which had reconverted to a day carrier. Radford also had the battleships *Iowa*, *Wisconsin*, and *Missouri*, two "battle cruisers"—*Alaska* (CB 1) and *Guam* (CB 2)—antiaircraft cruisers *Flint* (CLAA 97) and *San Diego* (CLAA 53), and sixteen destroyers. McCain's old Comairsopac chief of staff, Matt Gardner, had lost his sole remaining night carrier when a kamikaze struck the *Enterprise*, so he rotated home to a staff job. With twelve fast carriers, McCain's force was the same size as it had been in January, but it was down from the maximum of fifteen that Mitscher had enjoyed at times during his stint as TF-58 commander.[12]

On the twenty-fourth, while still at Ulithi, Radford had welcomed onboard the *Yorktown* a party of well-known and influential newsmen, eager to report on TF-38's pending operations in the Ryukyus. Henry Luce, the publisher of *Time*, *Life*, and *Fortune* magazines, led the powerful media contingent, which also included *Time*'s senior editor Roy Alexander and Cedric Foster, a nationally respected commentator for the Mutual Broadcasting System. After interviewing Radford and making the rounds of other ships in the fleet, among them Halsey's *Missouri*, Luce and his entourage transferred back to the *Yorktown* as it steamed with Radford's task group south of the Ryukyus, getting an opportunity to observe up close and report on the fast carriers' contributions to the Okinawa campaign.[13]

Though not immediately available because it had retired to rearm and replenish at its main base in Sydney on 25 May, the British TF-57 promised an additional four fast carriers to the forces deployed by Halsey and McCain. In the summer of 1944, with their fast carriers having little to do in the European war and the British Chiefs of Staff insistent that the Royal Navy contribute to victory in the Pacific, the British began agitating for a Central Pacific task force. While acknowledging that the British had a role to play in Southeast Asia and might help in retaking the Dutch East Indies, King believed they had no understanding of the logistical requirements in the Pacific or any experience with complex multicarrier operations. Nevertheless, over his objections, the Combined Chiefs of Staff agreed at the Quebec Conference in September 1944 to create the British Pacific Fleet (BPF), commanded by Admiral Sir Bruce Fraser. King and Nimitz insisted that the British must employ their own logistics network, although they did concede that the BPF could use American advance bases at Manus and Ulithi. Moreover, Nimitz agreed to provide bulk petroleum to the BPF, supply stores on an emergency basis, and assigned liaison officers to cooperate with Vice Admiral Rawlings, second in command of the fleet, and Rear Admiral Sir Philip L. Vian, who led the British carrier force. After proving themselves in a raid on Japanese airfields and oil refineries at Palembang on the island of Sumatra in January, four fast carriers from the BPF joined the Fifth Fleet in March, operating as TF-57 under Spruance's tactical command during the Okinawa campaign. There the British flattops shook off repeated kamikaze hits, belatedly vindicating McCain's advocacy of armored flight decks. So well did the British do at Okinawa that on Spruance's recommendation Nimitz determined that henceforth TF-37 would operate as a fully integrated component of McCain's task force.[14]

Not usually recognized as an advantage enjoyed by the fast carriers in their operations off the Ryukyus and the Japanese home islands was a secret network of radar navigation installations known as Loran (long-range radio navigation). First used in the Battle of the Atlantic in 1942 and then by ships and aircraft in most parts of the Pacific theater by the end of 1944, the system used "pulses" of high-power, low-frequency radio waves that could be detected at distances of up to 1,500 miles. Paired Loran stations transmitted signals within milliseconds of one another. A navigator using relatively simple receiving equipment picked up the transmissions from the twin stations and measured the time delay between them on an oscilloscope. He used the interval between the signals and plotted their intersection on special charts, which allowed him to determine his position easily and with unprecedented accuracy. By the end of 1944, eight Loran stations were in operation in the Marshalls and Marianas, all constructed and operated by the Coast Guard and invaluable to the ships and aircraft of the fast carrier task force.[15]

Cruising south and southeast of Okinawa, McCain's carriers continued to provide support for the operations ashore. On 29 May, McCain released Sherman's task group to refit at the new advance fleet anchorage in San Pedro Bay near Tacloban on Leyte, while the other two groups encountered unfavorable weather that limited air operations to combat air patrol flights over Okinawa that day. Late on the thirtieth, McCain turned over tactical command to Radford, whose TG-38.4 stayed in close support as Clark's group split off to refuel 250 miles to the south. Weather again hampered flights on the last day in May, although it was possible for some task force aircraft to fly CAP and generally be in position to assist ground troops. There was no enemy air opposition. On 1 June, the task groups swapped places as Clark's group took up position to provide cover while Radford's refueled from TG-30.8, now under the command of Rear Adm. Donald B. Beary. McCain resumed tactical control when the two groups reunited late on the first.[16]

For the next two days, the task force, augmented by the night carrier *Bon Homme Richard* (CV 31) in Clark's TG-38.1, launched fighter sweeps over Kyushu and a barrier patrol near Amami Gunto northeast of Okinawa to intercept enemy aircraft staging into Okinawa from southern Japan. The strikes resulted in eight Japanese aircraft shot down and another twenty-five destroyed on the ground; another thirty-four were damaged in the air and on the ground. Although after-action reporting and photography had improved by this time, poor weather over the targets on those days meant that the statistics for Japanese losses were again most likely exaggerated. The numbers of friendly losses were not. TF-38 lost twenty-three fighters and one torpedo bomber, along with twelve aviators on those two days; half of the losses were to AA fire, and the other half were operational. That the carriers stayed relatively close to Okinawa meant that they had to launch the Kyushu strikes from outside optimal range, which gave the Japanese ample warning of the approaching attackers and time to get defensive fighters into the air. Frustrated, McCain concluded that the operations, "while resolutely executed, were unproductive and relatively costly."[17]

On 5 June, McCain circulated a Cincpac intelligence report on the situation he and his forces faced as the Okinawa campaign went forward. Despite "enormous losses" before and during the battle, the Japanese had integrated their navy and army air commands into a single Sky Air Force to coordinate the flow of aircraft and personnel from Honshu, northern Kyushu, and Formosa. As a result, the enemy had maximized his resources and continued to mount attacks on American ground forces and shipping in Okinawa while at the same time holding fighter aircraft in reserve to intercept Army Air Forces and Navy attacks on the home islands. In sum, McCain's task force faced a resourceful enemy committed to defend the Japanese homeland, and he recommended that fast carrier strikes on airfields in rear areas be employed to interdict the movement of aircraft into south Kyushu, which offered an "excellent opportunity of disorganizing and destroying" both conventional and suicide attacks. He warned that it would not be easy because the Japanese had widely dispersed their aircraft, protected them in camouflaged revetments often ringed by antiaircraft installations, and made creative use of dummies and duds as decoys.[18]

In a dispatch on the same date (5 June), McCain warned that his airmen had encountered "experienced and skilled enemy fighter squadrons" in southern Kyushu, flying high-performance Kawanishi NiK-J Shiden ("George"), Nakajima Ki-84 Hayate ("Frank"), Kawasaki Ki-61 Hien

("Tony"), and Mitsubishi J2M Raiden ("Jack") fighters that were more than a match for the Corsair and Hellcat. Moreover, the Japanese defenders were "undoubtedly under ground radar control for interceptions." Four of Radford's TG-38.4 fighters had been shot down in a dogfight with the Japanese on the third. In this "first brush" with enemy fighters, TF-38 fliers had been shocked by the skill and competence of the Japanese, most likely because of what McCain believed was the "overconfidence and a degree of carelessness from easy shoot downs of enemy bombers and suicide groups." He extolled his carrier group commanders to remind their fighter pilots that the Japanese "can be beaten" by staying in tight formations "for mutual protection when [the] enemy has [the] initial advantage and by teamwork and use of high cover in offensive operations."[19]

If McCain was dissatisfied with the results of the strikes on the second and third, the next two days would trap him in circumstances that called into question his and Halsey's capacities to make timely and correct command decisions. The crisis manifested itself, improbably, in the sudden appearance of another small, fast-moving, and unpredictable typhoon. An indication of trouble first came in a report from 1 June of a disturbance in the Philippine Sea about a thousand miles south-southeast of Okinawa and tracking northwest. Two days later, a search aircraft from the Philippines spotted a storm several hundred miles east of Manila. Subsequently—and confusingly—this storm may have split in two, with half of it vanishing and the other half continuing to track northeast at an accelerating pace. McCain monitored reports from weather centrals in Guam, Leyte, and Manus and correlated them with his own aerological information to follow the track of the remaining storm.[20]

Early on the morning of the fourth, Clark's group, again separated from Radford's TG-38.4, began fueling from Beary's TG-30.8 oilers. By that time, McCain was convinced that the storm was moving northeast and recommended to Halsey that flight operations be suspended and that the task force retire to the east out of the path of the storm. Halsey concurred. At 0745, he ordered TGs 38.1 and 30.8 to change course to 110 degrees. But the weather held, and with McCain's permission Clark's group resumed fueling, which it completed later that afternoon. At 1435, McCain recommended a course of 90 degrees (due east) to take the task force farther away from what he now believed was a typhoon. Like McCain, Halsey knew the previously reported storm had broken in two. But which storm was going where? After consulting with Cdr. George Kosco, his aerological officer, Halsey believed that one of the storms had dissipated and that the other storm was farther west than previous weather reports indicated. He determined to wait for more information. That evening, Halsey ordered McCain to bring his two task groups together and assume a course at twelve knots a little farther to the south. McCain was also to prepare to refuel Radford's group at daybreak on the fifth from TG-30.8, which was to accompany Clark's TG-38.1 to the rendezvous point. At 2235, McCain received a message from Halsey recommending another course change toward the south (150 degrees), to which McCain replied that based on his analysis "the best solution was an increase of speed to the east" to clear the weather.[21]

At 2200 on the fourth, the *Ancon* (AGC 4), an amphibious command ship with the joint expeditionary force (TF-31), reported that its radar plot showed the storm to the southwest of the task force, barreling along a track to the northeast at about twenty-six knots. With the *Ancon* report in hand, but still thinking that the storm was farther to the west than indicated by the *Ancon* report, Halsey told McCain at 0042 on the fifth that he wanted the task force to come around to a course of 300 degrees to cross ahead of the storm. McCain complied at 0115. Both Clark and Beary thought the new course was "ill advised." At 0246, Beary radioed McCain: "Believe this course is running us back into storm." At about the same time, McCain recommended, with Halsey's approval, a turn to the right, bringing the ships to a heading due north at a speed of sixteen knots, sufficient, McCain believed to clear the storm safely.[22]

With the December typhoon disaster in mind, McCain sent a TBS to Radford at 0258 requesting him to "keep me advised how DD's are making out" as the wind and waves increased in intensity. Farther to the south and closer to the storm, Beary reported that his "Escort Carriers are riding very heavy" and that he was turning left to 300 degrees, thinking they would handle better, but which put his group on a collision course with the eye of the typhoon. Clark temporarily slowed his task group while one of his destroyers restored power and steering control, lost due to water ingress in the pounding seas. His flagship's radar at that time located the typhoon's center forty miles to the southwest bearing northeast. Clark sent a TBS at 0420: "I can get clear of center of the storm by heading 120—please advise." McCain replied, "We have nothing on our scope resembling storm center." Clark: "We very definitely have and we have had one for an hour and a half." Then silence for twenty minutes before McCain asked Clark to "please give me bearing and distance of storm center now." Clark immediately informed

McCain that the typhoon center was about thirty miles away and the leading edge of the storm was about half that distance. At 0446, McCain signaled that "we intend holding present course. Use your own judgment." This released Clark to pursue the optimal course either to avoid the storm or to ride it out most comfortably. Yet Clark hesitated, staying roughly on the same heading to the north until he radioed at 0518 that he was finally "maneuvering to find best course," adding that the winds had picked up to eighty knots.[23]

For the next two hours, Clark set one course after another to stay clear of the typhoon and ensure that his ships, especially the smaller ones, were as safe as possible. Nevertheless, at times even the heavy ships found it impossible to hold positions in the wind and waves, which peaked at 120 knots and sixty feet, respectively, at about 0600. After crossing and recrossing the track of the typhoon, the group entered the eye of the storm, on the other side of which the ships encountered relatively moderate weather, though still severe under any other circumstances. Few vessels escaped the tempest unscathed. None sank, mostly due to expert ship-handling and lessons learned from the December typhoon. By far the worst damage was to the *Pittsburgh*, which at 0640 had more than one hundred feet of its bow sliced off by two monster waves. Fortunately, the cruiser, completely "buttoned up" and in full damage control mode when it was struck, suffered no loss of life and was able to limp safely back to Guam on 10 June. The *Hornet* and *Bennington* had twenty-five feet of their forward flight decks collapse, while the *Belleau Wood* and *San Jacinto* suffered hull damage, as did the cruisers *Baltimore* and *Duluth*. Mostly because their bunkers were full, the destroyers generally fared well, with the only serious damage to the superstructure of the *Samuel N. Moore* (DD 747).[24]

Sixteen miles to the north of TG-38.1 and just brushing the northern edge of the storm, Radford's task group also encountered rough weather, but nothing like what TG-38.1 ran into early that morning. When some of the group's destroyers had steering problems in the heavy seas, McCain ordered slight course changes and an increase in speed to help the small ships ride better. The maximum wind velocity recorded on the *Shangri-La* a little before 0600 was fifty-four knots with eighteen-foot seas. By 0800, the winds and rain tapered off; three hours later, the skies were clear and the weather good enough for Radford's flattops to resume CAPs. Beary's group, on the other hand, south of Clark's ships, took various courses to avoid the storm, only to run into the typhoon's eye about 0530. The escort carrier *Windham*

Bay (CVE 92) reported seventy-five-foot waves and 127-knot winds. Damage was severe but could have been worse: the *Windham Bay* and *Salamaua* (CVE 96) saw large sections of their flight decks destroyed; an oiler suffered serious damage, and a destroyer escort lost most of its power plant and electronic gear.[25]

Compared to the catastrophe only six months previously, McCain's force got off lightly. Of ten ships damaged severely enough to require yard repairs, the *Hornet*, *Bennington*, *Belleau Wood*, and the two escort carriers were the worst, along with the *Pittsburgh*. Another dozen or so ships suffered minor damage, and 146 aircraft were damaged or destroyed. One officer and five enlisted seamen died, either from injuries on their ships or from being swept overboard. There were no offensive air operations on the fifth as the *Bennington* was released for repairs at Leyte and the remaining carriers regrouped and turned south to join Beary's logistics group about 135 miles southeast of Okinawa to refuel early the next day. That morning, the sixth, while the task force refueled in good weather and took on replacement aircraft, Clark came over to the *Shangri-La* to talk with McCain about the typhoon. Afterward, McCain and Clark, accompanied by Baker and Thach, boarded the *Missouri* for discussions with Halsey and his staff about the storm, about ship and aircraft damage, and about coordinating plans for another strike on Kyushu. That afternoon on the *Shangri-La* McCain and his staff briefed Radford and his operations officer on plans for the next few days. Both task groups resumed limited flight operations on the sixth, although the *Hornet* with its collapsed forward flight deck had to back down at eighteen knots to launch over the stern, a tribute to the flight deck crews and the ship-handling skill of the carrier's skipper, Capt. Austin K. ("Artie") Doyle. During routine patrols over Okinawa on the sixth, TF-38 airmen encountered two groups of Japanese fighters, downing seven of them; there was no enemy air opposition over Okinawa on the seventh.[26]

Rather than attack multiple installations on southern Kyushu as they had with mixed results on the second and third, McCain and Halsey decided to overwhelm a single target. McCain's Operation Stinger, articulated on 6 June, called for a concentrated fighter and fighter-bomber assault on a large airfield at Kanoya, where intelligence indicated at least 150 operational enemy aircraft had concentrated, many of them potential kamikazes. Turning north, McCain's carriers closed overnight to a position about 270 miles south of the target and launched late on the morning of 8 June. In five minutes, 199 TF-38 fighters and fighter-bombers swarmed over the air base, saturating the Japanese defenses and raining more than forty-four tons of VT-proximity-fuzed fragmentation bombs on the field and outlying facilities. They destroyed an estimated twenty-eight aircraft on the ground, many dispersed in well-protected revetments, shot down two aircraft, and damaged another forty-nine on the ground and one in the air. Only four Hellcats and Corsairs were lost in combat, and no aircrew were killed or injured. McCain was gratified with the results. He stressed that the success of the strike was primarily due to having "adequate time for preparation of target material and briefing pilots," compared to the previous attacks, which had been impeded by hasty and "superficial" planning. Favorable weather contributed to the success too.[27]

The carriers recovered their aircraft that afternoon and withdrew to refuel from Beary's oilers starting at dawn on 9 June. Just past noon, with most of his ships fueled, McCain's carriers (minus the *Bennington* and not including the *Bon Homme Richard*) launched fighters and bombers to strike Okino Daitō, Minami Daitō, and Kita Daitō, three tiny coral islands southeast of Okinawa. Although the archipelago had little strategic importance, McCain believed attacking the islands would give his airmen more experience with the VT-fuzed bombs and napalm canisters. In 178 sorties, Radford's group struck airfields and AA installations on Minami, and Clark's attacked a phosphate plant, a radio station, barracks, and antiaircraft positions on Okino and Kita, where fliers encountered unexpectedly heavy but inaccurate flak. Early on the tenth, about 200 TF-38 missions hit Minami, Okino, and Kita again. The task force lost no aircraft or flight crew on the ninth, but suffered three operational losses on the tenth; one each—a "lifeguard" submarine, dumbo flying boat, cruiser floatplane, and a destroyer—fished the airmen out of the water. At 1900, the task force set course for a much-anticipated break from combat operations at their advanced base in Leyte. TF-38 left behind the escort carrier *Anzio* (CVE 57) and a task group to continue CAP and transmit radio signals to deceive the Japanese that the big carriers were still on station.[28]

By noon on the thirteenth, Clark's task group had arrived at San Pedro Bay, Leyte, followed at intervals by the other carrier units, including TG-38.4 and the *Shangri-La*, which anchored about four hours later. All hands were startled when they saw the *Randolph*, which had been crashed and badly damaged on 7 June by an Army P-38 practicing dive-bombing. In an angry reaction, Sherman issued orders for ships to shoot down all AAF intruders. More temperate but equally urgent was Nimitz's dispatch admonishing the

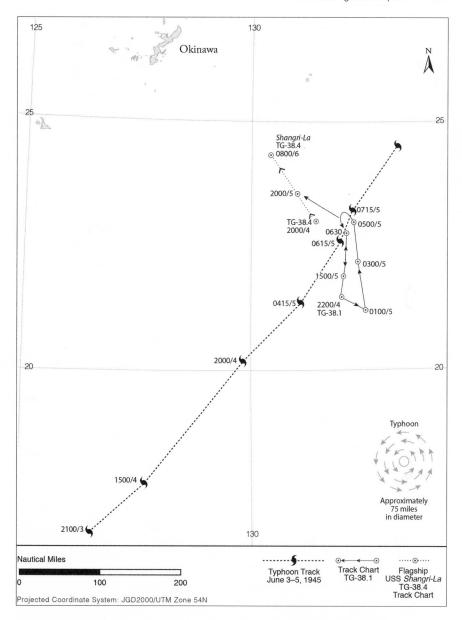

Map 7. Typhoon, 4–5 June 1945 (Morison, *Victory in the Pacific*; USS *Shangri-La* War Diary, June 1–30, 1945, www.Fold3.com, accessed April 16, 2016)

AAF to take immediate steps to "prevent any recurrence of this irresponsible conduct what has damaged a much needed fighting unit." Everyone and everything in McCain's force was worn out. It had been ninety-two days since the start of the Okinawa campaign, during which the ships and men had been subjected to almost unrelenting assault from the enemy and from the forces of nature. In remarks to the *Randolph's* Air Group 12, McCain stressed that it had "been a tough campaign" and that the aviators deserved their leaves at home. "Despite what you were up against, you have done a magnificent job," he continued. "You have swept the Jap back to his home-land. You hit him hard with your strikes against Japan. You led the way at Okinawa . . . by gaining and maintaining control of the air. Take pride in your record. It's a good one."[29]

Almost immediately on the carriers' arrival at Leyte, repairs began on ships and aircraft and the hot, back-breaking process of replenishment and rearming got under way as the crewmembers rotated off on liberty to the beaches and bars of San Antonio in northern Samar and to recreation cen-ters established at Tubabao and Calicoan islands on the eastern shores of Leyte Gulf. Halsey wanted Sherman's group to be ready for sea on twelve hours' notice, while Clark's and Radford's task groups were to complete their turnaround by 28 June. Early on the fourteenth, McCain boarded the *Missouri* for two hours of consultation with Halsey and his staff. There were also command changes in the task force: on the fifteenth, Rear Adm. Thomas L. Sprague in the repaired *Bennington* assumed command of TG-38.1 from Clark, who went back to the states with Doyle and the damaged *Hornet*; three days later, Bogan took over TG-38.3 from Sherman.[30]

For McCain the Ryukyu and Kyushu operations were lessons learned. He and Halsey agreed that tying the fast carriers to the beaches had been a costly error. In his 7 July action report, McCain was specific that the "employment of the Fast Carrier in direct ground support over protracted periods . . . is wasteful of force, and it fails to exploit the Fast Carrier assets of mobility, surprise, and concentration. It invites damage to the Fast Carriers through continued operation in restricted waters. Finally, it diverts the Fast Carriers from profitable targets only they can reach." In his endorsement of McCain's report, Halsey added that "the Fast Carrier Task Forces can best support landing operations by offensive action against enemy forces that threaten our invasion forces." Nimitz concurred. Carrier aircraft were vital for tactical support of amphibious operations, but they should fly from CVEs, "leaving the fast carriers free to engage in offensive operations more in keeping with their capabilities." In a separate communication that qual-ified his earlier assessment of Japanese fighters, McCain admitted that the

"Tony" had good performance but lacked reliability and that "our average VF squadrons are far superior in gunnery and tactics." "The Kamikaze attack against ships," he believed, "remains the only real threat against our naval operations."[31]

McCain also made another plea for reconstituting carrier air groups. He believed that planning was still rooted in "the early 1942 concept of the carrier striking force," which, based on recent operations, was totally obsolete. To support land operations, "VF and VBF are practically the only useful type." Torpedo and dive-bombers were vulnerable to antiaircraft fire and land-based fighters, whereas fighter-bombers in "strategic" operations when "properly and understandingly handled can carry greater punishment to the enemy over longer ranges than the VB type." He urged Murray as Comairpac to press for the acquisition of more fighters and recommended that light carriers immediately take on all-fighter air groups and in the future all air complements have 100 percent fighters and fighter-bombers. Murray recommended "strongly against" McCain's proposal, and Nimitz denied his request for the immediate transition to all-fighter air groups on light carriers. Nevertheless, there were important changes to the carriers' air complements starting in July. Although heavy carrier air groups would remain unchanged, all new light carrier air groups, as well as older ones when they were reconstituted, would be made up exclusively of fighters and fighter-bombers (Hellcats, Corsairs, and ultimately the new Grumman F8F Bearcat).[32]

Important as those considerations were, Nimitz wanted to know why TF-38 had blundered into another typhoon. King, too, needed answers and signaled Nimitz that the "inability of Taskforce 38 to avoid typhoon of 5 June is cause for concern particularly in connection [with] future operations." On 8 June, Nimitz constituted a court of inquiry, with Adm. John Hoover presiding, as he had in the previous investigation. George Murray was also on the court, as well as Vice Adm. Charles A. Lockwood, commander, Submarine Force Pacific Fleet, and Capt. Ira H. Nunn sitting as judge advocate. The court opened its hearings on the New Mexico at the Leyte anchorage on the fifteenth. Appearing before the panel two days later, Jocko Clark recounted developments early on the fifth as TG-38.1 unsuccessfully attempted to dodge the typhoon. He stressed that for some time he knew where the storm was and believed he could avoid it by heading east, yet he thought McCain wanted to maintain the integrity of the force on its northerly course and did not begin maneuvering independently until 0515. Part of his hesitation was due, he testified, to his thinking that Halsey "might have had information that I didn't have" and that "it was my duty to remain on my station until I had some real information to go on."[33]

Halsey's testimony followed Clark's. He emphasized that he had indications as early as 1 June that a storm had been forming to the south and that he had determined to move the fleet eastward and to "get sea room to maneuver and avoid the storm." With receipt of the *Ancon* report, Halsey and his staff realized that the storm was farther east than they had predicted, and he ordered the course changed to 300 degrees to cross in front of the storm. Neither he nor his staff had objected to McCain's idea of setting a new course due north, although they worried it might "keep us in the path of the storm a little bit longer." To Halsey the real problem had been a lack of accurate and timely weather information. "As the responsible commander in the combat zone I believe I am fully entitled to have every bit of information that can be made available about storms." Yet aircraft reports from untrained observers were badly in error and he did not receive the *Ancon* report until four and a half hours after it had been filed. "It is imperative that communications in regard to storms must be immediate. We are not telling the Japs anything when we tell them a typhoon is coming because they have nothing out there they can use it for." Finally, he reminded the court that Task Force 38 was back in action on the sixth and that it had carried out fighter and fighter-bomber raids on Kanoya just two days later.[34]

When McCain's turn came to testify before the court later in the afternoon of the seventeenth, he underscored Halsey's point that timely weather information was vital and that initially the thinking was that the typhoon was relatively far to the west. Early on the fifth, "I recommended that we go east. My reason for recommending this with an increase of speed was that I had a better idea of where this storm was on the assumption that the storm's course was northeast." McCain stated that he did not like Halsey's course of 300 degrees and insisted his own course due north was better, at least until it became apparent that the typhoon had picked up speed and was on a more northerly track than anticipated. By 0600, Radford's TG-38.4 group had "passed comfortably to the north" of the typhoon. "The wind was in the east. DDs were also riding comfortably." In comparison to what Clark's and Beary's groups were enduring only a short distance to the south, McCain found it "surprising what a difference sixteen miles made in the two task groups."[35]

Clark cross-examined McCain, first asking him if his radar plot of the storm and the course due north appeared "to be placing 38.1 in danger."

McCain replied that his radar "was showing that 38.1 had he remained in position would have just cleared the northeastern edge" of the storm. Then Clark demanded that he "would like to know why you did not release Task Group 38.1 at 0420 when you were advised, 'I can get clear of the center of the storm quickest by heading 120°. Please advise.'" "I debated that question for twenty minutes to find out if I knew something that Admiral Clark did not know," McCain responded. "I did know that course 120° would buck heavy seas but on finding that Admiral Clark did know this I told him to use his own judgment. If twenty minutes' delay made any difference, I'm sorry." It was an unfortunate statement. In hindsight, it is apparent that had McCain authorized the course change earlier and Clark had immediately taken a course of 120 degrees his group might well have missed the worst of the weather or avoided it altogether. Yet the court concluded that task group commanders, if not released from "prescribed courses and stations," also had responsibility for acting independently to "avoid storm danger."[36]

The court continued its hearings at Nimitz's headquarters in Guam, concluding the proceedings on 22 June. In its findings, the court concurred there were shortcomings in the Pacific weather forecasting and reporting system, yet it determined that Halsey bore "primary responsibility" for the damages suffered by the fleet on 5 June. Specifically, the course change to 300 degrees was "extremely ill advised" and that Halsey bore "primary responsibility" for the resultant material and personnel losses. Moreover, Halsey did not properly evaluate information he had received on the location and intensity of the storm, and he "failed to release major Fleet units from tactical concentration" when it was obvious they were endangered by the typhoon. For their parts, McCain, Clark, and Beary shared "responsibility, to a lesser degree" for the damage and losses in the storm. The court determined that McCain deserved "serious blame" for not carrying out "the spirit and letter" of Nimitz's 13 February fleet letter that had reminded commanders of their responsibilities to ensure the safety of ships and men in the face of severe weather. McCain "as OTC of Task Force 38 maintained his Task Force tactically concentrated until grave danger to ships of one of his Task groups was imminent." He "continued on courses and at speeds which eventually led [his] task groups into dangerous weather," especially when "better judgment dictated a course of action which would have taken them fairly clear of the typhoon path."[37]

The court went on to recommend that "letters of admonition" be sent to Halsey, McCain, Clark, and Beary and "that serious consideration be given to assigning Commander THIRD Fleet and Commander Task Force 38 to other duty." Forrestal was so inclined, but Nimitz and King were more circumspect. In his endorsement, Nimitz agreed with the court's findings, while calling attention to the need for more improvements in Pacific weather forecasting and reporting. But he disagreed with the recommendation that Halsey and McCain be relieved, for both had "outstanding combat records" and had, "during their present assignments, rendered services of great value in prosecuting the war against our enemies." King found that there was evidence that "there was ineptness in obtaining, disseminating and acting upon meteorological data with the result that certain units of the THIRD Fleet failed to avoid the path of a typhoon center and, in consequence, suffered storm damage that impaired to a serious degree the combat efficiency of that fleet." Furthermore, the "responsible officers" had "sufficient information to enable them to avoid the worst part of the storm area had they reacted to the situation as it developed with the weatherwise skill to be expected of professional seamen." "Notwithstanding the above," King added, "I recommend that no individual disciplinary measures be taken" against either Halsey or McCain. He did, "suggest, however, that the Secretary of the Navy address a letter to the Commander THIRD Fleet expressing dissatisfaction with the repeated inability of the THIRD Fleet to deal intelligently with typhoon conditions." Radford, who alone escaped criticism, concluded that Halsey was "culpably negligent" and that McCain bore "a lesser degree of responsibility" for the disaster.[38]

Not surprisingly, McCain devoted much of his 7 July action report to aerology, in effect presenting an addendum and supplementary defense of his actions during the typhoon. He asserted that part of the problem was too much information that had not been efficiently organized or distributed, thereby forcing fleet aerologists to sift through a sequence of periodic Weather Central broadcasts to ascertain the information needed in the immediate operational area. Reorganizing the broadcast schedule and retransmitting as needed would solve the problem. Belatedly he seemed to have learned a hard lesson from his experience in the South Pacific that frequent aircraft in-flight reports were essential to provide the task force with up-to-date information; summary reports at twelve and twenty-four-hour intervals were next to useless. Not only had the task force suffered from tardy information, but, even worse, Weather Central had provided "erroneous advice regarding the location of the typhoon." McCain did rightly admit that "an officer in a position of command is responsible for decisions made in the execution of the duties of his office." And he concluded, "Any deviation from an aggressive, intelligent policy of supplying the required timely weather information to the aerological advisors to officers in Command is a potential threat to the validity of decisions of officers in command."[39]

McCain had stated the obvious. More often than not, command at sea necessitates decisions based on limited and conflicting information. All naval officers faced the fundamental problem of uncertainty, which they were challenged to mitigate but never fully solve through experience, intelligence, communication, and close attention to command-and-control systems. The vicissitudes of combat—in this instance compounded by horrid weather—only heightened that uncertainty. Brooding on the subject decades later, Radford believed that McCain's indecision on course changes was a contributing factor to the calamity: "I have never been able to determine just how he judged the situation as it developed." From years of experience McCain knew, or should have known, that command in modern warfare demanded split-second decisions based on inadequate information.[40] Yet he stressed in his action reports and court of inquiry testimony that he did not have enough intelligence about the typhoon nor did he have it in time to make the right judgments about courses and speeds. Further, McCain understood that maneuvering a task group, especially in bad weather, took time, and he was uncharacteristically obtuse in testifying that he did not think twenty minutes made much difference. He understood that he would not be held blameless, that he shared major responsibility for the typhoon, and that he was accountable for fundamental errors that might jeopardize his continuation in combat command.

Indeed, as McCain's fast carriers readied to assault Japan in preparation for Olympic, King and Nimitz were in the process of making their own decisions, destined to affect McCain's future as a task force commander. Regardless of the immediate circumstances, Halsey and McCain were slated to rotate home when Spruance returned as Fifth Fleet commander for the invasion of Kyushu. King and Nimitz had decided, as well, that Mitscher, exhausted and in ill-health, would not take over TF-58 and that Sherman, who had been one of the most successful carrier task group commanders, would relieve him. It was also now clear to Nimitz that it was time to move John Towers into his long-coveted carrier task force command. Less than pleased with McCain's mistakes, Nimitz proposed, with King's concurrence, that Towers step in as McCain's relief as commander, Second Fast Carrier

Force Pacific in charge of TF-38 in Halsey's Third Fleet, and that Sherman, elevated to vice admiral, would assume Mitscher's billet as commander, First Fast Carrier Force Pacific and command of TF-58 under Spruance and Fifth Fleet. Towers learned on 19 June that he would relieve McCain when TF-38 retired about the end of August to the new advance fleet base at Eniwetok.[41]

It is not clear when McCain got unofficial word about the command shakeup, but it is probable he heard about it at the same time Towers did. On 25 June, McCain received notification from the Bureau of Naval Personnel that on or about 1 September he would be detached as Commander Second Fast Carrier Task Force, after which he was to fly to the West Coast and from there on to Washington to report to the Secretary of the Navy for his next duty assignment. That post was not specified. Yet rumors quickly spread that McCain would be relegated to a desk job as assistant administrator of veterans' affairs, a non-Navy billet that reflected King's and Nimitz's displeasure with McCain's recent performance as CTF-38. Halsey recalled that when McCain got the news he was "thoroughly sore" at what he "considered an insult" by his superiors in Washington. Not until 27 July did orders arrive about the veterans' affairs job, where he would serve under Army Gen. Omar Bradley.[42]

Much more was on McCain's mind than fretting about what the future held for his continued service, regardless of where, when, or what it was. Foremost was ensuring that the task force identified and struck objectives consistent with Nimitz's 15 May Op Plan 4-45 and that the flattops not be sidetracked by going after tempting but less important targets. McCain wrote that "live game in the hunting ground of the Fast Carriers has changed its spots during the course of the war. Some targets, old and familiar, have lost importance or ceased to exist. Other targets, important as ever, have become obscured in the clutter of tempting objectives presented to those pilots who fly over the Empire this season." "Vital" Japanese industrial areas should be the principal priority for "all hands" involved with planning, target selection, and briefings. Enemy airfields and aircraft that could threaten the task force had to be blanketed. Primacy also had to be accorded to "targets of great value and significance to Japanese war strength, but which at present are not being attacked by any means. These are the targets which . . . have survived high altitude area bombing" by the Army Air Forces. "They await destruction by carrier aircraft." Numbers mattered. Intelligence was needed to identify all targets within an entire industrial complex, and careful calculations employed to determine the tonnage of bombs that could be delivered during each operation. ACIOs had to ensure that the airmen had a thorough knowledge of their targets and were indoctrinated in the discipline necessary to avoid attacking more "juicy" targets like enemy warships. "It takes a priceless effort to carry bombs to Japan," he concluded. "Put them where they will do the most good!"[43]

Third Fleet and TF-38 had primary responsibility for softening up the Japanese in preparation for Olympic and the invasion of Kyushu. Halsey's Op Plan 9-45 adhered to the general outlines of his previous plans in stressing that the mission was to assault enemy naval and air forces, shipping, shipyards, and "assigned strategic objectives" as needed to weaken the Japanese "ability and will to resist." McCain's more detailed plan specified that TF-38 would sortie on 1 July, conduct Moose-trap and gunnery exercises, refuel, and then strike targets in and around Tokyo on 10 and 11 July. The emphasis was on aircraft, airfields, and aircraft factories, as well as on such strategic targets as electronic manufacturing facilities and the railroad ferries operating across the Tsugaru Strait separating Hokkaido and northern Honshu. On the fifteenth, the British TF-37 would join TF-38 and under McCain's command would take part in more raids in and around Tokyo on 16 and 17 July before the carriers retired late on the seventeenth. After 20 July, the flattops were to resume attacks on Japan, adhering to a routine of two days of strikes followed by a day refueling, then two more days of strikes in a different area, after which there would be two days of replenishment before repeating the cycle. The idea was to exploit the carriers' mobility so that the Japanese did not have time to respond defensively before the task force moved on to new targets. TF-38 would follow that pattern until withdrawing on or about 10 August to Leyte and Eniwetok. Nimitz had understood that radar, radar-jamming devices, and other products of the Japanese electronics industry were likely to be a threat as the carriers closed in on Japan, and he recommended that plants in the Tokyo area be added to the Third Fleet target list. The rail ferries, at first glance, would appear to be of low priority. But they carried the Hokkaido coal used for power generation, and if the system were successfully interdicted much of Japan's electric power grid would collapse. The final command rotation would take place at Eniwetok after the carriers retired and TF-38 again reverted to TF-58.[44]

According to McCain's Op Order 2-45 of 25 June, TF-38 consisted of three groups: TG-38.1 under Rear Admiral Sprague with the carriers *Bennington*, *Lexington*, *Hancock*, *Belleau Wood*, and *San Jacinto*; TG-38.3 with Bogan and the *Essex*, *Randolph*, *Monterey*, and *Bataan*; and TF-38.4, commanded by Radford with the *Yorktown, Shangri-La, Bon Homme Rich-ard, Independence,* and *Cowpens.* British TF-37, functioning as a task group, included four big flattops: *Implacable, Indefatigable, Victorious,* and *Formi-dable.* Two other task forces, TF-34 and TF-35, were heavy and light sur-face striking forces, respectively, and two more groups of surface ships were organized to conduct shore bombardment missions. McCain estimated that most Japanese aircraft were concentrated in Honshu, especially in and around Tokyo, as well as in northern Kyushu, with most of the suicide planes located on dispersed fields near Tokyo. The Japanese were likely to direct suicide attacks "against Fleet Units to the maximum extent of their capabil-ities," as well as carry out conventional bombing and torpedo missions "by highly trained units based near Tokyo." TF-38 was to strike strategic objec-tives in Tokyo and vicinity, northern Honshu, and Hokkaido. The primary objectives were to "reduce enemy tactical air strength" and to "destroy stra-tegic targets directly supporting [the] enemy war effort." A tertiary mission was to return photographic intelligence of Japanese war-making capabilities in northern Honshu and Hokkaido.[45]

Task Force 38 sortied from the San Pedro Bay–Leyte anchorage early on the morning of 1 July, the three task groups proceeding independently toward the fueling rendezvous planned for the eighth. A break from the rou-tine on the *Shangri-La* came at 1100 on the second when the crew assem-bled on the flight deck to witness DCNO (Air) Vice Adm. Aubrey Fitch administer the oath of office to John L. Sullivan as the new Assistant Secre-tary of the Navy for Air. Sullivan was nearing the end of a Pacific tour that had included stops at Pearl Harbor, Manus, Eniwetok, Ulithi, Guam, and Manila. Following the ceremony, Sullivan and Fitch flew over to the *York-town,* spending the afternoon with Radford and his staff. On the fourth, they visited the *Randolph* and *Bennington* to meet with Bogan and Sprague and on the sixth conferred with Halsey and his staff aboard the *Missouri.* Sul-livan and Fitch returned to the *Shangri-La* to observe the first day's strikes before transferring to a destroyer that took them to Iwo Jima. When the *Ticonderoga,* in Radford's group, suffered an engineering casualty on the third, the carrier had to retire to Guam for repairs. McCain's ships spent the eighth refueling from Beary's TG-30.8 oilers before hauling off at 1800 that evening for the run-in to the launch point for the raids on Honshu sched-uled for the tenth.[46]

In fair weather for a change, McCain's carriers made the twenty-five-knot approach to Honshu overnight, 9–10 July, launching the first fighter sweeps before sunrise at 0400 from 140 miles east-southeast of Tokyo. That metropolis occupied center stage, but the targets extended north and south from the capital along an arc stretching more than two hundred miles. The Japanese were totally surprised and dispatched only a handful of interceptors, although the carriers' CAP splashed two snoopers. TF-38's "Big Blue Blanket" smothered sixty-nine airfields—most of them on the Tokyo Plain—with bombs, rockets, and gunfire. Other targets were factories, a radio installation, a power house, a highway bridge, and a freight train. Racking up 1,160 strike sorties, in which 454 tons of bombs and 1,648 rockets were expended, TF-38 airmen destroyed 109 aircraft and damaged another 231. By this time, the task force had experience with dedicated photo planes, which accompanied fighter sweeps and early strike missions. Careful debriefing and statistical analysis had been instituted to ensure greater accuracy in assessing the damage, so the estimates were if anything conservative rather than exaggerated as they tended to be just six months earlier. Because McCain insisted that photos be processed within ninety minutes, it was even possible for airmen flying later missions to study photos taken after the initial strikes. It was still hard, though, to gauge the damage done to aircraft on the ground by VT-fuzed fragmentation bombs, so none of those aircraft were listed as destroyed. TF-38 suffered thirteen aircraft lost in combat and six more in operational accidents; thirteen pilots and crewmen were killed or missing in action.[47]

Part of McCain's scheme for the carrier raids involved dispatching the light cruiser *Tucson* (CL 98) from the task force on a radio deception mission. The cruiser left the flattops on the afternoon of the tenth, shaping a course intended to mask the actual location of the task force and lead the Japanese to misdirect their forces by transmitting radio signals simulating messages between Halsey and Cincpac in Guam. The gambit had precedent dating back at least to the Battle of Midway, when on 28–29 May, the *Tangier* in McCain's South Pacific command had broadcast signals mimicking carrier operations to deceive the Japanese into thinking that the Americans were still focusing on that theater and not the Central Pacific. Yet with the *Tucson*, there was a problem that some in the Third Fleet thought compromised the security of the task force and its mission. Following public relations policies and procedures, news releases went out explaining that TF-38 was operating under radio silence in the vicinity of Japan. Based on the press releases, a San Francisco radio station broadcast the news that for forty-eight hours the carriers had been in a "security blackout," which, if Tokyo had been listening, would have revealed the *Tucson* deception. For the present, the Japanese might have been misled into believing that the San Francisco broadcast was itself a deception and thus "deception pyramided upon deception." Yet in the future there had to be closer coordination between fleet intelligence officers and those responsible for disseminating information to the media.[48]

On the evening of the tenth, the task force withdrew to fuel at a position about four hundred miles east of northern Honshu in preparation for strikes on the thirteenth. While his ships took on oil and other supplies on the morning of the twelfth, McCain, along with Baker and Thach, discussed the forthcoming Honshu and Hokkaido operations with Halsey on the *Missouri*. In addition to attacks on aircraft and air installations in Honshu, northern Kyushu, and southern Hokkaido, Halsey anticipated "sustained strikes against naval combatant strength KURE-KOBE area." Nimitz had called for attacks on the remnants of the Japanese navy—in essence a fleet-in-being—assuming that the warships constituted a threat to Russia-bound North Pacific convoys. Halsey saw the ultimate destruction of the Japanese fleet as the symbolic payback for Pearl Harbor, but McCain was less sanguine. He and Thach saw the ships as "really no threat to us" and that giving the fleet precedence over airfields and aircraft was "just wrong timing." Shortly after the carriers parted company with the replenishment group and set a course to the west to close with the islands, the weather again turned sour. Early on 13 July, McCain canceled that day's strikes, hoping that a twenty-four-hour postponement would be enough time for the weather to clear. In the interim, the carriers flew weather missions and topped off the destroyers' bunkers. Finally, at 1730, the task force began the run-in to the launching point, only eighty miles east of northern Honshu.[49]

The weather was still not good on the fourteenth when the flattops launched their first strikes about an hour before sunrise. Fighters and fighter-bombers worked over airfields, destroying or damaging an estimated sixty-seven aircraft on the ground. Other targets were hangars, oil storage tanks, locomotives, a railroad bridge, and the Wanishi ironworks in Muroran, Hokkaido, which had functioned as a naval ordnance test facility. All the objectives were hit before heavy cloud cover led McCain to cancel afternoon strikes. Nearly 100,000 tons of shipping were destroyed or damaged, most notably eight of the ferries that shuttled coal-laden railcars between Hokkaido and Honshu. TF-38 flew 859 strike missions, delivering 336 tons of ordnance and firing 1,809 rockets. Sixteen aircraft went down in combat and eleven operationally, with the loss of five pilots and four aircrew in combat and four pilots and four aircrew operationally. Killed in an air-to-air collision was Lt. Cdr. Richard Crommelin, the commanding officer of the *Yorktown's* VF-88 and one of four Alabama-born brothers who became naval aviators. The railroad ferry strikes reduced coal shipments to 18 percent of their previous levels, crippling Japanese electric power production and other industries dependent on coal. The historian Richard B. Frank recognized the strategic importance of the ferry system and the role of the fast carriers in disrupting it: "this blow by carrier planes ranks as the most devastating single strategic-bombing success of all the campaigns against Japan."[50]

Not all the destruction wrought that day came from McCain's carriers. Halsey split off the battleships *Massachusetts, Indiana,* and *South Dakota* as Task Unit 34.8.1 to bombard the Kamaishi ironworks in northern Honshu on the fourteenth, and dispatched Task Unit 34.8.2, centered on the *Iowa, Missouri,* and *Wisconsin,* to blast the iron and steel works at Muroran early on the morning of the fifteenth. Thach questioned the value of using battle-wagons in this role. He calculated that if the three battleships achieved 20 percent accuracy, their shells delivered about 12,000 pounds of explosives on Kamaishi, approximately equivalent to what a sortie of 112 F6F fighter-bombers would accomplish, assuming that twenty-four of the planes, each carrying a 1,000-pound bomb, reached their targets. Furthermore, he estimated that only eight bombs were necessary if the Hellcats specifically targeted the vulnerable coke ovens at the ironworks. Thach was off the mark on the number of shells fired by the battleships and their weight of explosives. Yet he was right—and McCain agreed—that the need to provide air cover for surface ships placed more burdens on task group mission planners, disrupted strike schedules, and overtaxed already hard-working airmen and carrier crews.[51]

McCain's carriers repositioned themselves overnight for more raids on Hokkaido and northern Honshu beginning before dawn on 15 July. Again, low clouds concealed most of the airfields, so the airmen mauled shipping, railroad yards, factories, warehouses, oil storage facilities, and factories in coastal areas. Another of the vital Hokkaido-Honshu rail ferries went to the bottom. In 949 strike sorties, the task force dropped 335 tons of bombs and expended 2,093 rockets. Despite the weather, sixteen Japanese aircraft were destroyed or damaged on the ground. Ten of McCain's aircraft went down in combat, and another seven in operational accidents, with the loss of eight pilots and crewmembers. Although the Navy made a point of eschewing civilian targets, sometimes military objectives were located in population centers where it was impossible to avoid collateral damage. Twenty square blocks of the port city of Kushiro in eastern Hokkaido were inadvertently burned out in the 15 July strikes. That evening, reunited with the Muroran bombardment ships, the task force retired to the southeast to meet up with the service group for refueling early the next day.[52]

That morning, 16 July, while the task force replenished from Beary's oilers at the refueling point east of northern Honshu, McCain, Baker, Thach, and other officers transferred to the *Missouri* to meet with Halsey and his staff about the next phase of operations against airfields and naval targets in the Tokyo area. Halsey elaborated on changes to his Op Plan 9-45, stressing the need for coordination with the AAF, whose heavy bombers from the Marianas were scheduled for attacks on airfields and aircraft manufacturing facilities in the Tokyo vicinity for late July and early August. He expected that AAF fighter-bombers flying from Okinawa would be able to hit airfields on days when TF-38 was not available, thus providing continuous suppression of enemy air opposition. McCain modified his operational orders accordingly. Also present at the briefing were Admirals Rawlings and Vian and their staffs from TF-37, which had arrived early in the morning, minus the carrier *Indefatigable*, still in Sydney with mechanical problems. The British had departed from Manus on 6 July and refueled from their own service group on the fifteenth, so they were ready and eager to go when the Americans completed refueling that afternoon and turned south toward a position about two hundred miles east of Tokyo for the next phase of the aerial offensive.[53]

With the British ships, McCain now had four task groups with seventeen fast carriers. In a message to Nimitz on 17 July, McCain anticipated future task force operations, where more ships and task groups were likely to pose command-and-control problems. If the task force were to include four groups plus a night group, he recommended that instead of five carrier division commanders and staffs there should be six, ensuring that a task group commander and staff would always be held in reserve. Because it was "awkward" for a task force commander to handle four task groups and "difficult" for that officer to command five or six groups, he suggested that Nimitz consider dividing the fast carriers into two task forces, separated but still operating "in concert under one command." Nimitz was amenable to McCain's proposals. Through the middle of August, the task force organization would in effect have four carrier division officers (including the British commander), with two officers in "makee-learn" reserve status. To support Olympic, Nimitz planned to have carriers in TF-58 covering the amphibious operations on Kyushu while simultaneously TF-38 carriers would be unleashed to range up and down the home islands providing interdiction and strategic support.[54]

Once more, TF-38 ran afoul of the weather. After dispatching two strikes early on the morning of 17 July, McCain called off the rest of the strikes because the targets were impossible to see in the gloom. The carriers flew only 203 strike sorties, losing one Hellcat in combat and five more fighters operationally; four pilots were missing or dead. Although damage assessment was all but impossible, seven enemy aircraft were declared destroyed or damaged. Sinking a picket boat and other small craft, as well as destroying several locomotives and trains and miscellaneous targets in and around the city of Mito, provided some small consolation for the meager results that day, as did TF-37's destruction of thirteen aircraft on the ground. The three *Iowas* of Task Unit 34.8.2 hit Mito that night, with night fighters from the *Bon Homme Richard* flying cover. Not until late in the morning on the eighteenth did the weather improve enough to launch the first of three strikes on the naval base at Yokosuka, with the battleship *Nagato* in the aviators' crosshairs. In 153 sorties Bogan's Helldivers and Avengers plastered the dreadnought with 270 tons of ordnance, most in the form of 1,000-pound general-purpose bombs intended to detonate close aboard to maximize mining effects. It was mostly wasted effort, for the damage turned out to be relatively minor and the ship, remarkably, survived the war. Other strikes that day sank the ancient armored cruiser *Kasuga* and a small tanker and hit an estimated thirty-nine aircraft on the ground, as well as antiaircraft positions and hangars. Intense AA fire brought down thirteen task force planes, with another pair lost operationally. TF-37 claimed the destruction of thirteen aircraft on the ground at airfields north of Tokyo. American personnel losses were nineteen pilots and aircrew.[55]

The task forces separated to spend the next four days—19–22 July—regrouping and replenishing from their respective service groups before proceeding on a course that brought them roughly 325 miles south of Tokyo. On the morning of the twentieth, McCain met Halsey on the *Missouri* to fine-tune plans for the next operation, which focused on reducing Japanese land-based air power and eliminating remnants of the Japanese Navy's Mobile Fleet scattered throughout the Inland Sea between Shikoku and Honshu.

McCain's operation order (Op Order 3-45) noted that the Japanese were expanding their air forces in and around Tokyo, Nagoya, and Kobe in anticipation of the Allied amphibious landings in Kyushu. The task forces should expect "conventional" torpedo and bombing raids in addition to suicide attacks from units deployed in the home islands. McCain called on his carriers to "effect maximum attrition to enemy air, naval, and ground forces," specifically targeting enemy aircraft and airfields and assigning Radford's task group principal responsibility for strikes on naval forces in the Inland Sea. In preparation for the assault, what McCain touted as the "largest replenishing and rearming operation ever undertaken at sea," took place on 21–22 July, during which TF-38 took on nearly 380,000 barrels of oil, 1,600 tons of stores, more than 6,300 tons of ammunition, and 99 replacement aircraft. Now at full strength with the *Ticonderoga* back from repairs in Guam and falling in with Bogan's group, TF-38 had fifteen fast carriers equally divided among the three task groups. TF-37 (including the *Indefatigable*, just in from Manus) provided McCain with another four carriers as the four-group armada set course south and west to reach the launching point about 180 miles south of Kobe early on the morning of 24 July.[56]

At sunrise the carriers launched the first of six strikes that day, aimed at warships and airfields in Honshu, Shikoku, and Kyushu. The huge naval bastion at Kure near Hiroshima on the Inland Sea in southwestern Honshu was of particular importance. Roaring into Kure, TF-38 fighters and fighter-bombers found their targets widely distributed around the complex, some of them heavily camouflaged. Long pursued by TF-38, the battleship-carrier *Hyuga*, which had been targeted by TF-58 in March, was finally sent to the bottom in shallow water near the island of Nasake. The *Hyuga's* sister ship *Ise*, also hit by Mitscher's task force in March, was heavily damaged by five bombs, but remained stubbornly afloat off nearby Kurahashi island. Moored at Etajima, the battleship *Haruna* took a bomb hit that caused only light damage. At Mitsuko Jima the attackers damaged the carriers *Katsuragi* and *Amagi*, and at Beppu Wan on the other side of the Inland Sea, British TF-37 Avengers bombed but failed to sink the escort carrier *Kaiyō*. West of Kure at Nishinomi Shima, the heavy cruiser *Tone*, a Midway veteran, was bombed and sunk, but nearby the old carrier *Hosho* escaped the attack with only light damage. Another heavy cruiser, the *Aoba*, sustained multiple bomb hits and sank while moored not far from the Kure navy yard, and the light cruiser *Oyodo* was strafed, bombed, and badly damaged near Etajima. In

1,354 offensive sorties that day, TF-38 dropped 559 tons of bombs and fired more than 1,700 rockets, damaging or destroying twenty naval vessels of all types and sinking nearly 20,000 tons of merchant ships. American and British aviators claimed thirteen enemy aircraft shot down, including three by the task force CAP, and another forty destroyed on the ground. The Japanese exacted a price: a thick curtain of antiaircraft fire brought down thirty-two planes, and another seventeen were lost operationally, costing the task force thirty-nine aviators missing or dead, the fast carriers' heaviest losses in the last months of the war.[57]

TF-38's aerial assault on Kure resumed at dawn the next day. Shipping again took precedence, although it was hard to find targets that had somehow avoided McCain's fighters and bombers on the twenty-fourth. Nevertheless, they beat up a small patrol craft and a destroyer, and damaged twenty-one merchant ships. In attacks on air bases at Nagoya, Osaka, and Miho, task force planes destroyed or damaged nearly 130 aircraft, shot down another 18, and damaged four. Before the weather closed in, TF-38 flew 640 strike sorties, dropped 185 tons of bombs, and launched more than 1,100 rockets. That afternoon, as the carriers recovered the last of their strike sorties, radar picked up three separate groups of enemy aircraft closing on the task force. British CAP fighters intercepted one of the groups and splashed three Aichi B7A single-engine torpedo bombers. *Bon Homme Richard* night fighters downed an Aichi and two single-engine Nakajima C6N reconnaissance aircraft from another group of attackers. Allied losses were ten fighters in combat, and six, plus a Helldiver, that went down in operations. Only one aviator was killed.[58]

During the next two days, 26 and 27 July, the task force refueled and replenished from the service group about four hundred miles south of Nagoya. The *Wasp* joined TG-38.4 on the twenty-sixth, bringing Radford's group up to six fast carriers. That day, McCain spent more than three hours conferring with Halsey, Rawlings, and their staffs on the *Missouri* to coordinate the next phase of operations, aimed at targets on Kyushu, the Inland Sea, and central Honshu. As before, the British TF-37 would join the Americans in the strikes. Late in the morning of the twenty-seventh, TF-38 broke away from Beary's oilers and, accompanied by TF-37, began the overnight approach to their launch position ninety-six miles south of Shikoku.[59]

Before dawn on the twenty-eighth, the American and British carriers arrayed for another series of attacks on what remained of the Imperial Navy. The weather cooperated. A nearly continuous wave of Allied planes struck warships and merchant vessels in and around Kure, especially targeting the *Haruna*, which had only been scratched by a bomb on the twenty-fourth. This time bombers left the battleship beached, burning, and flooded as a result of multiple hits in the bow and stern. The *Ise* was finally sunk, as was the light cruiser *Oyodo*, and the sunken wreckage of the heavy cruiser *Tone* proved to be a tempting target. Two flattops, the *Amagi* and *Katsuragi*, damaged on the twenty-fourth, remained afloat, but their flight decks were wrecked. At Kure the old heavy cruisers *Iwate* and *Izumo* were sunk as was a destroyer escort and an oiler; two transports were believed to have been sunk, but were most likely only badly damaged. British aircraft sank two frigates. American fliers further damaged the escort carrier *Kaiyō* grounded at Beppu Wan. TF-38 aircraft flew 1,394 strike sorties that day, delivered a record 605 tons of bombs, and fired more than two thousand rockets. Twenty-one enemy aircraft were shot down and another 115 were destroyed on the ground. Thirty-seven aircraft and forty aircrew were lost. The loss of twenty-two SB2Cs in two days of raids on the Japanese fleet anchorages was vindication of McCain's insistence that the Helldivers be replaced by fighter-bombers in offensive operations.[60] Nevertheless, TF-38 airmen had left the Imperial Japanese Navy in ruins. No longer a navy at all, it had been mercilessly reduced to a faint shadow of the force that had once been the pride of the nation and its people, its warships aground, burning, or sunk in the shallows of the Inland Sea.

Overnight and the next day, 29 July, the task force relocated to a position only seventy miles south of Hammatsu for more strikes on Honshu. Covered by the *Bon Homme Richard*, the bombardment group broke off to shell industrial targets at Hammatsu after nightfall on the twenty-ninth. On the thirtieth, weather north of Tokyo pushed carrier aircraft to the south and west, where they struck shipping in Sagami Wan south of Tokyo Bay and at the Maizuru naval base on the Sea of Japan. Task force airmen found and destroyed or damaged nearly 260 aircraft camouflaged and widely dispersed around airfields at Nagoya. Targets of opportunity included aircraft plants at Omi and Fujisawa and the Japan International Aircraft Industries factory at Hiratsuka, believed to be a site for producing components for Ohka rocket-powered suicide bombs. Locomotives, trains, railroad yards and shops, bridges, and other infrastructure were bombed and rocketed, as were submarines, especially the "midgets" thought to be a threat as the task force closed on Japan. Six were strafed and damaged on the western shore of Sagami Wan. Carrier aircraft flew more than 1,200 offensive sorties in which 417 tons of ordnance were dropped and nearly 2,600 rockets expended. The task force lost sixteen aircraft and eleven pilots and crewmembers.[61]

McCain's carriers retired 330 miles south to refuel from Beary's ships in anticipation of renewing strikes on northern Honshu and Hokkaido scheduled for the fifth, after which the force would "shift full weight of attack to TOKYO area." When Halsey received reports of a typhoon in the area he decided not to take any chances and moved the fueling rendezvous farther south, where the task force hovered for the next three days while completing replenishment and waiting for the weather to improve. McCain met with Halsey on the *Missouri* on the morning of the fourth to discuss current and future operations. There was also time to carry out training exercises, since McCain received orders from Nimitz on the second to stay well offshore and not to undertake any missions over Kyushu, western Honshu, or Tokyo while awaiting the results of a "special operation" of the AAF 509th Bomb Group scheduled for the fifth or sixth. It is unclear whether McCain and Halsey had any prior knowledge that Hiroshima was the target of the atomic bomb on the sixth. Even if they had, it is doubtful they would have changed their plans to support Olympic. Moreover, recent scholarship has shown that the Japanese leadership was not at that time prepared to sue for peace. As far as McCain and TF-38 were concerned, the war would go on much as before.[62]

McCain's thinking was consistent with Nimitz's Op Plan 11-45 of 9 August, which presupposed that "the Japanese have not surrendered" and, though grievously weakened, were likely to fight on for some time. American and Allied forces were to continue their air and sea blockade of the home islands through "unremitting military pressure" and exact "maximum attrition" on Japan's "air, naval, and ground forces, merchant shipping and industrial capacity by all possible means in all areas." Third Fleet and TF-38 would continue operations leading up to and supporting Olympic, emphasizing, as before, the destruction of Japanese air forces and shipping. Halsey and McCain were also to target Japanese bases, resources, and lines of communication in Hokkaido and the southern Kuriles in support of American North Pacific and Soviet operations in those areas. Also necessary were strikes on airfields in northern Honshu, where intelligence indicated the Japanese were hoarding aircraft in anticipation of a mass attack on American positions in Okinawa.[63]

Following its extended hiatus from offensive operations, TF-38 shifted north to a position 120 miles off northern Honshu on 8 August, only to postpone strikes that day due to thick overcast. Detailed information on the destruction at Hiroshima trickled in to Cincpac headquarters, as well as notification that the 509th planned to strike Nagasaki on 9 August with another atomic bomb. Launching in better conditions nearly an hour before dawn on the ninth (coincidentally, McCain's sixty-first birthday), task force aircraft swept in against airfields and aircraft north of Tokyo. For the first time, the Japanese dispatched aircraft from fields in and around Tokyo for a concentrated attack on the Allied fleet. At 1455, a suicide plane hit the *Borie* (DD 704), one of the Tomcat destroyers in Bogan's group, damaging the ship so badly that it had to withdraw with scores of men dead or injured. Another kamikaze just missed the *Wasp*. Task force CAP and antiaircraft fire claimed seven of the attackers. Meanwhile, in a crescendo of high explosives, McCain's strike aircraft flew 1,468 sorties, pummeling enemy aircraft and airfields with 588 tons of bombs and more than 2,200 rockets. They claimed more than 290 aircraft destroyed or damaged on the ground and seven in the air, also counting a tanker sunk and two destroyer escorts damaged. TF-38 lost twenty-two aircraft—sixteen operationally—along with nine pilots and aircrew. Later that day, American battleships joined with British and New Zealand cruisers to bombard the Kamaishi ironworks for the second time.[64]

News that the second atomic bomb had devastated Nagasaki and that the Soviet Union had declared war on Japan reached the task force late on the ninth, as did the gist of King's message to Nimitz that Ultra intercepts indicated that Japan was ready to "bring about peace immediately." Realization that the war might soon be over brought smiles to McCain's and Baker's faces and elicited a general feeling throughout the fleet that it would not be long before the fighting ended. Morale then quickly plummeted when orders came through canceling the planned withdrawal to Eniwetok pending resolution of peace talks. Nimitz warned that "neither the Japanese nor Allied Forces have stopped fighting. Take precautions against treachery even if local or general surrender should be suddenly announced. Maintain all current reconnaissance and patrols. Offensive action shall be continued unless otherwise specifically directed." Accordingly, there was no letup in air operations on the tenth, when the task force launched 1,368 offensive sorties, primarily targeting airfields, where McCain's aviators claimed 255 enemy aircraft destroyed or damaged on the ground, but none in the air. McCain boasted that "enormous damage was inflicted upon airfield installations, oil storage, transportation facilities, docks, shipyards, and industrial buildings." Ordnance expended included 520 tons of bombs and 3,245 rockets. Seventeen TF-38 aircraft were lost, including ten pilots and crewmembers.[65]

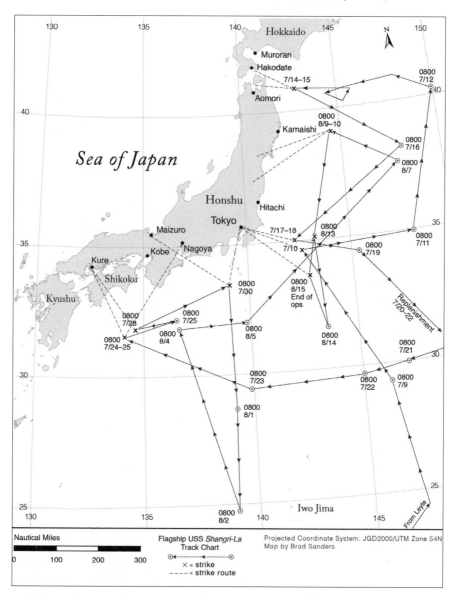

Map 8. Task Force 38 Operations against Japan, July–August 1945; USS *Shangri-La* Track Chart, July–August 1945 (USS *Shangri-La* Action Report, July 2–August 15, 1945, www.Fold3.com, accessed June 2, 2017)

Halsey's decision to continue offensive operations and not retire as previously scheduled disrupted British plans. Rawlings had anticipated withdrawing to Australia for repairs and replenishment in preparation for intensive strikes in support of Olympic. He could keep TF-37 on station for another day, but no longer, because the British logistics supply network was unable to adjust the movement of oilers and ammunition ships to continue supporting the task force. Halsey, McCain, and Rawlings met on 11 August and agreed that although the British task force had to withdraw, it was feasible to leave some ships behind so that the Royal Navy would have a token presence when the Japanese surrendered. Meeting in Guam, Nimitz and Fraser decided that the remaining British ships would constitute a new task group within TF-38. The next day, TG-38.5 was formed around the *Indefatigable* and a screen consisting of the battleship *King George V*, two cruisers, and ten destroyers.[66]

On the eleventh, the carriers refueled 350 miles east of northern Honshu before closing again on the island the next day in preparation for strikes in and around Tokyo. To dispel scuttlebutt that peace was imminent and to keep his men vigilant, McCain announced on the twelfth that "the war is not over yet. The Japanese may be playing their national game of judo waiting until we are close and unwary. Keep alert for Nipponese tricks and Banzai charges." Halsey signaled that the strikes planned for 13 August would proceed "as originally scheduled." McCain passed the word to the task force: "Show to all pilots. The fact that we are ordered to strike indicates that the enemy may have thrown an unacceptable joker into the surrender terms. This war could last many months longer. We cannot afford to relax. Now is the time to pour it on." Although the weather was less than optimal on the thirteenth, the carriers launched 1,167 offensive sorties, during which McCain's airmen delivered 380 tons of bombs and fired 2,175 rockets. No fewer than 403 aircraft were destroyed or damaged on the ground, the most claimed in a single day since operations against Japan began. Throughout the day and into the evening, bogeys approached the flattops, whose CAPs shot down twenty-one of the Japanese aircraft. None of the ships in the task force suffered damage, but the assault was a reminder that despite the second atomic bomb there still appeared to be no sign that the Japanese were ready to surrender.[67] TF-38 turned south to steam overnight to join Beary's oilers and logistics ships 325 miles southeast of Tokyo at first light the next morning. After forty-four consecutive days at sea, McCain was resolved—and the fast carriers prepared—to keep maximum pressure on the Japanese as long as necessary to assure victory over resolute foes seemingly determined to continue a bloody struggle they had no hope of winning.

CHAPTER 11

Triumph and Tragedy

T hroughout the day, 14 August, Adm. John McCain's carriers loitered with the refueling group well off Honshu, topping up the ships' bunkers while evading still another typhoon gathering to the south of the operating area. McCain, armed with what he considered accurate data from a variety of sources that the storm would track to the north and east of the task force, related in his action report that TF-38 "boldly and with assurance set course between the typhoon and the enemy coast" to close again on Honshu for more strikes on airfields in the Tokyo area. No longer an enemy, the weather was now an ally, masking the task force's approach to the launch point about 160 miles southeast of Tokyo. At 0415 on the fifteenth, the flattops got off their first deckload strikes. By now, Radford was having second thoughts about continuing operations. Later he reflected that "the war would be over within hours" and that he "hated to see our planes take off that morning."[1]

The second strike was en route to the targets at about 0615 when Halsey received an urgent message from Nimitz that the Japanese had finally agreed to a ceasefire and that Third Fleet was to suspend offensive operations. At 0633, McCain passed the word to the strike groups, which was enough time for the aircraft in the second sortie to return after jettisoning their ordnance. But the first strike mission was already over its objectives, where it met strong opposition from Japanese interceptors; the Americans downed twenty-six of the enemy. Only 240 strike sorties went out that morning, releasing twelve tons of bombs and 284 rockets. In this, the last offensive carrier operation of the war, eleven aircraft did not return, including three British Supermarine Seafires, along with seven pilots and crewmembers. Radford again: "Their loss was a personal tragedy to me on that day of victory. I felt I should have been able to convince Admiral McCain to delay offensive operations." Whether McCain agreed we will never know. Following the raids, the task force retired to what Halsey designated as "Area McCain" well clear of the coast about 280 miles southeast of Tokyo. McCain beefed up the carriers' CAP and cleared flight decks for fighter operations in antic-ipation of last-ditch enemy attacks. His caution was justified. Throughout the rest of the day, Japanese aircraft approached the task force, four of which were splashed by fighters (two claimed by Corsairs from the *Shangri-La*'s Air Group 85) and one shot down by antiaircraft fire.[2]

The next morning, 16 August, finally brought relief from the deadly rhythm of combat as the three American task groups came together at "Point Ready" in an unusually tight formation for aerial photographs. No one disputed that the exercise, dubbed Operation Snapshot, was at the time the world's largest concentration of air and sea power. The next day, in better weather, the task force repeated the evolution before turning north to rendezvous with TG-30.8 on the morning of the eighteenth. That morning, as the ships took on oil, aviation gas, provisions, and ammu-nition, McCain and members of his staff went over to the *Missouri* for conferences with Halsey and his subordinates. TF-38's assignment was to provide reconnaissance and air cover for a task force (TF-31) under the command of Rear Adm. Oscar C. Badger, which was to land Marines and sailors to secure the big Japanese air and naval base at Yokosuka south of Tokyo. Anticipation of the imminent command change became reality for McCain on the morning of the twenty-second, when Towers transferred from the destroyer *Healy* (DD 672) and broke his flag on the *Shangri-La*. Later that day, the carriers launched full deckloads, putting nearly a thou-sand aircraft in the sky over McCain's flagship for another photo opportu-nity as well as to provide a dress rehearsal for a mass flyover planned for the surrender ceremonies in Tokyo Bay.[3]

Meanwhile, the carriers stayed with Beary's service group for the next six days, taking a course southwest on the twenty-first to clear two more typhoons gestating some three hundred miles to the southeast. None of the ships in Radford's TG-38.4 or Sprague's TG-38.1 had any problems, but as luck would have it, Bogan's TG-38.3, in position further south, was clipped by one of the storms on 25 August, and the *Wasp* (recently detached from Radford's group) suffered damage to the forward end of its flight deck that forced the ship to leave the group for repairs. Due to the adverse weather, the schedule for Third Fleet ships to enter Tokyo Bay and for the occupation of Japanese naval facilities was set back from the twenty-sixth to the twenty-eighth, with the formal surrender delayed from 31 August to 2 September.[4]

According to Joint Staff Study Campus, promulgated on 9 August to outline operations consequent to a Japanese unconditional surrender,

Halsey was to command a force of battleships, cruisers, and destroyers drawn from the Third Fleet for the "emergency occupation" of Tokyo Bay. The study assumed that the pre-Olympic air campaign would result in the near destruction of Japanese air power and that any surviving enemy aircraft would be withdrawn out of range where they could not interfere with the occupation effort. Third Fleet fast carriers were to remain offshore in support of the occupation forces, making "a show of force at all times," carrying out "offensive demonstration flights," reconnaissance missions, and delivering air strikes if the occupation forces met any resistance. All aircraft, military as well as civil, were to remain grounded until Japanese officials provided full lists of numbers, types, locations, and conditions of the aircraft; all naval vessels would be similarly inventoried by the Japanese. With modifications to suit the immediate circumstances, Campus provided the outline for Third Fleet and task force operations subsequent to the Japanese capitulation.[5]

Generally adhering to Campus, McCain's three task groups cruised independently less than one hundred miles off the coast north and south of Tokyo. Flight operations resumed on the twenty-fifth. Reconnaissance missions showed that the Japanese had complied with the ceasefire agreement stipulating that all of their aircraft had to be brought from camouflaged dispersal areas into the open where they could be counted and photographed; some of the Japanese aircraft even had their propellers removed. Other tasks were flying CAP over surface ships in Sagami Wan and Tokyo Bay, covering the Navy and Marine landing forces at Yokosuka and Army troops who had occupied the air base at Atsugi, identifying defensive military installations, locating and monitoring shipping (including submarines still lurking in the area), and providing air-sea rescue for Navy and AAF aircraft. Heavy cloud cover caused Radford's group to cancel reconnaissance missions on the twenty-sixth, but all air groups were flying again the next day as the storms moved west into the Sea of Japan. On the twenty-eighth, a *Shangri-La* TBM set down at Atsugi, southwest of Tokyo, carrying among others Lt. Cdr. Donald B. Thorburn, McCain's public relations officer, earning the distinction of being the first American naval aircraft to land on Japanese soil since the war began.[6]

Of critical importance was locating Allied prisoner of war camps, aided by enthusiastic POWs, many of whom had suffered ill treatment during their months and years in captivity and were now anxious about retribution from their captors as Japan faced defeat. Pilots and aircrew pitched in to load seabags with rations, medicine, cigarettes, candy, and other supplies, attaching them to parachutes to drop from carrier bombers to the grateful prisoners at designated sites. The missions had the bonus of raising morale among the war-weary aviators, who returned to their carriers with "a feeling of having done a good deed for the day." Task force aircraft located seventy-seven camps, most of them in the Tokyo area, aided by identification panels and large white "PW" letters displayed on rooftops. From 16 August to the end of the month, the task force flew nearly 5,800 sorties, of which the bulk were CAP and reconnaissance missions, with another 606 devoted to POW search and relief flights. Although the enemy was no longer a threat, TF-38 lost eighteen aircraft, ten of which were Hellcats, while the British had six Seafires go down in operations. Most of the aircrew survived but five pilots and crewmembers did not, thus becoming the last casualties of the Pacific naval air war.[7]

While carrying out these operations, McCain, Towers, and their staffs met with Halsey on the *Missouri* for two hours on the morning of 23 August to work out the details of McCain's relief. Towers preferred to have his own staff, but because not all of them were immediately available he decided to retain Wilder Baker as his chief of staff, along with Noel Gayler and Bill Leonard. These experienced officers provided continuity as the task force underwent fundamental command and organizational changes. Halsey recalled that McCain was unhappy with the prospect of relinquishing command to Towers; his grandson, John S. McCain III, stated that he was "crushed" at the prospect of leaving the carriers. But he kept his feelings to himself; one member of Towers' staff recalled that "if McCain resented being relieved before the surrender" he never let on to junior officers. In a note to Kate on the twentieth, he had intimated that he was ready to hand things over to Towers sooner rather than later: "There is a high justice over and above that of commanders in chief. Am so glad to be in at the finish, and am gratified at great numbers of congrats to that effect. . . . It now looks as tho I may follow closely on the heels of this letter. To h__ with war and work. Want to sleep half a year."[8]

When Robert Carney, Halsey's chief of staff, met with McCain on the *Shangri-La*, he found McCain disheartened and tired. McCain told Carney to "go back and tell Bill that I've had it. I fought all the way from the South Pacific up to here. It's all over now, and I want to go home." Carney responded that Halsey wanted him at least to stay in command until the formal Japanese surrender, to take place on the *Missouri* in Tokyo Bay.

But McCain insisted: "I don't give a damn about seeing the surrender, I want to get the hell out of here." Nimitz, however, had the final word. He ordered McCain's relief to proceed as previously scheduled on the first, thus ensuring that Towers would have the carrier command when the war ended. Halsey acquiesced, at the same time insisting that McCain, "the old SOB," was "entitled to witness the surrender, and that's what he's going to do." He did promise that "the minute the thing is over, I'll put him on a plane and start him home." McCain confided to Kate that "All's well that ends well. Bill Halsey is, on his own, holding me in command until the surrender, now scheduled for Sept. 2. This will occasion some grief in some quarters. 'Cheers.' Further he says he will order me to attend on the *Missouri* which I take very kindly."[9]

McCain's action report—his last, and in many ways a valedictory— was a comprehensive analysis of the task force operations through the final month and a half of hostilities. "The War is Over," it began, "the long strenuous offensive waged by the Fast Carrier Task Force from Pearl to Japan" came to an end with the task force almost within sight of the Japanese coast. Notwithstanding the difficulty in accurately determining whether ships were sunk or aircraft destroyed, the statistics from the last six weeks of operations were impressive. McCain reported that in nearly 10,700 strike sorties more than 2,400 enemy aircraft were destroyed or damaged in the air and on the ground, and 274 ships totaling more than 800,000 tons were either damaged or sunk. Hangars, fuel dumps, factories, warehouses, docks, barracks, bridges, locomotives, railyards, radar facilities, and antiaircraft installations were destroyed or badly damaged. The task force suffered the loss of 197 pilots and aircrew, and another 49 killed or missing in action from the suicide attack on the *Borie*; more than 300 aircraft were lost during the campaign.[10]

McCain stressed that the carriers, regardless of their specific missions, were an essentially offensive force that had delivered staggering blows to Japanese land, sea, and air forces. Even their CAP, loosely identified as a defensive element of the carriers' air complement, was "rather an insurance or assurance of the hitting power of the task force." To McCain, as to Halsey, Mitscher, Towers, and others, the best defense of the task force and the guarantee of its offensive mission was the total "destruction of any enemy air that bears or that may be brought to bear on the task force and in the most offensive practical manner." He repeated his criticism of Nimitz's decision to strike the battered residue of the Japanese fleet. Rather, if the concentration had remained on enemy aircraft, McCain averred that within a month all actual and potential air opposition would have been eliminated and the rest of the mission in support of Olympic would have been "cold turkey." Related to this was McCain's long-held contention that carrier air groups should be made up almost entirely of F6F and F4U fighters and fighter-bombers and that there was "no place for a plane with the performance of the SB2C" on front-line carriers. "Until such time that a complement as is recommended here is made effective," he concluded, "the fast carriers can never deliver the punch of which they are potentially capable."[11]

On the whole, McCain believed that the task force had responded well to the kamikaze threat. The three-strike system and "Big Blue Blanket" he and Thach had instituted had worked satisfactorily, as did the Tomcat radar and fighter direction destroyers and the "delousing" methods that prevented attackers from infiltrating groups of friendly aircraft returning from strike missions. Radar, IFF, fighter direction, and careful monitoring and control of the aircraft returning to the carriers were also important factors in defending the task force from Japanese air attack. Only on 9 August, when the carriers had to operate from an unfavorable position within range of the Tokyo airfields, did the task force face a serious threat from suicide planes, one of which had sneaked through to hit the *Borie*. Also worrisome were indications that the Japanese were developing sophisticated radar countermeasures, which might neutralize or at least complicate task force air defense. Photography was essential. McCain believed that improved camera technology and prompt photo processing, coupled with more experienced photo interpreters, were vital to differentiating real aircraft from dummies and for locating dispersed and hidden planes, while more accurate damage assessment reduced claims for aircraft destroyed on the ground by 25 percent.[12]

Knowing that this was likely to be his last opportunity to justify his decisions and actions during the typhoons that struck TF-38, McCain had much to say in his action report about aerology. Once more, he emphasized the need for accurate and up-to-the-minute meteorological information, stressing that when he had such data TF-38 was able to thread the needle between storms and the Japanese coast during the night of 14–15 August, while still carrying out offensive operations. Implying that those above him in the chain of command had issued conflicting and confusing orders when he had encountered severe weather, McCain stated that it was vital for the officer in tactical command to have free rein to make decisions "as to how and where" to direct his ships to ensure that the task force accomplished its mission. Multiple "overlapping" weather broadcasts, many of which were hours late, had exacerbated the OTC's problems, as had inaccurate reports from fleet weather planes. There had been notable improvements in the weather service to the fleet since the beginning of July, yet "the need for a comprehensive, accurate and timely weather reporting service continues" especially as the Navy transitioned from war to peace and remained a strategic presence in the western Pacific.[13]

McCain was pleased that the recommendations he had made about public relations in his 26 January action report had been carried out, yet more still needed to be done. Not enough public information officers had been available: "We had the greatest show on earth, and tried to cover it with a handful of men." He recommended that reporters and news wire people be placed on every carrier and battleship in the fleet, that a fleet photographer coordinate the activities of the individual ship photographers, and that comprehensive press releases be prepared by officers on the scene and not by personnel outside the combat areas. It was imperative for the Navy to articulate "a clear, definitive public relations policy" so that everyone in and out of the service knew what the Navy was doing and why it was doing it. And that policy had to be promulgated and implemented by professionals.[14]

Woven through the report were McCain's estimates of future missions and requirements, both for the Navy in general and for the fast carriers specifically. Because it was "likely for some years at least that the fast carriers should be prepared to launch attacks against hostile littorals, and hence to contest the air against enemy land-based formations," fighters and fighter-bombers needed to be the carriers' "predominant" aircraft. He also anticipated that enemy long-range aircraft, "perhaps carrying atomic bombs," might threaten carriers operating far at sea, necessitating development of a high-altitude, long-range, radar-equipped interceptor. To provide an organic search-and-rescue capability, carrier complements should also include amphibian aircraft, possibly fitted with JATO rockets for rough-sea takeoffs. Cincpac intelligence reports had been vital for planning and target selection. In general, the Navy's intelligence apparatus had to be thoroughly assessed, starting with an intensive study of "problems faced and lessons learned," including high-level code-breaking through Ultra, which McCain could not discuss in a document classified only as "secret." As for the ACIOs, most of whom were older reserve officers leaving to return to civilian life, the Navy needed a training program where nonflying officers learned the basics of combat intelligence. McCain urged that carrier CICs and communication spaces be enlarged, and that radio, radar, and other electronic technologies be upgraded to cope with what he believed would be a new and challenging tactical environment.[15]

McCain foresaw and articulated a leading role, too, for the Navy and the carrier task force in the postwar world. He predicted that a "long and thankless period of domestic danger" loomed, during which the public had to understand how vital the Navy was to national security, and the Congress had to be deterred from seeking to limit expenditures by "scrapping valuable ships." Peril lay, as well, in renewed agitation for a unified department of defense, into which the Navy and naval aviation would be subsumed. After the bombing experiments off the Virginia Capes in 1921, the Navy in its tradition as "the 'silent service' had stood aside and let the public sink it" during Billy Mitchell's protracted propaganda war to reduce naval aviation to an auxiliary arm of a united air force. McCain warned that unless quick action were taken, "this sabotage of the Navy can happen again" when the war ended. Refuting a statement by AAF Gen. Curtis LeMay that the B-29 had rendered aircraft carriers obsolete, he wrote to Secretary of the Navy Forrestal in April 1945 that such statements convinced him that "the war after the war will be more bitter than the actual war." Proposals for "a unified command, a single service or department of national defense, will of necessity be an instrument for an extra-constitutional and an interested division of funds prior to submission to the disinterested Budget (Office of the President) and a presumably disinterested Congress." If the lessons of the past meant anything, critical interests would be jealously upheld and advanced by the Army, at much cost to the Navy and the public.[16]

Following the change of command ceremony on the *Shangri-La* at 1100 on Saturday, 1 September, McCain issued a brief farewell message: "I am glad and proud to have fought through my last year of active service with the renowned fast carriers. War and victory have forged a lasting bond among us. If you are to be as fortunate in peace as you have been victorious in war, I am now talking to 110,000 prospective millionaires. Goodbye, good luck, and may God be with you." That afternoon, the *Shangri-La*'s officers gathered in the middle of a drenching rain squall on the ship's fantail to offer best wishes to their departing commander and friend. At 1736, McCain, Baker, Thach, and Towers boarded the *Wallace L. Lind* (DD 703) for the overnight journey to Tokyo Bay. At 0645, on 2 September McCain and his party transferred from the *Lind* to the *Missouri* for the surrender ceremonies. MacArthur as supreme commander of the Allied powers was in charge. American and British flag officers stood in ranks behind and to his left on the battleship's starboard veranda deck as the Japanese dignitaries solemnly stepped forward to sign the surrender document laid out on one of the *Missouri*'s mess tables. One of the photos captured Nimitz signing for the United States; behind him was Halsey, off to his left was McCain in his khaki uniform, standing loosely at attention with his head slightly bowed in the front row of officers. At the conclusion of the formalities about 0930, Halsey singled out McCain, embraced him, and said, "Thank God you were in this fight with me." McCain replied, "Thank God you made me stay, Bill. You had better sense than I did." He could not help but take personal and professional pride as a mass formation of 349 aircraft from TGs 38.1 and 38.4 passed over the *Missouri*, punctuating the ceremonies and underscoring the critical role the fast carriers had played in achieving victory over Japan.[17]

That he did not leave for home earlier allowed McCain to meet his son, Jack, who had arrived in Tokyo Bay with the sub tender *Proteus* (AS 19) on the thirtieth. After being relieved of command of the submarine *Dentuda* (SS 335) on 15 August, the younger McCain, a decorated commander with a superlative combat record as skipper of the *Gunnel* (SS 253), had transferred to the *Proteus* in Guam. Off Yokosuka, McCain was among those dispatched from the *Proteus* to take command of the big Japanese submarine *I-401*, which had surrendered at sea to an American sub on 29 August. Present for the surrender ceremonies was Pacific submarine force commander Vice Adm. Charles Lockwood, who invited McCain and his son to lunch with him on the *Proteus*. The junior McCain remembered that at one point during the luncheon he and his father excused themselves. They met in the captain's stateroom. "We went back there," Jack recalled, "and we talked for a little while. And he was to every—and I knew him as well as anybody in this world, with the possible exception of my mother—he looked in fine health to me. And God knows his conversation was anything but that indicative of a man who was sick."[18]

Nothing in McCain's mien alerted his son that his father suffered from heart disease or any other potentially terminal illness. "That taught me a lesson in life, too, and that is, you cannot tell how good a man feels unless he wants to let you know how he feels, and that's it. The only thing I do know is that he and Mitscher and men of that stature were very tired when the war was over, for obvious reasons." Asked if his father and Marc Mitscher "were really casualties of war," McCain replied, "Absolutely. Without any question, they were casualties of the war." Yet the senior McCain may have had a sense that he might not live much longer. "My father said to me at that time . . . 'Son, there is no greater thing than to die for the principles— for the country and the principles that you believe in.' And that was one part of the conversation that came through—and I have remembered down through the years—with him at that time. And I considered myself very fortunate to have had a chance to see him at that particular moment."[19]

Thach also believed that McCain was not in good health. "When we got word of the cease-fire," he recalled, "I realized that Admiral McCain wasn't feeling very well physically. He went to his sea cabin and he didn't pop out frequently into the flag plot and enter into things as much as he had. I missed him and I'd go in there and talk to him and tell him what I wanted to do." Before going ahead with Snapshot, Thach had found his boss oddly uninterested and uncharacteristically detached. Thach "went in to recommend to Admiral McCain that we do this and this was one of the times when I realized he just wasn't feeling well at all, and he said: 'Okay, good idea. You go ahead and do it. Just go ahead and do it, no problem. Do whatever you want to.' Then I said, 'Admiral, you don't feel very well, do you?' He said, 'Well, this surrender has come as kind of a shock to all of us. I feel lost. I don't know what to do. I know how to fight, but now I don't know whether I know how to relax or not. I am in an awful letdown. I do feel bad.' He didn't look too well, either."[20]

Halsey was true to his word about letting McCain go. That evening, the second, McCain flew out of Tokyo with Thach, Charles Sisson, and other staff officers for the long multistop flight to Hawaii. At Pearl Harbor McCain met with reporters eager for a firsthand description of the surrender ceremonies. The "explosive little admiral" did not disappoint them. He said that he did not trust the Japanese, who even after the ceasefire had dispatched kamikazes to attack his ships: "They paid for it. We shot them down. Not a one got through to the task force's carriers." He "did not like the look in their eyes" as the Japanese dignitaries came aboard the *Missouri*. "They were just measuring us—just like you measure a man when you're going to hit him the next minute. They don't know they're licked yet. They don't know we are better men than they are." He agreed with Halsey's suggestion that the Japanese military leaders needed a "good kick in the face," although "it wasn't in the face I thought about kicking them." From Honolulu a NATS four-engine Douglas R5D Skymaster picked up McCain's party on the evening of the fourth for the overnight flight to

San Diego. He arrived at North Island shortly after noon on 5 September and quickly motored over to Coronado and his home at 625 A Avenue, where he had a little time to relax before he was scheduled to fly to Washington on the eighth.[21]

On the afternoon of 6 September, the McCains organized a homecoming party, to which they invited neighbors and friends as well as Thach, Charles Sisson, and other members of McCain's staff. The gathering went well at first. McCain entertained everyone with stories about the last phases of the naval air war and his impressions of the surrender ceremonies. But to some he appeared to be tired, and one of those present thought he was suffering from a cold, not surprising after his nearly two-day transpacific air odyssey. About 1600, he excused himself and went to his room. A half-hour later, Navy physician and nearby resident Capt. John W. Vann came over to have a look at him. He noted that McCain was in a "state of complete exhaustion" and that he "complained of a tight feeling in the chest." Otherwise, his respiration and pulse were normal. Vann administered an injection of morphine sulfate, which did not seem to alleviate the pain. Suddenly, at 1705, with Kate and Vann still at his side, McCain died. Vann reported that the cause of death was a coronary thrombosis, probably brought on by extreme fatigue. He was not quite a month beyond his sixty-first birthday.[22]

Condolences poured in, followed by scores of tributes and remembrances. Thach felt a deep personal loss: "I felt like I lost my father for a second time." When asked by reporters about what stood out most in his mind about his boss, Thach insisted that McCain's "whole life was wrapped up in carriers and carrier air groups" and that "he practiced the art of war on a basis of common sense. Like an experienced boxer he was never caught off guard and never let his opponent rest." Secretary Forrestal wrote to Kate to offer his sympathy: "I know from experience that words are of slight solace. . . . He was fighting man to his very fiber, and you know better than I the depth of affection in which he was held by his Navy friends." To McCain's son Jack, Forrestal offered that "it is a sad thing that he died so soon after the completion of the war, but I know that he was grateful for having been spared to see the job completed." King remarked that McCain had died "in the line of duty—killed by the stress and strain of war." The Navy and the nation, he added, had suffered a "grievous loss." Halsey said that "America has lost a great man" and that "for myself I can only say that I have lost a great and good friend." The *New York Times* editorialized that McCain "fell as he might have fallen in battle" and that "his indomitable spirit and brilliant performance will rank him high among the history makers of our time."[23] Only by luck and chance had he been able to witness the culmination of the great Pacific conflict, which in the end had cost him his life as well as those of tens of thousands of his shipmates.

A Navy plane left North Island on the evening of the eighth, carrying McCain's body to Washington for interment at Arlington. Funeral services were held at the Fort Myer chapel at 1130 on Monday, 10 September, organized in part by McCain's son Gordon, who worked for the Federal Communications Commission in Washington. Gordon, Kate, and the McCains' daughter Catherine made it to the service, but Jack, in the *Dentuda* escorting the *I-401* to Hawaii, could not be there. Among those attending were King, Forrestal, and Bill Leahy, who was now Truman's chief of staff. Alexander Vandegrift, now Marine Corps commandant, Jake Fitch, Leigh Noyes, and Matt Gardner were honorary pallbearers. Accompanied by the Navy band and contingents of bluejackets and Marines, a horse-drawn caisson carried the body to a shaded hillside in Arlington, where McCain was laid to rest to the mournful notes of "Abide with Me."[24]

Nearly three years later, Kate received a letter from Secretary of the Navy Forrestal that John Sidney had been elevated posthumously to full admiral in recognition of his wartime service and sacrifice. The honorary promotion was dated to 6 September 1945, the day of McCain's death. On 10 September 1949, Kate and other members of the family joined with Halsey on the *Valley Forge* (CV 45) at North Island for the formal promotion ceremony. Halsey, who had received his fifth star in 1946, used the occasion to remember his task force commander as "a very great man and a great sailor. . . . No man deserved more of his country than John Sidney McCain." Further recognition of McCain's service came with the USS *John S. McCain* (DL 3), a 3,700-ton *Mitscher*-class destroyer leader, launched at the Bath Iron Works on 12 July 1952 and commissioned three months later in Boston. Jack's wife Roberta was the ship's sponsor at the launching ceremonies. Halsey addressed the gathering, speaking from the heart about his friendship with his fallen shipmate before he was overcome with emotion and tearfully cut his speech short. The ship underwent a conversion to a guided missile destroyer (DDG 36) and returned to the fleet in 1969, remaining in service until it was stricken from the Navy lists in 1978 and scrapped a year later. Today (2018) a second *John S. McCain* (DDG 56), 6,900-ton *Arleigh Burke*-class destroyer commissioned in July 1994, is with the fleet, named for John Sidney, his son Jack, and grandson John S. McCain III.[25]

Following the war, during which he won Silver and Bronze Stars for his submarine service, Jack had a distinguished Navy career of his own. After serving as exec on the cruiser St. Paul (CA 73) during the Korean War, he went on to public relations assignments and congressional liaison duties, paralleling some of the work his father had done in Washington. As a vice admiral, he served as commander of the Atlantic Fleet Amphibious Force, during which he commanded the 1965 American invasion and occupation of the Dominican Republic. After a tour as commander of American naval forces in Europe, where coincidentally he succeeded then Adm. Jimmie Thach, McCain assumed the job of commander in chief, Pacific, the successor to Nimitz's wartime Cincpac. In what was regarded as the Navy's most prominent operational command, he had responsibility for American and Allied forces in Vietnam from 1968 to his retirement in 1972, during which he advocated a more aggressive strategy against the North Vietnamese. He died of a heart attack at the age of seventy when returning from a trip to Europe in 1981.[26]

Jack's son John III followed his father to the Naval Academy, where he graduated in 1958 before earning his wings in 1960. In his memoirs, he recalled that "like my grandfather and father, I loved life at sea, and I loved flying off carriers." Luck was with him when a Zuni missile misfired and struck his Douglas A-4 Skyhawk bomber on the carrier Forrestal (CVA 59) operating in the Tonkin Gulf on 29 July 1967. Video shows him leaping from the cockpit of his aircraft just moments after the exploding warhead ignited a catastrophic fire that killed 134 of his shipmates. Yet his fortune ran out three months later. Flying a strike mission from the carrier Oriskany (CVA 34) on 26 October, McCain's A-4 fell to a North Vietnamese surface-to-air missile. He ejected from the stricken airplane, was injured, was captured, and endured more than five years as a POW in the infamous "Hanoi Hilton." He retired from the Navy in 1981 and pursued a career in politics that included the Republican nomination for the presidency in 2008. At the time of his death from cancer in 2018 he was eighty-one and serving his sixth term as senator from Arizona. His son John IV ("Jack") carries on the McCain tradition as a 2009 Naval Academy graduate and naval aviator.[27]

Emerson wrote that "it's not the length of life, but the depth" that makes the difference. McCain came late to aviation; he was among the latest of the "Johnny-Come-Latelys." Yet this accorded him the advantage of what some refer to as the "fast second." The pioneers had nurtured naval aviation from infancy to adolescence, guiding technological change and ensuring that aviation and the airplane had a role with the fleet and a position in the naval bureaucracy. It fell to McCain and other officers to lead and sometimes follow naval aviation to maturity. That complex and not always linear process saw the airplane, naval aviation, and more specifically the aircraft carrier transformed from a tactical into a strategic weapon. More significant and to the point, the aircraft carrier was at the start of World War II considered a means of achieving sea control (in conjunction with the battleship and battle fleet). By the end of the conflict, the carrier had become the vital component of a colossal multiship and multidimensional task force capable of projecting power over unprecedented distances.[28]

McCain brought fresh ideas and innovative thinking to naval aviation. His wartime operations officer, Jimmie Thach, believed that such pioneers as Mitscher and Towers, fixated on ambitious visions of the future of naval air, were ironically more resistant to change and new ways of addressing tactical and strategic problems, unlike McCain and his black-shoe classmate Frank Jack Fletcher. Even his detractors concede that McCain had a creative mind. He was not a "brain" in the same category of contemporary flag officers Harold Stark, Charles McMorris, and Forrest Sherman. Rather, he was more of an adaptive and tenacious puzzle-solver seeking practical solutions to immediate problems, noteworthy being the need to suppress the kamikaze threat and his thinking about how the fighter-bomber could bring more flexibility to carrier air groups. He had a passion for gambling and horse racing; when he was with Spruance on the *Indianapolis* in June 1944, he remarked that "every commander must be a gambler." Spruance did not disagree, replying that he was "one of the professional variety" who "wanted all the odds I could get stacked in my favor."[29]

McCain's decision to stretch his task group's formation to expedite carrier launches during the Battle of Leyte Gulf underscores his willingness to take risks, yet he and Thach recognized that the experience of his carrier commanders minimized the dangers of the carefully choreographed maneuvers. Above all, few among his peers bore the burden of command in such broad dimensions of naval aviation—patrol aviation, carrier, task group, and task force command, administration, technological change, personnel, and logistics—as did McCain. He also embraced "jointness," so valued in the military of the twenty-first century, in the deadly cauldron of the Solomons. And had he not been robbed of just a handful of more years of life, his ideas about unification, the postwar Navy, and naval aviation would have resonated as the service navigated treacherous congressional and public waters. From the perspective of nearly three-quarters of a century, no one could ask more of a fighting admiral and a man who in the end made the ultimate sacrifice for his Navy and his country.

NOTES

Prologue

1. Vice Admiral J. S. McCain, Nov. 1944, Personal Interviews, Naval Records and Library, Records of the Chief of Naval Operations, Record Group (RG) 38, National Archives and Records Administration (NARA), Archives II, College Park, MD (unless otherwise noted, this document and all war diaries, action reports, and unit histories in RG 38, NARA Archives II were accessed from www.Fold3.com, 19 Dec. 2011–2 June 2017); Steve Ewing, *Thach Weave: The Life of Jimmie Thach* (Annapolis, MD: Naval Institute Press, 2004), 170; Alton Keith Gilbert, *A Leader Born: The Life of Admiral John Sidney McCain, Pacific Carrier Commander* (Philadelphia, PA: Casemate, 2006), 166–67; USS *Hancock* (CV 19), War Diary, 1 Nov. 1944–30 Nov. 1944, 19 Nov. 1944; John McCain with Mark Salter, *Faith of My Fathers: A Family Memoir* (New York: Random House, 1999), 95.

2. Summary, 31 Oct., 1, 2 Nov. 1944, Captain Steele's "Running Estimate and Summary," vol. 5, 1 Jan. 1944–31 Dec. 1944, War Plans, Cincpac Files, Archives Branch, Naval History and Heritage Command, Washington, DC, 2121–23, http://www.ibiblio.org/anrs/graybook.html (accessed 4 June 2017; hereafter cited as Graybook); Clark G. Reynolds, *The Fast Carriers: The Forging of an Air Navy* (1968; repr., Annapolis, MD: Naval Institute Press, 1992), 259, 284, 288; Thomas Alexander Hughes, *Admiral Bill Halsey: A Naval Life* (Cambridge, MA: Harvard University Press, 2016), 378; Commander Task Force 38, War Diary, 1 Nov.–30 Nov. 1944, 19 Nov. 1944. A 1947 joint Army-Navy assessment committee tabulated Japanese shipping losses; see http://www.ibiblio.org/hyperwar/Japan/IJN/JANAC-Losses/JANAC-Losses-4.html (accessed 15 Jan., 2 Sept. 2015, 20 Oct. 2016; hereafter cited as Japanese Shipping Losses).

3. Vice Admiral J. S. McCain, Nov. 1944, Personal Interviews, Naval Records and Library, Records of the Chief of Naval Operations, RG 38, NARA Archives II.

4. Reynolds, *Fast Carriers*, 321, 354. Of the four fleet admirals, only Halsey is the subject of a recent scholarly biography: Hughes, *Bill Halsey*. See also Robert Love, review of *Admiral Nimitz: The Commander of the Pacific Ocean Theater* by Brayton Harris, U.S. Naval Institute *Proceedings* 138 (May 2012): 151–52.

5. Capt. C. C. Felker, Introduction, CVN Debate, U.S. Naval Academy, Annapolis, MD, 9 Jan. 2015. For definitions of sea control and power projection, see Wayne P. Hughes Jr., *Fleet Tactics: Theory and Practice* (Annapolis, MD: Naval Institute Press, 1986), 220.

6. Clark G. Reynolds, *Admiral John H. Towers: The Struggle for Naval Air Supremacy* (Annapolis, MD: Naval Institute Press, 1991), 223.

7. Craig C. Felker, *Testing American Sea Power: U.S. Navy Strategic Exercises, 1923–1940* (College Station: Texas A&M University Press, 2007), 33–60; Edward S. Miller, "Eyes of the Fleet: How Flying Boats Transformed War Plan Orange," in *One Hundred Years of U.S. Navy Air Power*, ed. Douglas V. Smith (Annapolis, MD: Naval Institute Press, 2010), 31–42.

Chapter One. From Mississippi to the Sea

1. 1860 U.S. Census, Carroll County, Miss., 10 Sept. 1860, 11, 16–17 (Ancestry.com, accessed 4 Aug. 2009; courtesy of Angela Lakwete). For the average values of slaves, see Samuel H. Williamson and Louis P. Cain, "Measuring Slavery in 2011 Dollars," https://www.measuringworth.com/slavery.php, accessed 18 March 2016.

2. Elizabeth Spencer, *Landscapes of the Heart: A Memoir* (New York: Random House, 1998), 14; 1860 U.S. Census, Carroll County, Miss., 10 Sept. 1860, 11; William Addams Reitwiesner, "Ancestry of Sen. John McCain," http://www.wargs.com/political/mccain.html, accessed 26 May 2011. Other sources cite William Alexander's birth in 1813 and 1817; the manuscript census specifies that he was forty-six in September 1860. See also https://www.geni.com/people/Private-William-Alexander-McCain-CSA/6000000012917405598, accessed 18 March 2016.

3. Reitwiesner, "Ancestry of Sen. John McCain"; Spencer, *Landscapes*, 15–22, 55, 61–62.

4. Spencer, *Landscapes*, 33–36; Gilbert, *Leader Born*, 8–9. Gilbert had exclusive access to McCain family materials in the possession of McCain's granddaughter Margaret La Grange of San Diego.

5. Midshipman Personnel Jacket, John S. McCain, Record Group 405, Special Collections & Archives, Nimitz Library, U.S. Naval Academy, Annapolis, MD (hereafter cited as RG 405, Spec. Coll. & Archives, USNA).

6. Jack Sweetman, *The U.S. Naval Academy: An Illustrated History* (Annapolis, MD: Naval Institute Press, 1979), 142–44.

7. Record of Midshipmen, John Sidney McCain, Academic and Conduct Record of Cadets, 1902–1906, 1:373; 2:375; Midshipman Personnel Jacket, John S. McCain; both in RG 405, Spec. Coll. & Archives, USNA; *Annual Register of the United States Naval Academy, 1904–1905* (Washington, DC: Government Printing Office, 1904), 85; Gilbert, *Leader Born*, 9–10.

8. *Annual Register of the United States Naval Academy, 1903–1904* (Washington, DC: Government Printing Office, 1903), 23–25, 28; Hughes, *Bill Halsey*, 50; *Annual Register of the United States Naval Academy, 1904–1905*, 29, 34; *Annual Register of the United States Naval Academy, 1905–1906* (Washington, DC: Government Printing Office, 1905), 24, 33.

9. *Annual Register of the United States Naval Academy, 1903–1904*, 74–75; *Annual Register of the United States Naval Academy, 1904–1905*, 85; *Annual Register of the United States Naval Academy, 1905–1906*, 51; *Annual Register of the United States Naval Academy, 1906–1907* (Washington, DC: Government Printing Office, 1906), 48–49; Gilbert, *Leader Born*, 8; *Lucky Bag* (Springfield, MA: F. A. Bassette, 1906), 113; Physical

Record of Midshipmen, John Sidney McCain, Midshipman Personnel Jacket, John S. McCain, RG 405, Spec. Coll. & Archives, USNA.

10. *Dictionary of American Naval Fighting Ships*, 8 vols. (Washington, DC: Naval History Division, 1959–1981), 5:144 (hereafter cited as *DANFS*); *DANFS*, 1:89; Quarterly Reports on the Fitness of Midshipmen, April 12–June 30, 1906, July 1–Sept. 14, 1906, 14 Sept.–30 Sept. 1906, Sept. 30–Dec. 31, 1906, Dec. 31, 1906–7 Jan. 1907, Midshipman Personnel Jacket, John S. McCain, RG 405, Spec. Coll. & Archives, USNA; Officer Service, Vice Admiral John Sidney McCain, in John S. McCain, Official Military Personnel File, file no. V200114, National Personnel Records Center, St. Louis, MO (hereafter cited as McCain Personnel File, NPRC). See also McCain and Salter, *Faith of My Fathers*, 23–24.

11. *DANFS*, 5:208; Nimitz to Ernest Eller, 20 Aug. 1962, folder 4, Nimitz-General, Adm. Eller Collection, 1968–1969, box 115, Papers of Fleet Admiral Chester W. Nimitz, Archives Branch, Naval History and Heritage Command, Washington, DC (hereafter cited as Nimitz Papers, NHHC); Gilbert, *Leader Born*, 12–13.

12. *DANFS*, 2:89–90; Quarterly Reports on the Fitness of Midshipmen, July 9, 1907–Sept. 30, 1907, Sept. 30, 1907–Jan. 1, 1908, 1 Jan.–31 March 1908, Midshipman Personnel Jacket, John S. McCain, RG 405, Spec. Coll. & Archives, USNA; Record of Officers, Vice Admiral John Sidney McCain (hereafter cited as McCain Officer Record); Medical Record Ens. John S. McCain, 6 Feb. 1911; both in McCain Personnel File, NPRC.

13. *DANFS*, 2:166; *DANFS*, 5:322; McCain Officer Record, McCain Personnel File, NPRC; James R. Reckner, *Teddy Roosevelt's Great White Fleet* (Annapolis, MD: Naval Institute Press, 1988), 138–56.

14. McCain Officer Record, McCain Personnel File, NPRC; Gilbert, *Leader Born*, 14–15. Some sources cite 1876 and 1877 as years of Katherine's birth. Hers and John Sidney's headstone in Arlington has the 9 January 1878 date, verified by the California Death Index, Department of Public Health Services, https://familysearch.org/ark:/61903/1:1:VGRZ-6D2, accessed 24 March 2016.

15. *DANFS*, 8:125–29; McCain Officer Record, McCain Personnel File, NPRC; McCain and Salter, *Faith of My Fathers*, 52.

16. Victor Blue (Chief BuNav) to McCain, 22 April 1914; Josephus Daniels (SecNav) to McCain, 3 March 1915; McCain Officer Record; all in McCain Personnel File, NPRC; *New York Times*, 13 Oct. 1912; Gilbert, *Leader Born*, 15–16; *DANFS*, 2:145; *Coronado Eagle and Journal*, 22 March 2000, http://cdnc.ucr.edu/cgi-bin/cdnc?a=d&d=CJ20000322.2.95, accessed 28 Sept. 2016.

17. *DANFS*, 2:13–14; McCain Officer Record, McCain Personnel File, NPRC; Gilbert, *Leader Born*, 18.

18. McCain Officer Record; BuNav to McCain, 8 Aug. 1920; both in McCain Personnel File, NPRC; Gilbert, *Leader Born*, 23–24; *Annual Reports of the Secretary of the Navy for the Fiscal Year 1919* (Washington, DC: Government Printing Office, 1920), 377–78. Navy personnel statistics are from the Naval History and Heritage Command (http://www.history.navy.mil).

19. J. S. McCain, "A Personnel Survey," U.S. Naval Institute *Proceedings* 49 (Jan. 1923): 19–37.

20. *DANFS*, 4:257–59; McCain Officer Record; Report of Leave of Absence, Cdr. John S. McCain, 27 Jan. 1922; Medical History, Cdr. John Sidney McCain, 5 Jan. 1928; all in McCain Personnel File, NPRC; *New York Times*, 6, 13 Sept. 1922.

21. J. S. McCain, "The Staff Equalization Bill," U.S. Naval Institute *Proceedings* 50 (March 1924): 417–23; U.S. Congress, House, *Hearing on the Bill H.R. 4444 (Later Introduced as H.R. 9315) to Provide for the Equalization of Promotion of Officers of the Staff Corps of the Navy with Officers of the Line*, 68th Cong. 1st sess. (Washington, DC: Government Printing Office, 1924), 2332, 2367.

22. U.S. Congress, Senate, *Hearings before the Subcommittee of the Committee on Naval Affairs . . . on a Bill to Provide for the Equalization of Promotion of Officers of the Staff Corps of the Navy with Officers of the Line*, 68th Cong. 1st sess. (Washington, DC: Government Printing Office, 1924), 17–22.

23. Ibid., 43–69, 74, 76–77, 84, 89.

24. U.S. Congress, House, *Hearing on the Bill H.R. 4444 . . .* , 2332, 2337–38, 2345, 2349–61, 2436–45.

25. Hearings before the General Board of the Navy, 1924, vol. 1, micro roll 5, 144–60.

26. J. S. McCain, "Service since Graduation vs. Age in Grade Retirement," U.S. Naval Institute *Proceedings* 51 (May 1925): 737–45.

27. Thomas Wildenberg, *Billy Mitchell's War with the Navy: The Interwar Rivalry over Air Power* (Annapolis, MD: Naval Institute Press, 2013), 119–20, 141.

28. William F. Trimble, *Admiral William A. Moffett: Architect of Naval Aviation* (1994; repr., Annapolis, MD: Naval Institute Press, 2007), 7–8, 162–63.

29. U.S. President's Aircraft Board, *Hearings before the President's Aircraft Board*, 4 vols. (Washington, DC: Government Printing Office, 1925), 3:951–58.

30. Trimble, *Moffett*, 238–43; Reynolds, *Towers*, 191, 195. For an overview of aviation personnel policies and problems, see Donald Chisholm, "Big Guns versus Wooden Decks: Naval Aviation Officer Personnel, 1911–1941," in *One Hundred Years of U.S. Navy Air Power*, ed. Douglas V. Smith (Annapolis, MD: Naval Institute Press, 2010), 52–78.

31. Trimble, *Moffett*, 192–93; McCain to Stark, 18 Aug. 1939, folder 1–2, Corresp. 1935–1940, box 1, Papers of John Sidney McCain, Hoover Institution Library and Archives, Stanford University, Palo Alto, CA (hereafter cited as McCain Papers, HISU).

32. Washington to Randall Jacobs (Acting Chief BuNav), 14 Sept. 1940, McCain Personnel File, NPRC.

33. *DANFS*, 5:65–66; McCain Officer Record; Application for Transportation of Dependents, 10 June 1927; Lewis Porterfield to McCain, 20 June 1927; all in McCain Personnel File, NPRC; Henry H. Adams, *Witness to Power: The Life of Fleet Admiral William D. Leahy* (Annapolis, MD: Naval Institute Press, 1985), 54–57; Gilbert, *Leader Born*, 32.

34. Reminiscences of Vice Admiral William R. Smedberg III, U.S. Navy (Ret.), 2 vols., Annapolis, MD: U.S. Naval Institute, 1979, 1:38–39.

35. Application for Transportation of Dependents, 5 April 1928, McCain Personnel File, NPRC; Reynolds, *Towers*, 254–55.

36. McCain, John S., "The Causes of the Spanish American War, and the Naval and Combined Operations in the Atlantic, Including the Transfer of the Oregon," Student Theses, Record Group 13, Naval Historical Collection, Naval War College, Newport, RI (courtesy of Dara A. Baker).

37. McCain, John S., "The Foreign Policies of the United States," Student Theses, Record Group 13, Naval Historical Collection, Naval War College, Newport, RI (courtesy of Dara A. Baker).

38. McCain Officer Record; R. H. Leigh (Chief BuNav) to McCain, 26 Aug. 1929; BuNav to McCain, 1, 21 Feb., 20 May, 25 June 1930; Board of Medical Survey to Commandant Washington Navy Yard, 3 Sept. 1930; Medical Record, John Sidney McCain, 14 Nov. 1935; all in McCain Personnel File, NPRC.

39. *DANFS*, 5:97–98; McCain Officer Record; Chief BuNav to McCain, 25 Sept. 1931; Chief BuNav to McCain, 15 June 1932; all in McCain Personnel File, NPRC; *Nitro* Deck Logs, 9 June 1931–31 March 1933, Records of the Bureau of Naval Personnel, Record Group 24, National Archives and Records Administration, Archives I, Washington, DC (hereafter cited as RG 24, NARA Archives I).

40. *Nitro* Deck Log, 1 April 1933, RG 24, NARA Archives I; McCain to C. M. Austin, 16 Nov. 1933; McCain to L. B. Porterfield, 9 Jan. 1934; both in folder 1–1, Corresp. 1933–1934, box 1, McCain Papers, HISU; *New York Times*, 1 Jan. 1934, 1 Jan. 1935.

41. McCain to L. B. Porterfield, 25 Jan. 1934; McCain to J. F. Shafroth, 21 Feb. 1934; both in folder 1–1, Corresp. 1933–1934, box 1, McCain Papers, HISU; Robert Greenhalgh Albion, *Makers of Naval Policy, 1798–1947* (Annapolis, MD: Naval Institute Press, 1980), 237–55.

42. *New York Times*, 27 May, 4 June 1934; McCain to C. M. Austin, 12 March, 17 Oct. 1934; both in folder 1–1, Corresp. 1933–1934, box 1, McCain Papers, HISU; Report of Leave of Absence, 27 April 1934, McCain Personnel File, NPRC.

43. McCain Officer Record; McCain to Chief BuNav, 18 Jan. 1935; both in McCain Personnel File, NPRC; Gilbert, *Leader Born*, 28–29; Senator John S. McCain III, telephone interview with the author, 7 Oct. 2015.

Chapter Two. Naval Aviation

1. E. R. Stitt (Chief BuMed) to R. H. Leigh (Chief BuNav), 26 Jan. 1928, McCain Personnel File, NPRC; Gilbert, *Leader Born*, 39.

2. E. J. King (Chief BuAer) to Leahy, 1st endorsement, 22 Jan. 1935; P. S. Rossiter (Chief BuMed) to Leahy, 24 Jan. 1935; Report of Physical Examination, 27 Nov. 1935; Leahy to McCain, 30 Apr. 1935; Transportation of Dependents, 8 Oct. 1935; McCain Officer Record; all in McCain Personnel File, NPRC; Gilbert, *Leader Born*, 40.

3. Hill Goodspeed, "One Hundred Years at Pensacola," *Naval History* 28 (Dec. 2014): 48–53; Wesley Phillips Newton and Robert R. Rea, *Wings of Gold: An Account of Naval*

Aviation Training in World War II, the Correspondence of Aviation Cadet/Ensign Robert R. Rea (Tuscaloosa: University of Alabama Press, 1987), 12–13, 15; NAS Pensacola, Ground School Course Report, McCain, J. S., Flight Training Record, Capt. J. S. McCain, Emil Buehler Naval Aviation Library, National Naval Aviation Museum, Pensacola, FL (courtesy of Hill Goodspeed; hereafter cited as McCain Flight Record, NNAM); Roy A. Grossnick, ed., *United States Naval Aviation, 1910–1995* (Washington, DC: Naval Historical Center, 1995), 89.

4. Dual Instruction, 26 June, 5, 10, 16 July 1935; Check Flights, 24, 26 July 1935; all in McCain Flight Record, NNAM; Gilbert, *Leader Born*, 41.

5. Dual Instruction, 20, 28 Aug., 9–13 Sept., 4 Nov. 1935, 30 Jan.–19 Feb., 2, 11 March, 1–14 April 1936; Check Flights, 19 Dec. 1935, 16 Jan., 20, 24 Feb. 1936; all in McCain Flight Record, NNAM.

6. L. P. Davis, memo, 24 Feb. 1936, McCain Personnel File, NPRC; Chief BuAer to McCain, 16 March 1936; third endorsement, Aubrey W. Fitch, 24 April 1936; fourth endorsement, John H. Towers, 12 May 1936; all in McCain Flight Record, NNAM; Albert A. Nofi, "Aviation in the Interwar Fleet Maneuvers, 1919–1940," in *One Hundred Years of U.S. Navy Air Power*, ed. Douglas V. Smith (Annapolis, MD: Naval Institute Press, 2010), 112–13; Paolo E. Coletta, *Patrick N. L. Bellinger and U.S. Naval Aviation* (Lanham, MD: University Press of America, 1987), 186.

7. Check Flights, 12, 17, 18, 23 June, 16 July, 10 Sept 1936; Dual Instruction, 1 July 1935; summary of flights and hours, undated; C. A. Blakely to McCain 11 Sept. 1936; all in McCain Flight Record, NNAM; Reminiscences of Admiral Roy L. Johnson, USN (Ret.), Annapolis, MD: U.S. Naval Institute, 1982, 30; certificate, 24 Aug. 1936, McCain Personnel File, NPRC.

8. Chief BuNav to McCain, 25 Aug. 1936; McCain Officer Record; W. A. McCain message to BuNav, 13 Oct. 1936; all in McCain Personnel File, NPRC; Paolo E. Coletta, ed., *United States Navy and Marine Corps Bases, Overseas* (Westport, CT: Greenwood Press, 1985), 74–78; Michael D. Roberts, *Dictionary of American Naval Aviation Squadrons* (Washington, DC: Naval Historical Center, 2000), 2:262, 469–70, 515, 755.

9. Thomas B. Buell, *Master of Sea Power: A Biography of Fleet Admiral Ernest J. King* (Boston: Little, Brown and Company, 1980), 91–93; King to McCain, 12 Sept. 1936; McCain to King, 23 Oct. 1936; McCain to King, 29 March 1937; all in folder M–N, box 6, General Correspondence, 1908–1957, Ernest Joseph King Papers, Manuscript Division, Library of Congress, Washington, DC (hereafter cited as King Papers, MDLC); *New York Times*, 28 Feb. 1937; Gilbert, *Leader Born*, 44.

10. A. B. Cook (Chief BuAer) to Chief BuNav, 1 March 1937; Cook to Chief BuNav, 7 April 1937; McCain to Chief BuNav, 7 May 1937; all in McCain Personnel File, NPRC; *Ranger* Deck Logs, 1–5 June 1937, RG 24, NARA Archives I; Robert J. Cressman, *USS Ranger: The Navy's First Flattop from Keel to Mast, 1934–46* (Washington, DC: Brassey's Inc., 2003), 83; Gilbert, *Leader Born*, 44–46.

11. Norman Friedman, *U.S. Aircraft Carriers: An Illustrated Design History* (Annapolis, MD: Naval Institute Press, 1983), 69–77.

12. Cressman, *USS Ranger*, 84–87, 96–99; Register of Officers, *Ranger* Deck Log, 1 June 1937, RG 24, NARA Archives I; Gordon Swanborough and Peter M. Bowers, *United States Navy Aircraft since 1911* (Annapolis, MD: Naval Institute Press, 1976), 210–11, 216, 443.

13. *Ranger* Deck Logs, 4, 13 Sept. 1937, RG 24, NARA Archives I; Cressman, *USS Ranger*, 99–101.

14. Cressman, *USS Ranger*, 102–4; *Ranger* Deck Logs, 15–24 Sept. 1937, RG 24, NARA Archives I; *New York Times*, 19, 25 Sept., 5 Oct. 1937; Reminiscences of Rear Admiral Francis D. Foley, USN (Ret.), 2 vols., Annapolis, MD: U.S. Naval Institute, 1988, 1:186; Claude A. Swanson (SecNav) to McCain, 18 Nov. 1937, McCain Personnel File, NPRC.

15. *Ranger* Deck Logs, 15, 19 March 1938, RG 24, NARA Archives I; Nofi, "Aviation in the Interwar Fleet Maneuvers," 116; Cressman, *USS Ranger*, 106–10; Reynolds, *Towers*, 276.

16. *Ranger* Deck Logs, 28, 30 March 1938, RG 24, NARA Archives I; Reynolds, *Towers*, 276–78.

17. *Ranger* Deck Logs, 1–9, 21, 25, 26, 28 April 1938, RG 24, NARA Archives I; Nofi, "Aviation in the Interwar Fleet Maneuvers," 117; Reynolds, *Towers*, 278–79.

18. William F. Trimble, *Wings for the Navy: A History of the Naval Aircraft Factory, 1917–1956* (Annapolis, MD: Naval Institute Press, 1990), 186–94; Cressman, *USS Ranger*, 111–13.

19. McCain to CinC US Fleet, 29 Aug. 1938 (courtesy of Thomas Wildenberg); *Ranger* Deck Log, 24 Aug. 1938, RG 24, NARA Archives I; Rear Adm. D. S. Fahrney, "The History of Pilotless Aircraft and Guided Missiles," undated manuscript (probably 1958), Naval History and Heritage Command, 232–40.

20. McCain to CinC US Fleet, 29 Aug. 1938 (courtesy of Thomas Wildenberg); Fahrney, "History of Pilotless Aircraft and Guided Missiles," 232–40 (emphasis in original).

21. *Ranger* Deck Logs, 4, 18, 19, 31 Jan., 13, 17, 20 Feb. 1939, RG 24, NARA Archives I; Nofi, "Aviation in the Interwar Fleet Maneuvers," 117–18; Felker, *Testing American Sea Power*, 111.

22. *Ranger* Deck Logs, 21, 24, 25 Feb. 1939, RG 24, NARA Archives I; Nofi, "Aviation in the Interwar Fleet Maneuvers," 118–19; Felker, *Testing American Sea Power*, 112; Cressman, *USS Ranger*, 121–22.

23. *Ranger* Deck Logs, 26, 27 Feb. 1939, RG 24, NARA Archives I; Cressman, *USS Ranger*, 123.

24. Reynolds, *Towers*, 279; Nofi, "Aviation in the Interwar Fleet Maneuvers," 119.

25. *Ranger* Deck Logs, 2 April–18 May, 31 May 1939, RG 24, NARA Archives I; *New York Times*, 30 April, 1, 8 May 1939; McCain to King, 5 May 1939, folder J–R, 1939, box 7, General Correspondence, 1908–1957, King Papers, MDLC; Cressman, *USS Ranger*, 125–26.

26. J. O. Richardson (Chief BuNav) to McCain, 4 April 1939, McCain Personnel File, NPRC; *Ranger* Deck Log, 3 June 1939, RG 24, NARA Archives I; Archibald D. Turnbull and Clifford L. Lord, *History of United States Naval Aviation* (New Haven, CT: Yale

University Press, 1949), 303; Gilbert, *Leader Born*, 50–51; Reminiscences of Admiral James S. Russell, U.S. Navy (Ret.), Annapolis, MD: U.S. Naval Institute, 1976, 46.

27. Elretta Sudsbury, *Jackrabbits to Jets: The History of North Island, San Diego, California* (San Diego: Neyenesch Printers, 1967), 74–93, 204–41; McCain to C. W. Nimitz (Chief BuNav), 28 Aug. 1939, folder 1-2, Corresp. 1935–1940, box 1, McCain Papers, HISU; C. W. Nimitz (Chief BuNav) to McCain, 16 Feb. 1940, McCain Personnel File, NPRC.

28. McCrary to Chief BuAer, 8 Jan. 1941; 1st endorsement, Chief BuAer to CNO, 23 Jan. 1941; both in folder 1-5, Corresp. 1941 January–December, box 1, McCain Papers, HISU.

29. McCain to Bellinger, 3 Jan. 1941, folder 1-11, United States Navy File, Aircraft Scouting Force, 1941 January–1942 April, box 1, McCain Papers, HISU.

30. Friedman, *U.S. Aircraft Carriers*, 138–43, 213–14; McCain to SecNav, 1 March 1939, folder Memorandums, 1939, box 7, Gen. Corresp., 1908–1957, King Papers, MDLC; H. R. Stark (CNO) to McCain, 9 Dec. 1940; McCain to W. H. P. Blandy, 10 Feb. 1941; both in folder 1-10, United States Navy File, Aircraft Scouting Force 1939 June–1941 November, box 1, McCain Papers, HISU; Reynolds, *Towers*, 292–93.

31. Reynolds, *Towers*, 285–89; Gilbert, *Leader Born*, 55–56; Leahy to Chief BuNav, 13 May 1940; Washington to Chief BuNav, 14 Sept. 1940; both in McCain Personnel File, NPRC.

32. Roosevelt to McCain, 23 Jan. 1941; Frank Knox (SecNav) to McCain, 24 Jan. 1941; message 251946 January 1941, Comairscofor to Cincus, Comairbatfor; Comairscofor to Chief BuNav, 27 Jan. 1941; all in McCain Personnel File, NPRC; *New York Times*, 23 Jan. 1941; McCain to King, 23 Jan. 1941, folder 1-5, Corresp. 1941 January–December, box 1, McCain Papers, HISU; Reynolds, *Fast Carriers*, 26, 29.

33. Gardner to McCain, 10 Feb. 1941, folder 1-5, Corresp. 1941 January–December, box 1, McCain Papers, HISU; Reminiscences of Vice Admiral Herbert D. Riley, U.S. Navy (Ret.), Annapolis, MD: U.S. Naval Institute, 2004, 100–101.

34. Coletta, *Bellinger*, 239–40; Bellinger to McCain, 4 July 1941, folder 1-5, Corresp. 1941 January–December; McCain to Bellinger, 15 Feb. 1941; McCain to Brown, 6 March 1941; all in folder 1-10, United States Navy File, Aircraft Scouting Force 1939 June–1941 November, box 1, McCain Papers, HISU.

35. John S. McCain, "VPB—The Patrol Bomber," *Flying and Popular Aviation* 30 (Jan. 1942): 52, 54.

36. McCain to W. H. P. Blandy (BuOrd), 18 Feb. 1941, folder 1-10, United States Navy File, Aircraft Scouting Force 1939 June–1941 November, box 1, McCain Papers, HISU; Thomas Wildenberg and Norman Polmar, *Ship Killer: A History of the American Torpedo* (Annapolis, MD: Naval Institute Press, 2010), 72.

37. Blandy to McCain, 1 March 1941, file S70-S81-1 (17), box 20, BuOrd Secret Files, NARA Archives II (courtesy of Thomas Wildenberg); Wildenberg and Polmar, *Ship Killer*, 75–77, 85–86.

38. Reynolds, *Towers*, 347, 350–51; McCain to Thomas H. Robbins, 27 June 1941, folder 1-11, United States Navy File, Aircraft Scouting Force 1941 January–1942 April, box 1, McCain Papers, HISU.

39. McCain to Towers (Chief BuAer), 8 April 1941, folder 1-5, Corresp. 1941 January–December; McCain to Kimmel (Cincus), 31 July 1941, folder 1-11, United States Navy File, Aircraft Scouting Force 1941 January–1942 April; McCain to Capt. H. M. Briggs, 25 July 1941, folder 1-11, United States Navy File, Aircraft Scouting Force 1941 January–1942 April; all in box 1, McCain Papers, HISU; Comairscofor to BuNav, 3 May 1941; temporary additional duty, J. S. McCain, 11 July 1941; second endorsement, itinerary, 10 Aug. 1941; Cincus to McCain, 7 Aug. 1941; all in McCain Personnel File, NPRC.

40. Stimson to SecNav, 25 June 1941; Maj. Gen. Jacob E. Fickel to McCain, 25 Oct. 1941; both in McCain Personnel File, NPRC; McCain to Fickel, 22 May 1941, folder 1-5, Corresp. 1941 January–December, box 1, McCain Papers, HISU.

41. Temporary additional duty, J. S. McCain, 7 Oct. 1941; first endorsement, itinerary, 24 Oct. 1941; both in McCain Personnel File, NPRC; Bellinger to McCain, 6 Nov. 1941; McCain to Bellinger, 10 Nov. 1941; both in folder 1-10, United States Navy File, Aircraft Scouting Force 1939 June–1941 November, box 1, McCain Papers, HISU; Gordon W. Prange, with Donald M. Goldstein and Katherine V. Dillon, *At Dawn We Slept: The Untold Story of Pearl Harbor* (New York: McGraw-Hill Book Company, 1981), 410; *DANFS*, 2:220–21; *DANFS*, 7:40–41.

42. McCain to Brown, 5 Dec. 1941, folder 1–10, United States Navy File, Aircraft Scouting Force 1939 June–1941 November, box 1, McCain Papers, HISU.

43. McCain to Greenslade, 13 Dec. 1941, folder 1-10, United States Navy File, Aircraft Scouting Force 1939 June–1941 November, box 1, McCain Papers, HISU.

44. Prange, *At Dawn We Slept*, 539; Coletta, *Bellinger*, 265; McCain to Bellinger, 11 Jan. 1942, folder 1-7, 1942 January–1945 Aug.–Sept. Corresp. with John H. Towers, box 1, McCain Papers, HISU.

45. McCain to Greenslade, 13 Dec. 1941, folder 1-10, United States Navy File, Aircraft Scouting Force 1939 June–1941 November, box 1, McCain Papers, HISU; McCain to Towers, 17 Dec. 1941; Towers to McCain, 17 Dec. 1941; both in folder 1-10, United States Navy File, Aircraft Scouting Force 1939 June–1941 November, box 1, McCain Papers, HISU.

46. Towers to McCain, 19 Dec. 1941; McCain to Towers, 24 Dec. 1941; both in folder 1-10, United States Navy File, Aircraft Scouting Force 1939 June–1941 November; McCain to Towers, 13 April 1942, folder 1-7, 1942 January–1945 Aug.–Sept. Corresp. with John H. Towers; all in box 1, McCain Papers, HISU; McCain to F. S. Low, 14 March 1942, folder March 1942, box 2, Series I Correspondence and Memoranda, 1918–1955, Papers of Fleet Admiral Ernest J. King, Archives Branch, Naval History and Heritage Command, Washington, DC (hereafter cited as King Papers, NHHC).

47. Comairscofor to Commander Pacific Southern Naval Coastal Frontier, file A16-3 (0106), 2 Jan. 1942, www.Fold3.com, accessed 27 Feb. 2015; Aircraft, Southern Sector, Western Sea Frontier, War Diary, March 1942, Composition of Force, 2, 20, 21, 23, 26 March 1942; NAS San Diego, War Diary, Feb. 1 to Feb. 28, 1942; McCain to Culbert E. Olsen, 30 March 1942, folder 1-10, United States Navy File, Aircraft Scouting Force 1939 June–1941 November, box 1, McCain Papers, HISU; *New York Times*, 18 Feb. 1942.

Chapter Three. South Pacific Command

1. Richard B. Frank, "Picking Winners?" *Naval History* 25 (June 2011): 24–30. The Knox memo to Roosevelt, 9 March 1942, is in the "Safe Files" at the Franklin D. Roosevelt Presidential Library, available online at docs.fdrlibrary.marist.edu/psf/box4/a47a01.html, accessed 1 Aug. 2012.

2. Reynolds, *Towers*, 385.

3. Richard B. Frank, *Guadalcanal* (New York: Random House, 1990), 6–9.

4. Ibid., 9–10, 21–22; John B. Lundstrom, *Black Shoe Carrier Admiral: Frank Jack Fletcher at Coral Sea, Midway, and Guadalcanal* (Annapolis, MD: Naval Institute Press, 2006), 72.

5. Frank, *Guadalcanal*, 12–13.

6. John B. Lundstrom, *The First South Pacific Campaign: Pacific Fleet Strategy, December 1941–June 1942* (Annapolis, MD: Naval Institute Press, 1976), 201; Lundstrom, *Black Shoe Carrier Admiral*, 72–75.

7. Lundstrom, *Black Shoe Carrier Admiral*, 48–49, 101–2; message 122059 March 1942, Cincpac to Cominch, roll 6, CINC Pacific and U.S. Pacific Fleet (CINCPAC), Microfilm Copies of Dispatches (Microfilmed Incoming and Outgoing Dispatches and Chronological Message Traffic of CINC, Pacific and U.S. Pacific Fleet, 1940–45), Records of Naval Operating Forces, Record Group 313, National Archives and Records Administration, Archives II, College Park, MD (hereafter cited as Cincpac Dispatches and Message Traffic, RG 313, NARA Archives II). Copies courtesy of John Lundstrom.

8. World War II Administrative History, Western Sea Frontier (Washington, DC: Director of Naval History, 1946), 312–20, www.Fold3.com, accessed 17 April 2013.

9. Chief BuNav to McCain, 9 April 1942; ComPatWings Pacific Fleet to McCain, 27 April 1942; Chief BuAer to Chief BuNav, 1 May 1942; all in McCain Personnel File, NPRC; Lundstrom, *Black Shoe Carrier Admiral*, 117–18.

10. Lundstrom, *Black Shoe Carrier Admiral*, 118.

11. Ibid., 119–22.

12. McCain to Duncan, 29 April 1942 (emphasis in original); McCain to Towers, 29 April 1942; both in folder 1-11, United States Navy File, Aircraft Scouting Force, 1941 January–1942 April, box 1, McCain Papers, HISU.

13. Chief, BuPers to McCain, 3 June 1942, McCain Personnel File, NPRC; Aircraft Southern Sector, Western Sea Frontier, War Diary, 1 May 1942; message 180510 May 1942, Tangier to Comtaskfor 9, roll 12, Cincpac Dispatches and Message Traffic, RG 313, NARA Archives II; message 190839 May 1942, Comairsopac to Cincpac, Graybook, vol. 1, 7 Dec. 1941–31 Aug. 1942, 485.

14. *DANFS*, 4:332–33; Lundstrom, *Black Shoe Carrier Admiral*, 134; *Naval Aviation News* 54 (Jan. 1972), 2; USS *Tangier* (Flagship), War Diary, Designation: Commander Aircraft South Pacific Force, Confidential War Diary, Commander Aircraft South Pacific Force, May–August 1942, AirSoPac Jan. 42–Jan. 43, 21, 22 May 1942, vol. 1, box 76, World War II War Diaries, Records Relating to Naval Activity during World War II, Records of the Office of the Chief of Naval Operations, Record Group 38, National Archives and Records Administration, Archives II, College Park, MD (hereafter

cited as USS *Tangier*, War Diary, World War II War Diaries, RG 38, NARA Archives II); message 030145 May 1942, Cincpac, roll 10, Cincpac Dispatches and Message Traffic, RG 313, NARA Archives II.

15. McCain to Ghormley, 1 June 1942, file N10, Establishment of Land-Based Naval Aviation, box 6784, Records Relating to Operations (Red 182), 1942–1946, Records of Naval Operating Forces, Record Group 313, National Archives and Records Administration, Archives II, College Park, MD (hereafter cited as Operations Records (Red 182), RG 313, NARA Archives II); Ghormley to McCain, 2 June 1942, folder 1-4, Corresp. 1940–1941, box 1, McCain Papers, HISU; Reminiscences of Captain James R. Ogden, USN (Ret.), Annapolis, MD: U.S. Naval Institute, 1982, 92–93 (hereafter cited as Ogden Reminiscences).

16. Lt. Cdr. William J. Slattery, memo to Rear Adm. R. E. Byrd, 13 July 1942, Secret No. 2, folder 1 of 2, box 2, Commander, Aircraft South Pacific Forces (COMAIRSOPAC), Records Relating to Operations (Blue 242), 1942–1943, Records of Naval Operating Forces, Record Group 313, National Archives and Records Administration, Archives II, College Park, MD (hereafter cited as Comairsopac Records (Blue 242), RG 313, NARA Archives II); Hughes, *Bill Halsey*, 236–38; Kim Munholland, *Rock of Contention: Free French and Americans at War in New Caledonia, 1940–1945* (New York: Berghahn Books, 2005), 36–57, 93–107, 118–19.

17. USS *Tangier*, War Diary, Jan. 42–Jan. 43, 20 May 1942, vol. 1, box 76, World War II War Diaries, RG 38, NARA Archives II; War Plans—Daily Summary, Secret, War Diary, Commander in Chief, United States Pacific Fleet, May 1–15, 1942, 5, 10 May 1942, vol. 1, box 6, Cincpac: Apr. 1942 to May 1942, World War II War Diaries, Records Relating to Naval Activity during World War II, Records of the Office of the Chief of Naval Operations, Record Group 38, National Archives and Records Administration, Archives II, College Park, MD (hereafter cited as Cincpac War Diary, World War II War Diaries, RG 38, NARA Archives II); Lundstrom, *First South Pacific Campaign*, 170; "The AAF in the South Pacific to October 1942" (Washington, DC: Assistant Chief of Air Staff, Intelligence, Historical Division, 1944), 44, http://www.ibiblio.org/hyperwar/AAF/AAFHS/AAFHS-101.pdf, accessed 12 Feb. 2014.

18. Headquarters, Army Air Forces, Office of Assistant Chief of Air Staff, Intelligence, *Wings at War, No. 3: Pacific Counterblow*, 2–3, http://www.ibiblio.org/hyperwar/AAF/WW/WW-3-2.html, accessed 19 Dec. 2011; "The AAF in the South Pacific," 27–32; Comairsopac to Commanding generals, 19 June 1942, folder 1-4, Corresp., 1940–1941, box 1, McCain Papers, HISU.

19. "The AAF in the South Pacific," 47; L. G. Saunders, S-2 and S-3 Report, 24 Sept. 1942, folder GP-11-SU-OP-S (Bomb) 31 Jul 1942–6 Oct. 1942, IRIS no. 77779, box 14, Air Force Historical Research Agency, Maxwell AFB, AL (hereafter cited as AFHRA); *New York Times*, 28 Oct. 1942.

20. Message 181120 May 1942, Comairsopac to Cincpac, Graybook, vol. 1, 7 Dec. 1941–31 Aug. 1942, 485; McCain to Ghormley, 6 July 1942, folder 1-4, Corresp. 1940–1941; McCain to Harmon, folder 1-6, Corresp. 1942 April–September; both in box

1, McCain Papers, HISU; Saunders to Maj. Gen. Willis H. Hale, 18 Aug. 1942, folder GP-11-SU-OP Aug. 1942, IRIS no. 77773, box 10, AFHRA; Richard W. Bates, "The Battle of Savo Island, August 9th, 1942: Strategical and Tactical Analysis, Part 1" (Newport, RI: Naval War College, 1950), 332.

21. War Plans—Daily Summary, Cincpac War Diary, 22 May 1942, vol. 2, box 6, World War II War Diaries, RG 38, NARA Archives II. For the significance of VPs to American prewar plans and strategy, see Miller, "Eyes of the Fleet," 31–42.

22. War Plans—Daily Summary, Cincpac War Diary, 22 May 1942, vol. 2, box 6, World War II War Diaries, RG 38, NARA Archives II; message 232300 May 1942, Comairsopac to Cincpac, Graybook, vol. 1, 7 Dec. 1941–31 Aug. 1942, 528; message 262359 May 1942, Cominch to Comairsopac, Comsopac, roll 12; message 290205 May 1942, Comairsopac to Cincpac, roll 13; message 301430 May 1942, Cominch to Cincpac, roll 13; all in Cincpac Dispatches and Message Traffic, RG 313, NARA Archives II.

23. McCain to Nimitz, 26 May 1942, folder 1-6, Corresp. 1942 April–September; McCain to Nimitz, 10 June 1942, folder 1-4, Corresp. 1940–1941; both in box 1, McCain Papers, HISU.

24. Nimitz to McCain, 24 June 1942; McCain to Nimitz, 6 July 1942; both in folder 1-4, Corresp. 1940–1941, box 1, McCain Papers, HISU.

25. McCain to Low and Duncan, 21 June 1942, folder 1-4, Corresp. 1940–1941, box 1, McCain Papers, HISU.

26. McCain to ComGens, 19 June 1942, Secret No. 1, folder 1 of 2, box 2, Comairsopac Records (Blue 242), RG 313, NARA Archives II (emphasis in original). For the significance of scouting and the problems, see Hughes, *Fleet Tactics*, 166–67.

27. McCain to ComGens, 19 June 1942, Secret No. 1, folder 1 of 2, box 2, Comairsopac Records (Blue 242), RG 313, NARA Archives II. For the Navy's role in radar development, see David Kite Alison, *New Eye for the Navy: The Origin of Radar at the Naval Research Laboratory* (Washington, DC: Naval Research Laboratory, 1981). For operational limitations, see Richard C. Knott, *Black Cat Raiders of WWII* (Annapolis, MD: Nautical & Aviation Publishing Company of America, 1981), 61, 96, 148–49; and Capt. M. B. Gardner, USN, interview, Air Information Branch, Bureau of Aeronautics, 13 Jan. 1943, 15, www.Fold3.com (courtesy of John Lundstrom), accessed 24 Sept. 2012 (hereafter cited as Gardner interview).

28. Frank, *Guadalcanal*, 28–29; World War II Administrative History, Bureau of Aeronautics, Summary, 2 vols. (Washington, DC: Director of Naval History, 1957), 1:309 (hereafter cited as BuAer World War II Admin. History); USS *Tangier*, War Diary, 12 June 1942, vol. 1, box 76, World War II War Diaries, RG 38, NARA Archives II; message 212159 Aug. 1942, Comairsopac to Cincpac; message 231917 Aug. 1942, Cincpac to Comairsopac; both in roll 22, Cincpac Dispatches and Message Traffic, RG 313, NARA Archives II; John B. Lundstrom, *The First Team and the Guadalcanal Campaign: Naval Fighter Combat from August to November 1942* (Annapolis, MD: Naval Institute Press, 1994), 177.

29. USS *Tangier*, War Diary, 9 June 1942, Enclosure (A), vol. 1, box 76, World War II War Diaries, RG 38, NARA Archives II; John B. Lundstrom, *The First Team: Pacific Naval Air Combat from Pearl Harbor to Midway* (Annapolis, MD: Naval Institute Press, 1984), 205.

30. War Plans—Daily Summary, 18, 26 May 1942, Cincpac War Diary, vol. 2, box 6; War Plans—Daily Summary, 9 July 1942, Cincpac War Diary, vol. 1, box 7; USS *Tangier*, War Diary, 25 May 1942, vol. 1, box 76; all in World War II War Diaries, RG 38, NARA Archives II; message 092301 June 1942, Comairsopac to Cominch, roll 14; message 150516 June 1942, Efate to BuNav, roll 15; both in Cincpac Dispatches and Message Traffic, RG 313, NARA Archives II.

31. Gardner interview, 2–3 (emphasis in original); "The AAF in the South Pacific," 66–67; Kyle Crichton, "Navy Air Boss," *Collier's*, 23 Oct. 1943, 21.

32. James A. Michener, *Tales of the South Pacific* (New York: Macmillan Company, 1946), 2.

33. Message 191759 May 1942, Comgen Roses; message 200943 May 1942, Ghormley to Cincpac; message 050325 June 1942, Comairsopac to Comsopac; all in Graybook, vol. 1, 7 Dec. 1941–31 Aug. 1942, 485, 500, 607; USS *Tangier*, War Diary, 28 May 1942, vol. 1, box 76, World War II War Diaries, RG 38, NARA Archives II; Gardner interview, 2; McCain to Ghormley, 4 June 1942, file N10, Establishment of Land-Based Naval Aviation, box 6784, Operations Records (Red 182), RG 313, NARA Archives II.

34. McCain to Leary, 27 June 1942, folder 1-6, Corresp. 1942 April–September, box 1, McCain Papers, HISU; Ghormley to McCain, 1 June 1942; Comments by Captain Callaghan, 10 June 1942; both in file N10, Establishment of Land-Based Naval Aviation, box 6784, Operations Records (Red 182), RG 313, NARA Archives II; McCain to Towers, undated (probably late May or early June 1942), folder 1-3, Corresp. 1939–1941, Letters to John H. Towers, box 1, McCain Papers, HISU; Summary, 15 June, Graybook, vol. 1, 7 Dec. 1941–31 Aug. 1942, 593.

35. "The AAF in the South Pacific," 51; War Plans—Daily Summary, 5 July 1942, Cincpac War Diary, vol. 1, box 7; War Plans—Daily Summary, 29 July 1942, Cincpac War Diary, vol. 2, box 7; both in World War II War Diaries, RG 38, NARA Archives II; Gardner interview, 2–3; message 140616 June 1942, Comsopac to Cominch, roll 15; message 020854 Aug. 1942, Comairsopac to Comsopac, roll 20; both in Cincpac Dispatches and Message Traffic, RG 313, NARA Archives II.

36. McCain to Ghormley, 26 May 1942, file N10, Establishment of Land-Based Naval Aviation, box 6784, Operations Records (Red 182), RG 313, NARA Archives II; USS *Tangier*, War Diary, 29 May 1942, Enclosure (A), vol. 1, box 76, World War II War Diaries, RG 38, NARA Archives II; Lundstrom, *Black Shoe Carrier Admiral*, 217, 220.

37. McCain to Ghormley, 2 June 1942, folder 1 of 2, box 2, Comairsopac Records (Blue 242), RG 313, NARA Archives II (emphasis in original); McCain to Leary, 27 June 1942, folder 1-6, Corresp. 1942 April–September, box 1, McCain Papers, HISU; Frank, *Guadalcanal*, 30–31.

38. War Plans—Daily Summary, 31 May 1942, Cincpac War Diary, vol. 2, box 6: War Plans—Daily Summary, 8 July 1942, Cincpac War Diary, vol. 1, box 7; USS *Curtiss*, War Diary, 25 June 1942, vol. 1, box 76; all in World War II War Diaries, RG 38, NARA Archives II; message 110815 July 1942, Comairsopac to Comsopac, Cincpac, roll 18, Cincpac Dispatches and Message Traffic, RG 313, NARA Archives II; Knott, *Black Cat Raiders*, 73.

39. USS *Tangier*, War Diary, 26 May, 15 June 1942; USS *Curtiss*, War Diary, 16, 20, 28 June, 3 July 1942; all in vol. 1, box 76, World War II War Diaries, RG 38, NARA Archives II; message 180245 June 1942, Mackinac to Cincpac, roll 15; message 200745 June 1942, Comairsopac to Cincpac, roll 16; message 280830 June 1942, Comsopac to Cincpac, roll 16; all in Cincpac Dispatches and Message Traffic, RG 313, NARA Archives II; Daily Distribution of Operating Forces, 18 June 1942, War Diary, Cincpac, June 1–30, 1942, vol. 1, box 7, Cincpac: June 1942–July 31, 1942, World War II War Diaries, RG 38, NARA Archives II; *DANFS*, 4:184–85, 299–300; Ogden Reminiscences, 95.

40. Message 290121 June 1942, Cincpac to Compatwingspac; message 292139 June 1942, Compatwingspac to Cincpac; message 300408 June 1942, Compatwings to Comairsopac; message 081905 July 1942, Compatwing 2 to Comairsopac; all in roll 17, Cincpac Dispatches and Message Traffic, RG 313, NARA Archives II.

41. Message 240315 June 1942, Cincpac to Comairsopac; message 28083 June 1942, Comairsopac to Cincpac; both in roll 16, Cincpac Dispatches and Message Traffic, RG 313, NARA Archives II.

42. Lundstrom, *Black Shoe Carrier Admiral*, 308–14.

43. McCain to Chamberlin, 4 June 1942, folder 1-4, Corresp. 1940–1941, box 1, McCain Papers, HISU; Lundstrom, *Black Shoe Carrier Admiral*, 3, 118, 311. Lundstrom is the definitive source for Fletcher's Navy career.

44. Lundstrom, *Black Shoe Carrier Admiral*, 311–12, 314–16; "Best Course of Action, Discussion of Each Event," Graybook, vol. 1, 7 Dec. 1941–31 Aug. 1942, 740.

45. Lundstrom, *Black Shoe Carrier Admiral*, 319; Report of Informal Inquiry into the Circumstances Attending the Loss of the USS *Vincennes*, USS *Quincy*, USS *Astoria*, and HMAS *Canberra*, on August 9, 1942, in the Vicinity of Savo Island (Solomon Islands), 13 May 1943, 5, Naval War College Library, Newport, RI (hereafter cited as Hepburn Report).

46. Message 201300 July 1942, Comsopac to CTF 11, 16, 18, 44, Graybook, vol. 1, 7 Dec. 1941–31 Aug. 1942, 625.

47. Operation Plan No. 1-42, 25 July 1942, A4-3/A16-3, Serial 0016, in USS *Curtiss*, War Diary, vol. 1, box 76, World War II War Diaries, RG 38, NARA Archives II; Bates, "Savo Island," 16-A, 22-A-23, 25–26; "The AAF in the South Pacific," 52.

48. Lundstrom, *Black Shoe Carrier Admiral*, 340; Operation Plan No. 1-42, 25 July 1942, A4-3/A16-3, Serial 0016, in USS *Curtiss*, War Diary, vol. 1, box 76, World War II War Diaries, RG 38, NARA Archives II; Bates, "Savo Island," 26.

49. Annex "D," Operation Plan No. 1-42, 25 July 1942, A4-3/A16-3, Serial 0016, in USS *Curtiss*, War Diary, vol. 1, box 76, World War II War Diaries, RG 38, NARA Archives II; Bates, "Savo Island," 31–32.

50. USS *Curtiss*, War Diary, 26 July 1942, vol. 1, box 76, World War II War Diaries, RG 38, NARA Archives II; Lundstrom, *Black Shoe Carrier Admiral*, 327. Gilbert, *Leader Born*, 82, erroneously states that McCain was soaked with sour milk jettisoned from a garbage chute.

51. Lundstrom, *Black Shoe Carrier Admiral*, 325–40, is the most recent and thorough summary of the issues and controversy surrounding the *Saratoga* conference.

52. USS *Curtiss*, War Diary, 28, 30, 31 July, 1–5 Aug. 1942, vol. 1, box 76, World War II War Diaries, RG 38, NARA Archives II; "The AAF in the South Pacific," 56.

53. Lundstrom, *Black Shoe Carrier Admiral*, 337–40; message 020240 Aug. 1942, Comsopac to CTF 61, Graybook, vol. 1, 7 Dec. 1941–31 Aug. 1942, 631.

54. Lundstrom, *Black Shoe Carrier Admiral*, 338–39; *DANFS*, 1:58–59.

55. Daniel J. Callaghan, Report of Conference, 28 July 1942, folder 256, Cincpac Conference, Argonne, Noumea, box 24, Samuel Eliot Morison Office Files, Archives Branch, Naval History and Heritage Command, Washington, DC; Frank, *Guadalcanal*, 57; Lundstrom, *First Team and Guadalcanal*, 30.

56. Bates, "Savo Island," 26; Lundstrom, *Black Shoe Carrier Admiral*, 340; message 300820 July 1942, CTF 63 to CTF 61, Graybook, vol. 1, 7 Dec. 1941–31 Aug. 1942, 628.

57. Bates, "Savo Island," 22–1A. The numbers reflect the operational loss of aircraft in the last three days before the landings.

Chapter Four. Guadalcanal

1. USS *Curtiss*, War Diary, 6, 7 Aug. 1942, vol. 1, box 76, World War II War Diaries, RG 38, NARA Archives II; Roberts, *Dictionary of American Naval Aviation Squadrons*, 2:430; Pacific Wrecks, PBY-5 Catalina BuNo. 2389, http://www.pacificwrecks .com/aircraft/pby/2389.html, accessed 3 March 2017.

2. Saunders to Hale, 18 Aug. 1942, folder GP-11-SU-OP Aug. 1942, IRIS no. 77773, box 10, AFHRA. Numbers of ships and aircraft are from Lundstrom, *Black Shoe Carrier Admiral*, 343, 350, 520–22, and Frank, *Guadalcanal*, 57, 619–23.

3. Lundstrom, *Black Shoe Carrier Admiral*, 353–62; USS *Curtiss*, War Diary, 7 Aug. 1942, vol. 1, box 76, World War II War Diaries, RG 38, NARA Archives II.

4. Message 081233 Aug. 1942, Comairsopac to CTF 61, info. Comsopac, CTF 62, roll 20, Cincpac Dispatches and Message Traffic, RG 313, NARA Archives II; USS *Curtiss*, War Diary, 8 Aug. 1942, vol. 1, box 76, World War II War Diaries, RG 38, NARA Archives II.

5. Message 081233 Aug. 1942, Comairsopac to CTF 61, info. Comsopac, CTF 62, roll 20, Cincpac Dispatches and Message Traffic, RG 313, NARA Archives II; USS *Curtiss*, War Diary, 8 Aug. 1942, vol. 1, box 76, World War II War Diaries, RG 38, NARA Archives II.

6. Lundstrom, *Black Shoe Carrier Admiral*, 362, 368–73, 381, 384–86; message 081233 Aug. 1942, Comairsopac to CTF 61, roll 20, Cincpac Dispatches and Message Traffic, RG 313, NARA Archives II.

7. Lundstrom, *Black Shoe Carrier Admiral*, 590–91.

8. Lundstrom, *Black Shoe Carrier Admiral*, 384–96, and Frank, *Guadalcanal*, 83–123, provide good summaries of the battle. Denis Warner and Peggy Warner, with Sadao Seno, *Disaster in the Pacific: New Light on the Battle of Savo Island* (Annapolis, MD: Naval Institute Press, 1992), is detailed but not totally reliable.

9. Hepburn Report, 3, 42–43, 58–59.

10. Ibid., 1–3, 54–56, Nimitz letter following appendix E.

11. George Carroll Dyer, *The Amphibians Came to Conquer: The Story of Admiral Richmond Kelly Turner*, 2 vols. (Washington, DC: Department of the Navy, 1972), 1:370–72; Frank, *Guadalcanal*, 95. For an example of McCain's later search reports, see message 221210 Aug. 1942, Comairsopac to CTF 61, CTF 62, Comsopac, roll 22, Cincpac Dispatches and Message Traffic, RG 313, NARA Archives II.

12. Lundstrom, *Black Shoe Carrier Admiral*, 398–99, 406–8.

13. Ibid., 405, 376; Crichton, "Navy Air Boss," 21.

14. Lundstrom, *Black Shoe Carrier Admiral*, 398; USS *Curtiss*, War Diary, 9 Aug. 1942, vol. 1, box 76, World War II War Diaries, RG 38, NARA Archives II.

15. Daily Distribution of Operating Forces, 11 Aug. 1942, Cincpac War Diary, vol. 2, box 8: USS *Curtiss*, War Diary, 10, 11, 12, 13, 18, 19 Aug. 1942, vol. 1, box 76; all in World War II War Diaries, RG 38, NARA Archives II; message 091152 Aug. 1942, Comairsopac to CTF 63.5, roll 20; message 110200 Aug. 1942, CTF 61 to CTF 63, roll 21; both in Cincpac Dispatches and Message Traffic, RG 313, NARA Archives II; message 150746 Aug. 1942, Comsopac to CTF 63, Graybook, vol. 1, 7 Dec. 1941–31 Aug. 1942, 650.

16. USS *Curtiss*, War Diary, 15, 18, 19, 20 Aug. 1942, vol. 1, box 76, World War II War Diaries, RG 38, NARA Archives II; message 171114 Aug. 1942, Comairsopac to CTF 61; message 182105 Aug. 1942, Comairsopac to CTF 61, CTF 62; message 190229 Aug. 1942, Comairsopac to Comsopac; message 190548 Aug. 1942, Comsopac to CTF 63; message 190901 Aug. 1942, Comairsopac to Comsopac; all in roll 21, Cincpac Dispatches and Message Traffic, RG 313, NARA Archives II; Lundstrom, *Black Shoe Carrier Admiral*, 415.

17. War Plans—Daily Summary, 10 Aug. 1942, Cincpac War Diary, vol. 1, box 8; USS *Curtiss*, War Diary, 9, 15, 20, 24, 29 Aug. 1942, vol. 1, box 76; both in World War II War Diaries, RG 38, NARA Archives II; message 270411 Aug. 1942, Comairsopac to Comsopac, Graybook, vol. 1, 7 Dec. 1941–31 Aug. 1942, 667.

18. Summary, 10 August, Graybook, vol. 1, 7 Dec. 1941–31 Aug. 1942, 829; USS *Curtiss*, War Diary, 12, 19, 22 Aug. 1942, vol. 1, box 76; Daily Distribution of Operating Forces, 21 Aug. 1942, Cincpac War Diary, vol. 2, box 8; both in World War II War Diaries, RG 38, NARA Archives II; Vandegrift to Ghormley, 12 Aug. 1942, folder 1-6, Corresp. 1942 April–September, box 1, McCain Papers, HISU; Frank, *Guadalcanal*, 127; "The AAF in the South Pacific," 75; Lundstrom, *First Team and Guadalcanal*, 95, 96.

19. Lundstrom, *Black Shoe Carrier Admiral*, 410–15; McCain to Harmon, 21 Aug. 1942, folder 1-6, Corresp. 1942 April–September, box 1, McCain Papers, HISU.

20. Lundstrom, *Black Shoe Carrier Admiral*, 418–19; USS *Curtiss*, War Diary, 20, 21, 22 Aug. 1942, vol. 1, box 76, World War II War Diaries, RG 38, NARA Archives II;

message 201118 Aug. 1942, Comairsopac to Curtiss, info. CTF 61, CTF 62, roll 22, Cincpac Dispatches and Message Traffic, RG 313, NARA Archives II; McCain to Ghormley, 21 Aug. 1942, folder 1-6, Corresp. 1942 April–September, box 1, McCain Papers, HISU.

21. Lundstrom, *Black Shoe Carrier Admiral*, 410–11, 426; Frank, *Guadalcanal*, 159–72.

22. USS *Curtiss*, War Diary, 23 Aug. 1942, vol. 1, box 76, World War II War Diaries, RG 38, NARA Archives II; Lundstrom, *Black Shoe Carrier Admiral*, 427–31. John Lundstrom and James Sawruk provided specific information on Lieutenant Riley and the 23 August VP searches.

23. USS *Curtiss*, War Diary, 24 Aug. 1942, Enclosure (A), vol. 1, box 76, World War II War Diaries, RG 38, NARA Archives II; message 240020 Aug. 1942, Comsopac to CTF 63, info. CTF 61, 62, Cincpac, roll 22, Cincpac Dispatches and Message Traffic, RG 313, NARA Archives II; Lundstrom, *Black Shoe Carrier Admiral*, 435–39, 456.

24. Lundstrom, *Black Shoe Carrier Admiral*, 435, 436, 444.

25. Message 240300 Aug. 1942, CTF 63 to CTF 61, CTF 62, Comsopac; message 240365 Aug. 1942, Mackinac to Comairsopac; message 240703 Aug. 1942; Comairsopac to CTF 61; all in roll 22, Cincpac Dispatches and Message Traffic, RG 313, NARA Archives II; Lundstrom, *Black Shoe Carrier Admiral*, 435–38, 442–45.

26. Lundstrom, *Black Shoe Carrier Admiral*, 444–55.

27. USS *Curtiss*, War Diary, 24 Aug. 1942, vol. 1, box 76, World War II War Diaries, RG 38, NARA Archives II; "The AAF in the South Pacific," 70.

28. Lundstrom, *Black Shoe Carrier Admiral*, 453, 455–57; USS *Curtiss*, War Diary, 25 Aug. 1942, Enclosure (A), vol. 1, box 76, World War II War Diaries, RG 38, NARA Archives II; message 260231 Aug. 1942, Comsopac to CTF 63, roll 22, Cincpac Dispatches and Message Traffic, RG 313, NARA Archives II.

29. USS *Curtiss*, War Diary, 25, 26 Aug. 1942, Enclosure (A), vol. 1, box 76, World War II War Diaries, RG 38, NARA Archives II; Lundstrom, *Black Shoe Carrier Admiral*, 455–56.

30. USS *Curtiss*, War Diary, 27–29 Aug. 1942, vol. 1, box 76, World War II War Diaries, RG 38, NARA Archives II; message 270350 Aug. 1942, Comsopac to Cincpac, Graybook, vol. 1, 7 Dec. 1941–31 Aug. 1942, 662.

31. USS *Curtiss*, War Diary, 29 Aug. 1942, vol. 1, box 76, World War II War Diaries, RG 38, NARA Archives II; Lundstrom, *Black Shoe Carrier Admiral*, 468–69; Samuel Eliot Morison, *History of United States Naval Operations in World War II*, vol. 5, *The Struggle for Guadalcanal, August 1942–February 1943* (Boston: Little, Brown and Company, 1950), 121; message 050815 Sept. 1942, CTG 63.5 to Comairsopac; message 061120 Sept. 1942, Comsopac to Comairsopac; both in roll 23, Cincpac Dispatches and Message Traffic, RG 313, NARA Archives II; Japanese Shipping Losses.

32. Lundstrom, *Black Shoe Carrier Admiral*, 471–74, 483; message 302203 Aug. 1942, Comairsopac to McFarland, roll 23, Cincpac Dispatches and Message Traffic, RG 313, NARA Archives II.

33. USS *Curtiss*, War Diary, 30, 31 Aug. 1942, vol. 1, box 76, World War II War Diaries, RG 38, NARA Archives II; Gilbert, *Leader Born*, 92–93.

34. Message 310402 Aug. 1942, Comairsopac to Cincpac, Comsopac, roll 23, Cincpac Dispatches and Message Traffic, RG 313, NARA Archives II.

35. Lundstrom, *First Team and Guadalcanal*, 173; Frank, *Guadalcanal*, 214–16; message 301010 Aug. 1942, Forrestal to SecNav, Cominch, Gates, Graybook, vol. 1, 7 Dec. 1941–31 Aug. 1942, 664.

36. Message 060156 Sept. 1942, Comairsopac to Comsopac, roll 23, Cincpac Dispatches and Message Traffic, RG 313, NARA Archives II; McCain to Ghormley, 10 Sept. 1942, folder 1-4, Corresp. 1940–1941, box 1, McCain Papers, HISU; Lundstrom, *First Team and Guadalcanal*, 181–82.

37. Lundstrom, *First Team and Guadalcanal*, 182–83, 188; Frank, *Guadalcanal*, 229–31; message 110233 Sept. 1942, Comairsopac to Comgencactus, roll 24, Cincpac Dispatches and Message Traffic, RG 313, NARA Archives II. Gilbert, *Leader Born*, 85, mistakenly specifies that a Navy Douglas R4D flew McCain and Turner into Henderson.

38. Lundstrom, *First Team and Guadalcanal*, 193–201; message 130933 Sept. 1942, Comairsopac to Comsopac, roll 24, Cincpac Dispatches and Message Traffic, RG 313, NARA Archives II.

39. Lundstrom, *First Team and Guadalcanal*, 188–90; message 100425 Sept. 1942, Cincpac to Cominch, Comsopac, roll 24, Cincpac Dispatches and Message Traffic, RG 313, NARA Archives II.

40. Message 102355 Sept. 1942, Comairsopac to All Taskforcoms; message 110010 Sept. 1942, Comairsopac to All Taskforcoms; message 110130 Sept. 1942, Guadalcanal to Comsopac, Comairsopac; message 112157 Sept. 1942, Cincpac to Cominch; message 111028 Sept. 1942, Comairsopac to *Mackinac*; message 120228 Sept. 1942, Comairsopac to All Ships, Comgens; message 120329 Sept. 1942, Comairsopac to All Ships, Comgens; message 121001 Sept. 1942, ComTF63 to ComTF61; all in roll 24, Cincpac Dispatches and Message Traffic, RG 313, NARA Archives II; *Wings at War, No. 3: Pacific Counterblow*, 31, http://www.ibiblio.org/hyperwar/AAF/WW/WW-3-2.html.

41. Message 130302 Sept. 1942, Plane 48, Flight 35 to Curtiss and All Ships Sopac; message 140040 Sept. 1942, Comairsopac to All Ships, TFs; message 140115 Sept. 1942, Comairsopac to Comsopac, CTF 61; message 151134 Sept. 1942, Comairsopac to Cincpac; all in roll 24, Cincpac Dispatches and Message Traffic, RG 313, NARA Archives II; Lundstrom, *Black Shoe Carrier Admiral*, 332, 477; Lundstrom, *First Team and Guadalcanal*, 220–22.

42. Lundstrom, *First Team and Guadalcanal*, 222–29.

43. Lt. C. C. Colt, memo, 15 Sept. 1942, untitled folder 2 of 2, Misc. memos, reports, etc., July–Sept. 1942, box 1, Comairsopac Records (Blue 242), RG 313, NARA Archives II; message 290607 Aug. 1942, Comairsopac to Comsopac, roll 22, Cincpac Dispatches and Message Traffic, RG 313, NARA Archives II.

44. McCain to Vandegrift and Geiger, 14 Sept. 1942, folder 1-6, Corresp. 1942 April–September, box 1, McCain Papers, HISU (emphasis in original).

45. Reynolds, *Towers*, 401; Lundstrom, *Black Shoe Carrier Admiral*, 483.

46. Reynolds, *Towers*, 401; Lundstrom, *Black Shoe Carrier Admiral*, 483, 487; Conference Notes, 7 Sept. 1942, Graybook, vol. 2, 1 Sept. 1942–31 Dec. 1942, 1027; message

091844 Sept. 1942, Com 12 to Comsopac, roll 24, Cincpac Dispatches and Message Traffic, RG 313, NARA Archives II.

47. Reynolds, *Towers*, 402.

48. Message 141301 Sept. 1942, Comairsopac to Comsopac; message 141807 Sept. 1942, BuPers to Comairsopac; message 142007 Sept. 1942, BuPers to Comairpac; message 152315 Sept. 1942, Cincpac to Comsopac; message 160429 Sept. 1942, Comairwing 1 to Comairsopac; message 171252, Sept. 1942, Comairsopac to CTF 17; all in roll 24; message 201133 Sept. 1942, Comsopac to Cincpac, roll 25; all in Cincpac Dispatches and Message Traffic, RG 313, NARA Archives II.

49. Lundstrom, *First Team and Guadalcanal*, 236, 238–39; message 251957 Sept. 1942, Comairpac to Cominch, roll 25, Cincpac Dispatches and Message Traffic, RG 313, NARA Archives II.

50. Lundstrom, *Black Shoe Carrier Admiral*, 508–9; Gilbert, *Leader Born*, 99; McCain to Vandegrift, 20 Sept. 1942, folder 1-6, Corresp. 1942 April–September, box 1, McCain Papers, HISU; Geiger to McCain, 19 Sept. 1942, Secret No. 4, folder 1 of 2, box 2, Comairsopac Records (Blue 242), RG 313, NARA Archives II.

51. Message 220300 Sept. 1942, Comsopac to Cincpac; message 230852 Sept. 1942, *Curtiss* to Cincpac; message 240110 Sept. 1942, Suva to White Poppy; message 241848 Sept. 1942, Suva to Canton; message 250727 Sept. 1942, Cincpac to Palmyra; message 272013 Sept. 1942, Cincpac to Cominch; all in roll 25, Cincpac Dispatches and Message Traffic, RG 313, NARA Archives II; Lundstrom, *Black Shoe Carrier Admiral*, 485, 487.

52. *New York Times*, 16, 20 Sept. 1942; *Time*, 28 Sept. 1942, 57, 12 Oct. 1942, 6–8, 2 Nov. 1942, 10.

53. Conference Notes, 27 Sept. 1942, Graybook, vol. 2, 1 Sept. 1942–31 Dec. 1942, 1046; Lundstrom, *First Team and Guadalcanal*, 328.

54. Lisle A. Rose, *Power at Sea*, vol. 2, *The Breaking Storm, 1919–1945* (Columbia: University of Missouri Press, 2007), 253–54; David C. Evans and Mark R. Peattie, *Kaigun: Strategy, Tactics, and Technology in the Imperial Japanese Navy, 1887–1941* (Annapolis, MD: Naval Institute Press, 1997), 499–500.

55. Gerald E. Wheeler, *Kinkaid of the Seventh Fleet: A Biography of Admiral Thomas C. Kinkaid, U.S. Navy* (Washington, DC: Naval Historical Center, 1995), 271–73; Douglas V. Smith, *Carrier Battles: Command Decision in Harm's Way* (Annapolis, MD: Naval Institute Press, 2006), 175–76, 179; Michael A. Palmer, *Command at Sea: Naval Command and Control since the Sixteenth Century* (Cambridge, MA: Harvard University Press, 2005), 16–17.

Chapter Five. The War in Washington

1. Message 272013 Sept. 1942, Cincpac to Cominch, roll 25, Cincpac Dispatches and Message Traffic, RG 313, NARA Archives II; Ghormley to McCain, 21 Sept. 1942, McCain Personnel File, NPRC; Lundstrom, *Black Shoe Carrier Admiral*, 485, 488.

2. Gilbert, *Leader Born*, 103, 107; Crichton, "Navy Air Boss," 24; U.S. Naval Air Station, San Diego, California, War Diary, October 1, 1942–October 31, 1942, 1 Oct.

1942; Report of Physical Exam, 21 Sept. 1942; Application for Transportation for Dependents, 21 Oct. 1942, both in McCain Personnel File, NPRC; 2 Oct. 1942 entry, folder 4, 7 Jan.–2 Oct. 1942, Diaries, box 1, Papers of John H. Towers, Manuscript Division, Library of Congress, Washington, DC (hereafter cited as Towers Papers, MDLC).

3. BuAer World War II Admin. History, 2: 188–91; Julius Augustus Furer, *Administration of the Navy Department in World War II* (Washington, DC: Department of the Navy, 1959), 382.

4. Trimble, *Moffett*, 66–81; Wildenberg, *Billy Mitchell's War with the Navy*, 30–82.

5. Trimble, *Moffett*, 7–8, 10, 134–40, 190–92.

6. Reynolds, *Towers*, 403.

7. *New York Times*, 14 Oct. 1942; Frank Knox (SecNav), Distinguished Service Medal citation, 30 Oct. 1942, McCain Personnel File, NPRC.

8. Reynolds, *Towers*, 289–93, 302–35, 346–51.

9. Ibid., 356.

10. Furer, *Administration of the Navy Department in World War II*, 364; Geoffrey L. Rossano, *Stalking the U-Boat: U.S. Navy Aviation in Europe during World War I* (Gainesville: University Press of Florida, 2010), 29, 74–75.

11. Reynolds, *Towers*, 357–60.

12. BuAer World War II Admin. History, 2:58–64.

13. Reynolds, *Towers*, 375–76; BuAer World War II Admin. History, 3:94–95.

14. BuAer World War II Admin. History, 3:95–97.

15. Reynolds, *Towers*, 400; BuAer World War II Admin. History, Summary, 1:77–78; BuAer World War II Admin. History, 6:259–60.

16. BuAer World War II Admin. History, 6:260–61.

17. Ibid., 91–93.

18. Ibid., 681–82; Trimble, *Wings for the Navy*, 221–22.

19. BuAer World War II Admin. History, 6:685–91.

20. Furer, *Administration of the Navy Department in World War II*, 367–68, 370–74; BuAer World War II Admin. History, Summary, 1:446.

21. ChiefBuPers to McCain, 24 Nov. 1942; Randall Jacobs (ChiefBuPers) to McCain, 5 Jan. 1943, with attachments; both in McCain Personnel File, NPRC.

22. Graybook, vol. 3, 1 Jan. 1943–30 June 1943, 1276, 1370; Towers to Roy Grumman, 13 Jan. 1943, Towers Personal File, Correspondence, folder 3, box 3, Towers Papers, MDLC; E. B. Potter, *Nimitz* (Annapolis, MD: Naval Institute Press, 1976), 214–16; *New York Times*, 6 Feb. 1943.

23. Potter, *Nimitz*, 216; McCain and Salter, *Faith of My Fathers*, 31.

24. Randall Jacobs (ChiefBuPers) to McCain, 5 Jan. 1943, with attachments, McCain Personnel File, NPRC; Notes on the Conference held at Noumea, January 23, 1943, Graybook, vol. 3, 1 Jan. 1943–30 June 1943, 1343–48; Reynolds, *Towers*, 417.

25. Randall Jacobs (ChiefBuPers) to McCain, 5 Jan. 1943, with attachments, McCain Personnel File, NPRC; Graybook, vol. 3, 1 Jan. 1943–30 June 1943, 1352, 1354.

26. Furer, *Administration of the Navy Department in World War II*, 369; BuAer World War II Admin. History, 5:71–90.

27. Chief BuAer to VCNO, 24 March 1943, Aer-PL-51-DSC, A1-1/P16 A16-1, vol. 4, box 8, Bureau of Aeronautics Confidential Correspondence, 1922–1944, Record Group 72, NARA Archives II (hereafter cited as BuAer Confid. Corresp., 1922–1944, RG 72, NARA Archives II); BuAer World War II Admin. History, 5:141–47.

28. BuAer World War II Admin. History, 6:255–61; Reynolds, *Towers*, 304; Swanborough and Bowers, *United States Navy Aircraft*, 166–68; *New York Times*, 10 Feb. 1941; E. T. Wooldridge, ed., *Carrier Warfare in the Pacific: An Oral History Collection* (Washington, DC: Smithsonian Institution Press, 1993), 103–4.

29. *New York Times*, 15 Jan. 1943; BuAer World War II Admin. History, Summary, 2:34–37; Wooldridge, ed., *Carrier Warfare in the Pacific*, 103.

30. Reynolds, *Fast Carriers*, 59; Swanborough and Bowers, *United States Navy Aircraft*, 238–39.

31. BuAer World War II Admin. History, 8:42–55.

32. Ibid., 69–79; Towers to McCain, 2 May 1943, Towers Personal File, Correspondence, folder 3, box 3, Towers Papers, MDLC; Reynolds, *Towers*, 414–15.

33. BuAer World War II Admin. History, 6:244–49.

34. Reynolds, *Towers*, 387–93; BuAer World War II Admin. History, 17:73–74, 92; Trimble, *Wings for the Navy*, 248–49.

35. Trimble, *Wings for the Navy*, 186–204, 258–64; Reynolds, *Towers*, 382.

36. Fahrney, "History of Pilotless Aircraft and Guided Missiles," 383–84.

37. Ibid., 385–88.

38. Reynolds, *Towers*, 359–60, 379, 402; Furer, *Administration of the Navy Department in World War II*, 384; Newton and Rea, *Wings of Gold*, 21–23.

39. *New York Times*, 21 March 1943; BuAer World War II Admin. History, 12:224–26.

40. McCain to Towers, 11 March 1943, Towers Personal File, Correspondence, folder 3, box 3, Towers Papers, MDLC; BuAer World War II Admin. History, 12:226–29.

41. Chief BuAer to SecNav, 9 Dec. 1942, Aer-A-MAO'D QR8 EN11, file EN 11 42&43, box 478, BuAer Confid. Corresp., 1922–1944, RG 72, NARA Archives II; BuAer World War II Admin. History, 12:55–65; Bureau of Naval Personnel, Administrative History: Women's Reserve, vol. 1 (Washington, DC: Historical Section, Bureau of Naval Personnel, no date), 6–7 (hereafter cited as BuPers Admin. History: Women's Reserve).

42. BuAer World War II Admin. History, 12:65–67; BuPers Admin. History: Women's Reserve, 1:7.

43. BuAer World War II Admin. History, 12:65–67.

44. Reynolds, *Towers*, 380, 400; BuAer World War II Admin. History, Summary, 2:238–41; BuAer World War II Admin. History, 19:10.

45. Rear Adm. Harry C. Train to ChiefBuAer, 3 Oct. 1942, Op-16-X A3-1/EN11 (SCA8-1, Serial 01623316); McCain to DNI, 26 Oct. 1942, Aer-PL-71-MKB/ERT EN11, both in file EN 11 42&43, box 478, BuAer Confid. Corresp., 1922–1944, RG 72, NARA Archives II.

46. BuAer World War II Admin. History, 19:10–12.

47. BuAer World War II Admin. History, 11:95–111, 130; ChiefBuAer to Cdr., Air Force Atlantic Fleet, 4 March 1943, Aer-PL-3-LG (A16-O-Allocations FF13-7), vol. 3, file A16, box 180, BuAer Confid. Corresp., 1922–1944, RG 72, NARA Archives II.

48. BuAer World War II Admin. History, 11:128–29.

49. Ibid., 111–14, 124, 126; Newton and Rea, *Wings of Gold*, 31–37.

50. Grossnick, ed., *United States Naval Aviation, 1910–1995*, 30, 121, 127; "Patuxent River," http://www.globalsecurity.org/military/facility/patuxent-river.htm, accessed 9 Aug. 2012; BuAer World War II Admin. History, 10:55–57.

51. Reynolds, *Towers*, 394, 412; BuAer World War II Admin. History, 3:61–65.

52. Arthur B. Ferguson, *The Antisubmarine Command* [USAF Historical Study 107] (Washington, DC: Historical Division, Assistant Chief of Air Staff, Intelligence, 1945), 57–58, http://www.afhra.af.mil/shared/media/document/AFD-09055–043 .pdf, accessed 20 Feb. 2014; BuAer World War II Admin. History, 3:99–101; Daniel F. Harrington, "The Missing Man: Joseph McNarney and Air Force Leadership," draft chapter excerpt, 1–3 (courtesy of the author). I am indebted to retired Air Force historians Harrington and George Cully for information about this and other wartime interservice controversies.

53. BuAer World War II Admin. History, 3:97, 102–3; Ferguson, *Antisubmarine Command*, 68–69; Harrington, "Missing Man," draft chapter excerpt, 4; Ladislas Farago, *The Tenth Fleet* (New York: Ivan Obolensky, Inc., 1962), 163–68.

54. King, memo to Marshall, 23 May 1943, 001015, folder 23 Gen. Marshall/Adm. King—A/S Air, box 38, 00 file, Office files of the CNO, 1941–1946, RG 38, NARA Archives II; BuAer World War II Admin. History, 3:97, 104–6 (emphasis in original).

55. Larry I. Bland, ed., *The Papers of George Catlett Marshall* (Baltimore: Johns Hopkins University Press, 1996), vol. 4, 7–9.

56. BuAer World War II Admin. History, 3:65, 106–8; Gardner, memo to King, 10 June 1943, in BuAer World War II Admin. History, 3:196–97.

57. King, memo for Chief of Staff, U.S. Army, 14 June 1943, FF1/A16–3(9), serial 001177; Marshall, memo to King, 15 June 1943; King, memo to Marshall, 19 June 1943, serial no. 001216; Marshall, memo to King, 28 June 1943; King, memo to Marshall, 3 July 1943; all in folder 23 Gen. Marshall/Adm. King—A/S Air, box 38, 00 file, Office files of the CNO, 1941–1946, RG 38, NARA Archives II; Harrington, "Missing Man," draft chapter excerpt, 7–8.

58. Harrington, "Missing Man," draft chapter excerpt, 10–13.

Chapter Six. Washington and the Pacific

1. World War II Administrative History, Office of the Deputy Chief of Naval Operations DCNO (Air) (Washington, DC: Historical Section, Office of the Chief of Naval Operations, 1945), 1:19–32 (hereafter cited as DCNO [Air] World War II Admin. History).

2. Ibid., 41–42; Reynolds, *Towers*, 373; Albion, *Makers of Naval Policy*, 533–35.

3. Reynolds, *Towers*, 378; Albion, *Makers of Naval Policy*, 536–37; DCNO (Air) World War II Admin. History, 1: 52–53.

4. DCNO (Air) World War II Admin. History, 1:61–67. See also Jeffrey G. Barlow, *From Hot War to Cold: The U.S. Navy and National Security Affairs, 1945–1955* (Stanford, CA: Stanford University Press, 2009), 18–23.

5. Albion, *Makers of Naval Policy*, 536–38; DCNO (Air) World War II Admin. History, 1:56–58, 64–65; DCNO (Air) World War II Admin. History, 14:28–29 (emphases in original).

6. DCNO (Air) World War II Admin. History, 1:74–87; 14:29–30.

7. BuAer World War II Admin. History, Appendix, 2:383.

8. Ibid., 384–86; BuAer World War II Admin. History, Summary, 1:86; BuAer World War II Admin. History, 3:18.

9. House Committee on Naval Affairs, Naval Aviation Report, 21 March 1944, EN 11, vol. 1, Jan. 1, 1944–May 10, 1944, box 487, file EN 11, BuAer Confid. Corresp., 1922–1944, RG 72, NARA Archives II; Clark G. Reynolds, "Admiral Ernest J. King and the Strategy for Victory in the Pacific," in *Eagle, Shield and Anchor: Readings in American Naval History*, ed. James C. Bradford (New York: American Heritage Custom Publishing Group, 1993), 233–34; Reynolds, *Fast Carriers*, 41; Buell, *Master of Sea Power*, 348.

10. Reynolds, *Fast Carriers*, 42; Knox to McCain, 6 Aug. 1943; Randall Jacobs (ChiefBuPers) to King, 6 Aug. 1943; Report of Physical Examination, 17 March 1944; all in McCain Personnel File, NPRC; Buell, *Master of Sea Power*, 347.

11. BuAer World War II Admin. History, 2:72–73; Buell, *Master of Sea Power*, 352; Reynolds, *Towers*, 432; *New York Times*, 21 Aug. 1943.

12. Buell, *Master of Sea Power*, 346–47; Reynolds, *Towers*, 431. A synopsis of the Yarnell report is in DCNO (Air) World War II Admin. History, 1:88–104.

13. Reynolds, *Towers*, 421, 432, 440, 497; Reynolds, *Fast Carriers*, 47–48.

14. Buell, *Master of Sea Power*, 348.

15. Ibid., 348–50.

16. Ibid., 351–52.

17. DCNO (Air) World War II Admin. History, 1:108–10 (emphases in original).

18. Ibid., 369.

19. Crichton, "Navy Air Boss," 24; *New York Times*, 30 Aug. 1943.

20. U.S. Congress, House, *Proposal to Establish a Single Department of Armed Forces, Hearings before the Select Committee on Post-War Military Policy*, 78th Cong., 2d sess. (Washington, DC: Government Printing Office, 1944), 238–40; Forrestal to Nimitz, 9 July 1944, James V. Forrestal Papers, Seeley G. Mudd Manuscript Library, Princeton University, http://findingaids.princeton.edu/MC051/c02852.pdf, accessed 2 Nov. 2016 (hereafter cited as Forrestal Papers, MMLPU).

21. DCNO (Air) World War II Admin. History, 1:116–20, 132–33; Furer, *Administration of the Navy Department*, 165; Reynolds, *Fast Carriers*, 69.

22. BuAer World War II Admin. History, Summary, 2:268–69; BuAer World War II Admin. History, 3:34–42.

23. *New York Times*, 2 Sept. 1943; Randall Jacobs (Chief BuPers) to McCain, 8 Oct. 1943; P. V. Mercer (for Cincpac) to McCain, 25 Oct. 1943; both in McCain Personnel File, NPRC; 23, 26 Oct. 1943 entries, folder 5, 23 Aug. 1943–1 Jan. 1944, Diaries, box 1, Towers Papers, MDLC; Reynolds, *Towers*, 443.

24. McCain to Randall Jacobs (Chief BuPers), 25 Jan. 1944; Jacobs to McCain, 26 Jan. 1944; Nimitz to McCain, 10 Feb. 1944; all in McCain Personnel File, NPRC; Reynolds, *Towers*, 464.

25. BuAer World War II Admin. History, Summary, 1:88–89, 590–92.

26. Reynolds, *Fast Carriers*, 130, 135, 229, 458; Reynolds, *Towers*, 428–29, 441, 459, 464; BuAer World War II Admin. History, 5:204–5; BuAer World War II Admin. History, 2:98.

27. BuAer World War II Admin. History, Summary, 1:89–93, 95, 590, 592, 596–97, 600–601.

28. BuAer World War II Admin. History, 5:220–21; BuAer World War II Admin. History, Summary, 1:88, 96–97.

29. BuAer World War II Admin. History, Summary, 1:92–93, 95, 597, 600–601; BuAer World War II Admin. History, 5:207.

30. BuAer World War II Admin. History, Summary, 1:642–45; Reynolds, *Fast Carriers*, 129–30; Vern A. Miller, "Our Coral Carriers Helped Turn the Tide of Battle," http://www .wartimepress.com/archive-article.asp?TID=This%20is%20CASU&MID=68&q =114&FID=746, accessed 26 Nov. 2012.

31. BuAer World War II Admin. History, Summary, 1:97, 617–22; 2:47; BuAer World War II Admin. History, 2:98, 107–8; BuAer World War II Admin. History, 5:229–33.

32. BuAer World War II Admin. History, Summary, 1:95–96.

33. Reynolds, *Towers*, 446, 480–81; Reynolds, *Fast Carriers*, 136, 149–50, 236. Frederick Sherman was not related to Forrest Sherman.

34. Reynolds, *Fast Carriers*, 96–101, 143.

35. Ibid., 70, 77, 88–89, 93–96, 101–5, 127–28, 133–35; Reynolds, *Towers*, 468.

36. Reynolds, *Fast Carriers*, 71, 74, 110, 125, 127–28, 136–41, 145; Craig L. Symonds, "Mitscher and the Mystery of Midway," *Naval History* 26 (June 2012): 46–52. The most recent biography of Mitscher is Paolo E. Coletta, *Admiral Marc A. Mitscher and U.S. Naval Aviation* (Lewiston, NY: Edwin Mellen Press, 1997).

37. Reynolds, *Towers*, 452–54, 464, 466; Forrestal to Nimitz, 9 July 1944, Forrestal Papers, MMLPU.

38. Reynolds, *Fast Carriers*, 232–33, 385–86.

39. R. T. Lyman Jr. (by direction ChiefBuPers) to McCain, 4 March 1944; Randall Jacobs (ChiefBuPers) to McCain, 6 March 1944; both in McCain Personnel File, NPRC; Ewing, *Thach Weave*, 37–39, 64–78, 93.

40. Ewing, *Thach Weave*, 108–9; *Reminiscences of Admiral John Smith Thach, U.S. Navy (Retired)* (Annapolis, MD: Naval Institute Press, 1977), 2 vols., 1:310–12, 318.

41. Randall Jacobs (ChiefBuPers) to McCain, 11 May 1944; Jacobs to McCain, 16 May 1944; both in McCain Personnel File, NPRC; ComThird Fleet, War Diary, 15 June 1944; Reynolds, *Towers*, 473; Ewing, *Thach Weave*, 112.

42. Message 251233 May 1944, Com5thFlt to Indianapolis, etc., roll 122, Cincpac Dispatches and Message Traffic, RG 313, NARA Archives II; USS *Indianapolis*, War Diary, 26 May, 2 June 1944; Barrett Tillman, *Clash of the Carriers: The True Story of the Marianas Turkey Shoot of World War II* (New York: NAL Caliber, 2005), 16, 51; Samuel Eliot Morison, *History of United States Naval Operations in World War II*, vol. 8, *New Guinea and the Marianas, March 1944–August 1944* (Boston: Little, Brown and Company, 1953), 158–59.

43. Morison, *New Guinea and the Marianas*, 158–59, 233; Tillman, *Clash of the Carriers*, 51, 301–5; W. D. Dickson, *The Battle of the Philippine Sea* (London: Ian Allan Ltd., 1975), 186–87.

44. USS *Indianapolis*, War Diary, 3–9 June 1944; Timothy S. Wolters, *Information at Sea: Shipboard Command and Control in the U.S. Navy from Mobile Bay to Okinawa* (Baltimore: Johns Hopkins University Press, 2013), 175, 186–87, 195–201, 204–13; World War II Administrative History, Office of the Deputy Chief of Naval Operations DCNO (Air), History of Naval Fighter Direction (Washington, DC: Aviation History Unit, Office of the Chief of Naval Operations, 1946), 1:139–46, 163–65, 191–99, 212–14; Carrier Combat Information Center Doctrine, 14 May 1944, folder A2–11(5) Air Pac Letters, box 1, Commander 2nd Carrier Task Force—Administrative Messages, Operation Plans, Action Reports, Logs, Award Recommendations (Blue 627) 1944–1945, Records of Naval Operating Forces, Record Group 313, National Archives and Records Administration, Archives II, College Park, MD (hereafter cited as Com 2nd Carrier TF (Blue 627), RG 313, NARA Archives II); Thach *Reminiscences*, 1:332–33.

45. Tillman, *Clash of the Carriers*, 39, 50–51, 65–66, 76–77, 101–2; Morison, *New Guinea and the Marianas*, 179–83; Gilbert, *Leader Born*, 123.

46. John Prados, *Combined Fleet Decoded: The Secret History of American Intelligence and the Japanese Navy in World War II* (New York: Random House, 1995), 561, 572; John Prados, *Storm over Leyte: The Philippine Invasion and the Destruction of the Japanese Navy* (New York: NAL Caliber, 2016), 74.

47. Tillman, *Clash of the Carriers*, 48–49; Dickson, *Philippine Sea*, 48–50, 53, 55, 62, 63, 70; Morison, *New Guinea and the Marianas*, 242; message 170314 June 1944, Cincpac to Com5thFleet, roll 129, Cincpac Dispatches and Message Traffic, RG 313, NARA Archives II.

48. Dickson, *Philippine Sea*, 77–78, 80; Tillman, *Clash of the Carriers*, 88–93, 96–97.

49. Tillman, *Clash of the Carriers*, 100–101, 107–8; Reynolds, *Fast Carriers*, 187–89.

50. Tillman, *Clash of the Carriers*, 108–9, 119, 125–31, 135–36, 139, 146–60, 162–82, 196, 199, 322; Dickson, *Philippine Sea*, 108, 119, 121; Reynolds, *Fast Carriers*, 192–93.

51. Tillman, *Clash of the Carriers*, 197, 201, 204; Dickson, *Philippine Sea*, 140–41.

52. Tillman, *Clash of the Carriers*, 207–9, 212–14, 219, 238–62, 276.

53. Ibid., 265–69, 276–84; Reynolds, *Fast Carriers*, 202–4, 238; Reeves to McCain, 26 June 1944, McCain Personnel File, NPRC; message 211108 June 1944, Spruance to CTF58; message 222117 June 1944, Halsey to Spruance; both in roll 130, Cincpac Dispatches and Message Traffic, RG 313, NARA Archives II; USS *Indianapolis*, War Diary, 21 June 1944.

54. Reynolds, *Towers*, 476; Reynolds, *Fast Carriers*, 205–6; Ewing, *Thach Weave*, 118.

55. Message 181153, June 1944, Ballard to Com5thFleet; message 190359 June 1944, Spruance to CTG59.3; both in roll 129, Cincpac Dispatches and Message Traffic, RG 313, NARA Archives II; Tillman, *Clash of the Carriers*, 106–8, 276; Dickson, *Philippine Sea*, 95–96; Reynolds, *Fast Carriers*, 238; Coletta, *Mitscher*, 246.

56. Tillman, *Clash of the Carriers*, 54–63, 123–25, 202; Reynolds, *Fast Carriers*, 222–23; Ewing, *Thach Weave*, 170.

Chapter Seven. Task Force Command

1. Randall Jacobs (ChiefBuPers) to McCain, 25 July 1944; Nimitz to McCain, 9 Aug. 1944; both in McCain Personnel File, NPRC; 8 Aug. 1944 entry, folder 6, 1 Jan.–31 Dec. 1944, Diaries, box 1, Towers Papers, MDLC; Reynolds, *Fast Carriers*, 233, 238, 243.

2. Reynolds, *Fast Carriers*, 238; Minutes of Pacific Conference, Headquarters, Commander in Chief, Pacific Ocean Areas, First Day, 13 July 1944, folder Conferences, Minutes, 1944, box 10, Conference Materials, King Papers, NHHC.

3. Reynolds, *Fast Carriers*, 240–42, 244–46.

4. McCain to Chief BuPers, 28 July 1944, McCain Personnel File, NPRC; Gilbert, *Leader Born*, 127; transcripts FDR logs, 19–21 July 1944, in http://www.fdrlibrary .marist.edu/daybyday/daylog/july-21st-1944/, accessed 19 April 2017.

5. Reynolds, *Fast Carriers*, 236, 239; 8, 9, 13–16 Aug. 1944 entries, folder 6, 1 Jan.–31 Dec. 1944, Diaries, box 1, Towers Papers, MDLC; Montgomery C. Meigs, *Slide Rules and Submarines: American Scientists and Subsurface Warfare in World War II* (Washington, DC: National Defense University Press, 1990), 51–52, 58; Ewing, *Thach Weave*, 122–23.

6. Ewing, *Thach Weave*, 123–24; Barrett Tillman, with Henk van der Lugt, *VF-11/111 "Sundowners," 1942–45* (Oxford: Osprey Publishing Ltd., 2010), 28; Reminiscences of Admiral Noel A. M. Gayler, USN (Ret.), Annapolis, MD: U.S. Naval Institute, 1983–1984: 130–31 (hereafter cited as Gayler Reminiscences).

7. USS *Wasp*, War Diary, 18 Aug. 1944; USS *Lexington* Deck Log, 18 Aug. 1944, RG 24, NARA Archives II (courtesy of Michael Kern); Gilbert, *Leader Born*, 130–31. Theodore Taylor, *The Magnificent Mitscher* (New York: Norton, 1954), 247–48, mistakenly places the meeting at Majuro, but it is clear the *Lexington* lay at Eniwetok and not Majuro in late August.

8. USS *Wasp*, War Diary, 21, 26 Aug. 1944; Commander Third Fleet, War Diary, 22 July, 1, 8 Aug. 1944; message 180417 Aug. 1944, CTF 58 to Com3rdFleet, roll 149, Cincpac Dispatches and Message Traffic, RG 313, NARA Archives II; Reynolds, *Fast Carriers*, 243, 246; ComThird Fleet, Operation Plan No. 14-44, 1 Aug. 1944, Commander Western Pacific Task Forces & Commander Third Fleet, Op Plan 14-44 (1 of 2) folder, box 99, Com 2nd Carrier TF (Blue 627), RG 313, NARA Archives II.

9. Reynolds, *Fast Carriers*, 246–47; Hughes, *Bill Halsey*, 334; USS *Wasp*, War Diary, 29 Aug. 1944; Commander Third Fleet, War Diary, 24, 31 Aug. 1944; message 092147 Aug. 1944, Comservpac to NYPH, roll 145; message 250724 Aug. 1944, CTF38 to task groups, roll 151; both in Cincpac Dispatches and Message Traffic, RG 313, NARA Archives II; Commander Task Group 38.1 Operation Order No. 1-44, CTG 38.1-Op Order 1-44 folder, box 91, Com 2nd Carrier TF (Blue 627), RG 313, NARA Archives II.

10. Commander Third Fleet, War Diary, 30, 31 Aug. 1944; Commander Task Group Thirty-Eight Point One, Operations . . . 29 Aug.–28 Sept. 1944, Enclosure C, NWC Library; Ewing, *Thach Weave*, 122–23, 178; Tillman, with van der Lugt, *VF-11–111*, 29–30.

11. Commander Task Group Thirty-Eight Point One, War Diary, 6, 7, 8 Sept. 1944; Commander Task Group Thirty-Eight Point One, Operations . . . 29 Aug.–28 Sept. 1944, Enclosure A, NWC Library; Reynolds, *Fast Carriers*, 225, claimed that napalm was first used in the Marianas.

12. Commander Task Group Thirty-Eight Point One, War Diary, 9, 10, 11, 12, 13 Sept. 1944.

13. Ibid., 14, 15, 16 Sept. 1944; Commander Task Group Thirty-Eight Point One, Operations . . . 29 Aug.–28 Sept. 1944, Enclosure A, NWC Library; Reynolds, *Fast Carriers*, 249–50; summary TG-38.1, 14, 15 Sept. 1944, Graybook, vol. 5, 1 Jan. 1944–31 Dec. 1944, 2068.

14. USS *Hornet*, War Diary, 12 Sept. 1944; Commander Task Group Thirty-Eight Point One, Operations . . . 29 Aug.–28 Sept. 1944, Enclosure A, NWC Library; E. B. Potter, *Bull Halsey* (Annapolis, MD: Naval Institute Press, 1985), 277–78; messages 130230, 130300 Sept. 1944, Com3rdFleet to Cincpac; all in Graybook, vol. 5, 1 Jan. 1944–31 Dec. 1944, 2064.

15. Commander Task Group Thirty-Eight Point One, War Diary, 17, 18, 19, 20 Sept. 1944; USS *Wasp*, Action Report, 17 Sept. 1944; Commander Task Group Thirty-Eight Point One, Operations . . . 29 Aug.–28 Sept. 1944, Enclosure A, NWC Library.

16. Commander Task Group Thirty-Eight Point One, War Diary, 21 Sept. 1944; USS *Wasp*, Action Report, 21 Sept. 1944; Commander Task Group Thirty-Eight Point One, Operations . . . 29 Aug.–28 Sept. 1944, Enclosure A, NWC Library; Barrett Tillman, *Hellcat: The F6F in World War II* (Annapolis, MD: Naval Institute Press, 1979), 124–25; Towers to Pierre Towers, 21 Sept. 1944, Towers Personal File, Correspondence, folder 9, box 2, Towers Papers, MDLC; Japanese Shipping Losses.

17. Commander Task Group Thirty-Eight Point One, War Diary, 22 Sept. 1944; USS *Hornet*, Action Report, 21, 22 Sept. 1944; USS *Wasp*, Action Report, 21, 22 Sept. 1944; Commander Task Group Thirty-Eight Point One, Operations . . . 29 Aug.–28 Sept. 1944, Enclosure A, NWC Library; Japanese Shipping Losses.

18. Commander Task Group Thirty-Eight Point One, War Diary, 24–28 Sept. 1944; Commander Task Group Thirty-Eight Point One, Operations . . . 29 Aug.–28 Sept. 1944, Enclosures A, C, NWC Library; Reynolds, *Fast Carriers*, 251.

19. Commander Task Group Thirty-Eight Point One, Operations . . . 29 Aug.–28 Sept. 1944, Enclosure B, NWC Library; Tillman, *Clash of the Carriers*, 153, 188, 198–99; Richard W. Bates, "The Battle for Leyte Gulf, October 1944, Strategical and Tactical Analysis. Vol. 1, Preliminary Operations" (Newport, RI: Naval War College, 1953), 450.

20. Commander Task Group Thirty-Eight Point One, Operations . . . 29 Aug.–28 Sept. 1944, 5–6, 16–19, Enclosure B, NWC Library.

21. Ibid., 2–4, 7, 9–10, 15.

22. Samuel Eliot Morison, *History of United States Naval Operations in World War II*, vol. 12, *Leyte, June 1944–January 1945* (Boston: Little, Brown and Company, 1961), 428–29; Commander Task Group Thirty-Eight Point One, Operations . . . 29 Aug.–28 Sept. 1944, 11, NWC Library.

23. Reynolds, *Fast Carriers*, 248–49; Samuel Eliot Morison, *History of United States Naval Operations in World War II*, vol. 14, *Victory in the Pacific, 1945* (Boston: Little, Brown and Company, 1960), 4–5.

24. Reynolds, *Fast Carriers*, 248–49, 255–56; Potter, *Bull Halsey*, 279–80; Morison, *Leyte*, 57–58; ComThird Fleet, OpOrder 21-44, 3 Oct. 1944, folder A4-3(2), box 76, Com 2nd Carrier TF (Blue 627), RG 313, NARA Archives II.

25. Halsey to Nimitz, 6 Oct. 1944, folder Nimitz, Chester, Dec. 1943–1947, box 15, Special Correspondence, Papers of William F. Halsey, Manuscript Division, Library of Congress, Washington, DC (hereafter cited as Halsey Papers, MDLC); Reynolds, *Fast Carriers*, 247, 259; Commander Third Fleet, War Diary, 19 July 1944; Morison, *Leyte*, 424–28.

26. Morison, *Leyte*, 424–25; Commander 2nd Carrier Task Force, Task Group 38.1, Operation Order No. 2-44, 8 Oct. 1944, folder 38.1, OpOrder 2-44, box 90, Com 2nd Carrier TF (Blue 627), RG 313, NARA Archives II.

27. Reynolds, *Fast Carriers*, 253–54; Richard W. Bates, "The Battle for Leyte Gulf, October 1944, Strategical and Tactical Analysis. Vol. 2, Operations from 0719 October 17th until October 20th D-Day" (Newport, RI: Naval War College, 1955), 2: xl, 209.

28. Bates, "Battle for Leyte Gulf," 1:91–92; Commander Task Group Thirty-Eight Point One, Action Report, 2 Oct.–29 Oct. 1944, Enclosure A, 3, folder CTG 38.1, Action Report 2 Oct.–29 Oct. 1944, box 92, Com 2nd Carrier TF (Blue 627), RG 313, NARA Archives II; USS *Wasp*, Action Report, 2–10 Oct. 1944.

29. Bates, "Battle for Leyte Gulf," 1:96, 98–99, 101–2; Reynolds, *Fast Carriers*, 259–60.

30. Commander Task Group Thirty-Eight Point One, Action Report, 2 Oct.–29 Oct. 1944, Enclosure A, 5–6, folder CTG 38.1, Action Report 2 Oct.–29 Oct. 1944, box 92, Com 2nd Carrier TF (Blue 627), RG 313, NARA Archives II; USS *Wasp*, Action Report, 12 Oct. 1944, Fighting Squadron Fourteen, History, 2 Dec 1944, 11–12; David C. Evans, ed., *The Japanese Navy in World War II: In the Words of Former Japanese Naval Officers*, 2d ed. (Annapolis, MD: Naval Institute Press, 1986), 347.

31. Commander Task Group Thirty-Eight Point One, Action Report, 2 Oct.–29 Oct. 1944, Enclosure A, 6, folder CTG 38.1, Action Report 2 Oct.–29 Oct. 1944, box 92, Com 2nd Carrier TF (Blue 627), RG 313, NARA Archives II; USS *Wasp*, Action Report, 13 Oct. 1944; Bates, "Battle for Leyte Gulf," 1:106–7.

32. Commander Task Group Thirty-Eight Point One, Action Report, 2 Oct.–29 Oct. 1944, Enclosure A, 7, folder CTG 38.1, Action Report 2 Oct.–29 Oct. 1944, box 92, Com 2nd Carrier TF (Blue 627), RG 313, NARA Archives II. In Donald M. Goldstein and Katherine V. Dillon, eds., *Fading Victory: The Diary of Admiral Matome Ugaki, 1941–1945* (Pittsburgh: University of Pittsburgh Press, 1991), 469, Ugaki specifies that *Gingas* (P1Ys) and "land torpedo bombers" (Bettys) flew in raids on 12 October. Morison, *Leyte*, 95–98, details the salvage operation.

33. Commander Task Group Thirty-Eight Point One, Action Report, 2 Oct.–29 Oct. 1944, Enclosure A, 8, folder CTG 38.1, Action Report 2 Oct.–29 Oct. 1944, box 92, Com 2nd Carrier TF (Blue 627), RG 313, NARA Archives II; Bates, "Battle for Leyte Gulf," 1:114–15, 118–19.

34. Commander Task Group Thirty-Eight Point One, Action Report, 2 Oct.–29 Oct. 1944, Enclosure A, 8–10, folder CTG 38.1, Action Report 2 Oct.–29 Oct. 1944, box 92, Com 2nd Carrier TF (Blue 627), RG 313, NARA Archives II; USS *Hornet*, Action Report, 2 Oct.–27 Oct. 1944, Enclosure G, 422–26; Bates, "Battle for Leyte Gulf," 1:115–16.

35. Commander Task Group Thirty-Eight Point One, Action Report, 2 Oct.–29 Oct. 1944, Enclosure A, 9–10, folder CTG 38.1, Action Report 2 Oct.–29 Oct. 1944, box 92, Com 2nd Carrier TF (Blue 627), RG 313, NARA Archives II; USS *Wasp*, Action Report, 14 Oct. 1944. Ugaki, in Goldstein and Dillon, *Fading Victory*, 472, identified both Franceses and Bettys in the 14 October attack.

36. Commander Task Group Thirty-Eight Point One, Action Report, 2 Oct.–29 Oct. 1944, Enclosure A, 10–12, folder CTG 38.1, Action Report 2 Oct.–29 Oct. 1944, box 92, Com 2nd Carrier TF (Blue 627), RG 313, NARA Archives II.

37. Bates, "Battle for Leyte Gulf," 1:126–27, 132; Commander Task Group Thirty-Eight Point One, Action Report, 2 Oct.–29 Oct. 1944, Enclosure A, 12, folder CTG 38.1, Action Report 2 Oct.–29 Oct. 1944, box 92, Com 2nd Carrier TF (Blue 627), RG 313, NARA Archives II; Morison, *Leyte*, 103–4; Navy Cross citation, 24 Oct. 1946, McCain Personnel File, NPRC. For a thorough study of the *Houston* salvage operation, see John Grider Miller, *The Battle to Save the Houston, October 1944 to March 1945* (Annapolis, MD: Naval Institute Press, 1985), esp. 35–137.

38. Reynolds, *Fast Carriers*, 260; Bates, "Battle for Leyte Gulf," 1:450; Commander Task Group Thirty-Eight Point One, Action Report, 2 Oct.–29 Oct. 1944, Enclosure B, 1–5, 10–12, folder CTG 38.1, Action Report 2 Oct.–29 Oct. 1944, box 92, Com 2nd Carrier TF (Blue 627), RG 313, NARA Archives II.

39. Commander Task Group Thirty-Eight Point One, Action Report, 2 Oct.–29 Oct. 1944, Enclosure A, 12, folder CTG 38.1, Action Report 2 Oct.–29 Oct. 1944, box 92, Com 2nd Carrier TF (Blue 627), RG 313, NARA Archives II; Bates, "Battle for Leyte Gulf," 2:32–34, 37–38, 307.

40. Goldstein and Dillon, *Fading Victory*, 480; Reynolds, *Fast Carriers*, 220, 259–63.

41. Commander Task Group Thirty-Eight Point One, Action Report, 2 Oct.–29 Oct. 1944, Enclosure A, 12–13, folder CTG 38.1–Action Report 2 Oct.–29 Oct. 1944, box 92, Com 2nd Carrier TF (Blue 627), RG 313, NARA Archives II; Commander Carrier Air Group Fourteen, Aircraft Action Reports, 10–26 October 1944, 3.

42. Morison, *Leyte*, 130–56; Commander Task Group Thirty-Eight Point One, Action Report, 2 Oct.–29 Oct. 1944, Enclosure A, 13–14, Enclosure B, 6–8, folder CTG 38.1, Action Report 2 Oct.–29 Oct. 1944, box 92; Commander Second Carrier Task Force to Task Group Commanders, 24 Nov. 1944, Enclosure A, Diagram of Task Group Formation, folder A4-3 Operations (3 of 3), box 75; both in Com 2nd Carrier TF (Blue 627), RG 313, NARA Archives II.

43. Potter, *Bull Halsey*, 287; Commander Third Fleet, Action Report, 23–26 October 1944, Enclosure A, 4; Commander Task Group Thirty-Eight Point One, Action Report, 2 Oct.–29 Oct. 1944, Enclosure A, 14, folder CTG 38.1, Action Report 2 Oct.–29 Oct. 1944, box 92, Com 2nd Carrier TF (Blue 627), RG 313, NARA Archives II.

44. Message 232330 Oct. 1944, Com2ndCarTaskForPac to Cominch and others, Gray-book, vol. 5, 1 Jan. 1944–31 Dec. 1944, 2391; Gilbert, *Leader Born*, 155–56; message 230351 July 1944, Cincpac to CTF 58, Com5thFleet, roll 139; message 200036 Aug. 1944, Comairpac to CNO, roll 149; both in Cincpac Dispatches and Message Traffic, RG 313, NARA Archives II; Nimitz to King, 23 Oct. 1944, Personal Correspondence of Fleet Admiral Nimitz with Cominch, Series XV, box 121, Nimitz Papers, NHHC.

45. Reynolds, *Fast Carriers*, 262–63; Morison, *Leyte*, 169–76; Commander Third Fleet, Action Report, 23–26 October 1944, Enclosure A, 2, 6; Commander Task Group Thirty-Eight Point One, Action Report, 2 Oct.–29 Oct. 1944, Enclosure A, 14, folder CTG 38.1, Action Report 2 Oct.–29 Oct. 1944, box 92, Com 2nd Carrier TF (Blue 627), RG 313, NARA Archives II; Richard W. Bates, "The Battle for Leyte Gulf, October 1944, Strategical and Tactical Analysis, Vol. 5, Battle of Surigao Strait, October 24th–25th" (Newport, RI: Naval War College, 1958), 44, 46, 163–65, 168, 178. Morison, *Leyte*, 170, states that Halsey learned of the submarine contacts at 0630 on the twenty-third. Time discrepancies in the *Wasp* and other action reports are because TG-38.1 en route to Ulithi had lost an hour transiting from Item (Z-9) time zone east to King (Z-10) time zone.

46. Bates, "Battle for Leyte Gulf," 5:179; Reynolds, *Fast Carriers*, 264–66.

47. Reynolds, *Fast Carriers*, 267–68, 271–73.

48. Commander Task Group Thirty-Eight Point One, War Diary, 22–25 Oct. 1944; Commander Third Fleet, Action Report, 23–26 October 1944, Enclosure A, 33, 34. It is possible that McCain's group received Halsey's message an hour earlier and that in the confusion that morning recorded King (Z-10) times from the day before rather than Item (Z-9) times.

49. Commander Task Group Thirty-Eight Point One, War Diary, 25 Oct. 1944; Commander Third Fleet, Action Report, 23–26 October 1944, Enclosure A, 34; Commander Task Group Thirty-Eight Point One, Action Report, 2 Oct.–29 Oct. 1944, Enclosure A, 15, folder CTG 38.1, Action Report 2 Oct.–29 Oct. 1944, box 92, Com 2nd Carrier TF (Blue 627), RG 313, NARA Archives II; Reminiscences of Vice Admiral Gerald F. Bogan, U.S. Navy (Ret.), Annapolis, MD: U.S. Naval Institute, 1970/1986, 117 (hereafter cited as Bogan Reminiscences). Thach stated (*Reminiscences*, 1:381) that there were delays in receiving messages that day due to the volume of radio traffic.

50. Thach, *Reminiscences*, 1:381–86; Clark G. Reynolds, *On the Warpath in the Pacific: Admiral Jocko Clark and the Fast Carriers* (Annapolis: MD: Naval Institute Press, 2005), 234, 331–32.

51. Commander Third Fleet, Action Report, 23–26 October 1944, Enclosure A, 33; Potter, *Bull Halsey*, 302–4; Morison, *Leyte*, 330.

52. Commander Task Group Thirty-Eight Point One, War Diary, 25 Oct. 1944; Commander Task Group Thirty-Eight Point One, Action Report, 2 Oct.–29 Oct. 1944, Enclosure A, 16, Enclosure B, 9, folder CTG 38.1, Action Report 2 Oct.–29 Oct. 1944, box 92, Com 2nd Carrier TF (Blue 627), RG 313, NARA Archives II; Commander Torpedo Squadron Fourteen, Aircraft Action Reports, 25 Oct. 1944, 2–6;

Commander Carrier Air Group Eleven, Aircraft Action Reports, 25 Oct 1944, 166–71; USS *Hancock*, War Diary, 25 Oct. 1944; Morison, *Leyte*, 296–300, 309–10.

53. Commander Task Group Thirty-Eight Point One, War Diary, 25 Oct. 1944; Commander Task Group Thirty-Eight Point One, Action Report, 2 Oct.–29 Oct. 1944, Enclosure A, 16, Enclosure B, 9–10, 12, folder CTG 38.1, Action Report 2 Oct.–29 Oct. 1944, box 92, Com 2nd Carrier TF (Blue 627), RG 313, NARA Archives II; Commander Carrier Air Group Eleven, Aircraft Action Reports, 25 Oct 1944, 179–82, 302–8; Morison, *Leyte*, 296–300, 309–10.

54. Commander Task Group Thirty-Eight Point One, War Diary, 26 Oct. 1944; Commander Third Fleet, Action Report, 23–26 October 1944, Enclosure A, 44.

55. Commander Task Group Thirty-Eight Point One, War Diary, 26 Oct. 1944; Commander Task Group Thirty-Eight Point One, Action Report, 2 Oct.–29 Oct. 1944, Enclosure A, 18–19, Enclosure B, 9–10, 12, folder CTG 38.1, Action Report 2 Oct.–29 Oct. 1944, box 92, Com 2nd Carrier TF (Blue 627), RG 313, NARA Archives II; USS *Wasp*, Action Report, 26 Oct. 1944; Commander Torpedo Squadron Fourteen, Aircraft Action Reports, 25 Oct 1944, 16–17; Morison, *Leyte*, 311; Goldstein and Dillon, *Fading Victory*, 500.

56. USS *Wasp*, Action Report, 26 Oct. 1944; Commander Third Fleet, Action Report, 23–26 October 1944, Enclosure A, 62, 64, 66, 68; Commander Task Group Thirty-Eight Point One, War Diary, 26 Oct. 1944; Morison, *Leyte*, 300–307.

57. Commander Task Group Thirty-Eight Point One, Action Report, 2 Oct.–29 Oct. 1944, Enclosure A, 18–19, folder CTG 38.1, Action Report 2 Oct.–29 Oct. 1944, box 92, Com 2nd Carrier TF (Blue 627), RG 313, NARA Archives II; Commander Task Group Thirty-Eight Point One, War Diary, 28, 29 Oct. 1944; USS *Wasp*, Action Report, 26, 27 Oct. 1944.

58. Commander Task Group Thirty-Eight Point One, Action Report, 2 Oct.–29 Oct. 1944, 4–6, Enclosure F, folder CTG 38.1, Action Report 2 Oct.–29 Oct. 1944, box 92, Com 2nd Carrier TF (Blue 627), RG 313, NARA Archives II.

59. Reynolds, *Fast Carriers*, 278.

60. Bates, "Battle for Leyte Gulf," 2:30–32; Morison, *Leyte*, 175.

61. Reynolds, *Fast Carriers*, 278–80; Reynolds, *Towers*, 493; Hughes, *Bill Halsey*, 372–74, 404–7.

62. Reynolds, *Fast Carriers*, 282–83; Hughes, *Bill Halsey*, 373; Wheeler, *Kinkaid*, 405–6, 489.

63. Thach, *Reminiscences*, 1:381–86, 388.

Chapter Eight. Task Force 38

1. USS *Wasp*, War Diary, 30 Oct. 1944; USS *Lexington*, War Diary, 30, 31 Oct. 1944; Coletta, *Mitscher*, 292.

2. Reynolds, *Fast Carriers*, 286–87; Morison, *Leyte*, 341–43.

3. Reynolds, *Fast Carriers*, 287; Lundstrom, *Black Shoe Carrier Admiral*, 499–500.

4. Message 130338 Oct. 1944, Com3rdFlt to Cincpac; message 140445 Oct. 1944, Cincpoa to Com3rdFlt; message 260814 Oct. 1944, Com3rdFlt to Cincpoa; all in

Graybook, vol. 5, 1 Jan. 1944–31 Dec. 1944, 2098, 2112; John S. McCain, "So We Hit Them in the Belly, I," *Saturday Evening Post*, 14 July 1945, 12; Reynolds, *Fast Carriers*, 284, 288; Bates, "Battle for Leyte Gulf," 1:93, 5:47, 163.

5. Summary, 31 Oct., 1, 2 Nov. 1944, Graybook, vol. 5, 1 Jan. 1944–31 Dec. 1944, 2121–23; USS *Wasp*, War Diary, 2 Nov. 1944; Commander Task Force Thirty-Eight, War Diary, 1, 2 Nov. 1944; Morison, *Leyte*, 345–46.

6. Commander Task Force Thirty-Eight, War Diary, 3, 4, 5 Nov. 1944; Morison, *Leyte*, 347–48.

7. Morison, *Leyte*, 348; Goldstein and Dillon, *Fading Victory*, 507; Commander Task Force Thirty-Eight, War Diary, 5, 6 Nov. 1944; McCain, "So We Hit Them in the Belly, I," 12; Hughes, *Bill Halsey*, 378. *Nachi* tabular record of movement, 5 Nov. 1944, in www.combinedfleet.com/nachi_t.htm, accessed 4 April 2013; Japanese Shipping Losses.

8. Commander Task Force Thirty-Eight, War Diary, 5, 6 Nov. 1944.

9. Commander Task Force Thirty-Eight, Action Report, 30 October 1944–26 January 1945, Enclosure A, 13, box 92, Com 2nd Carrier TF (Blue 627), RG 313, NARA Archives II; Commander Task Force Thirty-Eight, War Diary, 8–9 Nov. 1944; message 280135 Oct. 1944, CTG 38.1 to Com 3rd Flt, CTF 38; message 280174 Oct. 1944, Com 3rd Flt to Comairpac; both in roll 174, Cincpac Dispatches and Message Traffic, RG 313, NARA Archives II; Carrier Air Group Fourteen History, 15 September 1943–29 November 1944, 2–3.

10. Commander Task Force Thirty-Eight, Action Report, 30 October 1944–26 January 1945, Enclosure A, 13–14; Tillman, *Hellcat*, 152; Commander Task Force Thirty-Eight, War Diary, 8–13 Nov. 1944; USS *Wasp*, Action Report, 11–13 Nov. 1944.

11. Commander Task Force Thirty-Eight, Action Report, 30 October 1944–26 January 1945, Enclosure E, 65; McCain to Halsey, 12 Nov. 1944, folder A1-Plans, Projects & Policies, box 74, Com 2nd Carrier TF (Blue 627), RG 313, NARA Archives II; message 200043 Nov. 1944, Cincpoa to Com3rdFlt, info Com2dCarTF, Graybook, vol. 5, 1 Jan. 1944–31 Dec. 1944, 2418; Reynolds, *Fast Carriers*, 286, 326.

12. Commander Task Force Thirty-Eight, War Diary, 18 Nov. 1944; Commander Task Group Thirty-Eight Point One, Action Report, 2 Oct.–29 Oct. 1944, 5–6, Enclosure F, folder CTG 38.1, Action Report 2 Oct.–29 Oct. 1944; Commander Task Force Thirty-Eight, Action Report, 30 October 1944–26 January 1945, 5; both in box 92, Com 2nd Carrier TF (Blue 627), RG 313, NARA Archives II; Wolters, *Information at Sea*, 215–16.

13. Reynolds, *Fast Carriers*, 290; Ewing, *Thach Weave*, 146–48; Commander Task Force Thirty-Eight to Task Group Commanders, 11 Nov. 1944, Enclosure A, folder P11–1, box 88, Com 2nd Carrier TF (Blue 627), RG 313, NARA Archives II.

14. Memo, *Enterprise* Fighter Director Officer to Air Officer, 15 Nov. 1944, folder P11-1, box 88, Com 2nd Carrier TF (Blue 627), RG 313, NARA Archives II.

15. Commander Task Force Thirty-Eight, War Diary, 13 Nov. 1944; Commander Task Force Thirty-Eight, Action Report, 30 October 1944–26 January 1945, Enclosure B, 41, box 92, Com 2nd Carrier TF (Blue 627), RG 313, NARA Archives II; *Kiso* tabular record of movement, 13 Nov. 1944, in www.combinedfleet.com/kiso_t.htm, accessed 4 April 2013; Japanese Shipping Losses.

16. Message 122156 January 1945, Cominch to Cincpac, roll 200; message 152007 January 1945, roll 201; both in Cincpac Dispatches and Message Traffic, RG 313, NARA Archives II; *Tachibana Maru* tabular record of movement, 5 Nov. 1944, http://www .combinedfleet.com/Tachibana_t.htm; *Muro Maru* tabular record of movement, 13 Nov. 1944, in www.combinedfleet.com/muro_t.htm, accessed 4 April 2013; VB-3 ACA Report, 13 Nov. 1944; Department of State, memo to Spanish Embassy, 26 March 1945, *Foreign Relations of the United States: Diplomatic Papers, 1945, The British Commonwealth, The Far East, Volume VI, Document 321*, https://history.state.gov/ historicaldocuments/frus1945v06/d321, accessed 18 Aug. 2016.

17. Commander Task Force Thirty-Eight, Action Report, 30 October 1944–26 January 1945, Enclosure A, 14, box 92, Com 2nd Carrier TF (Blue 627), RG 313, NARA Archives II; Commander Task Force Thirty-Eight, War Diary, 14 Nov. 1944; Edward P. Stafford, *The Big E: The Story of the USS* Enterprise (New York: Dell Publishing Co., Inc., 1964), 445; Japanese Shipping Losses.

18. Commander Task Force Thirty-Eight, War Diary, 15–17 Nov. 1944; USS *Wasp*, Action Report, 16 Nov. 1944.

19. Commander Task Force Thirty-Eight, War Diary, 19 Nov. 1944.

20. Vice Admiral J. S. McCain, Nov. 1944, Personal Interviews, Naval Records and Library, Chief of Naval Operations, www.Fold3.com, accessed 25 Jan. 2016.

21. McCain to Halsey, 22 Nov. 1944, folder McCain, J. S., 1940, 1943–44, box 15, Special Corresp., Halsey Papers, MDLC; USS *Bunker Hill*, War Diary, 16 Nov. 1944; USS *Enterprise*, War Diary, 21, 22 Nov. 1944; USS *San Jacinto*, War Diary, 22 Nov. 1944; Commander Task Force Thirty-Eight, War Diary, 20–23 Nov. 1944.

22. Commander Task Force Thirty-Eight, War Diary, 25 Nov. 1944; *Kumano* tabular record of movement, 5–25 Nov. 1944, in www.combinedfleet.com/kumano_t.htm, accessed 4 April 2013; Japanese Shipping Losses.

23. Commander Task Force Thirty-Eight, Action Report, 30 October 1944–26 January 1945, Enclosure A, 15–16, box 92, Com 2nd Carrier TF (Blue 627), RG 313, NARA Archives II; USS *Essex*, War Diary, 25 Nov. 1944; USS *Hancock*, Action Report, 14 November–27 November 1944, Enclosure A, 12–14; McCain, "So We Hit Them in the Belly, I," 41; Morison, *Leyte*, 358.

24. Morison, *Leyte*, 360, 367–68; Reynolds, *Fast Carriers*, 291; USS *Enterprise*, War Diary, 22–27 Nov. 1944; USS *San Jacinto*, War Diary, 22–28 Nov. 1944; Commander Task Force Thirty-Eight, War Diary, 27–30 Nov. 1944; USS *Essex*, War Diary, 1–2 Dec. 1944.

25. Wheeler, *Kinkaid*, 408–13; message 290400 Nov. 1944, Com3rdFlt to Cincpac; message 301311 Nov. 1944, GHQ Sowespac to Cincpoa; both in Graybook, vol. 5, 1 Jan. 1944–31 Dec. 1944, 2431, 2435.

26. Commander Task Force Thirty-Eight, War Diary, 1–2 Dec. 1944.

27. McCain, "So We Hit Them in the Belly, I," 15, 40.

28. Commander Task Force Thirty-Eight, Action Report, 30 October 1944–26 January 1945, 5, box 92, Com 2nd Carrier TF (Blue 627), RG 313, NARA Archives II.

29. Ewing, *Thach Weave*, 148–49; Thach, *Reminiscences*, 1:401–4.

30. Message 220615 Nov. 1944, CTF38 to CTGs, Graybook, vol. 5, 1 Jan. 1944–31 Dec. 1944, 2292–93.

31. McCain, "So We Hit Them in the Belly, I," 44; Lt. Cdr. W. N. Leonard, memo to McCain, 27 Nov. 1944, folder A2–11(2) Memos, box 74; Davison to Rear Adm. George Murray (Comairpac), 5 Dec. 1944, folder A4–3(1) Operation Orders (2 of 2), box 75; both in Com 2nd Carrier TF (Blue 627), RG 313, NARA Archives II; Radford to Pownall, 7 Dec. 1944, folder 10, box 29, Arthur Radford Papers, Archives Branch, Naval History and Heritage Command, Washington, DC (hereafter cited as Radford Papers, NHHC).

32. CNO to Comairpac, 3 Jan. 1945, folder A4–3(1) Operation Orders (2 of 2), box 75, Com 2nd Carrier TF (Blue 627), RG 313, NARA Archives II; Tillman, *Hellcat*, 155–56.

33. McCain to Task Group Commanders, 30 Nov. 1944, folder A4-3 Operations (3 of 3), box 75, Com 2nd Carrier TF (Blue 627), RG 313, NARA Archives II. For a discussion of Japanese torpedo and dive-bombing tactics, see Mark R. Peattie, *Sunburst: The Rise of Japanese Naval Air Power, 1909–1941* (Annapolis, MD: Naval Institute Press, 2001), 138–47.

34. Thach, *Reminiscences*, 1:394; Samuel Eliot Morison, *History of United States Naval Operations in World War II*, vol. 13, *The Liberation of the Philippines: Luzon, Mindanao, the Visayas, 1944–1945* (Boston: Little, Brown and Company, 1959), 53–54; Reynolds, *Fast Carriers*, 291–92.

35. McCain to Halsey, 12 Nov. 1944, folder A1-Plans, Projects & Policies, box 74, Com 2nd Carrier TF (Blue 627), RG 313, NARA Archives II; Potter, *Halsey*, 316; *Building the Navy's Bases in World War II: History of the Bureau of Yards and Docks and the Civil Engineer Corps, 1940–1946*, 2 vols. (Washington, DC: Department of the Navy Bureau of Yards and Docks, 1947), 2:332–34.

36. Thach, *Reminiscences*, 1:408; message 210935 Nov. 1944, Cincpoa to Com3rdFlt; message 240354 Nov. 1944, Com3rdFlt to CTF 38; both in Graybook, vol. 5, Jan. 1944–31 Dec. 1944, 2421, 2424.

37. Commander 2nd Carrier Task Force, Pacific, Operation Order No. 4-44, 7 Dec. 1944, folder A6-5(2) Speedletters, box 76, Com 2nd Carrier TF (Blue 627), RG 313, NARA Archives II.

38. USS *Hancock* (CV 19), Action Report, 10 December–24 December 1944, Enclosure A, 1–4; USS *Hancock*, War Diary, 8, 10–12 Dec. 1944; Commander Task Force Thirty-Eight, War Diary, 10–12 Dec. 1944; USS *Yorktown*, War Diary, 10 Dec. 1944; Morison, *Liberation of the Philippines*, 316.

39. Commander Task Force Thirty-Eight, War Diary, 12–14 Dec. 1944; Commander Task Force Thirty-Eight, Action Report, 30 October 1944–26 January 1945, Enclosure B, 28, 32, 42–44, 52, box 92, Com 2nd Carrier TF (Blue 627), RG 313, NARA Archives II.

40. Commander Task Force Thirty-Eight, Action Report, 30 October 1944–26 January 1945, Enclosure B, 28, 32, 42–43, 52, box 92, Com 2nd Carrier TF (Blue 627), Naval Operating Forces, RG 313, NARA Archives II; Japanese Shipping Losses. For the *Oryoku Maru*, see Lee A. Gladwin, "American POWs on Japanese Ships Take a Voyage into Hell," *Prologue* 35 (Winter 2003): 30–39.

41. Morison, *Liberation of the Philippines*, 17–32.

42. Commander Task Force Thirty-Eight, Action Report, 30 October 1944–26 January 1945, Enclosure A, 18, Enclosure B, 28, 32, 42–44, 52, box 92, Com 2nd Carrier TF (Blue 627), RG 313, NARA Archives II; USS *Hancock*, War Diary, 16 Dec. 1944.

43. Commander Task Force Thirty-Eight, War Diary, 17 Dec. 1944; C. Raymond Calhoun, *Typhoon: The Other Enemy* (Annapolis, MD: Naval Institute Press, 1981), 32; Morison, *Liberation of the Philippines*, 63.

44. Message 130520 Dec. 1944, Cincpac to Alpac, roll 190; message 010533 Nov. 1944, Comair7th Fleet to ComForwardArea Central Pacific, roll 175; both in Cincpac Dispatches and Message Traffic, RG 313, NARA Archives II; USS *Hornet*, Typhoon of 15–21 December 1944, 13 Jan. 1945, 1; Calhoun, *Typhoon*, 141–42.

45. Calhoun, *Typhoon*, 43–44, 141, 150, 161; USS *Hornet*, Typhoon of 15–21 December 1944, 13 Jan. 1945, 1; Patrol Bombing Squadron Twenty-One, War Diary, 17–21 Dec. 1944; Commander Task Force Thirty-Eight, War Diary, 17 Dec. 1944.

46. Commander Task Force Thirty-Eight, War Diary, 17–18 Dec. 1944; Morison, *Liberation of the Philippines*, 64–65, 78.

47. Calhoun, *Typhoon*, 43–45; Commander Task Force Thirty-Eight, War Diary, 18 Dec. 1944.

48. Calhoun, *Typhoon*, 33, 45–46; Commander Task Force Thirty-Eight, War Diary, 18 Dec. 1944.

49. Calhoun, *Typhoon*, 37, 46; Commander Task Force Thirty-Eight, War Diary, 18 Dec. 1944.

50. Commander Task Force Thirty-Eight, War Diary, 18 Dec. 1944; Friedman, *U.S. Aircraft Carriers*, 191.

51. Commander Task Force Thirty-Eight, War Diary, 18 Dec. 1944. *Wasp* radar screen photos are in Calhoun, *Typhoon*, 182–85. See also sketches from the *Yorktown*'s radar: USS *Yorktown*, Operations against Enemy Airfields on Luzon . . . 14 to 16 December 1944, Enclosure D, 136.

52. Calhoun, *Typhoon*, 49.

53. Commander Task Force Thirty-Eight, War Diary, 19–24 Dec. 1944. Bob Drury and Tom Clavin, *Halsey's Typhoon: The True Story of a Fighting Admiral, an Epic Storm, and an Untold Rescue* (New York: Atlantic Monthly Press, 2007), 224; Record of Proceedings of a Court of Inquiry Convened on Board the U.S.S. *Cascade* . . . , December 26, 1944, 3, microfilm NRS 1978-43, Archives Branch, Naval History and Heritage Command, Washington, DC (hereafter cited as Record of Proceedings . . . Archives Branch, NHHC).

54. Buell, *Master of Sea Power*, 465.

55. Record of Proceedings of a Court of Inquiry Convened on Board the U.S.S. *Cascade* . . . , December 26, 1944, 72–73, microfilm NRS 1978–43, Archives Branch, NHHC; Morison, *Liberation of the Philippines*, 83, 85–86.

56. Record of Proceedings of a Court of Inquiry Convened on Board the U.S.S. *Cascade* . . . , December 26, 1944, 75–77, microfilm NRS 1978-43, Archives Branch, NHHC.

57. Ibid., 5–7; Morison, *Liberation of the Philippines*, 83; Calhoun, *Typhoon*, 86.

58. Morison, *Liberation of the Philippines*, 83–84.

59. Ibid., 85–87.

60. Thach, *Reminiscences*, 1:430–35.

61. Reynolds, *Fast Carriers*, 295; Calhoun, *Typhoon*, 172.

Chapter Nine. Luzon and the South China Sea

1. Morison, *Leyte*, 77–78, 80; War History, USS *Jason*, 23 April 1946; ComServron10 report, 21 Dec. 1944, Graybook, vol. 5, 1 Jan. 1944–31 Dec. 1944, 2177.

2. Cincpoa summary, 30 Dec. 1944; message 232318 Dec. 1944, Com3rdFlt to CTF38; message 232254 Dec. 1944, Com3rdFlt to CTF38; all in Graybook, 1 Jan. 1944–31 Dec. 1944, 2186, 2473, 2477–78; Morison, *Liberation of the Philippines*, 87, 158, 161; McCain, "So We Hit Them in the Belly, I," 44.

3. Morison, *Liberation of the Philippines*, 37–43; Commander 2nd Carrier Task Force, Pacific, Operation Order No. 5-44, 27 Dec. 1944, folder A4-3(1) Operation Orders (2 of 3), box 76, Com 2nd Carrier TF (Blue 627), RG 313, NARA Archives II.

4. Reynolds, *Fast Carriers*, 289; Commander 2nd Carrier Task Force, Pacific, Operation Order No. 5-44, 27 Dec. 1944, folder A4-3(1) Operation Orders (2 of 3), box 76; Commander Task Force Thirty-Eight, Action Report, 30 October 1944–26 January 1945, 5, box 92; both in Com 2nd Carrier TF (Blue 627), RG 313, NARA Archives II.

5. Message 250550 Dec. 1944, CTF38 to Comairpac, Graybook, vol. 5, 1 Jan. 1944–31 Dec. 1944, 2475; message 030321 Jan. 1945, Cincpac to Com3rdFlt, Com2ndCarrierTaskForce, Graybook, vol. 6, 1 Jan. 1945–1 July 1945, 2737.

6. C.T.G. 30.8, War Diary, 29–31 Dec. 1944; Commander Task Force Thirty-Eight, War Diary, 25–30 Dec. 1944; USS *Hancock*, War Diary, 1–2 Jan. 1945; Commander Task Force Thirty-Eight, War Diary, 1–2 Jan. 1945.

7. Commander Task Force Thirty-Eight, War Diary, 3 Jan. 1945; Commander Task Force Thirty-Eight, Action Report, 30 October 1944–26 January 1945, Enclosure B, 28, 45, 46, 48, 49, 53, box 92, Com 2nd Carrier TF (Blue 627), RG 313, NARA Archives II; Morison, *Liberation of the Philippines*, 101, 103–4; Japanese Shipping Losses.

8. Commander Task Force Thirty-Eight, War Diary, 4 Jan. 1945; Commander Task Force Thirty-Eight, Action Report, 30 October 1944–26 January 1945, Enclosure B, 29, 32, 45, 46, 48, 49, 53, box 92, Com 2nd Carrier TF (Blue 627), RG 313, NARA Archives II; USS *Hancock*, War Diary, 4 Jan. 1945; Japanese Shipping Losses.

9. Commander Task Force Thirty-Eight, War Diary, 5 Jan. 1945; Stafford, *Big E*, 452–53.

10. Commander Task Force Thirty-Eight, War Diary, 6 Jan. 1945; Commander Task Force Thirty-Eight, Action Report, 30 October 1944–26 January 1945, Enclosure B, 29, 45, 46, 48, 49, 53, box 92, Com 2nd Carrier TF (Blue 627), RG 313, NARA Archives II; War Diary, Marine Fighting Squadron Two Thirteen, Marine Fighting Squadron One Twenty Four, 1–10 Jan. 1945; Japanese Shipping Losses.

11. Message 061824 Jan. 1945, CTF 77 to Com3rdFlt, Cincpac; message 070312 Jan. 1945, Cincpoa to CincSWPa; message 071044 Jan. 1945, Com3rdFlt to Cincpoa;

message 071207 Jan. 1945, CincSWPa to Cincpoa, info Com3rdFlt; message 072207 Jan. 1945, Cincpoa to Com3rdFlt, info CincSWPa; all in Graybook, vol. 6, 1 Jan. 1945–1 July 1945, 2945, 2946–49; Commander Task Force Thirty-Eight, War Diary, 6 Jan. 1945.

12. Commander Task Force Thirty-Eight, Action Report, 30 October 1944–26 January 1945, Enclosure B, 29, 45, 46, 48, 49, 53, box 92, Com 2nd Carrier TF (Blue 627), RG 313, NARA Archives II; USS *Hancock*, War Diary, 7 Jan. 1945; Japanese Shipping Losses.

13. Message 011102 Jan. 1945, CTF 77 to all TFs, info Cincpac, Cominch, Graybook, vol. 6, 1 Jan. 1945–1 July 1945, 2736; Morison, *Liberation of the Philippines*, 158–59.

14. Cincpoa summaries, 8, 9 Jan. 1945; message 050651 Jan. 1945, CTF77 to CTF71; all in Graybook, vol. 6, 1 Jan. 1945–1 July 1945, 2504–05, 2942–43; message 090900 Jan. 1945, Com3rdFlt to Cincpac, roll 199, Cincpac Dispatches and Message Traffic, RG 313, NARA Archives II. For Japanese naval air operations against China, see Peattie, *Sunburst*, 104–5.

15. Commander Task Force Thirty-Eight, War Diary, 9 Jan. 1945; Commander Task Force Thirty-Eight, Action Report, 30 October 1944–26 January 1945, Enclosure B, 29, 45, 47–49, box 92, Com 2nd Carrier TF (Blue 627), RG 313, NARA Archives II; Thach, *Reminiscences*, 1:409; notes considering his career, June 18, no year, envelope 3, box 25, John S. Thach Papers, Emil Buehler Naval Aviation Library, National Naval Aviation Museum, Pensacola, FL (hereafter cited as Thach Papers, NNAM); Japanese Shipping Losses.

16. Commander Task Force Thirty-Eight, War Diary, 9–10 Jan. 1945; USS *Hancock*, War Diary, 10 Jan. 1945. The war diaries do not agree on the location of the Japanese aircraft shot down; the *Hancock*'s is more specific and appears to be more accurate.

17. Commander Task Force Thirty-Eight, War Diary, 11 Jan. 1945.

18. Ibid., 12 Jan. 1945.

19. Ibid.; John S. McCain, "So We Hit Them in the Belly, II," *Saturday Evening Post*, 21 July 1945, 24; Commander Task Force Thirty-Eight, Action Report, 30 October 1944–26 January 1945, Enclosure B, 29, 45, 47–48, box 92, Com 2nd Carrier TF (Blue 627), RG 313, NARA Archives II; Japanese Shipping Losses.

20. Commander Task Force Thirty-Eight, War Diary, 13 Jan. 1945; McCain, "So We Hit Them in the Belly, II," 24.

21. USS *Hancock*, War Diary, 13, 14 Jan. 1945; message 121241 Jan. 1945, Cominch to Cincpac; message 121606 Jan. 1945, CincPoa to Com3rdFlt; both in Graybook, vol. 6, 1 Jan. 1945–1 July 1945, 2958, 2960.

22. Commander Task Force Thirty-Eight, War Diary, 15 Jan. 1945; Commander Task Force Thirty-Eight, Action Report, 30 October 1944–26 January 1945, Enclosure B, 30, 45, 47–48, box 92, Com 2nd Carrier TF (Blue 627), RG 313, NARA Archives II; Japanese Shipping Losses.

23. Commander Task Force Thirty-Eight, War Diary, 16 Jan. 1945; Commander Task Force Thirty-Eight, Action Report, 30 October 1944–26 January 1945, Enclosure B, 47–48, Enclosure I, 80, box 92, Com 2nd Carrier TF (Blue 627), RG 313, NARA

Archives II; message 191933 Jan. 1945, Cincpoa to Secnav, roll 203; message 201355 Jan. 1945, Cominch to Cincpac, roll 204; both in Cincpac Dispatches and Message Traffic, RG 313, NARA Archives II; History of Bombing Squadron Seven, 16 Jan. 1945.

24. Commander Task Force Thirty-Eight, War Diary, 16 Jan. 1945; Commander Task Force Thirty-Eight, Action Report, 30 October 1944–26 January 1945, Enclosure B, 30, 33, Com 2nd Carrier TF (Blue 627), RG 313, NARA Archives II; Reynolds, *Fast Carriers*, 297; Japanese Shipping Losses.

25. Commander Task Force Thirty-Eight to Commander Third Fleet, 24 Jan. 1945, folder 3–5, United States Navy File, Second Carrier Task Force, 1944 Nov. 13–1945 Jan. 1, box 3, McCain Papers, HISU.

26. Commander Task Force Thirty-Eight, War Diary, 17 Jan. 1945.

27. Ibid., 18 Jan. 1945; USS *Hancock*, War Diary, 18 Jan. 1945.

28. Message 160211 Jan. 1945, Com3rdFlt to Cincpac; message 161836 Jan. 1945, Cincpac to Cominch, info Com3rdFlt, etc.; message 170243 Jan. 1945, Com3rdFlt to Cincpac; all in Graybook, vol. 6, 1 Jan. 1945–1 July 1945, 2971–72, 2974.

29. Message 112239 Jan. 1945, Com3rdFlt to 3rdFlt, info. Cincpac, etc.; message 181001 Jan. 1945, Com3rdFlt to Cincpac; both in Graybook, vol. 6, 1 Jan. 1945–1 July 1945, 2958–59, 2983; Reynolds, *Fast Carriers*, 297.

30. Message 181837 Jan. 1945, Cincpoa to Com3rdFlt; message 182308 Jan. 1945, Com-3rdFlt to Cincpac; message 190438 Jan. 1945, Com3rdFlt to Cincpac; all in Graybook, vol. 6, 1 Jan. 1945–1 July 1945, 2985, 2987.

31. Commander Task Force Thirty-Eight, War Diary, 19 Jan. 1945; USS *Hancock*, War Diary, 19 Jan. 1945.

32. Commander Task Force Thirty-Eight, War Diary, 20, 21 Jan. 1945; Commander Task Force Thirty-Eight, Action Report, 30 October 1944–26 January 1945, Enclosure B, 45, box 92, Com 2nd Carrier TF (Blue 627), RG 313, NARA Archives II; message 202314 Jan. 1945, Com3rdFlt to Cincpac, roll 204, Cincpac Dispatches and Message Traffic, RG 313, NARA Archives II.

33. USS *Hancock*, War Diary, 21 Jan. 1945; Commander Task Force Thirty-Eight, Action Report, 30 October 1944–26 January 1945, 23, Enclosure B, 45–49, 55, box 92, Com 2nd Carrier TF (Blue 627), RG 313, NARA Archives II; Japanese Shipping Losses.

34. Commander Task Force Thirty-Eight, War Diary, 21 Jan. 1945; USS *Langley*, Action Report, 21 Jan. 1945.

35. USS *Ticonderoga*, Action Report, 3–21 January 1945, Part I, 4–6, Part III, 63, Part IV, 80–82; Morison, *Liberation of the Philippines*, 181.

36. USS *Hancock*, Action Report, 21 Jan. 1945, Enclosure A, 52–54; Thach, *Reminiscences*, 1:427–28.

37. Commander Task Force Thirty-Eight, War Diary, 22 Jan. 1945; Commander Task Force Thirty-Eight, Action Report, 30 October 1944–26 January 1945, Enclosure B, 33, 49–50, 55, Enclosure K, 86–87, box 92, Com 2nd Carrier TF (Blue 627), RG 313, NARA Archives II; USS *Langley*, Action Report, 30 December 1944–25 January 1945, Part VI, 106–7; Stafford, *Big E*, 457–60; Japanese Shipping Losses.

38. Commander Task Force Thirty-Eight, War Diary, 23–25 Jan. 1945; USS *Hancock*, War Diary, 26 Jan. 1945.

39. Commander Task Force Thirty-Eight, War Diary, 26–31 Jan. 1945; message 271900 Jan. 1945, ADO Majuro to Johnston I.; message 280929 Jan. 1945, NAS Pearl Harbor; both in roll 207, Cincpac Dispatches and Message Traffic, RG 313, NARA Archives II.

40. Commander Task Force Thirty-Eight, Action Report, 30 October 1944–26 January 1945, 2–4, box 92, Com 2nd Carrier TF (Blue 627), RG 313, NARA Archives II.

41. Ibid., Enclosure C, 56–57, Enclosure H, 72.

42. Ibid., 5, Enclosure D, 58–60.

43. Ibid., 7, Enclosure H, 73–77.

44. Gilbert, *Leader Born*, 111, 129–30, 162; Reynolds, *On the Warpath*, 387.

45. Commander Task Force Thirty-Eight, Action Report, 30 October 1944–26 January 1945, Enclosure M, 91–94, box 92, Com 2nd Carrier TF (Blue 627), RG 313, NARA Archives II; message 070815 Jan. 1945, Cincpac to Com3rdFlt, info CTF38, Graybook, vol. 6, 1 Jan. 1945–1 July 1945, 3244; message 170311 Jan. 1945, Cincpac to Com2ndCarTaskFor, roll 202, Cincpac Dispatches and Message Traffic, RG 313, NARA Archives II.

46. Commander Task Force Thirty-Eight, Action Report, 30 October 1944–26 January 1945, 8, Enclosure N, 95, box 92, Com 2nd Carrier TF (Blue 627), RG 313, NARA Archives II; USS *Hancock*, Action Report, 30 December 1944–25 January 1945, Enclosure A, 167–68.

47. Com 3d Fleet to Com TF-38, 1st endorsement on C2CTF serial 00168, 13 Feb. 1945, in Commander Task Force Thirty-Eight, Action Report, 30 October 1944–26 January 1945, 96, box 92, Com 2nd Carrier TF (Blue 627), RG 313, NARA Archives II; Cincpac to Cominch, 1st endorsement on Com 3d Fleet serial 0081, 8 March 1945, in Commander Third Fleet, Report on Operations of the Third Fleet, 30 December 1944 to 23 January 1945, 19.

48. Bogan Reminiscences, 118; Reynolds, *Fast Carriers*, 296, 297, 299–300.

49. Thach, *Reminiscences*, 1:423–24, 438–39 (emphasis in original); Robert B. Carney, "In Defense of Halsey," *Naval History* 30 (April 2016): 26; comments on Chapter 39 (1959), folder 1946–1960 Various Correspondents, box 2, E. B. Potter Papers, Special Collections & Archives, Nimitz Library, U.S. Naval Academy; Molteni to Clark Reynolds, 17 July 1966, Reynolds Correspondence, folder 2, box 14, Towers Papers, MDLC.

50. Palmer, *Command at Sea*, 254, 261–62.

51. McCain, "So We Hit Them in the Belly, II," 39; 27 Jan. 1945 entry, folder 7, 1 Jan.–30 Dec. 1945, Diaries, box 1, Towers Papers, MDLC; Reynolds, *Towers*, 497.

Chapter Ten. Carriers against Japan

1. Message 310316 Jan. 1945, Comairpac to Cincpac, roll 208, Cincpac Dispatches and Message Traffic, RG 313, NARA Archives II; CincPac to McCain, 7 Feb. 1945, McCain Personnel File, NPRC; 8 Feb. 1945 entry, Diaries, folder 7, 1 Jan.–30 Dec. 1945, box 1, Towers Papers, MDLC; Gilbert, *Leader Born*, 181.

2. Cominch to McCain, 21 Feb. 1945, McCain Personnel File, NPRC; Thach, *Reminiscences*, 1:437–38.

3. Third Fleet Operations, 1 November 1944–19 September 1945, folder Third Fleet Operations, 1943–45, box 37, Military File, Halsey Papers, MDLC; Reynolds, *Fast Carriers*, 320–21.

4. Reynolds, *Fast Carriers*, 338–46; Morison, *Victory in the Pacific*, 89.

5. Reynolds, *Towers*, 507; Richard B. Frank, *Downfall: The End of the Imperial Japanese Empire* (New York: Random House, 1999), 30, 35–37, 117–18.

6. First endorsement, Cominch to McCain, 21 Feb. 1945, McCain Personnel File, NPRC; press release, Eleventh Naval District, 2 March 1945, folder 18.11.1.16, box 3, Thach Papers, NNAM.

7. McCain, "So We Hit Them in the Belly, I," 12–15, 40–44; McCain, "So We Hit Them in the Belly, II," 22–24, 39; Forrestal to McCain, 19 July 1945, Forrestal Papers, MMLPU.

8. Halsey to SecNav, 12 Feb. 1945; Gold Star citation, 5 March 1945; ComFairWest to McCain, 3 April 1945; Comairpac to McCain, 5 April 1945; Cominch to SecNav, 11 April 1945; all in McCain Personnel File, NPRC; 4 April 1945 entry, Diaries, folder 7, 1 Jan.–30 Dec. 1945, box 1, Towers Papers, MDLC; Commander Second Carrier Task Force, Pacific, War Diary, 1–8 May 1945; Gilbert, *Leader Born*, 182–83.

9. Cincpoa Operation Plan No. 4-45, 15 May 1945, folder Operation Plan 4-45, box 37, Military File, Halsey Papers, MDLC; message 200400 May 1945, Com3rdFlt to CTF51 . . . info Cincpac, Graybook, vol. 6, 1 Jan. 1945–1 July 1945, 3130–32; Commander Third Fleet, War Diary, 16–18 May 1945.

10. Message 260842 May 1945, Cincpac to Com3rdPhibFor, Graybook, vol. 6, 1 Jan. 1945–1 July 1945, 3142; Reynolds, *Fast Carriers*, 322–24.

11. Commander Second Carrier Task Force, Pacific, War Diary, 9–29 May 1945; message 181035 May 1945, Com2ndCarTaskFor to Cincpac, Graybook, vol. 6, 1 Jan. 1945–1 July 1945, 2905; Reynolds, *Fast Carriers*, 342–45. Commander Second Carrier Task Force, Pacific, War Diary, 1 May–31 May 1945, records that McCain assumed command on 17 May, failing to add a day after crossing the International Date Line. Gilbert, *Leader Born*, 183, repeats the 17 May date.

12. Reynolds, *Fast Carriers*, 330, 342, 345–47; Commander Second Carrier Task Force Thirty-Eight, Action Report, 28 May–1 July 1945, Enclosure G, 1, folder 4-1, United States Navy File, Second Carrier Task Force, 1944 Dec.–1945 Aug. 22, box 4, McCain Papers, HISU.

13. Message 210845 May 1945, Cincpac to CTG 58.4, roll 265, Cincpac Dispatches and Message Traffic, RG 313, NARA Archives II; War Diary for USS *Monssen*, 24 May 1945; War Diary, USS *Cushing* (DD 797), 30 May 1945.

14. Reynolds, *Fast Carriers*, 301–3, 311–12, 314–17, 344–46; David Hobbs, *The British Pacific Fleet: The Royal Navy's Most Powerful Strike Force* (Annapolis, MD: Naval Institute Press, 2011), 17–19, 74–107; message 300732 June 1945, Cincpac to CincBritPac-Flt, roll 289, Cincpac Dispatches and Message Traffic, RG 313, NARA Archives II.

15. BuAer World War II Admin. History, Summary, 1:362–63; message 140006 Jan. 1945, ComgenAAFPoa to Cincpoa, roll 201, Cincpac Dispatches and Message Traffic, RG 313, NARA Archives II; BuAer World War II Admin. History, Summary, 1:362–63;

The Coast Guard at War, Loran IV, 2 vols. (Coast Guard Headquarters, 1946), 2:143–47, http://www.loran-history.info/LORAN_Implementation_Planning_Installation_ and_Termination/1942–1949/THE%20COAST%20GUARD%20AT%20WAR. pdf, accessed 20 July 2016.

16. Commander Second Carrier Task Force, Pacific, War Diary, 29–31 May 1945.

17. Commander Second Carrier Task Force Thirty-Eight, Action Report, 28 May–1 July 1945, 2–3 June 1945, Enclosure B, 2–4, Enclosure C, 3, Enclosure D, 1, folder 4-1, United States Navy File, Second Carrier Task Force, 1944 Dec.–1945 Aug. 22, box 4, McCain Papers, HISU.

18. Charles A. Sisson (by direction CTF38 to Com3rdFlt and CTGs), 5 June 1945, folder 3-5, United States Navy File, Second Carrier Task Force, 1944 Nov. 13–1945 Jan. 1, box 3, McCain Papers, HISU.

19. Message 050255 June 1945, CTF38 to all carriers TF 38; message 050648 June 1945, Com3rdFlt to Cincpac; both in roll 272, Cincpac Dispatches and Message Traffic, RG 313, NARA Archives II.

20. Summary of Report of Court of Inquiry on Damage to Ships of the Third Fleet in the Typhoon of 5 June 1945, 11 Aug. 1945, 2, Flag File Screening Documents, 1941–1963, Cincpac 1945, box 45, RG 38, NARA Archives II; message 030322 June 1945, Weather Central Leyte to TFCs, roll 271, Cincpac Dispatches and Message Traffic, RG 313, NARA Archives II; Morison, *Victory in the Pacific*, 298.

21. Summary of Report of Court of Inquiry, 2–3, Flag File Screening Documents, 1941–1963, Cincpac 1945, box 45, RG 38, NARA Archives II; Commander Second Carrier Task Force, Pacific, War Diary, 4 June 1945; USS *Hornet* (CV 12), War Diary, 4 June 1945.

22. Morison, *Victory in the Pacific*, 299–300; Record of Proceedings of a Court of Inquiry . . . into the circumstances connected with the damage of ships of the Third Fleet in a typhoon . . . off Okinawa, 3–4, Flag File Screening Documents, 1941–1963, Cincpac 1945, box 45, RG 38, NARA Archives II; USS *Hornet* (CV 12), Action Report, TBS #1 Log, 4. Times vary among the *Hornet* TBS Log, war diaries, Court of Inquiry documents, and Morison's account. I have primarily relied on the *Hornet* log and war diaries.

23. Morison, *Victory in the Pacific*, 300–301; USS *Hornet* (CV 12), Action Report, TBS #1 Log, 4–6; Record of Proceedings of a Court of Inquiry, 4, Flag File Screening Documents, 1941–1963, Cincpac 1945, box 45, RG 38, NARA Archives II.

24. USS *Hornet* (CV 12), Action Report, 5 June 1945; Summary of Report of Court of Inquiry, 4, Flag File Screening Documents, 1941–1963, Cincpac 1945, box 45, RG 38, NARA Archives II; Morison, *Victory in the Pacific*, 301–6.

25. Commander Second Carrier Task Force, Pacific, War Diary, 5 June 1945; USS *Shangri-La* (CV 38), Action Report, 5 June 1945, Part 3 (B), 13–14; Morison, *Victory in the Pacific*, 306–7; Arthur W. Radford, *From Pearl Harbor to Vietnam: The Memoirs of Admiral Arthur W. Radford*, ed. Stephen Jurika Jr. (Stanford, CA: Hoover Institution Press, 1980), 59.

26. Morison, *Victory in the Pacific*, 307; Reynolds, *Fast Carriers*, 349; Commander Second Carrier Task Force, Pacific, War Diary, 5–6 June 1945; Commander Third Fleet, War Diary, 5 June 1945; USS *Hornet* (CV 12), War Diary, 6 June 1945.

27. Commander Second Carrier Task Force Thirty-Eight, Action Report, 8 June 1945, Enclosure B, 1–4; Com TF-38 to distribution list, 6 June 1945, Operation Stinger; both in folder 4-1, United States Navy File, Second Carrier Task Force, 1944 Dec.–1945 Aug. 22, box 4, McCain Papers, HISU.

28. Commander Second Carrier Task Force Thirty-Eight, Action Report, 8–10 June 1945, Enclosure B, 2, folder 4-1, United States Navy File, Second Carrier Task Force, 1944 Dec.–1945 Aug. 22, box 4, McCain Papers, HISU; Commander Second Carrier Task Force, Pacific, War Diary, 9–10 June 1945; USS *Shangri-La* (CV 38), Action Report, 24 May 1945–13 June 1945, Part 6 (B), 24; Commander Third Fleet, War Diary, 10 June 1945.

29. Reynolds, *Fast Carriers*, 350; Commander Third Fleet, War Diary, 12–14 June 1945; Commander Second Carrier Task Force Thirty-Eight, Action Report, 11–13 June 1945, folder 4-1, United States Navy File, Second Carrier Task Force, 1944 Dec.–1945 Aug. 22, box 4, McCain Papers, HISU; message 080219 June 1945, Cincpoa to Cincfoa, roll 274, Cincpac Dispatches and Message Traffic, RG 313, NARA Archives II; CO, Air Group Twelve to COs VF-12, VBF-12, VB-12, VT-12, 23 June 1945, www.Fold3.com, accessed 25 Jan. 2017.

30. Commander Third Fleet, War Diary, 14–18 June 1945; Commander Second Carrier Task Force Thirty-Eight, Action Report, 11–13 June 1945, folder 4-1, United States Navy File, Second Carrier Task Force, 1944 Dec.–1945 Aug. 22, box 4, McCain Papers, HISU; Reynolds, *Fast Carriers*, 349, 360–61; *Building the Navy's Bases*, 2:383–86; 14 June, Third Fleet Log, May 21–Sept. 18, 1945, box 36, Military File, Halsey Papers, MDLC.

31. Commander Second Carrier Task Force Thirty-Eight, Action Report, 28 May–1 July 1945, 3, Halsey 1st Endorsement, Cincpac 2d endorsement, folder 4-1, United States Navy File, Second Carrier Task Force, 1944 Dec.–1945 Aug. 22, box 4, McCain Papers, HISU; message 100612 June 1945, CTF 38 to Cincpac, Graybook, vol. 6, 1 Jan. 1945–1 July 1945, 3175.

32. Message 120245 June 1945, CTF38 via Com3rdFlt to Comairpac; message 232208 June 1945, Comairpac Admin; message 260352 June 1945, Cincpoa; all in Graybook, vol. 6, 1 Jan. 1945–1 July 1945, 3173, 2709, 2711; Reynolds, *Fast Carriers*, 357.

33. Message 091847 June 1945, Cominch to Cincpac, roll 274, Cincpac Dispatches and Message Traffic, RG 313, NARA Archives II; Summary of Report of Court of Inquiry, 1; Record of Proceedings of a Court of Inquiry, 39–45; both in Flag File Screening Documents, 1941–1963, Cincpac 1945, box 45, RG 38, NARA Archives II.

34. Record of Proceedings of a Court of Inquiry, 47–50, Flag File Screening Documents, 1941–1963, Cincpac 1945, box 45, RG 38, NARA Archives II.

35. Commander Third Fleet, War Diary, 18 June 1945; Record of Proceedings of a Court of Inquiry, 53–54, Flag File Screening Documents, 1941–1963, Cincpac 1945, box 45, RG 38, NARA Archives II.

36. Record of Proceedings of a Court of Inquiry, 54–55; Summary of Report of Court of Inquiry, 5; both in Flag File Screening Documents, 1941–1963, Cincpac 1945, box 45, RG 38, NARA Archives II; Reynolds, *Fast Carriers*, 348.

37. Summary of Report of Court of Inquiry, 5–6, Flag File Screening Documents, 1941–1963, Cincpac 1945, box 45, RG 38, NARA Archives II; Morison, *Victory in the Pacific*, 308.

38. Hughes, *Bill Halsey*, 390; Summary of Report of Court of Inquiry, 7; Nimitz to Judge Advocate General, 24 July 1945; King to SecNav, 31 July 1945; Flag File Screening Documents, 1941–1963, Cincpac 1945, box 45, RG 38, NARA Archives II; Radford, *Pearl Harbor to Vietnam*, 59.

39. Commander Second Carrier Task Force Thirty-Eight, Action Report, 28 May–1 July 1945, Enclosure C, 1–8, folder 4-1, United States Navy File, Second Carrier Task Force, 1944 Dec.–1945 Aug. 22, box 4, McCain Papers, HISU.

40. Radford, *Pearl Harbor to Vietnam*, 59. For the importance of rapid decision making in World War II naval warfare, see Palmer, *Command at Sea*, 263.

41. Reynolds, *Towers*, 505–7.

42. BuPers order, 25 June 1945; Chief, Naval Personnel to Judge Advocate General, 27 July 1945; both in McCain Personnel File, NPRC; William F. Halsey and J. Bryan III, *Admiral Halsey's Story* (New York: Whittlesey House, McGraw-Hill Book Company, Inc., 1947), 284.

43. McCain to Task Force Thirty-Eight, 26 June 1945, folder 3-5, United States Navy File, Second Carrier Task Force, 1944 Nov. 13–1945 Jan. 1, box 3, McCain Papers, HISU.

44. Message 261225 June 1945, Com3rdFlt to CTGs, CTFs, Cominch, Cincpac; message 211415 June 1945, CTF38 to All Flag Officers TF38, CTF37; message 300525 May 1945, Cincpac to Com3rdFlt; all in Graybook, vol. 6, 1 Jan. 1945–1 July 1945, 3148, 3185–86, 3189–90; CTF38, Concept-Third Fleet Operations, July 1945, folder A4-3(1), (2 of 4), box 74, Com 2nd Carrier TF (Blue 627), RG 313, NARA Archives II; Gayler Reminiscences, 131; Reynolds, *Fast Carriers*, 367.

45. Reynolds, *Fast Carriers*, 365–66; Commander Second Carrier Task Force, Op Order No. 2-45, 25 June 1945, folder A4-3(1) Operations Orders (2 of 4), box 74, Com 2nd Carrier TF (Blue 627), RG 313, NARA Archives II.

46. Commander Second Carrier Task Force, Pacific, War Diary, 2, 6, 10 July 1945, folder 4-1, United States Navy File, Second Carrier Task Force, 1944 Dec.–1945 Aug. 22, box 4, McCain Papers, HISU; Reynolds, *Fast Carriers*, 366.

47. Commander Second Carrier Task Force, Pacific, Action Report, 2 July 1945–15 August 1945, Enclosure C, 5, 8–9, 11, 14–15, folder 3-6, United States Navy File, Second Carrier Task Force, 1944 Dec.–1945 Aug. 22, box 3, McCain Papers, HISU.

48. Lundstrom, *Black Shoe Carrier Admiral*, 217; memo, Communication Security Unit, TG-30.2, 15 July 1945, folder A6-1 Communications, box 76, Com 2nd Carrier TF (Blue 627), RG 313, NARA Archives II.

49. Commander Second Carrier Task Force, Pacific, War Diary, 11–14 July 1945, folder 4-1, United States Navy File, Second Carrier Task Force, 1944 Dec.–1945 Aug. 22, box 4; Commander Second Carrier Task Force, Pacific, Action Report, 2 July 1945–15 August 1945, Enclosure A, 1, folder 3-6, United States Navy File, Second Carrier Task Force, 1944 Dec.–1945 Aug. 22, box 3; both in McCain Papers, HISU; message

110828 July 1945, Cincpac to Com3rdFlt; message 132105 July 1945, Com3rdFlt to CTF 37, CTF 38, info. Cincpac, Cominch; both in Graybook, vol. 7, 1 July 1945–31 Aug. 1945, 3322, 3389; Thach, *Reminiscences*, 2:468.

50. Commander Second Carrier Task Force, Pacific, War Diary, 14 July 1945, folder 4-1, United States Navy File, Second Carrier Task Force, 1944 Dec.–1945 Aug. 22, box 4; Commander Second Carrier Task Force, Pacific, Action Report, 2 July 1945–15 August 1945, Enclosure C, 5–6, annex 1, 1, folder 3-6, United States Navy File, Second Carrier Task Force, 1944 Dec.–1945 Aug. 22, box 3; both in McCain Papers, HISU; Frank, *Downfall*, 157.

51. Summary 14 July, Graybook, vol. 7, 1 July 1945–31 Aug. 1945, 3261; Ewing, *Thach Weave*, 162; Commander Second Carrier Task Force, Pacific, Action Report, 2 July 1945–15 August 1945, Enclosure A, 1, folder 3-6, United States Navy File, Second Carrier Task Force, 1944 Dec.–1945 Aug. 22, box 3, McCain Papers, HISU; Thach, memo to McCain, 20 July 1945, folder A2-11(3), Staff Memos—Officers, box 1; McCain to Halsey, 19 June 1945, folder A1—Plans, Projects & Policies, box 74; both in Com 2nd Carrier TF (Blue 627), RG 313, NARA Archives II. Frank, *Downfall*, 157–58, lists 802 shells expended on Kamaishi and 860 on Muroran.

52. Commander Second Carrier Task Force, Pacific, War Diary, 15 July 1945, folder 4-1, United States Navy File, Second Carrier Task Force, 1944 Dec.–1945 Aug. 22, box 4; Commander Second Carrier Task Force, Pacific, Action Report, 2 July 1945–15 August 1945, Enclosure C, 5–6, annex 1, 16, folder 3-6, United States Navy File, Second Carrier Task Force, 1944 Dec.–1945 Aug. 22, box 3; both in McCain Papers, HISU.

53. Commander Second Carrier Task Force, Pacific, War Diary, 16 July 1945, folder 4-1, United States Navy File, Second Carrier Task Force, 1944 Dec.–1945 Aug. 22, box 4, McCain Papers, HISU; message 132145 July 1945, Com3rdFlt to Cincpac, Graybook, vol. 7, 1 July 1945–31 Aug. 1945, 3389–90; 15–16 July, Third Fleet Night Order Book, July–Aug. 1945, box 36, Military File, Halsey Papers, MDLC; Hobbs, *British Pacific Fleet*, 252–56, 260.

54. Commander Second Carrier Task Force, Pacific to Cincpac, 17 July 1945, folder A3-1, box 4, Com 2nd Carrier TF (Blue 627), RG 313, NARA Archives II; Reynolds, *Fast Carriers*, 365–68.

55. Commander Second Carrier Task Force, Pacific, War Diary, 17–18 July 1945, folder 4-1, United States Navy File, Second Carrier Task Force, 1944 Dec.–1945 Aug. 22, box 4; Commander Second Carrier Task Force, Pacific, Action Report, 2 July 1945–15 August 1945, Enclosure A, 1, Enclosure C, 5–6, annex 1, 16, folder 3-6, United States Navy File, Second Carrier Task Force, 1944 Dec.–1945 Aug. 22, box 3; both in McCain Papers, HISU; message 171356 July 1945, Com3rdFleet to Cincpac; message 211300 July 1945, Com3rdFleet to Cincpac; both in Graybook, vol. 7, 1 July 1945–31 Aug. 1945, 3328, 3332; Com2dCarTF, Supplementary Strike Plans, 11 July 1945, folder A4-3(1), Operation Orders (2 of 2), box 75, Com 2nd Carrier TF (Blue 627), RG 313, NARA Archives II; Japanese Shipping Losses.

56. Commander Second Carrier Task Force, Pacific, War Diary, 19–23 July 1945, folder 4-1, 1944 Dec.–1945 Aug. 22; Commander Second Carrier Task Force, Pacific, Operation Order No. 3-45, 20 July 1945, folder 4-3, 1945 July–August; both in United

States Navy File, Second Carrier Task Force, box 4, McCain Papers, HISU; Morison, *Victory in the Pacific*, 330–31; Hobbs, *British Pacific Fleet*, 264–67.

57. Commander Second Carrier Task Force, Pacific, War Diary, 24 July 1945, folder 4-1, United States Navy File, Second Carrier Task Force, 1944 Dec.–1945 Aug. 22, box 4; Commander Second Carrier Task Force, Pacific, Action Report, 2 July 1945–15 August 1945, Enclosure A, 2, Enclosure C, 5–6, annex 1, 28, folder 3-6, United States Navy File, Second Carrier Task Force, 1944 Dec.–1945 Aug. 22, box 3; both in McCain Papers, HISU; Frank, *Downfall*, 158; Hobbs, *British Pacific Fleet*, 266–67; Japanese Shipping Losses. Additional information on Japanese losses is at http://www.combinedfleet.com, accessed 2 Sept. 2015.

58. Commander Second Carrier Task Force, Pacific, War Diary, 25 July 1945, folder 4-1, United States Navy File, Second Carrier Task Force, 1944 Dec.–1945 Aug. 22, box 4; Commander Second Carrier Task Force, Pacific, Action Report, 2 July 1945–15 August 1945, Enclosure A, 2, Enclosure C, 5–6, annex 1, 40, folder 3-6, United States Navy File, Second Carrier Task Force, 1944 Dec.–1945 Aug. 22, box 3; both in McCain Papers, HISU; Hobbs, *British Pacific Fleet*, 267–68; Japanese Shipping Losses.

59. Commander Second Carrier Task Force, Pacific, War Diary, 26–27 July 1945, folder 4-1, United States Navy File, Second Carrier Task Force, 1944 Dec.–1945 Aug. 22, box 4, McCain Papers, HISU.

60. Commander Second Carrier Task Force, Pacific, War Diary, 28 July 1945, folder 4-1, United States Navy File, Second Carrier Task Force, 1944 Dec.–1945 Aug. 22, box 4; Commander Second Carrier Task Force, Pacific, Action Report, 2 July 1945–15 August 1945, Enclosure A, 2, Enclosure C, 5–6, annex 1, 41, folder 3-6, United States Navy File, Second Carrier Task Force, 1944 Dec.–1945 Aug. 22, box 3; both in McCain Papers, HISU; Japanese Shipping Losses.

61. Commander Second Carrier Task Force, Pacific, War Diary, 29–30 July 1945, folder 4-1, United States Navy File, Second Carrier Task Force, 1944 Dec.–1945 Aug. 22, box 4; Commander Second Carrier Task Force, Pacific, Action Report, 2 July 1945–15 August 1945, Enclosure A, 2, Enclosure C, 5–6, annex 1, 53, folder 3-6, United States Navy File, Second Carrier Task Force, 1944 Dec.–1945 Aug. 22, box 3; both in McCain Papers, HISU; summary 30 July, Graybook, vol. 7, 1 July 1945–31 Aug. 1945, 3282.

62. Commander Second Carrier Task Force, Pacific, Action Report, 2 July 1945–15 August 1945, Enclosure A, 2, folder 3-6, United States Navy File, Second Carrier Task Force, 1944 Dec.–1945 Aug. 22, box 3, McCain Papers, HISU; summary 2 Aug.; message 092115 Aug., Com3rdFlt to Cincpac, info. CTF 38, CTF 37; both in Graybook, vol. 7, 1 July 1945–31 Aug. 1945, 3286, 3438; *Shangri-La* Deck Log, 4 Aug. 1945, RG 24, NARA Archives II; Frank, *Downfall*, 293–99.

63. Commander Pacific Ocean Areas, Operation Plan No. 11-45, 9 Aug. 1945, folder CINCPOA, Op Plan 11-45, box 91, Com 2nd Carrier TF (Blue 627), RG 313, NARA Archives II; message 040747 Aug. 1945, Cincpac to Com3rdFleet, Graybook, vol. 7, 1 July 1945–31 Aug. 1945, 3428.

64. Commander Second Carrier Task Force, Pacific, Action Report, 2 July 1945–15 August 1945, Enclosure A, 2–3, Enclosure C, 5–6, folder 3-6, United States Navy

File, Second Carrier Task Force, 1944 Dec.–1945 Aug. 22, box 3, McCain Papers, HISU; summary 8 Aug., Graybook, vol. 7, 1 July 1945–31 Aug. 1945, 3292.

65. Reynolds, *Fast Carriers*, 374; *New York Times*, 13 Aug. 1945; Commander Second Carrier Task Force, Pacific, Action Report, 2 July 1945–15 August 1945, Enclosure A, 3, Enclosure C, 5–6, folder 3-6, United States Navy File, Second Carrier Task Force, 1944 Dec.–1945 Aug. 22, box 3, McCain Papers, HISU; "Cease Offensive Action . . . ," folder Third Fleet Operations, 1943–45, box 36, Military File, Halsey Papers, MDLC; message 101614 Aug. 1945, Cincpac to Alpoa; message 101135 Aug. 1945, Cominch to Cincpac; both in Graybook, vol. 7, 1 July 1945–31 Aug. 1945, 3439, 3510.

66. Hobbs, *British Pacific Fleet*, 286–88; *Shangri-La* Deck Log, 11 Aug. 1945, RG 24, NARA Archives II.

67. Commander Second Carrier Task Force, Pacific, Action Report, 2 July 1945–15 August 1945, Enclosure A, 3, Enclosure C, 5–6, folder 3-6, United States Navy File, Second Carrier Task Force, 1944 Dec.–1945 Aug. 22, box 3, McCain Papers, HISU; Ship's Activity, *Shangri-La*, 12 Aug. 1945, http://www.kellycrawford.org/ShangriLa/logbook.html#AUG12, accessed 8 Jan. 2016.

Chapter Eleven. Triumph and Tragedy

1. Commander Second Carrier Task Force, Pacific, Action Report, 2 July 1945–15 August 1945, Enclosure D, 4–5, folder 3-6, United States Navy File, Second Carrier Task Force, 1944 Dec.–1945 Aug. 22, box 3, McCain Papers, HISU; Radford, *Pearl Harbor to Vietnam*, 65.

2. Commander Second Carrier Task Force, Pacific, Action Report, 2 July 1945–15 August 1945, Enclosure A, 3, Enclosure C, 5–6; folder 3-6, United States Navy File, Second Carrier Task Force, 1944 Dec.–1945 Aug. 22, box 3, McCain Papers, HISU; Commander Third Fleet, War Diary, 15 Aug. 1945; Radford, *Pearl Harbor to Vietnam*, 65.

3. Commander Third Fleet, War Diary, 16–24 Aug. 1945; Commander Second Carrier Task Force, Pacific, Action Report, 15 August–2 September 1945, Enclosure A, 5.

4. Commander Third Fleet, War Diary, 25 Aug. 1945; summary 21 Aug.; summary 25 Aug.; both in Graybook, vol. 7, 1 July 1945–31 Aug. 1945, 3308, 3312; Reynolds, *Fast Carriers*, 377.

5. Cincpac/Cincpoa, Joint Staff Study Campus, 9 Aug. 1945, folder CINCPAC-CINCPOA Joint Staff Study, box 90, Com 2nd Carrier TF (Blue 627), RG 313, NARA Archives II.

6. Commander Third Fleet, War Diary, 25–26 Aug. 1945; Commander Second Carrier Task Force, Pacific, Action Report, 15 August–2 September 1945, Enclosure A, 5–6; USS *Shangri-La* (CV 38), Action Report, 28 Aug. 1945; *New York Times*, 29 Aug. 1945.

7. Commander Second Carrier Task Force, Pacific, Action Report, 15 August–2 September 1945, Enclosure A, 4, Enclosure C, 13; Hill Goodspeed, "POW Relief and the End of World War II," *Foundation* 36 (Fall 2015): 20–25.

8. Sen. John S. McCain III, telephone interview by author, 7 Oct. 2015; Gilbert, *Leader Born*, 217; Peter G. Molteni Jr. to Clark Reynolds, 17 July 1966, folder 2, box 14, Towers Papers, MDLC.

9. Reynolds, *Towers*, 508–10; Potter, *Bull Halsey*, 350; Gilbert, *Leader Born*, 215–16.

10. Commander Second Carrier Task Force, Pacific, Action Report, 2 July 1945–15 August 1945, 3–4, folder 3-6, United States Navy File, Second Carrier Task Force, 1944 Dec.–1945 Aug. 22, box 3, McCain Papers, HISU.

11. Ibid., 4–7.

12. Ibid., 4, 8, Enclosure C, 9, 11–12, 14–15, Enclosure E, 4–5.

13. Ibid., 9, Enclosure D, 1–5.

14. Ibid., Enclosure G, 1–3.

15. Ibid., 8–10, Enclosure C, 18–19, 21, Enclosure E, 4–5.

16. Ibid., Enclosure G, 1–3; Albion, *Makers of Naval Policy*, 601.

17. Commander Second Carrier Task Force, Pacific, Action Report, 15 August–2 September 1945, Enclosure A, 2–3; Gayler Reminiscences, 137–38; USS *Shangri-La* (CV 38), Ship's History, 13 June 1945–20 September 1945, 107; Commander Task Group Thirty-Eight Point Four, Action Report, 1 Sept. 1945; Gilbert, *Leader Born*, 218. For the number of aircraft in the 2 September flyover (some of which are absurdly high), see Barrett Tillman, "Comment and Discussion," U.S. Naval Institute *Proceedings* 141 (Sept. 2015): 9, 86. The number cited here is from Commander Second Carrier Task Force, Pacific, Action Report, 15 August–2 September 1945, Enclosure A, 2.

18. USS *Proteus* (AS 19), Ship's History, to 15 September 1945, 16–19; Reminiscences of Admiral John S. McCain Jr., U.S. Navy (Ret.), Annapolis, MD: U.S. Naval Institute, 1999, 5 (hereafter cited as McCain Reminiscences). For the *I-401* see http://www.combinedfleet.com/I-401.htm. Some sources mistakenly place the *Dentuda* in Tokyo Bay on 2 September.

19. McCain Reminiscences, 6.

20. Thach, *Reminiscences*, 2:481–82.

21. NAS San Diego to BuPers, 13 Dec. 1945; confid. dispatch, 042144 Sept. 1945; both in McCain Personnel File, NPRC; *New York Times*, 5 Sept. 1945; excerpt from the *Honolulu Star-Bulletin*, 4 Sept. 1945, folder McCain, John S., VADM, box 104, Samuel Eliot Morison Office Files, NHHC; Gilbert, *Leader Born*, 219.

22. *New York Times*, 7 Sept. 1945; certificate of death, 29 Sept. 1945, McCain Personnel File, NPRC; Gilbert, *Leader Born*, 219–20.

23. Thach, *Reminiscences*, 2:484; Forrestal to Mrs. John S. McCain 17 Sept. 1945; Forrestal to John S. McCain Jr., 7 Sept. 1945; both in James V. Forrestal Papers, MMPLU; *New York Times*, 8, 9 Sept. 1945.

24. *New York Times*, 8, 9, 11 Sept. 1945; undated, unidentified article, probably a few days after 6 Sept. 1945, folder McCain, John S., VADM, box 104, Samuel Eliot Morison Office Files, NHHC; Gilbert, *Leader Born*, 226.

25. Gilbert, *Leader Born*, 227; Hughes, *Bill Halsey*, 401; McCain and Salter, *Faith of My Fathers*, 45; *DANFS*, 3:547–50. The newest *John S. McCain* was badly damaged in a

fatal collision with a merchant tanker in 2017. John S. McCain III's name was added to the ship in 2018.

26. McCain and Salter, *Faith of My Fathers*, 58–60, 93–96, 258–88; *New York Times*, 24 March 1981; *Washington Post*, 24 March 1981.

27. McCain and Salter, *Faith of My Fathers*, 118–257, 289–342, esp. 157.

28. Reynolds, *Fast Carriers*, 18–20, 320–21, 353–54, 381.

29. Lundstrom, *Black Shoe Carrier Admiral*, 515; Gilbert, *Leader Born*, 54; Notes by Admiral Raymond A. Spruance for E. B. Potter, The United States and World Sea Power, 4 Jan. 1959, folder 1956 March 3–1959 February 21, box 1, E. B. Potter Papers, Special Collections & Archives, Nimitz Library, USNA.

BIBLIOGRAPHY

Manuscript and Archival Material

Air Force Historical Research Agency, Maxwell AFB, AL
        Folder GP-11-SU-OP-S (Bomb) 31 Jul 1942–6 Oct 1942, IRIS no. 77779.
        Folder GP-11-SU-OP Aug. 1942, IRIS no. 77773.
Hoover Institution Library and Archives, Stanford University, Palo Alto, CA
        McCain, John Sidney. Papers.
            Action Reports
            Commander Second Carrier Task Force Thirty-Eight, Action Report,
                28 May–1 July 1945.
            Commander Second Carrier Task Force, Pacific, Action Report, 2 July
                1945–15 August 1945.
            Operation Order
            Commander Second Carrier Task Force, Pacific, Operation Order No.
                3-45, 20 July 1945.
            War Diary
            Commander Second Carrier Task Force, Pacific, War Diary, 1 July
                1945–31 July 1945.
Library of Congress, Manuscript Division, Washington, DC
        Halsey, William F. Papers.
        King, Ernest Joseph. Papers.
        Towers, John H. Papers.
National Archives and Records Administration [unless indicated by * all action reports,
    war diaries, and unit histories are from www.Fold3.com, accessed 19 Dec. 2011–2 June
    2017]
        Records of the Bureau of Naval Personnel, Record Group 24
            Lexington Deck Log, 18 Aug. 1944 (courtesy of Michael Kern).
            Nitro Deck Logs, 9 June 1931–31 March 1933.
            Ranger Deck Logs, 1 June 1927–3 June 1939.
            Shangri-La Deck Logs, 4 Aug.–1 Sept. 1945.
        Records of the Office of the Chief of Naval Operations, Records Relating to
            Naval Activity during World War II, Record Group 38
            00 file, Office files of the Chief of Naval Operations, 1941–1946.
            Flag File Screening Documents, 1941–1963.
            Record of Proceedings of a Court of Inquiry . . . into the circumstances
                connected with the damage of ships of the Third Fleet in a typhoon
                . . . off Okinawa, Cincpac 1945.

Action Reports

Commander Carrier Air Group Eleven, Aircraft Action Reports, 29 Oct. 1944.

Commander Carrier Air Group Fourteen, Aircraft Action Reports, 10–26 October 1944.

Commander Second Carrier Task Force, Pacific, Action Report, 15 August–2 September 1945.

Commander Task Group Thirty-Eight Point Four, Action Report, 16 August to 2 September 1945.

Commander Third Fleet, Action Report, 23–26 October 1944.

Commander Third Fleet, Report on Operations of the Third Fleet, 30 December 1944–23 January 1945.

Commander Torpedo Squadron Fourteen, Aircraft Action Reports, 25–26 Oct 1944.

USS *Hancock*, Action Report, 14 November–27 November 1944.

USS *Hancock* (CV 19), Action Report, 10 December–24 December 1944.

USS *Hancock*, Action Report, 30 December 1944–25 January 1945.

USS *Hornet*, Action Report, 7–24 Sept. 1944.

USS *Hornet*, Action Report, 2–27 Oct. 1944.

USS *Hornet* (CV 12), Action Report, 28 May–10 June 1945.

USS *Langley*, Action Report, 30 December 1944–25 January 1945.

USS *Shangri-La* (CV 38), Action Report, 24 May 1945–13 June 1945.

USS *Shangri-La* (CV 38), Action Report, 2 July 1945–15 August 1945.

USS *Shangri-La* (CV 38), Action Report, 16 August 1945–2 September 1945.

USS *Ticonderoga*, Action Report, 3–21 January 1945.

USS *Wasp*, Action Report, 29 Aug.–24 Sept. 1944.

USS *Wasp*, Action Report, 2 Oct.–27 Oct. 1944.

USS *Wasp*, Action Report, 11 November–24 November 1944.

USS *Yorktown*, Operations against Enemy Airfields on Luzon . . . 14–16 December 1944.

VB-3 ACA Report, 13 Nov. 1944.

War Diaries; Ships', Air Group, and Squadron Histories

Aircraft, Southern Sector, Western Sea Frontier, War Diary, March 1942.

Aircraft Southern Sector, Western Sea Frontier, War Diary, 1 May 1942.

Bombing Squadron Seven, History.

Carrier Air Group Fourteen, History, 15 September 1943–29 November 1944.

*Commander in Chief, United States Pacific Fleet, War Diary, May 1–15, 1942, War Plans—Daily Summary, Cincpac: Apr 1942–May 1942.

*Commander in Chief, United States Pacific Fleet, War Diary, 1 July 1942–15 July, 1942, War Plans—Daily Summary, Cincpac: June 1942–July 31, 1942.

*Commander in Chief, United States Pacific Fleet, War Diary, August
    1, 1942–August 15, 1942, War Plans—Daily Summary, Cincpac:
    Aug. 1942–Sept. 1942.

*Commander in Chief, United States Pacific Fleet, War Diary,
    Cincpac, June 1–30, 1942, Daily Distribution of Operating Forces,
    Cincpac: June 1942–July 31, 1942.

*Commander in Chief, United States Pacific Fleet, War Diary,
    Cincpac, August 16, 1942–August 31, 1942, Daily Distribution of
    Operating Forces, Cincpac: Aug. 1942–Sept. 1942.

Commander Second Carrier Task Force, Pacific, War Diary, 1 May–31
    May 1945.

Commander Second Carrier Task Force, Pacific, War Diary, 1 June–30
    June 1945.

Commander Task Force Thirty-Eight, War Diary, 1 Nov.–30 Nov. 1944.

Commander Task Force Thirty-Eight, War Diary, 1 December–31
    December 1944.

Commander Task Force Thirty-Eight, War Diary, 1 January–31 January
    1945.

Commander Task Group Thirty-Eight Point One, War Diary, 1
    Sept.–30 Sept. 1944.

Commander Task Group Thirty-Eight Point One, War Diary, 1
    Oct.–31 Oct. 1944.

Commander Third Fleet, War Diary, 15 June–31 Aug. 1944.

Commander Third Fleet, War Diary, 1 Feb.–31 May 1945.

Commander Third Fleet, War Diary, 1–30 June 1945.

Commander Third Fleet, War Diary, 1–31 August 1945.

C.T.G. 30.8, War Diary, 1 December 1944–31 December 1944.

Fighting Squadron Fourteen History, 2 Dec. 1944.

Marine Fighting Squadron Two Thirteen, Marine Fighting Squadron
    One Twenty Four, War Diary . . . 1–31 January 1945.

NAS San Diego, War Diary, 1 February–28 February 1942.

Patrol Bombing Squadron Twenty-One, War Diary, 1 December
    1944–31 December 1944.

U.S. Naval Air Station, San Diego, California, War Diary, 1 October
    1942–31 October 1942.

USS Bunker Hill, War Diary for the Month of November 1944.

*USS Curtiss (Flagship), Comairsopac, Jan. 42–Jan. 43, War Diary.

USS Cushing (DD 797), War Diary, 18 May 1945–31 May 1945.

USS Enterprise, War Diary for November 1944.

USS Essex, War Diary, Month of November 1944.

USS Essex, War Diary for the Month of December 1944.

USS Hancock, War Diary, 1 October–31 October 1944.

USS Hancock (CV 19), War Diary, 1 November 1944–30 November
    1944.

USS *Hancock*, War Diary, 1 December 1944–31 December 1944.

USS *Hancock*, War Diary, 1 January 1945–31 January 1945.

USS *Hornet*, Typhoon of 15–21 December 1944.

USS *Hornet*, War Diary, 1–30 Sept. 1944.

USS *Hornet* (CV 12), War Diary, 1–30 June 1945.

USS *Indianapolis*, War Diary, May 1944.

USS *Indianapolis*, War Diary, June 1944.

USS *Jason*, War History, 23 April 1946.

USS *Lexington*, War Diary, 1–31 October 1944.

USS *Monssen* (DD 798), War Diary for May 1945.

USS *Proteus* (AS 19), Ship's History, to 15 September 1945.

USS *San Jacinto*, War Diary, 1 Nov.–30 Nov. 1944.

USS *Shangri-La* (CV 38), Ship's History, 13 June 1945–20 September 1945.

USS *Shangri-La* (CV 38), War Diary, 1 June 1945–30 June 1945.

*USS *Tangier* (Flagship), Commander Aircraft South Pacific Force, Confidential War Diary, Commander Aircraft South Pacific Force, War Diary, May–August 1942.

USS *Wasp*, War Diary, 1 Aug.–31 Aug. 1944.

USS *Wasp*, War Diary, 1 Oct.–31 Oct. 1944.

USS *Wasp*, War Diary, 1 Nov.–30 Nov. 1944.

USS *Yorktown*, War Diary—Month of December 1944.

Records of the Bureau of Aeronautics, Record Group 72

Confidential Correspondence, 1922–1944.

Records of Naval Operating Forces, Record Group 313

Commander 2nd Carrier Task Force—Administrative Messages, Operation Plans, Action Reports, Logs, Award Recommendations (Blue 627), 1944–1945.

*Commander Task Force Thirty-Eight, Action Report, 30 October 1944–26 January 1945.

*Commander Task Group Thirty-Eight Point One, Action Report, 2 Oct.–29 Oct. 1944.

Microfilm Copies of Dispatches (Microfilmed Incoming and Outgoing Dispatches and Chronological Message Traffic of CINC, Pacific and U.S. Pacific Fleet, 1940–45).

Records Relating to Operations (Blue 242), 1942–1943.

Records Relating to Operations (Red 182), 1942–1946.

National Naval Aviation Museum, Emil Buehler Naval Aviation Library, Pensacola, FL

McCain, J. S. Flight Training Record.

Thach, John S. Papers.

National Personnel Records Center, St. Louis, MO.

McCain, John S. Official Military Personnel File, file no. V200114.

Naval History and Heritage Command, Archives Branch, Washington, DC
  Captain Steele's "Running Estimate and Summary" (Graybook; http://www
      .ibiblio.org/anrs/graybook.html, accessed 4 June 2017).
          Vol. 1, 7 Dec. 1941–31 Aug. 1942.
          Vol. 2, 1 Sept. 1942–31 Dec. 1942.
          Vol. 3, 1 Jan. 1943–30 June 1943.
          Vol. 5, 1 Jan. 1944–31 Dec. 1944.
          Vol. 6, 1 Jan. 1945–1 July 1945.
          Vol. 7, 1 July 1945–31 Aug. 1945.
  King, Fleet Admiral Ernest J. Papers.
  Morison, Samuel Eliot. Office Files.
  Nimitz, Fleet Admiral Chester W. Papers.
  Radford, Arthur. Papers.
  Record of Proceedings of a Court of Inquiry Convened on Board the U.S.S.
      Cascade . . . , December 26, 1944, microfilm NRS 1978–43.
Naval War College Library, Naval War College, Newport, RI
  Commander Task Group Thirty-Eight Point One, Operations . . . 29 Aug.–28
      Sept. 1944.
  Naval Historical Collection, Student Theses, RG 13
          McCain, John S. "The Causes of the Spanish American War, and the
              Naval and Combined Operations in the Atlantic, Including the
              Transfer of the Oregon."
          McCain, John S. "The Foreign Policies of the United States."
  Report of Informal Inquiry into the Circumstances Attending the Loss of the
      USS *Vincennes*, USS *Quincy*, USS *Astoria*, and HMAS *Canberra*, on August
      9, 1942, in the Vicinity of Savo Island (Solomon Islands), 13 May 1943
      (Hepburn Report).
Princeton University, Seeley G. Mudd Manuscript Library, Princeton, NJ
  Forrestal, James V. Papers. http://findingaids.princeton.edu/MC051/c02852.pdf.
      Accessed 2 Nov. 2016.
U.S. Naval Academy, Nimitz Library, Special Collections & Archives, Annapolis, MD
  McCain, John S. Midshipman Personnel Jacket. Record Group 405.
  McCain, John Sidney. Record of Midshipmen, Academic and Conduct Record of
      Cadets, 1902–1906.
  Potter, E. B. Papers.

Public Documents

"The AAF in the South Pacific to October 1942." Washington, DC: Assistant Chief of
    Air Staff, Intelligence, Historical Division, 1944. http://www.ibiblio.org/hyperwar/
    AAF/AAFHS/AAFHS-101.pdf. Accessed 12 Feb. 2014.
Army Air Forces, Headquarters, Office of Assistant Chief of Air Staff, Intelligence.
    Wings at War, No. 3: Pacific Counterblow. http://www.ibiblio.org/hyperwar/AAF/
    WW/WW-3–2.html. Accessed 19 Dec. 2011.

Bates, Richard W. "The Battle for Leyte Gulf, October 1944, Strategical and Tactical Analysis. Vol. 1, Preliminary Operations." Newport, RI: Naval War College, 1953.

———. "The Battle for Leyte Gulf, October 1944, Strategical and Tactical Analysis. Vol. 2, Operations from 0719 October 17th until October 20th D-Day." Newport, RI: Naval War College, 1955.

———. "The Battle for Leyte Gulf, October 1944, Strategical and Tactical Analysis, Vol. 5, Battle of Surigao Strait, October 24th–25th." Newport, RI: Naval War College, 1958.

———. "The Battle of Savo Island, August 9th, 1942: Strategical and Tactical Analysis, Part 1." Newport, RI: Naval War College, 1950.

Bureau of Naval Personnel, Administrative History: Women's Reserve, vol. 1. Washington, DC: Historical Section, Bureau of Naval Personnel, no date.

The Coast Guard at War, Loran IV, 2 vols. Coast GuardHeadquarters, 1946. http://www .loran-history.infoLORAN_Implementation_Planning_Installation_and_Termination /1942–1949/THE%20COAST%20GUARD%20AT%20WAR.pdf. Accessed 20 July 2016.

Ferguson, Arthur B. *The Antisubmarine Command* [USAF Historical Study 107]. Washington, DC: Historical Division, Assistant Chief of Air Staff, Intelligence, 1945. http://www.afhra.af.mil/shared/media/document/AFD-09055–043.pdf. Accessed 20 Feb. 2014.

Foreign Relations of the United States: Diplomatic Papers, 1945, The British Commonwealth, The Far East, Volume VI, Document 321. https://history.state.gov/historicaldocuments/ frus1945v06/d321. Accessed 18 Aug. 2016.

General Board of the Navy. Hearings, 1924, vol. 1.

U.S. Census, 1860. Carroll County, Miss., 10 Sept. 1860. Ancestry.com. Accessed 4 Aug. 2009.

U.S. Congress, House. *Hearing on the Bill H.R. 4444 (Later Introduced as H.R. 9315) to Provide for the Equalization of Promotion of Officers of the Staff Corps of the Navy with Officers of the Line*, 68th Cong. 1st sess. Washington, DC: Government Printing Office, 1924.

U.S. Congress, House. *Proposal to Establish a Single Department of Armed Forces, Hearings before the Select Committee on Post-War Military Policy*, 78th Cong., 2nd sess. Washington, DC: Government Printing Office, 1944.

U.S. Congress, Senate. *Hearings before the Subcommittee of the Committee on Naval Affairs . . . on a Bill to Provide for the Equalization of Promotion of Officers of the Staff Corps of the Navy with Officers of the Line*, 68th Cong. 1st sess. Washington, DC: Government Printing Office, 1924.

U.S. President's Aircraft Board. *Hearings before the President's Aircraft Board*, 4 vols. Washington, DC: Government Printing Office, 1925.

World War II Administrative History, Bureau of Aeronautics. Summary, vols. 1, 2, 3, 5, 6, 8, 10, 11, 12, 17, 19. Washington, DC: Director of Naval History, 1957.

World War II Administrative History, Office of the Deputy Chief of Naval Operations DCNO (Air), vols. 1, 14. Washington, DC: Historical Section, Office of the Chief of Naval Operations, 1945.

World War II Administrative History, Office of the Deputy Chief of Naval Operations DCNO (Air), History of Naval Fighter Direction, vol. 1. Washington, DC: Aviation History Unit, Office of the Chief of Naval Operations, 1946.

World War II Administrative History, Western Sea Frontier. Washington, DC: Director of Naval History, 1946.

Interviews and Oral Histories

Bogan, Vice Admiral Gerald F., U.S. Navy (Ret.). Reminiscences. Annapolis, MD: U.S. Naval Institute, 1970, 1986.

Foley, Rear Admiral Francis D., USN (Ret.). Reminiscences. Annapolis, MD: U.S. Naval Institute, 1988, 2 vols.

Gardner, Captain M. B. USN. Interview in the Air Information Branch, Bureau of Aeronautics, 13 Jan. 1943, www.Fold3.com. Courtesy of John Lundstrom. Accessed 24 Sept. 2012.

Gayler, Admiral Noel A. M., USN (Ret.). Reminiscences. Annapolis, MD: U.S. Naval Institute, 1983–1984.

Johnson, Admiral Roy L., USN (Ret.). Reminiscences. Annapolis, MD: U.S. Naval Institute, 1982.

McCain, Vice Admiral J. S. Interview, Nov. 1944. Personal Interviews, Naval Records and Library, Chief of Naval Operations, www.Fold3.com. Accessed 25 Jan. 2016.

McCain, Admiral John S. Jr., U.S. Navy (Ret.). Reminiscences. Annapolis, MD: U.S. Naval Institute, 1999.

McCain, Sen. John S. III. Telephone interview by author, 7 Oct. 2015.

Ogden, Captain James R., USN (Ret.). Reminiscences. Annapolis, MD: U.S. Naval Institute, 1982.

Reminiscences of Admiral John Smith Thach, U.S. Navy (Retired). 2 vols. Annapolis, MD: Naval Institute Press, 1977.

Riley, Vice Admiral Herbert D., U.S. Navy (Ret.). Reminiscences. Annapolis, MD: U.S. Naval Institute, 2004.

Russell, Admiral James S., U.S. Navy (Ret.). Reminiscences. Annapolis, MD: U.S. Naval Institute, 1976.

Smedberg, Vice Admiral William R. III, U.S. Navy (Ret.). Reminiscences. 2 vols. Annapolis, MD: U.S. Naval Institute, 1979.

Books

Adams, Henry H. Witness to Power: The Life of Fleet Admiral William D. Leahy. Annapolis, MD: Naval Institute Press, 1985.

Albion, Robert Greenhalgh. Makers of Naval Policy, 1798–1947. Annapolis, MD: Naval Institute Press, 1980.

Alison, David Kite. New Eye for the Navy: The Origin of Radar at the Naval Research Laboratory. Washington, DC: Naval Research Laboratory, 1981.

Annual Register of the United States Naval Academy, 1903–1904. Washington, DC: Government Printing Office, 1903.

Annual Register of the United States Naval Academy, 1904–1905. Washington, DC: Government Printing Office, 1904.

Annual Register of the United States Naval Academy, 1905–1906. Washington, DC: Government Printing Office, 1905.

Annual Register of the United States Naval Academy, 1906–1907. Washington, DC: Government Printing Office, 1906.

Annual Reports of the Secretary of the Navy for the Fiscal Year 1919. Washington, DC: Government Printing Office, 1920.

Barlow, Jeffrey G. *From Hot War to Cold: The U.S. Navy and National Security Affairs, 1945–1955*. Stanford, CA: Stanford University Press, 2009.

Bland, Larry I., ed. *The Papers of George Catlett Marshall*. Vol. 4. Baltimore: Johns Hopkins University Press, 1996.

Buell, Thomas B. *Master of Sea Power: A Biography of Fleet Admiral Ernest J. King*. Boston: Little, Brown and Company, 1980.

Building the Navy's Bases in World War II: History of the Bureau of Yards and Docks and the Civil Engineer Corps, 1940–1946. 2 vols. Washington, DC: Department of the Navy Bureau of Yards and Docks, 1947.

Calhoun, C. Raymond. *Typhoon: The Other Enemy*. Annapolis, MD: Naval Institute Press, 1981.

Coletta, Paolo E. *Admiral Marc A. Mitscher and U.S. Naval Aviation*. Lewiston, NY: Edwin Mellen Press, 1997.

———. *Patrick N. L. Bellinger and U.S. Naval Aviation*. Lanham, MD: University Press of America, 1987.

———, ed. *United States Navy and Marine Corps Bases, Overseas*. Westport, CT: Greenwood Press, 1985.

Cressman, Robert J. *USS Ranger: The Navy's First Flattop from Keel to Mast, 1934–46*. Washington, DC: Brassey's Inc., 2003.

Dickson, W. D. *The Battle of the Philippine Sea*. London: Ian Allan Ltd., 1975.

Dictionary of American Naval Fighting Ships. Vol. 1. Washington, DC: Naval History Division, 1959.

———. Vol. 2. Washington, DC: Naval History Division, 1963.

———. Vol. 4. Washington, DC: Naval History Division, 1969.

———. Vol. 5. Washington, DC: Naval History Division, 1970.

———. Vol. 7. Washington, DC: Naval Historical Center, 1981.

———. Vol. 8. Washington, DC: Naval Historical Center, 1981.

Drury, Bob, and Tom Clavin. *Halsey's Typhoon: The True Story of a Fighting Admiral, an Epic Storm, and an Untold Rescue*. New York: Atlantic Monthly Press, 2007.

Dyer, George Carroll. *The Amphibians Came to Conquer: The Story of Admiral Richmond Kelly Turner*. 2 Vols. Washington, DC: Department of the Navy, 1972.

Evans, David C., ed. *The Japanese Navy in World War II: In the Words of Former Japanese Naval Officers*. 2d ed. Annapolis, MD: Naval Institute Press, 1986.

Evans, David C., and Mark R. Peattie. *Kaigun: Strategy, Tactics, and Technology in the Imperial Japanese Navy, 1887–1941*. Annapolis, MD: Naval Institute Press, 1997.

Ewing, Steve. *Thach Weave: The Life of Jimmie Thach*. Annapolis, MD: Naval Institute Press, 2004.

Farago, Ladislas. *The Tenth Fleet*. New York: Ivan Obolensky, Inc., 1962.

Felker, Craig C. *Testing American Sea Power: U.S. Navy Strategic Exercises, 1923–1940*. College Station: Texas A&M University Press, 2007.

Frank, Richard B. *Downfall: The End of the Imperial Japanese Empire*. New York: Random House, 1999.

———. *Guadalcanal*. New York: Random House, 1990.

Friedman, Norman. *U.S. Aircraft Carriers: An Illustrated Design History*. Annapolis, MD: Naval Institute Press, 1983.

Furer, Julius Augustus. *Administration of the Navy Department in World War II*. Washington, DC: Department of the Navy, 1959.

Gilbert, Alton Keith. *A Leader Born: The Life of Admiral John Sidney McCain, Pacific Carrier Commander*. Philadelphia: Casemate, 2006.

Goldstein, Donald M., and Katherine V. Dillon, eds. *Fading Victory: The Diary of Admiral Matome Ugaki, 1941–1945*. Pittsburgh: University of Pittsburgh Press, 1991.

Grossnick, Roy A., ed. *United States Naval Aviation, 1910–1995*. Washington, DC: Naval Historical Center, 1995.

Halsey, William F., and J. Bryan III. *Admiral Halsey's Story*. New York: Whittlesey House, McGraw-Hill Book Company, Inc., 1947.

Hobbs, David. *The British Pacific Fleet: The Royal Navy's Most Powerful Strike Force*. Annapolis, MD: Naval Institute Press, 2011.

Hone, Thomas C., Norman Friedman, and Mark D. Mandeles. *Innovation in Carrier Aviation*. Newport, RI: Naval War College Press, 2011.

Hughes, Thomas Alexander. *Admiral Bill Halsey: A Naval Life*. Cambridge, MA: Harvard University Press, 2016.

Hughes, Wayne P. Jr. *Fleet Tactics: Theory and Practice*. Annapolis, MD: Naval Institute Press, 1986.

Knott, Richard C. *Black Cat Raiders of WWII*. Annapolis, MD: The Nautical & Aviation Publishing Company of America, 1981.

Lucky Bag. Springfield, MA: F. A. Bassette, 1906.

Lundstrom, John B. *Black Shoe Carrier Admiral: Frank Jack Fletcher at Coral Sea, Midway, and Guadalcanal*. Annapolis, MD: Naval Institute Press, 2006.

———. *The First South Pacific Campaign: Pacific Fleet Strategy, December 1941–June 1942*. Annapolis, MD: Naval Institute Press, 1976.

———. *The First Team: Pacific Naval Air Combat from Pearl Harbor to Midway*. Annapolis, MD: Naval Institute Press, 1984.

———. *The First Team and the Guadalcanal Campaign: Naval Fighter Combat from August to November 1942*. Annapolis, MD: Naval Institute Press, 1994.

McCain, John, with Mark Salter. *Faith of My Fathers: A Family Memoir*. New York: Random House, 1999.

Meigs, Montgomery C. *Slide Rules and Submarines: American Scientists and Subsurface Warfare in World War II*. Washington, DC: National Defense University Press, 1990.

Michener, James A. *Tales of the South Pacific*. New York: Macmillan Company, 1946.

Miller, John Grider. *The Battle to Save the* Houston, *October 1944 to March 1945*. Annapolis, MD: Naval Institute Press, 1985.

Morison, Samuel Eliot. *History of United States Naval Operations in World War II*. Vol. 5. *The Struggle for Guadalcanal, August 1942–February 1943*. Boston: Little, Brown and Company, 1950.

———. *History of United States Naval Operations in World War II*. Vol. 8. *New Guinea and the Marianas, March 1944–August 1944*. Boston: Little, Brown and Company, 1953.

———. *History of United States Naval Operations in World War II*. Vol. 12. *Leyte, June 1944–January 1945*. Boston: Little, Brown and Company, 1961.

———. *History of United States Naval Operations in World War II*. Vol. 13. *The Liberation of the Philippines: Luzon, Mindanao, the Visayas, 1944–1945*. Boston: Little, Brown and Company, 1959.

———. *History of United States Naval Operations in World War II*. Vol. 14. *Victory in the Pacific, 1945*. Boston: Little, Brown and Company, 1960.

Munholland, Kim. *Rock of Contention: Free French and Americans at War in New Caledonia, 1940–1945*. New York: Berghahn Books, 2005.

Newton, Wesley Phillips, and Robert R. Rea. *Wings of Gold: An Account of Naval Aviation Training in World War II, the Correspondence of Aviation Cadet/Ensign Robert R. Rea*. Tuscaloosa: University of Alabama Press, 1987.

Palmer, Michael A. *Command at Sea: Naval Command and Control since the Sixteenth Century*. Cambridge, MA: Harvard University Press, 2005.

Peattie, Mark R. *Sunburst: The Rise of Japanese Naval Air Power, 1909–1941*. Annapolis, MD: Naval Institute Press, 2001.

Potter, E. B. *Bull Halsey*. Annapolis, MD: Naval Institute Press, 1985.

———. *Nimitz*. Annapolis, MD: Naval Institute Press, 1976.

Prados, John. *Combined Fleet Decoded: The Secret History of American Intelligence and the Japanese Navy in World War II*. New York: Random House, 1995.

———. *Storm over Leyte: The Philippine Invasion and the Destruction of the Japanese Navy*. New York: NAL Caliber, 2016.

Prange, Gordon W., with Donald M. Goldstein and Katherine V. Dillon. *At Dawn We Slept: The Untold Story of Pearl Harbor*. New York: McGraw-Hill Book Company, 1981.

Radford, Arthur W. *From Pearl Harbor to Vietnam: The Memoirs of Admiral Arthur W. Radford*. Edited by Stephen Jurika Jr. Stanford, CA: Hoover Institution Press, 1980.

Reckner, James R. *Teddy Roosevelt's Great White Fleet*. Annapolis, MD: Naval Institute Press, 1988.

Reynolds, Clark G. *Admiral John H. Towers: The Struggle for Naval Air Supremacy*. Annapolis, MD: Naval Institute Press, 1991.

———. *The Fast Carriers: The Forging of an Air Navy*. 1968. Reprint Annapolis, MD: Naval Institute Press, 1992.

———. *On the Warpath in the Pacific: Admiral Jocko Clark and the Fast Carriers*. Annapolis: MD: Naval Institute Press, 2005.

Roberts, Michael D. *Dictionary of American Naval Aviation Squadrons*. Vol. 2. Washington, DC: Naval Historical Center, 2000.

Rose, Lisle A. *Power at Sea*. Vol. 2. *The Breaking Storm, 1919–1945*. Columbia: University of Missouri Press, 2007.

Rossano, Geoffrey L. *Stalking the U-Boat: U.S. Navy Aviation in Europe during World War I*. Gainesville: University Press of Florida, 2010.

Smith, Douglas V. *Carrier Battles: Command Decision in Harm's Way*. Annapolis, MD: Naval Institute Press, 2006.

Spencer, Elizabeth. *Landscapes of the Heart: A Memoir*. New York: Random House, 1998.

Stafford, Edward P. *The Big E: The Story of the USS* Enterprise. New York: Dell Publishing Co., Inc., 1964.

Sudsbury, Elretta. *Jackrabbits to Jets: The History of North Island, San Diego, California*. San Diego: Neyenesch Printers, 1967.

Swanborough, Gordon, and Peter M. Bowers. *United States Navy Aircraft since 1911*. Annapolis, MD: Naval Institute Press, 1976.

Sweetman, Jack. *The U.S. Naval Academy: An Illustrated History*. Annapolis, MD: Naval Institute Press, 1979.

Taylor, Theodore. *The Magnificent Mitscher*. New York: Norton, 1954.

Tillman, Barrett. *Clash of the Carriers: The True Story of the Marianas Turkey Shoot of World War II*. New York: NAL Caliber, 2005.

———. *Hellcat: The F6F in World War II*. Annapolis, MD: Naval Institute Press, 1979.

Tillman, Barrett, with Henk van der Lugt. *VF-11/111 "Sundowners," 1942–45*. Oxford: Osprey Publishing Ltd., 2010.

Trimble, William F. *Admiral William A. Moffett: Architect of Naval Aviation*. 1994. Reprint Annapolis, MD: Naval Institute Press, 2007.

———. *Wings for the Navy: A History of the Naval Aircraft Factory, 1917–1956*. Annapolis, MD: Naval Institute Press, 1990.

Turnbull, Archibald D., and Clifford L. Lord. *History of United States Naval Aviation*. New Haven, CT: Yale University Press, 1949.

Warner, Denis, and Peggy Warner, with Sadao Seno. *Disaster in the Pacific: New Light on the Battle of Savo Island*. Annapolis, MD: Naval Institute Press, 1992.

Wheeler, Gerald E. *Kinkaid of the Seventh Fleet: A Biography of Admiral Thomas C. Kinkaid, U.S. Navy*. Washington, DC: Naval Historical Center, 1995.

Wildenberg, Thomas. *Billy Mitchell's War with the Navy: The Interwar Rivalry over Air Power*. Annapolis, MD: Naval Institute Press, 2013.

Wildenberg, Thomas, and Norman Polmar. *Ship Killer: A History of the American Torpedo*. Annapolis, MD: Naval Institute Press, 2010.

Wolters, Timothy S. *Information at Sea: Shipboard Command and Control in the U.S. Navy from Mobile Bay to Okinawa*. Baltimore: Johns Hopkins University Press, 2013.

Wooldridge, E. T., ed. *Carrier Warfare in the Pacific: An Oral History Collection*. Washington, DC: Smithsonian Institution Press, 1993.

Articles and Book Chapters

Carney, Robert B. "In Defense of Halsey." *Naval History* 30 (April 2016): 26.

Chisholm, Donald. "Big Guns versus Wooden Decks: Naval Aviation Officer Personnel, 1911–1941." In *One Hundred Years of U.S. Navy Air Power*, edited by Douglas V. Smith, 52–78. Annapolis, MD: Naval Institute Press, 2010.

Crichton, Kyle. "Navy Air Boss." *Collier's*, 23 Oct. 1943, 21, 24.

Frank, Richard B. "Picking Winners?" *Naval History* 25 (June 2011): 24–30.

Gladwin, Lee A. "American POWs on Japanese Ships Take a Voyage into Hell." *Prologue* 35 (Winter 2003): 30–39.

Goodspeed, Hill. "One Hundred Years at Pensacola." *Naval History* 28 (Dec. 2014): 48–53.

———. "POW Relief and the End of World War II." *Foundation* 36 (Fall 2015): 20–25.

Love, Robert. Review of *Admiral Nimitz: The Commander of the Pacific Ocean Theater* by Brayton Harris. U.S. Naval Institute *Proceedings* 138 (May 2012): 151–52.

McCain, J. S. "A Personnel Survey." U.S. Naval Institute *Proceedings* 49 (Jan. 1923): 19–37.

———. "Service since Graduation vs. Age in Grade Retirement." U.S. Naval Institute *Proceedings* 51 (May 1925): 737–45.

———. "So We Hit Them in the Belly, I." *Saturday Evening Post*, 14 July 1945, 12–15, 40–44.

———. "So We Hit Them in the Belly, II." *Saturday Evening Post*, 21 July 1945, 22–24, 39.

———. "The Staff Equalization Bill." U.S. Naval Institute *Proceedings* 50 (March 1924): 417–23.

———. "VPB—The Patrol Bomber." *Flying and Popular Aviation* 30 (Jan. 1942): 51–56.

Miller, Edward S. "Eyes of the Fleet: How Flying Boats Transformed War Plan Orange." In *One Hundred Years of U.S. Navy Air Power*, edited by Douglas V. Smith, 31–42. Annapolis, MD: Naval Institute Press, 2010.

Nofi, Albert A. "Aviation in the Interwar Fleet Maneuvers, 1919–1940." In *One Hundred Years of U.S. Navy Air Power*, edited by Douglas V. Smith, 94–130. Annapolis, MD: Naval Institute Press, 2010.

Reitwiesner, William Addams. "Ancestry of Sen. John McCain." http://www.wargs.com/political/mccain.html. Accessed 26 May 2011.

Reynolds, Clark G. "Admiral Ernest J. King and the Strategy for Victory in the Pacific." In *Eagle, Shield and Anchor: Readings in American Naval History*, edited by James C. Bradford, 229–38. New York: American Heritage Custom Publishing Group, 1993.

Symonds, Craig L. "Mitscher and the Mystery of Midway." *Naval History* 26 (June 2012): 46–52.

Tillman, Barrett. "Comment and Discussion." U.S. Naval Institute *Proceedings* 141 (Sept. 2015): 9, 86.

Williamson, Samuel H., and Louis P. Cain. "Measuring Slavery in 2011 Dollars." https://www.measuringworth.com/slavery.php. Accessed 18 March 2016.

Newspapers and Magazines

Collier's
Coronado Eagle and Journal
Flying and Popular Aviation
Foundation
Naval Aviation News
Naval History
Naval Institute *Proceedings*
New York Times
Prologue
Saturday Evening Post
Time
Washington Post

Miscellaneous

California Death Index, Department of Public Health Services. https://familysearch.org/ ark:/61903/1:1:VGRZ-6D2. Accessed 24 March 2016.

CO, Air Group Twelve to COs VF-12, VBF-12, VB-12, VT-12, 23 June 1945. www .Fold3.com. Accessed 25 Jan. 2017.

Fahrney, Rear Adm. D. S. "The History of Pilotless Aircraft and Guided Missiles." Undated manuscript (probably 1958). Washington, DC: Naval History and Heritage Command.

Felker, Capt. C. C. Introduction, CVN Debate, U.S. Naval Academy, Annapolis, MD, 9 Jan. 2015.

Harrington, Daniel F. "The Missing Man: Joseph McNarney and Air Force Leadership." Draft chapter excerpt, 1–3. Courtesy of the author.

Japanese Shipping Losses. http://www.ibiblio.org/hyperwar/Japan/IJN/JANAC-Losses/ JANAC-Losses-4.html.

Japanese warship movements. www.combinedfleet.com.

Knox, memo to Roosevelt, 9 March 1942, "Safe Files." Franklin D. Roosevelt Presidential Library. docs.fdrlibrary.marist.edu/psf/box4/a47a01.html. Accessed 1 Aug. 2012.

Miller, Vern A. "Our Coral Carriers Helped Turn the Tide of Battle." http://www.war timepress.com/archive-article.asp?TID=This%20is%20CASU&MID=68&q=114& FID=746. Accessed 26 Nov. 2012.

Pacific Wrecks, PBY-5 Catalina BuNo. 2389. http://www.pacificwrecks.com/aircraft/ pby/2389.html. Accessed 3 March 2017.

"Patuxent River." http://www.globalsecurity.org/military/facility/patuxent-river.htm. Accessed 9 Aug. 2012.

Ship's Activity, *Shangri-La*, 12 Aug. 1945. http://www.kellycrawford.org/ShangriLa/log book.html#AUG12. Accessed 8 Jan. 2016.

Transcripts FDR logs, 19–21 July 1944. http://www.fdrlibrary.marist.edu/daybyday/day log/july-21st-1944/. Accessed 19 April 2017.

INDEX

ABOUT THE AUTHOR

William F. Trimble is Professor Emeritus at Auburn University in Alabama. His most recent book is *Hero of the Air: Glenn Curtiss and the Birth of Naval Aviation* (Naval Institute Press, 2010). He is also the author of *Wings for the Navy: A History of the Naval Aircraft Factory*; *Admiral William A. Moffett: Architect of Naval Aviation*; *Jerome C. Hunsaker and the Rise of American Aeronautics*; and *Attack from the Sea: A History of the U.S. Navy's Seaplane Striking Force*, among other books and articles.

The Naval Institute Press is the book-publishing arm of the U.S. Naval Institute, a private, nonprofit, membership society for sea service professionals and others who share an interest in naval and maritime affairs. Established in 1873 at the U.S. Naval Academy in Annapolis, Maryland, where its offices remain today, the Naval Institute has members worldwide.

Members of the Naval Institute support the education programs of the society and receive the influential monthly magazine *Proceedings* or the colorful bimonthly magazine *Naval History* and discounts on fine nautical prints and on ship and aircraft photos. They also have access to the transcripts of the Institute's Oral History Program and get discounted admission to any of the Institute-sponsored seminars offered around the country.

The Naval Institute's book-publishing program, begun in 1898 with basic guides to naval practices, has broadened its scope to include books of more general interest. Now the Naval Institute Press publishes about seventy titles each year, ranging from how-to books on boating and navigation to battle histories, biographies, ship and aircraft guides, and novels. Institute members receive significant discounts on the Press' more than eight hundred books in print.

Full-time students are eligible for special half-price membership rates. Life memberships are also available.

For a free catalog describing Naval Institute Press books currently available, and for further information about joining the U.S. Naval Institute, please write to:

Member Services
U.S. Naval Institute
291 Wood Road
Annapolis, MD 21402-5034
Telephone: (800) 233-8764
Fax: (410) 571-1703
Web address: www.usni.org